LANDMARKS IN Rhetoric AND Public Address

LANDMARKS IN Rhetoric and Public Address

ALSO IN THIS SERIES

CICERO ON

ORATORY AND ORATORS

Translated or Edited by J. S. Watson

Introduction by Ralph A. Micken

Foreword by David Potter

With a New Preface by Richard Leo Enos

Southern Illinois University Press

Carbondale and Edwardsville

Library of Congress Cataloging-in-Publication Data

Cicero, Marcus Tullius.
   Cicero on oratory and orators.

   (Landmarks in rhetoric and public address)
   Translation of: De oratore.
   Bibliography: p.
   Includes index.
   1. Oratory, Ancient.   I. Watson, J. S. (John Selby),
1804–1884. II. Title. III. Series.
PA6308.D6W3   1986   808.5'1   85-26258
ISBN 0-8093-1293-X (pbk.)

07   9 8 7

CONTENTS

FOREWORD

By David Potter

HOYT HUDSON had concluded a particularly challenging
session on *De Oratore*. Despite the miserable summer heat,
most of the graduate students were unwilling to leave
Cicero as they milled around the entrance to Annie Mae
Swift Hall. Several of us dragged lawn chairs from the
School of Education and buzzed with excitement.

"Let's do a Cicero in Modern dress."

"We could feature a series of contemporary experts presenting conflicting theories of rhetoric and oratory—
maybe of communication. The students would have to
arrive at their own decisions—as in the *De Oratore*."

"I'll do the section on humor."

"Hey, Joe Miller Ehninger!"

S. Marion Tucker, then a visiting Professor of Speech
at Northwestern, joined the group. "A good idea, putting
De Oratore in modern dress," he volunteered. "I've been
playing with a *De Oratore* for business and professional
men. But I don't think the book will sell—the readers
I know don't want to make the smallest of decisions.
They prefer to be told and then gripe about it."

Our enthusiasm was redirected.

"Why not a new edition of *De Oratore* in which we combine the language of today with the general usefulness of
the old Watson edition?"

"A good idea but could we offer a better translation?
Maybe what we ought to try is a new Watson—adding

an introductory essay in which Cicero could be placed in the mainstream of rhetorical theory."

"We could add some information about Watson, too. A fascinating character!"

Some three decades later, faced with the impossibility of obtaining good one-volume editions of the classic, we commissioned Dr. Ralph A. Micken, Chairman of the Department of Speech at Southern Illinois University, to prepare the definitive edition of *De Oratore*. After examining every English translation of the book, Micken concluded that the Watson was still the best complete edition despite the often quaint language. Then, drawing upon forty years of research in the area of classical rhetoric and poetic, wide familiarity with Roman history and literature, as well as extensive platform and publishing experience, he completed an unusually comprehensive, readable, and entertaining introductory essay. Using as our model a clean copy of the Harper edition of *De Oratore* published in 1878, we have enlarged the original type by 12 percent. The consequence is a volume which pleases us immensely. We hope you will share our excitement.

PREFACE

By Richard Leo Enos

ONE OF THE pleasant, if not originally anticipated, requirements for the new edition of Watson's *Cicero on Oratory and
Orators* is an addendum to Ralph A. Micken's fine introduction. Those who initially participated in this contribution to
the Landmarks in Rhetoric and Public Address series could
hardly have imagined the growth and development of research
on Cicero's rhetoric and oratory in the ensuing fifteen years.
To think that Professor Micken's discussion, "The Influence of
Cicero on Western Thought," would require a rather extensive
update would have appeared unlikely given the relative length
and stability of Ciceronian scholarship through the centuries.
Yet, it is a compliment to those who served on the original
enterprise that now—after such a short period of time—a
preface must be added.

That Cicero's importance and impact has extended beyond
the province of traditional, classical scholarship is the result of
two intellectual forces which have prospered since the original
Landmarks text appeared. First, a number of academic so-
cieties have emerged within the last two decades which facili-
tated the interaction of researchers interested in Ciceronian
scholarship. The International Society for the History of Rhetoric was instrumental in providing the structure for such ex-
changes, and in their biannual conferences research on Cicero
is consistently featured. ISHR's *Rhetorica* has provided another arena for scholarly essays, while the Rhetoric Society of
America's *Rhetoric Society Quarterly* published an extensive
bibliography of Ciceronian rhetoric in their Spring 1976 issue.

So active has this scholarship become that *College Composition and Communication* regularly devotes issues to the history of rhetoric, and the Summer 1984 issue of the *Central States Speech Journal* offered a "Special Report" on studies in Cicero's *Opera Rhetorica*. Such scholarly activity is a clear index of the revived interest in the history of rhetoric in general and Cicero in particular.

The activity of Ciceronian research apparent in scholarly organizations and journals has been complemented by a canon of secondary sources for researchers and teachers in the history of rhetoric. George A. Kennedy's two excellent volumes, *The Art of Rhetoric in the Roman World: 300 B.C.–A.D. 300* and *Classical Rhetoric and Its Christian and Secular Tradition from Ancient to Modern Times*, are apt illustrations of prominent texts which fix Cicero and his contributions securely in the history of rhetoric. Further, such well-established works as James J. Murphy's *Rhetoric in the Middle Ages* and Wilbur Samuel Howell's *Logic and Rhetoric in England, 1500–1700* have provided readers with a sense of coherence about the enduring impact of Ciceronian rhetoric.

Such attention to Ciceronian scholarship has been enhanced recently by three major collections. Winifred Bryan Horner's edited volume, *Historical Rhetoric: An Annotated Bibliography of Selected Sources in English*, synthesizes and summarizes the best scholarship on Cicero in the English language. Her editing of the companion edition, *The Present State of Scholarship in Historical and Contemporary Rhetoric*, provides a detailed review of current research. Most recently, Southern Illinois University Press's publication of *Speech Communication in the 20th Century* chronicles this surge of activity of Ciceronian research in speech communication.

While the lively activity of Ciceronian scholarship in the last two decades can be partially attributed to the architecture which has made the discussion and publication of such scholarship possible, another compatible factor has emerged during this interim period which provides further inducement to Ciceronian scholarship. Specialists in writing have rediscovered that theories of classical rhetoric provide powerful and sensitive paradigms for composition and generate important hypotheses for research. To that end, important articles and texts have emerged which have stressed the pedagogical importance of classical rhetoric in writing in general and Ciceronian contributions as one of the principal topics. More than any other single text, Edward P. J. Corbett's *Classical Rhetoric and the Modern Student* established the utility of classical rhetoric in the teaching and study of composition. Specific discussion of Cicero's utility in composition is evident throughout the festschrift honoring Corbett, *Essays on Classical Rhetoric and Modern Discourse*. In fact, the Ciceronian influence has even been the basis for S. Michael Halloran and Merrill D. Whitburn's argument for curricular reform in writing in the recent MLA publication, *The Rhetorical Tradition and Modern Writing*. Such works provide a second dimension to the study of Cicero's rhetoric, for they complement the inherent interest in historical scholarship with a contemporary application of principles of discourse for current research on writing processes.

Of course, traditional scholarship on Cicero's rhetoric has steadily marched forward. Donovan J. Och's analysis of Ciceronian invention in *Explorations in Rhetoric: Studies in Honor of Douglas Ehninger* contributes a lucid statement on heuristic processes. Similarly, G. V. Sumner's *The Orator in Cicero's "Brutus": Prosopography and Chronology*, L. P. Wilkinson's comprehensive summary of Ciceronian oratory and its relationship to literature in *The Cambridge History of Classical Literature*, and the *Index Verborum in Ciceronis Rhetorica* are all examples of the sustained richness of traditional scholarship.

The emergence of these various intellectual dimensions forecast not only a promising future for Ciceronian scholarship but a compatibility with other researchers who recognize both the wealth and utility of such knowledge in their own disciplines. It is no small tribute to the Watson translation and the efforts of Ralph A. Micken that such a preface is required for this new edition. Rather, it is a testimonial to the diverse benefits which the history of rhetoric can offer and how rapidly such benefits can have an impact on the intellectual communities which utilize them. My fondest hope is that this preface quickly becomes obsolete by developments as impressive as those which have taken place in the past two decades.

INTRODUCTION

By Ralph A. Micken

The Influence of Cicero on Western Thought

IN THE *Classical Weekly*, March 8, 1954, Walter Allen Jr. published a survey of selected Ciceronian Bibliography covering the years 1939–53. Although he severely limited the citation of works which could not readily be discovered by a simple interlibrary loan, left out works written in languages other than Latin, French, German, Italian, and English, and gave very little notice, as he puts it, to articles on the philosophical and rhetorical works, he nonetheless reports on hundreds of books and articles. This is indication enough of the continued preoccupation of modern scholars with Cicero. Annotated editions of his orations, volumes dealing with his vast correspondence, comments on his philosophical treatises and studies of his struggles to preserve the Republic continue to be published. As Dr. John C. Rolfe[1] comments in *Cicero and His Influence:* "The story of the influence of Cicero is one to command admiration and wonder. Such movements as Christianity, The Renaissance and the French Revolution drew direct inspiration from this Roman of long ago . . . Centuries after his death, Cicero has remained a living presence, real to members of the English Parliament, real to Thomas Jefferson, and for us he remains an immortal who, above all, demonstrates the unity

[1] John C. Rolfe, *Cicero and His Influence* (New York, 1963), p. v.

of civilization and the common aspirations of the race."

Not only has Cicero influenced the political thought, the statesmanship, and the philosophical considerations of generations of men, he has had what at times amounted to an almost unbelievable impact upon the language of western culture. Dr. Johnson, the Great Cham of English literature, sedulously imitated the Ciceronian sentence, while Edmund Burke attempted to catch the style and flavor of the great orations.

In the Renaissance adherence to the classical Latin of Cicero assumed the proportions of a cult. Followers of the Ciceronian ideal reached the point where words and syntax which could not be specifically found in the great Roman's writings were rejected. Arguments went on about the propriety of certain scholastic treatises in terms of whether or not they were written in language purely Ciceronian. The *Thesaurus Ciceronianus* of Mario Nizzoli purported to be a compendium of all pure Ciceronian language and some scholars refused to accept any expressions not found in it.

The preoccupation with Cicero in the Middle Ages and the Renaissance was not limited to his style. St. Augustine found it difficult to put aside his deep respect for the great orator, and at least one of the church fathers, St. Jerome, was confronted in a dream with a choice between Cicero and Christ.

Donald Bryant[2] states extremely well the importance of Cicero in rhetoric: "The great source of the rhetorical tradition throughout the Renaissance and on into the seventeenth and the eighteenth centuries, in England and America and on the continent, was Cicero, directly and indirectly, and after him Quintilian and Aristotle."

After centuries of admiration and acceptance, it is not surprising that there was somewhat of a revulsion. In modern times we find certain scholars, notably Drumann and Mommsen, so bitterly hostile, so unnaturally anxious to condemn the man on all counts that the vehemence of

[2] Donald Bryant, "Aspects of the Rhetorical Tradition; The Intellectual Foundation," *Quarterly Journal of Speech* 36, No. 2 (April, 1950), 174.

their distaste induces doubt of reasonable judgment. Cicero has been condemned on the grounds of style, called an Asian, a wordmonger, accused of being fascinated with his own verbosity, a stylistic show-off. He has been minimized and ridiculed as a thinker. His philosophical essays have been called simply the parroting of the thoughts of true philosophers, his political pronouncements meaningless because of his failure to apply them to his own life. His humor has been said to range from the crude and malicious to the merely precious and silly. Even in his writings on rhetoric and public address, he has occasionally been dismissed as a shallow eclectic. He has been assailed as a man—called a vacillating spineless weakling, a vainglorious braggart, a pusillanimous deserter from good causes, and a pseudo-intellectual. Unfortunately for Cicero, at least as regards the hostile critics, he made himself vulnerable with an amazingly revealing record of his day-to-day life—in fact a running account of each thought and feeling he had. In the hundreds of letters that he himself more or less arranged to have published (at least he encouraged his friend Atticus in this pursuit) he tells all, to use the colloquial phrase. There is nothing like this in the whole history of literature. It seems that every good and every bad, every weak and every strong reaction that this busy man had to life is revealed somewhere in the letters. We know more about the day-to-day Cicero from his twenty-sixth year forward than we can claim to know about most of our contemporaries. This incredibly articulate and industrious Roman not only left a remarkable supply of personal correspondence but it was the correspondence of a compulsive self-analyst. He never had a doubt or misgiving, a hope or an ambition that he didn't report to Atticus, his other friends, or his family in the letters. We know of his religious doubts, his moral concerns, his suspicion of his wife's mismanagement of the family funds, and his political torment. Also, his kindness (revealed in his thoughtful and affectionate treatment of Tiro, a freedman), his inordinate love of his daughter Tullia, who somehow never seemed to have merited it particularly, his pathetic efforts to procure for himself a tri-

umph in honor of accomplishments that meant little or
nothing to his Senatorial friends.

But this full revelation of thought and feeling is not
limited to the letters. His rhetorical works, taken in order
of their writing also reveal his growth and his every shift
in judgment concerning rhetorical principles and practices. Crassus in *De Oratore* itself may well be identified
as the spokesman of Cicero but so at times, was Antony,
and even the elderly Scaevola may express some of the
author's misgivings about the importance of the power
of eloquence in society generally. Who can doubt that
the discourse on humor attributed to Caesar sets forth
the author's own approach? We accept the idea that Cicero planned to use Crassus as his spokesman in the dialogues, and, as Baldwin put it, "Certainly Cicero sym-
pathizes (and expects us to sympathize) with Crassus."
It is Cicero, not merely Crassus, who pleads that the teaching of the orator be "not the imparting of tricks . . . ,
but the gradual bringing to bear of the whole man."[3]
Nevertheless in Book II Antony's comments on *Inventio*
are certainly endorsed by the author, and as noted earlier
Scaevola's rejection of the idea that the philosopher-
statesman-orator was the greatest civilizing influence as
being a bit overdrawn may very well mirror Cicero's own
occasional concern about a possible overemphasis of the
idea.

MARCUS TULLIUS CICERO

Marcus Tullius Cicero lived in the last years of the
Roman republic. He was born on January 3, 106 B.C.,
near Arpinum about sixty miles southeast of Rome. Arpinum was a relatively small community in which his
parents were prosperous and respected citizens. We know
very little about his parents and nothing of that is particularly relevant except for the certainty that the family
was able to recognize the special talent of their eldest son

[3] C. S. Baldwin, *Ancient Rhetoric and Poetic* (New York, 1924),
p. 46.

and to indulge in their ambition to provide him with the best training available. While Marcus was a boy, the family moved to Rome, and Cicero tells us that he was put under the tutelage of Greek teachers in rhetoric and philosophy. Under one of these, Molo the rhetorician, he was able to study once again during a visit to Greece and Rhodes.

In the tradition of prosperous Roman youths with ambitions, he was put under the guidance of the greatest lawyer of the day—in this case Mucius Scaevola. He also benefitted from the advice of Crassus and other great orators. During the period when Cicero was growing up in Rome, momentous historic events were occurring. The Senatorial party, which had more or less presided over the development of Roman dominance throughout Europe and parts of Asia and Africa, was beginning to have more and more difficulty in controlling the situation. A great struggle was going on between two generals, Marius and Sulla, for the control of Rome. In their conflicts it became evident that military power was necessary if one were to enforce political control. One might say that the struggles of Marius and Sulla provided the handwriting on the wall for Senatorial government. As a matter of fact, Julius Caesar, a contemporary and rival of Cicero, was destined to precipitate the fall of the Roman Republic, and it was Octavianus, a young man very well known to the great orator, who became the first emperor under the title Augustus. If we accept the theory so often advanced that rhetoric prospers and burgeons in times when society is free, and reaches its greatest heights when freedom is being threatened, an ambitious orator could scarcely have hoped for a more favorable time.

Since Cicero chose early in life to work his way up in the Senatorial party, and since he chose the route of civil leadership rather than military accomplishment, he had ample opportunity to practice the art of oratory. He was attracting attention as a lawyer at the age of twenty-six, having successfully defended Roscius in an important case in the year 80. For reasons which are not altogether clear,

Cicero, his brother Quintus, and a cousin departed for Greece and Asia Minor where he studied under the philosophers and rhetoricians of the Academy in Athens and where he was able to improve his speaking habits, apparently in order to relieve the strain on his ailing throat and lungs. We do not know what therapy was involved, although there are stories that Molo of Rhodes made certain recommendations involving toning down his voice. Perhaps this period of travel and study cannot be described better than Haskell describes it—post-graduate study in Athens.

At the age of thirty, he was back in Rome and busy in the law courts, married to Terentia and the proud father of a daughter, Tullia. Shortly thereafter, the young man began to receive some attention from the government. He became finance officer in Sicily and is credited with having engaged in archaeological work there leading to the discovery of the tomb of Archimedes at Syracuse. At the age of thirty-six, he was elected *Curule Aedile*, the official in charge of public works. Three years later he took the next step in the sequence of civil honors in Rome when he became praetor. In 63 B.C. at the age of forty-three, Cicero as consul suppressed the uprising headed by Catiline, delivered the philippics for which he is best remembered, and was acclaimed Father of His Country by the Senate. Perhaps more important historically, Julius Caesar was elected Pontifex Maximus, and Pompey, the great military hero of the time, joined with Crassus and Caesar to form the first triumvirate.

Five years later, Cicero was driven into exile for having put to death certain of the Catilinarian conspirators without due process of law. A law was passed permitting his recall in 57 B.C. and he returned to Rome but soon discovered that his period of power and influence in the Capitol had passed. It had never been as great as he would have liked to believe. The triumvirate of Pompey, Crassus, and Caesar was renewed and Cicero was forced to acquiesce. In 55 B.C., while Caesar was away in Gaul establishing himself even more firmly in the popular esteem

of Rome, Cicero, pretty much out of things, took the time
to write *De Oratore*. From this time on, things deteriorated rapidly both for Cicero and his beloved Republic.
After an interlude while Cicero served as proconsul to
Cilicia in Asia Minor, the great orator returned to Rome
to find things approaching a crisis between Caesar and
Pompey. After a year of agonized indecision Cicero took
sides with Pompey and soon found himself defeated and
discredited. Caesar treated him with kindness and consideration, however, and let him return to Rome in 46 B.C.
He composed several of his books on oratory and rhetoric
during this period. These include *De Partitione Oratore*,
Brutus de Claris Oratoribus, and *Orator*. The assassina-
tion of Caesar took place in 44 B.C. and Cicero returned to
Rome to deliver a series of bitter attacks against Antony
who was trying to take over the control of Rome left by
Caesar. With characteristic bad luck or bad judgment,
Cicero and his party chose Octavian against Antony and
even expected help from Lepidus. These three men had
already agreed upon the second triumvirate for control
of affairs in Rome. When the conspirators led by Brutus
and Cassius had been defeated, Cicero was doomed, and
he was killed by order of the triumvirate on December 7,
43 B.C., when he was sixty-three years of age. This recital
of the bare chronological details of the life of Cicero indicates an unusually busy existence.

One cannot fail to be impressed with his industry when
one considers that, quite aside from the political acts which
tie him to the history of Western civilization, the man delivered scores of forensic orations, wrote many of the
world's best-known essays on subjects ranging from the
Aristotelean *Topics* to old age, made a half dozen brilliant
contributions to the literature of rhetoric and public address, wrote eight hundred letters of which we have definite
record, managed (perhaps mismanaged) extensive proper-
ties throughout the Mediterranean area, and found time
to spoil his son Marcus Jr. and to suffer through the mari-
tal misadventures of his beloved Tulliola, whose death left
him a bitter and shaken man.

THE RHETORICAL WORKS OF MARCUS TULLIUS CICERO

A review of Cicero's rhetorical product may prove helpful at this point. His first book on rhetoric was *De Inventione*, actually part one of a projected work, *Rhetorica
Libri*, which was to have been followed by sections on the
other areas of arrangement, style, delivery, and memory.
It was, as the title indicates, an attempt to provide the
young Roman with material on the discovery of ideas and
subject matter. Professor Petersson regrets that it was
not finished. As he says it would have left a full report on
how rhetoric was taught in the time of Cicero's youth.[4]

In the introduction Cicero states a position popular in
Greek rhetoric from the time of Isocrates and Aristotle,
"that wisdom without eloquence does too little for the
good of the states, but that eloquence without wisdom is
generally highly disadvantageous and is never helpful."

But after dealing briefly with the good done by eloquence, he then enters into a tedious analysis of the rules
in the tradition of the school rhetoricians. It is well identified by M. L. Clarke as "severely technical."[5] It seems
strange that this work by Cicero and the *Ad Herrenium*,
erroneously attributed to him, were the treatises most frequently referred to by scholars throughout most of the
Middle Ages as Ciceronian sources.

In the *De Oratore* Cicero considered the *De Inventio* to
be somewhat boyish and professed to be substituting for
this textbook approach something more indicative of his
mature thinking on the true nature of the orator. In other
words, the greatest of the Roman rhetoricians did not
make a fetish of absolute consistency nor did he hesitate
to change ideas and emphases in his thoughts on his chosen
subject. Few twentieth-century experts in rhetoric would
quarrel with him on this point.

Certainly Cicero himself was pleased with *De Oratore*.
Shortly after it was completed, he recommended it to his
friend Lentulus for the instruction of his son, and con-

---

[4] T. Petersson, *Cicero: A Biography* (New York, 1963), p. 369.
[5] M. L. Clarke, *Rhetoric at Rome* (New York, 1963), p. 53.

tinued to be well satisfied with it a decade later. In a letter to Atticus written in 45 B.C. we find the oft quoted comment: "Sunt etiam de oratore nostri tres, vehementer probati."[6] As we have said, Cicero seemed to have felt that the *De Oratore* provided an adequate statement of his best thinking on the subject. We do not know how he felt about the later works as compared to his masterpiece. They cannot be said, however, to have revealed any changes in or additions to his basic thinking after 55 B.C.

In the *De Partitione Oratoria*, done a few years after the *De Oratore* in 46 or 45 B.C. (according to Petersson, probably written shortly after 54 B.C.), Cicero reverts again, in an interesting question-and-answer format, to pretty much the dry, bookish rules and principles of the middle and new Academies. But his reason here is quite clear. This book was designed to provide a kind of short course in speaking for his son Marcus, Jr. and all that we know about this young man would indicate that the broad philosophical approach of *De Oratore* would have been wasted on him. Young Marcus seems to have shown none of the scholarly interest or aptitude of his father.

The *Topica*, 44 B.C., professes to be an exposition of Aristotle's theory of *topoi*. Even the fact that the author admitted to having written it from memory while on a sea voyage, to help his friend *Trebatius* understand the work of the great Greek in this aspect of rhetoric, does not explain the wide deviation of this treatment from Aristotle. Petersson[7] suggests that the *Topica* represents the contemporary teaching on topics that went under Aristotle's name in Rome at that time.

The *Brutus*, done in 46 B.C., is primarily a history of Roman orators but actually made use of the best practices of Rome's great speakers to defend Cicero's own point of view about what constituted effective oratory. It also initiated an attack on the severely logical style practiced by some of the young men of the city who called themselves Attici.

---

[6] Ad Atticum xiii 19.
[7] Petersson, *Cicero: A Biography*, p. 370.

In the *Orator*, which appears to have followed the *Brutus*, although quite likely in the same year, 46 B.C., Cicero continues his attack on the Attic approach practiced by Catulus and the young Brutus. The ideal orator is described in what is unmistakably a defense of the author's own style. Although his position had not essentially changed on the true art and function of the orator, this book provides a much more elaborate exposition of rhythmic prose, particularly as it affects the *clausula* in Ciceronian prose. This had been discussed rather vaguely in Book III of the *De Oratore;* in the *Orator* Cicero enters into the subject in some detail. Professor Albert Curtis Clark in his article on Cicero in the *Encyclopedia Britannica*, 1959 edition, explains the trochaic foot in the *clausula* and hails the work of Dr. Zielinski of Warsaw in discovering, after an examination of all the endings in Cicero's speeches, that they are governed by trochaic cadence. While these refinements of prose rhythm are quite interesting in the *Orator*, there is little reason to doubt that they had been worked out by Cicero before the writing of the *De Oratore*. After all, Cicero's consistent refusal to go into elaborate and systematic detail in the *De Oratore* is well known and led to much criticism on the part of those who insist upon severe adherence to elaboration of theory. It drew, for instance, an ex cathedra blast from Bishop Whately in his *Elements of Rhetoric*.[8] In the introduction to that work, Whately, after pronouncing Aristotle, "the best of the systematic writers on Rhetoric," goes on as follows, "Cicero is hardly to be reckoned among the number for he delighted so much more in the practice than in the theory of his art, that he is perpetually drawn off from the rigid philosophical analysis of its principles, into discursive declamations, always eloquent indeed, and often highly interesting, but adverse to regularity of system and frequently as unsatisfactory to the practical student as to the philosopher."

Nothing essentially new appears in *De Optimo Genere*

---

[8] Richard Whately, *Elements of Rhetoric*, ed. D. Ehninger (Carbondale, Ill., 1963), p. 7.

Oratorum, the fragmented introductory essay which apparently accompanied the author's translations of the speeches of Demosthenes and Aeschines on the Crown in 46 B.C.

Another work of approximately the same year, *Paradoxa Stoicorum*, is an attempt to put six of the Stoic paradoxes into oratorical form for argument.

References to the art of rhetoric occur from time to time in Cicero's philosophical essays. An interesting instance occurs in *De Fato* wherein the discussion of fate is interrupted while Hirtius and Cicero talk about the importance of oratory and its relationship to philosophy, but nothing new comes of this. One may conclude that of all of Cicero's work on oratory and orators, the *De Oratore* provides the best and fullest expression. It has been praised by scholars over the years.

EVALUATION OF THE *De Oratore* BY SCHOLARS

A. S. Wilkins,[9] in the introduction to his authoritative Latin text of *Ciceronis De Oratore Libri Tres* says that *De Oratore* is one of the most finished and perfect of all Cicero's works. He comments on its excellence in these terms:

> But in the *De Oratore* we have the greatest of Roman orators in the very prime of his power giving us the ripe results of his own experience in the art by which the *novus homo* of Arpinum had risen to the highest post in the Roman State. . . . He is giving us no mere theories for the school of declaimers: nothing is more noteworthy throughout the book than the contempt with which he flings aside the tricks and flourishes which are fit only for the wrestling school and its unguents and the steadiness with which he keeps in view the practical requirements of one who wishes to play the part of a true Roman in the conflicts of the Assembly and the law courts.

Wilkins then goes on to praise the wealth of illustration, the thoughtful selection of time and place, and finally the

[9] A. S. Wilkins, *Ciceronis De Oratore Libri Tres* (Oxford, 1892), Introduction, p. 1.

supreme mastery of the Roman style revealed in the language.

If this were not praise enough Baldwin in *Ancient Rhetoric and Poetic* writes, "It is worth insisting on that the practitioner here [in *De Oratore*] coincides with the philosopher, and both with the theory and practice of rhetoric in the best days of the ancient tradition."[10]

Petersson, in his *Cicero: A Biography* writes of this dialogue, "It is not easy to give a conception of the infinite variety, the sanity, the charm, and the enthusiasm of this work."[11]

M. L. Clarke, in *Rhetoric at Rome*, testifies thus, "And even if none of the ideas or precepts in *De Oratore* is new— and it was difficult to be original in such a well-known field—the choice and combination remain Cicero's as do the force and conviction and the eloquence and charm with which they are presented."[12] It must be admitted that Clarke follows this with an expression of disappointment at Cicero's inconclusiveness.

In the introduction of *Cicero: De Oratore*, Books I and II translated by Sutton and Rackham, we find this: "The present work is indeed worthy of the greatest of Roman orators. . . ."[13]

In the first published English translation of *De Oratore* done by G. P. and printed in London in 1723, the author says in his preface, "I have endeavor'd to relate intelligibly, the genuine sense of my Author and to avoid all excursions, rather leaving out, than adding. For tho' Tully is not more correct nor concise in any part of his writings, than in his beloved Book, *De Oratore*, yet to express his sincerity in as short sentences and as few Words as possible, must be suitable in a translation of him, because, as Quintilian observes, Nihil demi potest Demosthenes nihil addi Tullio!"[14]

---

[10] Baldwin, *Ancient Rhetoric*, p. 40.
[11] Petersson, *Cicero: A Biography*, p. 413.
[12] Clarke, *Rhetoric at Rome*, p. 51.
[13] E. W. Sutton and H. Rackham, *Cicero: De Oratore Books I and II* (London, 1942), p. xi.
[14] G. P., A translation of *Tully de Oratore* (London, 1723), preface, p. i.

In the preface to his 1742 translation, William Guthrie concedes admiringly that, "The character and qualifications of an Orator are so well, and so fully handled in the following that it would be the height of presumption to say anything farther on those Heads."[15]

Calvert in his well-known translation, *The De Oratore of Cicero*, 1870, pays tribute to his author in the Argument as follows, "Of all the treatises which have come down to us in this, their favorite form of discussion, none has a stronger claim to notice, for ingenuity of construction, excellence of matter, and exquisite finish of style than Cicero's celebrated dialogue on the character of the orator."[16]

CICERO AND MODERN RHETORICIANS

Perhaps it has been a misfortune that the Latin scholars and translators of ancient works on persuasion have often been rhetoricians themselves only incidentally. M. L. Clarke in his excellent study of *Rhetoric at Rome* is a case in point. Quoting Thomas de Quincey to the effect that the Age of Rhetoric, like that of Chivalry, "had passed amongst forgotten things," Professor Clarke concedes that, in a sense, persuasion is always with us, but makes clear that rhetoric, as taught by such as Cicero, survives "only in America with her professors of rhetoric and university departments of speech."[17] He doesn't seem to expect any interest in his book beyond that of the historian, the student of Roman affairs, and the classical language scholar. This is not to say that the Latinist who ponders such a work as *De Oratore* can remain unaware of the rhetorical emphasis; rather that his is not essentially the viewpoint of the rhetorician. But there are rhetoricians today, and they remain interested in the masterpiece of the great *doctus orator*, Cicero. People in the field of speech are guilty of a continuing preoccupation with the rhetorical

[15] William Guthrie (tr.), *M. T. Cicero de Oratore* (London, 1742), preface, p. iii.
[16] F. B. Calvert (tr.), *The De Oratore of Cicero* (Edinburgh, 1870), preface, p. xi.
[17] Clarke, *Rhetoric at Rome*, p. vi.

theory and practice of the great ancient rhetoricians. Some of us remain interested in tracing the development of thinking on rhetoric in terms of both qualitative and instrumental meanings as well as evaluative symbols among the ancient writers in Western culture. This being the case, we study Cicero and spend considerable time absorbing and thoughtfully exploring his ideas. We do this to relate them historically to the earlier Greek rhetoricians and the succeeding writers on the subject throughout the Middle Ages, the Renaissance, into the modern world and down to the present.

We also read a work like the *De Oratore* in order to extract from it such practical theory as may be of continuing use to us at the present time. And on this second point, there have been widely varied opinions and practices in recent times. It seems to many of those of us who review Cicero's advice and recommendations in his five works on the subject, that one could do a surprisingly good job of producing effective speakers in our own day simply by using his materials. Cicero, of course, did not view himself as a teacher of rhetoric and yet, taking him as a whole, he provides us with a solid basis in the characteristics and practices of the superior speaker in the areas of invention, arrangement, style, delivery, and memory. Much ancient rhetoric remains surprisingly teachable. Fairly recently, indeed, certain professors have undertaken to teach the basic speech course from Aristotle's *Rhetoric*, but, of course, such total and direct application of ancient theory is not what most of us have in mind when we continue to consider such works as the *De Oratore* in the twentieth century. Rather, we find in such a work much which is pertinent to our theory and to the things which help to identify problems with which we are still struggling. As an excellent example of the latter, we find Cicero in the first century B.C. pondering over where the proper emphasis ought to be placed as between idea and technique. Quite evidently, the great Roman was no more successful in discovering a completely satisfactory position on this problem than are we. How can we achieve an acceptable balance, a proper coincidence and relationship, between the man and his method? How can we emphasize adequately the philosopher-statesman concept without neglecting the admittedly less attractive but still very important matters of language and oral presentation? Cicero did not solve this problem in his day but his comments are useful. Shortly Quintilian was found not to be so insistent upon philosophy for the orator, and the rhetoricians of the empire for the most part soon turned away to the empty stylized approach. There might be a warning here for scholars of the second half of this century with all of our communications theory, behavioral modification studies and narrowly focused research projects based upon statistics.

It is evident that many innovators and initiators of concepts of rhetoric in our day have not moved in their new directions without having first taken proper cognizance of Cicero and the other ancients. I. A. Richards (1936) who dismisses much of the old rhetoric up to and including the works of Whately is nonetheless forced to refer to ancient sources more or less as a point of departure. Hence, in his work on metaphor in *The Philosophy of Rhetoric* he goes back to Aristotle and then makes the following comment: "Throughout the history of rhetoric, metaphor has been treated as a sort of happy extra trick with words, an opportunity to exploit the accidents of their versatility, something in place occasionally but requiring unusual skill and caution. In brief, a grace or ornament or *added* power of language, in its constitutive form."[18]

The sociologist Hugh Duncan (1962) in his work, *Communication and Social Order*, in an analytical review of Kenneth Burke's *Rhetoric of Social Order* has the following interesting statement, "but neither, as Aristotle, Cicero, Quintilian, Augustine, and now Burke warn us, will the theory of rhetoric be of any value unless it can be applied to the affairs of men and society. Classical rhetoricians are much more concerned with *how* to persuade than with the abstract principles of persuasion. They *assumed* that everyone knew that language, motives, and society could

[18] I. A. Richards, *The Philosophy of Rhetoric* (New York, 1965), p. 90.

not be separated.   Thus, for them, the argument was not whether language served to create and sustain social bonds, but *how* it did so."   He goes on to make the point that though classical rhetoricians were not involved with the questions about audiences which haunt those who must appeal successfully to the varied and extensive audiences of our time, this did not mean that they were unaware of the power of nonrational appeal.[19]   Certainly Cicero was not unaware.   He has some interesting things to say about emotional appeal.

A. Craig Baird in his work, *Rhetoric: A Philosophical Inquiry*, (1965) refers frequently to Cicero's comments in all the areas of rhetoric.   There are, of course, a number of papers in the *Quarterly Journal of Speech* bearing upon historical and theoretical matters which draw generously upon Cicero's works, particularly the *De Oratore*.

At the present time, now that scholars in oral communications are returning to rhetoric after a brief separation from the term, there is little doubt that the works of such ancients as Cicero will bear examination.   Such a work as the *De Oratore* may serve as a point of departure for students of the rhetoric of motivation, the rhetoric of creative interchange, the rhetoric of disequilibrium and balance, the rhetoric of frustration and protest, perhaps even the rhetoric of affluence and poverty.

The Watson Version of the *De Oratore*

LET US TURN to the specific translation of the *De Oratore* found in this volume.   It is that of John Selby Watson.   You will observe in Watson's preface that he identifies Barnes' translation as the groundwork for his text.   This leads Wilkins to report on the Barnes' translation as follows: "Barnes, 1762, revised by Watson, 1855."   Watson says quite accurately that every page of the Barnes was carefully corrected and many pages rewritten.   A careful comparison of both texts page by page gives a definite im-

[19] Hugh Duncan, *Communication and Social Order* (New York, 1962), p. 172.

pression that by the time the revision was completed we have, for all practical purposes, a completely new version and we cannot help but admire Watson for his modesty. As nearly as can be determined, Barnes does not indicate what text he uses. But Watson made his text conformable to that of Orellius (1826) or the second edition completed by Baiter and Holm (1846). There is no reason to doubt that Watson had access to excellent textual scholarship for his work. He is familiar with the Ellendt text. This is the same Ellendt whose notes were used by A. S. Wilkins in the preparation of his definitive edition in 1892. To quote Wilkins, "The present edition, the first which has been published with an English commentary, is largely indebted to the notes of Ellendt, Piderit, and Sorof."[20]

John Selby Watson's *Cicero on Oratory and Orators; With His Letters to Quintus and Brutus* was first published in 1848 as a part of the Bohn Classical Library. It was published by George Bell in 1855, and by Bell and Daldy in 1871. In 1878 it was printed as part of Harper's Classical Library, and was reprinted several times by Harper. After 1897 the *De Oratore* section appeared with an introduction by Edward Brooks, Jr. published by David McKay. The Watson version was widely used—almost certainly the most widely used of all translations for a half century. Appearing as it did in the two popular series of translations prior to 1948, the Bohn and the Harper, it represented Cicero in English to a generation of scholars. It still remains an excellent source though the English is inevitably a bit crabbed and old-fashioned. The language is quite clear and thoroughly understandable. A careful check of more recent versions indicates that Watson has done as well as any with the numerous passages which can never be rendered into English without some awkwardness. The textual and historical notes accompanying the Watson are still pertinent and reliable, and add a good deal to the text both in interest and in information. Some of the background these notes supply is particularly useful to the person who is not able to read the Latin.

[20] Wilkins, *Ciceronis de Oratore Libri Tres*, p. 71.

Since the English text sought for this series had to be readable and at the same time adequate in scholarship the Watson recommended itself. The translator of the *De Oratore* in this volume brought good credentials to the task. Educated at first by his grandfather, he earned the Bachelor of Arts Degree from Trinity College (Dublin) in 1838, receiving a gold medal in classics, and the Master of Arts from the same institution in 1844. In 1854, he was admitted to Oxford for advanced work. Watson continued his classical studies throughout his life. He published annotated editions of some works of Aeschylus and Sallust. As an indication of his wide acceptance as a classical scholar, we note that the Bohn Classical Library included in addition to his *Oratory and Orators*, his translations of Sallust, Lucretius, Quintilian, Xenophon, Paterculus, and Nepos.

In addition to his translations, he did a number of biographical works including lives of John Wilkes, Bishop Warburton, and George Fox. His interests did not end there. He was also the author of *Geology: A Poem in Seven Books* and a treatise on *Reasoning Power in Animals*. Watson was a most fascinating figure. A brief review of his life apart from his academic and scholarly accomplishments proves interesting and a few items might be worth mentioning. The article appearing under his name in the *Dictionary of National Biography* identifies him rather startlingly as follows: "Watson, John Selby (1804–84) author and murderer." He is reported to have been the son of humble Scottish parents. We have reviewed his educational background but he also led a busy and, at times, exciting existence outside the world of scholarship. He was ordained Deacon in 1839 and Priest in 1840 and served the curacy of Langport in Somerset for three years. From 1844 to 1870 he served as headmaster of a grammar school in Stockwell near London. The school was prosperous for many years but when it began to lose popularity he was dismissed from its management. In 1871, he killed his wife. He was found guilty of murder but the death sentence was commuted to penal servitude for life. A volume of psychological studies of his married life, with evidence leading up to the murder was published in Berlin in 1875. Of more interest to classical scholars perhaps, is the fact that he may well be the only scholar in British history on whose Latin usage the British cabinet divided. One of his remarks during the murder trial was "Saepe olim semper debere nocuit debitori." The division was called for on the question of whether this was good or bad Latin.

THE LATIN TEXT OF THE *De Oratore*

It is hard for us today to appreciate the dedication and industry of Renaissance and modern scholars in accumulating old manuscripts, collating texts, and even, at times, sorting out quantities of material which might prove to contain a few pages from each of several works all grouped together. The surviving manuscripts of *De Oratore* may be thought of as falling into three classes: all those discovered up to 1422 were not only fragmented, but showed signs of mutilation through the errors of copyists and the erroneous choices of scholars as regards meaning in certain passages. In the introduction to Augustus S. Wilkins' 1892 edition of the *De Oratore*, widely accepted as the best available, that scholar tells us how a final satisfactory text was arrived at after years of painstaking research. The Codex Abrincensis from the ninth century consists of sixty leaves of parchment, only fifty of which were from the *De Oratore*. Another of the earliest remains is Codex Harleianus, again dating from the ninth century. It contains parts of all three books of the *De Oratore*, is much more complete and, Wilkins says, equal in excellence to the Codex Abrincensis.

Codex Erlangensis, tenth century, contains the same passages as the Abrincensis but has additional materials from the dialogues. These three primary sources provide the scholars in Ancient Latin with a basis for working out the presently accepted text. Since these mutilated texts go far back in history and yet reveal a remarkable consistency they make it possible for scholars to arrive with certainty at the original language of the *De Oratore*. A second group of mutilated and fragmented manuscripts are of less value. They come from the fourteenth and fifteenth centuries mainly and are simply copies of the earlier remains. Ellendt is said to have relied on these although he knew of the older copies when he did his annotated text in 1840. The third class of manuscripts are the complete texts. Most notable of these is that called Codex Laudensis, found at Lodi in 1422. The complete *Brutus* and *Oratore* as well as the *De Oratore* were included in this discovery. The original soon disappeared but Ellendt quotes from twenty-two copies of this text, and dozens more have been found. For a detailed analysis and evaluation of the various Latin sources, the reader is referred to the introduction to the Wilkins work in 1892. The comments are in English, whereas in later editions the introduction is greatly reduced in content and is written in Latin.

ENGLISH TRANSLATIONS OF THE *De Oratore*

While a well-established Latin text was being arrived at laboriously, and also since comparative agreement has been reached, a number of translations into modern language have been attempted. Those in English should claim most of our attention. A translation of *Tully de Oratore* was printed in London for an author who was identified simply by the initials G. P. The publication date is 1723. In the preface, the translator announces,

> the part I have translated contains the most modern Precepts and Instructions of the Whole Book. What Need is there then for surfeiting of the Reader with a Repetition of the same Arguments, or a Multiplicity of needless ones which will probably have no other effect but to hinder him from attending to, or reaping an advantage from any of them . . . the Design of this Work, at present, is to prove that not only the Art of speaking well, but a general knowledge is requisit to the Qualifications of a just Oratour; for many other Arts have no dependence upon anything else: But to talk handsomely, that is with Judgment, Closeness, and Elegance, is no limited Province; nor confined to one

Subject: He must discourse well of everything that is disputable who pretends to be an Oratour or he must resign his Pretentions to it.

G. P. does not tell us of his original Latin source but in his quaint and rather pompous way manages to catch the sense of Cicero remarkably well.

In the 1742 edition of the often reprinted translation of William Guthrie, *M. T. Cicero de Oratore, or His Three Dialogues Upon the Character and Qualifications of an Orator*, that scholar faces up squarely to the problem of translation. In his introductory remarks, he writes,

all that is left to a translator is to endeavour that his Original may not be Disgrac'd by his Copy and that the Friends of Cicero may not Blush at the Mean Appearance he makes in a modern Language. But it is impossible with any Propriety to introduce my great Author to the Public in the following Translation without at the same time acquainting the World with the Motives, I had almost said with the Necessity of the present undertaking. Men of learning are divided, with regard to the Merit of Translations in general; I shall not pretend to decide upon either side; but I will venture to say, that if the present Taste in Learning should gain Ground, this Nation will soon have no other means left of being acquainted with the good sense of the Antients, but thro' Translations. It is upon this Footing only that I will justify the Translation of a Prose Author.

Guthrie goes on to justify translation of this Latin work. He argues as already indicated that he feared greatly that, what with the weakening of training in the ancient languages as a result of the tendency of the curricula to stress subjects useful in trade, much of the ancient wisdom would become inaccessible to the young British scholar of his and succeeding generations. It is interesting to note in the justification for this translation of a prose work, the same assumption which still seems to survive among educated Englishmen that there is scarcely any excuse for the scholar being unable to read ancient works in the original Latin, *particularly prose works*. Apparently the Latinists in the British public schools and universities felt justified in calling for help on the verses of Vergil and Horace.

It cannot be said that Guthrie's translation warrants his concern lest he embarrass the great Roman in his English version. Actually, the translation reads rather well and, at times, seems to catch the true Ciceronian flavor of utterance better than the efforts of the other translators. The text upon which this translation was based is that of Zacharias Pearce, as may be deduced from the fact that at the end of the volume page sources are given from Pearce, whose second edition had come out at Cambridge in 1732.

In 1762, George Barnes published a translation in London under the title, *Cicero and the Complete Orator*. The work has been mentioned earlier. This effort was recognized by Wilkins as being somewhat better than those of Guthrie and Calvert. Again, the translator severely limits his objectives and makes no claim of having captured the style of the original. In his notes and illustrations of *Book The First*, he writes about his translation of *De Oratore* which he claims to have "considered only as an interpretation to render the understanding of the original more easy, happy if I have not mistaken the author's sense without having the vanity to think that I have anywhere caught his stile or manner."

In 1870 F. B. Calvert published a translation under the title *The De Oratore of Cicero*. He revealed the usual misgivings as he approached the task. In fact, his comments are so much to the point that it is worthwhile to quote from them at considerable length. He says in his preface:

> In the somewhat ambitious attempt to convert a work of Cicero into English style, making even remote approximation to any of the higher qualities of his own superb Latin, the translator has come to his task not only with a full conviction of his difficulties, but with an oppressive feeling that many of those difficulties are absolutely insurmountable. The transference of one modern language into another has its own well-known and peculiar impediments, but in the attempt to make the ancient world speak both intelligibly and eloquently to the modern, those impediments are multiplied a hundredfold. Irrespective of the total difference of

construction, and other considerations too obvious to be mentioned, the material itself to be employed is not only so different in kind, but, as an exponent of Cicero especially, so inferior in quality, that whoever attempts to translate his largely rounded and polished periods into the comparatively rude and fragmentary dialects of the North, will find himself in imminent danger of reversing the proud boast of Augustus, and of reducing the massive marble of the Roman orator to brick, or mere adobe.

Cicero possesses in a pre-eminent degree that which embalms and confers immortality on thought in a style of surpassing grandeur, beauty, grace, and harmony. This constitutes his characteristic excellence, and this it is which opposes the great and insuperable barrier to the successful efforts of every translator; and if he who has now made the attempt could have supposed for one moment that an adequate reproduction of the matchless cadence of Cicero would be looked for in these pages, he must have thrown down his pen at once, and abandoned the undertaking in despair. But such an achievement, he feels assured, will not be expected from him; for, although fully aware that a perfect translation should faithfully reflect the minutest particle of the author's meaning, with all the graces and peculiarities of his style, and combine with these the free and unembarrassed flow of original composition, such perfection, he knows, though in different degrees approachable and approached, has rarely, if ever, yet been realized, and he therefore reposes confidently in the conviction, that this consideration will win for him the indulgent appreciation of every candid reader, and temper the severity of criticism.   The latitude allowed to translation is thus defined by Dr. Johnson in his Life of Dryden, "when correspondence cannot be obtained, it is necessary to be content with something equivalent."

A translation of Book I was made by E. N. P. Moor in 1893 and this translation has been widely praised as being the best, both in terms of meaning and the capturing of the Ciceronian style.   It is unfortunate that Books II and III were never completed.

In 1942 the dialogues were translated by E. W. Sutton and H. Rackham.   Theirs is the version which appears in the Loeb Classical Library series, having been revised and reprinted in 1948 and 1959.   Mr. Sutton is credited by Mr. Rackham with having done the work on Book I and part of

Book II. Sutton, in turn, acknowledges his indebtedness to Charles Stuttaford for the text of Book I. This translation, appearing first near the middle of the twentieth century is currently in wide use. The scholars involved expressed no concern for the difficulties in catching the thought and style of Cicero.

Without being in any way conclusive, a parallel sampling of the work of several of the translators of the *De Oratore* should be interesting. It should reveal, to an extent, the difficulties of achieving exact meaning and the variety with which different translators have attempted to approximate in English the Ciceronian style. It seems futile, one might almost say unnecessary, to attempt fine language in the English version. It is, on the other hand, of great importance to the scholar of rhetoric that the thought come through clearly and unmistakably. Consider what various scholars have done with the following Latin text taken from the 1901 edition by Wilkins.

> *Ac mihi quidem saepenumero in summos homines ac summis ingeniis praeditos intuenti quaerendum esse visum est, quid esset cur plures in omnibus rebus quam in dicendo admirabiles exstitissent. Nam, quocumque te animo et cogitatione converteris, permultos excellentes in quoque genere videbis non mediocrium artium, sed prope maximarum.*

This passage has been selected at random in order not to favor any one translator. Cicero is often more troublesome, but this is fairly typical of some of the problems his style presents. For example, the complex structure sustained for twenty-eight words in the first sentence and the piling up of modifiers.

Calvert has this passage as follows:

> Often, indeed, when passing in review before me the men of greatest note and most distinguished by the splendour of their genius, the question has forced itself upon my mind, how it is that more have stood forth in every art to challenge the admiration of mankind than in the art of oratory. For in whatever direction you turn your thoughts, when reflecting on this subject, you will find multitudes pre-eminent, not only in the subordinate but in the very highest departments of art.

Guthrie has the following which it is only fair to note might have been less strange to the eye of his contemporaries in the eighteenth century than it is to us. "I own indeed I have been frequently at a Loss to account, upon a Review of the greatest and ablest men, why fewer have been distinguish'd in Eloquence than in any other Art. For to whatever Point of Science you direct your View and Reflection, you shall find many, excelling in every kind, not only of the midling Arts, but of those which require almost the greatest Compass of Genius."

Sutton and Rackham have the following version of this material:

And for my own part, when, as has often happened, I have been contemplating men of the highest eminence and endowed with the highest abilities, it has seemed to me to be a matter for inquiry, why it was that more of them should have gained outstanding renown in all other pursuits, than have done so in oratory. For in whatever direction you turn your mind and thoughts, you will find very many excelling in every kind, not merely of ordinary arts, but of such as are almost the greatest.

E. N. P. Moor uses the following language in his version of the same passage:

For my own part, when I contemplate the world's greatest and most gifted men, it has often seemed to me a question well worth the asking, why it is that more men have won distinction in all other arts than in oratory; for, turn your thoughts and attention where you will, you will find that in any given branch of art (in those of the highest importance, I may say, as well as in the less important) a very large number have attained to excellence.

In our text J. S. Watson uses the following language:

Often, indeed, as I review in thought the greatest of mankind, and those endowed with the highest abilities, it has appeared to me worthy of inquiry what was the cause that a greater number of persons have been admirable in every other pursuit than in speaking. For which way soever you direct your view in thought and contemplation, you will see numbers excellent in every species, not only of the humble, but even of the highest arts.

It might be interesting to append the Barnes version upon which Watson tells us he based his translation of the *De Oratore*.

And often when I set before my view the greatest men, and those endued with the utmost abilities, I have thought it worthy of enquiry to what cause it was owing that more have been admirable in all things than in speaking. For which way soever you turn your mind in contemplation, you will see numbers excellent in every kind, not only in the mean but most liberal arts.

THE DIALOGUE FORM USED IN THE *De Oratore*

As we have already indicated, these dialogues are supposed to have been written for Cicero's brother Quintus in response to a request for something more polished and complete on the subject of the orator. Cicero throws in parenthetically what was perhaps his real motive which was to offset the impression created by the earlier *De Inventione*, a work which as he says, is scarcely worthy of his present standing in life and his thirty years of added experience in pleading important causes.

A great deal has been written on whether the form of the dialogues is Platonic or Aristotelean. The difference of opinion among reputable scholars is perhaps best revealed when we find Baldwin saying flatly, "the form is obviously the Platonic dialogue"[21] whereas Rackham says "its method is very different from that of the dialogues of Plato."[22] There is an equally troublesome question when we come to the subject of the dialogue of Aristotle because no examples survive, although there is evidence that he wrote some. We are compelled to assume that Aristotle's dialogue must have been, as is Cicero's, one in which the questions to be considered and the answers to be made have all been worked out in advance and where the genuine dramatic interchange is at a minimum. This latter modification is, perhaps, the result of Cicero's and Aristotle's lack of dramatic genius such as that revealed by Plato in

[21] Baldwin, *Ancient Rhetoric*, p. 40.
[22] Sutton and Rackham, *De Oratore*, p. xi.

the Socratic dialogues. Actually, we are, perhaps being a bit too hard on the Roman when we deny him all skill in creating a realistic atmosphere of conversation. In the *De Oratore* one too frequently finds oneself bothered by such chitchat as gossip from the forum and chair hunting in the very midst of the pursuit of absorbing problems.

The *dramatis personae* include Lucius Crassus, Marcus Antonius, Quintus Mucius Scaevola, Caius Aurelius Cotta, Julius Caesar Strabo Vopiscus, Publius Sulpicius Rufus and Quintus Lutatius Catulus. These names are all those of real figures in Roman history. Crassus and Antonius are discussed in the *Brutus* as the outstanding orators of their period and Cotta and Sulpicius are similarly identified as outstanding speakers. There is, of course, no way to be sure that the Romans named here are characterized as they were in real life.

Here again, we have a difference of opinion about the effectiveness of the dialogue. Baldwin says that there is very little imaginative realization once the characters are introduced.[23] Petersson on the other hand says, "The persons are made into living personalities . . . He tried to make a character consistent and convincing."[24] One can agree on this. He did go to considerable pains to introduce little personal notes about the speakers.

It is usually assumed that Crassus speaks for Cicero and Antonius for brother Quintus. This is, however, a division that can be overstressed. As we have said elsewhere, Antonius must certainly represent Marcus Cicero on the subject of invention, and Julius Caesar Vopiscus is surely the author's spokesman on the subject of humor.

The conversations are supposed to have occurred in 91 B.C. at the Tusculan villa of Crassus.

A SUMMARY OF IDEAS TREATED IN THE *De Oratore*

Attention has already been called to the fact that the *De Oratore* has been purposely made discursive and nontechnical. Cicero demonstrates elsewhere—in the *De*

[23] Baldwin, *Ancient Rhetoric*, p. 40.
[24] Petersson, *Cicero: A Biography*, p. 417.

Inventione and *The Partitiones Oratoriae*—that he is capable of presenting the materials of rhetoric in the technical format. In his masterpiece he deals with the orator, his theories and his characteristics in what Mr. Clarke has well described as "the elegant humane manner of a cultured and experienced man of letters and of affairs."[25] As we have already indicated this approach provides digressions and invites parenthetic comments. Nevertheless, when one has enjoyed the experience of reading through the total work one discovers that most of the areas of rhetoric have been given thorough treatment.

Book I After a few pages of opening remarks to Quintus bearing upon the troublesome times and on the fascinations and difficulties of oratory, with some comments on the intent of the dialogues and some words on the historical setting, the discussion begins. Crassus starts talking to his four companions about the importance of oratory in society and government. We are told that states are established and maintained primarily through the leadership of eloquent men. Scaevola casts some doubt upon the importance of the art of the orator, giving Crassus an opportunity to elaborate his thesis. In the course of his response, Crassus notes how brilliant was the rhetoric of Plato when he was ridiculing rhetoric. He argues that rhetoric is a science and that the orator must be well-versed in all the fields of knowledge. The orator must be a philosopher-statesman-orator as previously claimed by Isocrates.

Antonius has two objections to this concept. First, such a wide range of knowledge is unattainable by most men; second, the vast knowledge demanded by Crassus would only result in a vagueness and abstractness which would prevent the orator from being listened to and understood by the average listener. He suggests that effective speaking is primarily a matter of natural aptitude, although it can be improved with practice. The orator, he

[25] Clarke, *Rhetoric at Rome*, p. 50.

says, may wish to go to the learned philosopher for ideas from time to time but this does not demand that the orator himself be a repository of all knowledge.

Crassus then discusses the requirements of the orator, conceding that natural talent is essential for the highest accomplishment. Recognizing natural gifts in Sulpicius and Cotta, he recommends a course of training. This is usually assumed to be a recital of Cicero's method for developing supreme skill.

One must study the rhetoric of the schools in order to learn: 1] the duties of the orator; 2] the purposes of speaking; 3] the kinds of subjects; 4] the determination of *status;* 5] the three kinds of oratory—forensic, deliberative, and panegyric—with a brief reference to commonplaces; 6] the five divisions of oratory on a functional basis—invention, arrangement, style, memory, and delivery; 7] the divisions of speech; and 8] rules for the use of language. This rhetorical system is useful but of itself will not produce the best oratory. Practice is extremely important and *declamatio* seems to be recommended here. Writing is useful both in the development of style and for the practice in ideas and arguments. Training in voice and gesture are necessary. He talks of public speaking, debate practice, gathering a store of information in matters historical, legal, and political. The importance of wide knowledge is stressed again. Dignity and force are important for effective speaking.

Antonius takes issue once again. He says its important that the orator speak well on public questions but he does not need to have a wide cultural background. To work on the emotions, worldly wisdom will suffice the orator. Philosophers might actually disapprove of certain effective courtroom techniques. A detailed knowledge of law is not important. It is apparent that in legal controversy experts disagree on the law and eloquence wins cases. Rather oddly, Antonius, after conceding that such matters as voice control and a collection of historic examples need some study, goes on to say that their study should not be allowed to take up time needed for practice of the speech.

Book II   Book II begins with comments to Quintus on the learning possessed by Crassus and Antonius and the claim by Cicero that the material to follow will spring from more practical experience in oratory than could be claimed by any other writers on the subject of rhetoric. There is a charming comment on one orator being enough for one family and the oft quoted reference to the bashfulness which was said to have prevented the great rhetorician, Isocrates, from delivering his speeches in public.

Antonius begins a discussion of invention and arrangement. He repeats his previous statement that oratory cannot be properly called a science. Good speaking on any subject is oratory. No rules are needed for demonstration; there is no rhetoric of history. He discusses Herodotus and Thucydides on the matters of ideas and composition. Forensic oratory is the most difficult kind. Antonius gives examples of useless rules of rhetoric. He ridicules the Greeks who lay down rules for the obvious. He teases about the five functions or steps and suggests that common sense would clearly indicate that a speaker would begin with an idea and progress through the various stages until he is ready to present it. At this point, it does not take a rhetorician to tell him that it should now be delivered. Antonius urges constant practice with the imitation of good models. An original mind, of course, can dispense with the model. He goes on to talk briefly about the point at issue which will be a matter of fact, nature, or definition. He talks about commonplaces, says the general propositions and specific instances need not take up the time of the orator. Antonius says the Stoic system is of little use, talks about *topoi* but dismisses them as unimportant, then turns to emotions. Emotions must be felt by the speaker if they are to be felt by the audience.

Vopiscus, referred to in the dialogue as Caesar, talks about humor. He deals with its use, its nature, when it is appropriate. He talks of humor of expression and humor of ideas. He gives several examples of each. Antonius then takes over, gives some practical advice on argument, suggesting that the strongest arguments be put at the beginning or end of the speech. He talks about speeches of

advice, suggesting the importance of *ethos* in gaining cre-
dence. He notes the Greek masters of panegyric and recommends comparison with great people as a way of
praising. He then gives some advice on *memoria*, safely
arguing that although there are techniques to stimulate
recall, natural endowment is the prime requisite.

Book III The death of Crassus is reported and Cicero
suggests that the old orator might have been fortunate to
die peacefully considering what happened later on in real
life to the other participants in the dialogue.
  Returning to Cotta's report of the discussion, Crassus
agrees to talk on style: Style is not limited to certain areas
of thought. We respond in different senses to different
media but excellence of expression applies to all. Praise
may be merited for a variety of excellences, too, just as it
may among poets and playwrights. Isocrates possessed
sweetness (suavitatem); Lysias, delicacy (subtilitatem);
Hyperides, pointedness (acumen); Aeschines, sound (soni-
tum); Demosthenes, energy (vim). The list is continued
to the conclusion that each of them deserves praise although for such divergent qualities. Crassus contrasts
himself with Antonius in his manner of speaking. Antonius is bold, full of energy and action, well-armed with
evidence and argument. Crassus, on the other hand, is
quieter, more careful in choosing words than in subject
matter. There are almost as many kinds of eloquence as
of orators. Nevertheless, men of diverse talent may all
benefit from a particular course of instruction. Isocrates
and his students are set forth as examples of this. What
style can be better than pure Latin with perspicuity,
gracefulness, aptitude, and adaptation to the subject.
(quam ut Latine, ut plane, ut ornate, ut ad id quocumque
agetur apte congruenter que dicamus.) Embellishment
(ornatus) is important. Delivery, of course, is important.
There is not only a pure Latin language but a certain Roman tone of voice. A warning is given that if the style
should be confused and ill-arranged, a speech may produce
such a jumble that language which ought to throw light

upon things actually serves to make them obscure. The faculty of thinking and speaking was thought by the ancient Greeks to be wisdom itself. The Socratic point of view seems to suggest divorce of the tongue from the heart but eloquence has been related to philosophy both among the Peripatetics and the Academicians. The ideas of the Stoics do not apply. Wide knowledge remains more important than the systems of the rhetoricians, although the speaker trained in rhetorical skill may have more effect than the philosopher with no such skill. There is no more difficult pursuit or one that requires more aids from learning than oratory. The oratory must not seem too contrived, too "fine." It is well for the speaker to be praised with such remarks as "very well" or "excellent" but he should be bothered to hear "beautifully" come too often. A detailed treatment of the ornate style follows (Handled more thoroughly in the *Orator*). Choice of language and combination of words, rhythm, and figures of speech are discussed. "A metaphor is a brief similitude contracted into a single word."

Propriety has to do with adjusting the style to the subject, the audience and the occasion. No one style will cover everything. Judgment must be depended upon to determine whether plain, middle, or fuller style should be used.

Finally, Crassus discusses delivery. Delivery, he says, has the sole and supreme power in oratory. Without effective delivery, a brilliant man cannot impress listeners whereas a mediocre person who speaks well can exert influence. Here the old story about Aeschines' praise of Demosthenes comes in.

In everything, of course, truth has the advantage over imitation but truth cannot transcend poor delivery. Thus, one should study delivery—facial expression, tone of voice, gesture—in order to portray the emotions and to give force to ideas. The voice is most important along with bodily action and facial expression. One can only wish for a fine voice but through variation and alteration of tone one may make the best use of such voice as he has. Crassus concludes by saying "I have said what I could, although not as I wished but as the shortness of time obliged me; it is wise to lay the blame on time when you cannot add more even if you desire."

THE BRUTUS

The translation of the *Brutus* found in this volume is that of E. Jones published in 1776. It has been impossible to check the Jones version against the one reprinted here. We may accept Watson's statement in the preface to the effect that it was published with but very little variation. G. L. Hendrickson in the introduction to his translation of the *Brutus* in the Loeb Classical Library in 1962, dismisses the Jones translation as "for the most part little more than a free paraphrase, with occasional happy renderings which may justify the title of elegant." Watson, of course, was the author of the statement about the Jones translation's "deserving reputation of combining fidelity with elegance." It is not the purpose of this essay to depart significantly from the relatively slight emphasis that Watson places upon the *Brutus* in this volume. It was, as we have said, primarily a history of outstanding orators or, as Hendrickson puts it, an historical exemplification of Ciceronian theory, but it is also a controversial treatise. In it Cicero, being challenged in what he thought to be the height of his power, was trying to establish his style as superior to that of the Attic group. This group, exemplified pretty much by Calvus and Brutus, was advocating a departure from the Asiatic grandiloquence of Cicero. They professed, of course, to be closer to the clarity and purity of utterance of such Greeks as Lysias. Cicero, through a discussion of the development of oratory up to his time, suggests that his is the full fruition of the Latin style for the orator. One does detect, in a reading the account of great Roman orators, a certain defensive spirit as regards the ornate style which he had developed to such perfection. The members of the dialogue are Marcus Junius Brutus, Titus Pomponius Atticus, and Cicero. Greek oratory is reviewed from its beginnings—a nonhistorical summary of early Roman oratory up to Cathegus at about 204 B.C.

Marcus Cato and Scipio Minor are mentioned. Servius Galba is compared with Laellius. The former appears to have been the first Latin orator to employ consciously the proper resources of true oratory. M. Aemilius Lepidus is credited with having first achieved a true Latin written style. The Gracchi are treated along with such other orators as Rufus.

The account moves to 99 B.C. when the two outstanding orators are the Crassus and Antonius of the *De Oratore.* These men approached the quality of the great Greek orators. There is talk about the difference between the orators in the Italian provinces and those of the city of Rome itself. Julius Caesar Strabo, Sulpicius, and Cotta, three people who also appear in the *De Oratore,* were considered. Cicero, when he finally comes to mention Calvus, develops the theme of the revolt of the Atticists. He concludes by reviewing Hortensius, praising him but finally relegating him to a place inferior to his own.

Summary of Cicero's Position on Rhetoric

OVER A PERIOD of approximately forty years, Cicero made a practice of writing down his ideas on the orator and oratory and finally left us a fairly detailed rhetoric. Whether this rhetoric is his own or simply a rehash of earlier rhetoric is a question that has often been asked. Actually, the question is probably irrelevant. As a thoughtful scholar and purposive practitioner of rhetoric, Cicero knew his Aristotle, Isocrates, Plato, and their successors; nor, as a matter of fact, did he ever deny this knowledge. Consequently, when he wished to review useful theory on persuasion and eloquence for his generation, he found himself referring to the thinkers who had gone before; just, one supposes, as did Aristotle and Isocrates in their day. Of course, there was an element of the eclectic in his work on rhetoric and he was glad to acknowledge it.

Perversely, another question which comes up frequently among critics has to do with the directness and accuracy of Cicero's references to the sources. Did he really read Aristotle or did he simply report the teachings of the late

Peripatetics? Did he know his Plato or did he simply assume the theories of the New Academy to be Platonic? Did he read Isocrates or did he merely take at third or fourth hand the Isocratic teachings of Molo and other members of the Rhodian school? Did his knowledge of the dialectic of the Stoics come from the early founders of that philosophy or did he simply give a perverted version learned from Diodotus? Did his ideas on Topica in his treatise by that name represent a fragmentation and mis-conception of the Aristotelean thinking or a perfectly de-fensible system of *loci* worked out by Cicero himself, modifying the thinking of the great Greek? Did his addi-tion of the term "philosopher" to the orator-statesman theory mean simply that he couldn't understand the *Anti-dosis* and *Against the Sophists,* or do we see in the *De Oratore* an up-to-date Roman improvement and extension of Isocrates' teaching? It is impossible to answer these questions with any hope of complete agreement, but cer-tainly it is fair to grant that in a culture so centered upon rhetoric and oratory as that of the first century B.C., it seems scarcely fair to be too hard on Cicero. Of course he knew what the ancients had said, after all he had studied in Greece and Rhodes. It is equally certain that he knew what the more recent theorists had done with the thinking of the earlier leadership. But as a number of scholars have said, the product of his thought, couched in brilliant lan-guage and modified to meet the conditions that existed in the Rome of his day, forms a body of Ciceronian rhetoric which is worthy of our respect. We cannot ignore the rhetorical product of Cicero for another reason. As we have said before, he dominated the thinking on eloquence and persuasion of practically all the scholars of the Medie-val Age and Renaissance and, hence, provides the main connection between the ancient and the modern world.

How nearly can we state the Ciceronian position? In the first place, he believes firmly in the importance of the orator's being a philosopher and a statesman as well as an accomplished speaker.

He speaks repeatedly for the supremacy of idea over delivery.

On the question of style, even though he spends a great deal of time on rhythm and balance, he believes that natural talent is paramount. In the area of delivery, he holds for a nice balance between natural vocal and personal endowment improved through training. He decries the over-stylized utterance and the excessively dramatic action, yet he agrees with Demosthenes that presentation or delivery is of the greatest importance to the speaker.

On the question of pathetic appeal, he gives a great deal of importance to the emotions, developing the theory that the emotion must be felt by the speaker before it can be generated in the listener.

His position on the rhetoric of the schools is this: He rejects complete preoccupation with their systems, saying that the best orators cannot be produced along those lines. Occasionally speakers in the *De Oratore* ridicule the whole school approach. He admits that his own rather exhaustive earlier treatise in that tradition, the *De Inventione*, no longer satisfies him when he writes the *De Oratore*.

Nevertheless, he presents a modified list of eighteen *loci* for what they are worth, and discusses the use of *stasis* in forensic and to a lesser degree in deliberative and panegyric invention, although he has Antonius say that something like common sense can make their use unnecessary to the man preparing his arguments. Admittedly, it is difficult to make a satisfactory statement on just what the Romans meant when they discussed commonplaces. D. J. Ochs in an exhaustive study of classical doctrines of rhetorical *topoi*, has done a remarkable job of examining and ordering the ancient thinking on the subject ("The Tradition of the Classical Doctrines of Rhetorical Topoi" by Donovan J. Ochs, dissertation, Iowa State University, 1966).

On the use of *controversiae* and *suasoriae* in polishing the speaker, Cicero seems to compromise. He concedes that *declamationes* have some value, admits that he was obliged to use them in his early education and confesses that he kept up the practice of composing or reciting well into his mature years.

It seems quite clear that Cicero had considerable difficulty in reconciling his concept of the original, natural, and philosophically centered orator with the limited, un-inspired, and wearisome approach of school rhetoric. We can only say that his convictions on the one and his ability to recognize the shortcomings of the other deserve considerable credit.

On the question of style it would seem that although we must give Cicero credit for recognizing the virtues of plainness and spontaneity, he frequently seems to favor what most of us would consider overly embellished and excessively studied diction.

On the question of imitation his answer seemed to be in the affirmative; good models could, of course, be advantageously studied and imitated. He has some telling points on the folly of innovation when the best ways of saying things had already been discovered. He professes to have translated works of the Greek masters as a method of improving style. When it comes to the kinds of style, he identifies the plain, middle, and the grand.

In summary, one may say that Cicero, having reviewed the theory of rhetoric in terms of its functions and methods and having examined it in all of its ramifications, returns to the Isocratic emphasis. To Cicero, rhetoric was training for leadership. The product of that training was a man learned in all fields, a philosopher, skilled in all the arts of speaking.

REFERENCES

Compiled by James Jasinski

PRIMARY SOURCES

Latin Texts and Translations

Ellendt, Fridericus (ed.). *M. Tullii Ciceronis De Oratore, Libri tres.* Regimontii Prussorum, 1840.

Ernesti, J. A. (ed.). *M. T. Cicero De Oratore.* Rotterdam, 1804.

Orelli, Johann Kaspar. *Complete Works of M. Tullius Cicero.* Zurich, 1826.

Pearce, Zacharias (ed.). *M. Tullii Ciceronis and Quintum Fratrem.* Leipzig, 1816.

Piderit, Karl Wilhelm (ed.). *Cicero De Oratore.* Leipzig, 1873; rev. Leipzig, 1876.

Sorof, G. (ed.). *M. Tullius Ciceronis, De Oratore Libri tres.* Berlin, 1875.

Wilkins, Augustus S. (ed.). *M. Tullii Ciceronis De Oratore Libri tres.* Oxford, 1892.

Latin and English

Cicero. *De Oratore.* Books I and II tr. E. W. Sutton; Book III tr. H. Rackham. Loeb Classical Library. London, 1942.

English

Barnes, George. *Cicero on the Complete Orator.* London, 1762.

Calvert, F. B. *The De Oratore of Cicero.* Edinburgh, 1870.

G. P. *Tully De Oratore.* London, 1723.

Guthrie, William. *M. T. Cicero De Oratore.* Tr. T. Waller. London, 1742.

Moor, E. N. P. *Cicero De Oratore, Book I.* London, 1892.

SECONDARY SOURCES

Books on Cicero

Abbott, Kenneth Morgan, William Abbott Oldfather, Howard Vernon Canter, et al. *Index Verborum in Ciceronis Rhetorica.* Urbana, 1964.

Bailey, David R. S. *Cicero.* New York, 1971.
Cowell, F. R. *Cicero and the Roman Republic.* Middlesex, 1956.
Delayan, Gaston. *Cicero.* Tr. F. Symons. New York, 1931.
Dorey, T. A. (ed.). *Cicero.* London, 1964.
Haskell, H. J. *This Was Cicero.* New York, 1942 (rpt. 1964).
Hunt, Harold. *The Humanism of Cicero.* Carlton, 1954.
Jeans, T. E. *The Life and Letters of M. T. Cicero.* London, 1891.
Lacy, Walter K. *Cicero and the End of the Roman Empire.* London, 1978.
Laurand, L. *De M. T. Ciceronis, Studiis Rhetoricis.* Paris, 1907.
Martyn, John R. C. (ed.). *Cicero and Virgil: Studies in Honor of Harold Hunt.* Amsterdam, 1972.
Mitchell, Thomas N. *Cicero: The Ascending Years.* New Haven, 1979.
Petersson, Torsten. *Cicero: A Biography.* Berkeley, 1920 (rpt. New York, 1963).
Rawson, Elizabeth. *Cicero: A Portrait.* London, 1975.
Rolfe, John C. *Cicero and His Influence.* New York, 1963.
Sumner, G. V. *The Orator in Cicero's "Brutus": Prosopography and Chronology.* Toronto, 1973.
Trollope, Anthony. *The Life of Cicero.* 2 vols. London, 1880.
Tyrell, Robert Y. *The Correspondence of M. Tullius Cicero.* Dublin, 1885.
Watson, Albert H. (ed.). *Cicero: Select Letters.* 4th edition. Oxford, 1891.
Wooten, Cecil W. *Cicero's Philippics and Their Demosthenic Model: The Rhetoric of Crisis.* Chapel Hill, 1983.

Books on Greek and Roman Rhetorical Theory and Practice

Baldwin, Charles S. *Ancient Rhetoric and Poetic.* New York, 1924.
Bonner, S. *Roman Declamation in the Late Republic and Early Empire.* Liverpool, 1959.
Caplan, Harry. *Of Eloquence: Studies in Ancient and Medieval Rhetoric.* Ithaca, 1970.
Clark, Donald L. *Rhetoric in Greco-Roman Education.* New York, 1957.
Clarke, M. L. *Rhetoric at Rome: A Historical Survey.* London, 1953 (rpt. New York, 1962).
Gomperz, Heinrich. *Sophistik und Rhetorik.* Leipzig, 1912.

Grimaldi, William, S.J. *Studies in the Philosophy of Aristotle's Rhetoric*. Weisbaden, 1972.

———. *Aristotle, Rhetoric I: A Commentary*. New York, 1980.

Grube, G. M. A. *The Greek and Roman Critics*. London, 1965.

Gwynn, Aubrey. *Roman Education from Cicero to Quintilian*. London, 1926.

Havelock, Eric A., and Hershbell, Jackson. *Communication Arts in the Ancient World*. New York, 1978.

Hubbell, Harry M. *The Influence of Isocrates on Cicero, Dionysius, and Aristides*. New Haven, 1913.

Ijsseling, Samuel. *Rhetoric and Philosophy in Conflict*. Tr. Paul Dunphy. The Hague, 1976.

Jaeger, Werner. *Paideia: The Ideals of Greek Culture*. Tr. Gilbert Highet. New York, 1939.

Kahn, Victoria. *Rhetoric, Prudence, and Skepticism in the Renaissance*. Ithaca, 1985.

Kennedy, George A. *The Art of Persuasion in Greece*. Princeton, 1963.

———. *The Art of Rhetoric in the Roman World*. Princeton, 1972.

———. *Classical Rhetoric and Its Christian and Secular Tradition*. Chapel Hill, 1980.

Leeman, A. D. *Orationis Ratio: The Stylistic Theories and Practice of the Roman Orators, Historians, and Philosophers*. Amsterdam, 1963.

Marrou, H. I. *A History of Education in Antiquity*. Tr. George Lamb. New York, 1956.

Marsh, David. *The Quattrocento Dialogue: Classical Tradition and Humanist Innovation*. Cambridge, 1980.

Martin, Josef. *Antike Rhetorik: Technik und Methode*. Munich, 1974.

Murphy, James J. *Rhetoric in the Middle Ages: A History of Rhetorical Theory from St. Augustine to the Renaissance*. Berkeley, 1974.

Ong, Walter J., S.J. *Rhetoric, Romance, and Technology: Studies in the Interaction of Expression and Culture*. Ithaca, 1971.

Romilly, Jacqueline de. *Magic and Rhetoric in Ancient Greece*. Cambridge, 1975.

Seigel, Jerrold. *Rhetoric and Philosophy in Renaissance Humanism*. Princeton, 1968.

Untersteiner, Mario. *The Sophists*. Tr. Kathleen Freeman. Oxford, 1964.

Vernant, Jean-Pierre. *The Origins of Greek Thought*. Ithaca, 1982.

Volkmann, Richard. *Die Rhetorik der Griechen und Romer in systematischer Ubersicht*. Leipzig, 1885 (rpt. Hildesheim, 1963).

Articles on Cicero

Beasey, Mary Fowler. "It's What You Don't Say: *Omissio* in Cicero's Speeches." *Southern States Communication Journal*, 39 (1973), 11–20.

Dilorenzo, Raymond. "The Critique of Socrates in Cicero's *De Oratore: Ornatus* and the Nature of Wisdom." *Philosophy and Rhetoric*, 11 (1978), 247–61.

Enos, Richard Leo. "The Epistemological Foundation for Cicero's Litigation Strategies." *Central States Speech Journal*, 26 (1975), 207–14.

————. "The Advocates of Pre-Ciceronian Rome: Cicero's Standard for Forensic Oratory." *Communication Quarterly*, 27 (1979), 54–62.

Enos, Richard Leo, and Constant, Dean N. "A Bibliography of Ciceronian Rhetoric." *Rhetoric Society Quarterly*, 6 (1976), 21–28.

Enos, Richard Leo, and McClaran, Jeanne L. "Audience and Image in Ciceronian Rome: Creation and Constraints of the *Vir Bonus* Personality." *Central States Speech Journal*, 29 (1978), 98–106.

Fernandes, James J. "The Public Letters of Cicero." *Communication Quarterly*, 26 (1978), 21–26.

Flemming, Edwin G. "A Comparison of Cicero and Aristotle on Style." *Quarterly Journal of Speech*, 4 (1918), 61–71.

Gaines, Robert N., et al. "Special Reports: Studies in Cicero's *Opera Rhetorica*." *Central States Speech Journal*, 35 (1984), 120–31.

Halloran, S. Michael, and Whitburn, Merrill D. "Ciceronian Rhetoric and the Rise of Science: The Plain Style Reconsidered." In *The Rhetorical Tradition and Modern Writing*, ed. James J. Murphy. New York, 1982.

McNally, J. Richard. "Comments on Rhetoric and Oratory in Cicero's Letters." *Southern Speech Communication Journal*, 39 (1973), 21–32.

Meador, Prentice A., Jr. "Skeptic Theory of Perception: A Philosophical Antecedent of Ciceronian Probability." *Quarterly Journal of Speech*, 54 (1968), 340–51.

————. "Rhetoric and Humanism in Cicero." *Philosophy and Rhetoric*, 3 (1970), 1–12.

Murphy, James J. "Cicero's Rhetoric in the Middle Ages." *Quarterly Journal of Speech*, 53 (1967), 334–41.

Ochs, Donovan J. "Cicero's Rhetorical Theory." In *A Synoptic History of Classical Rhetoric*, ed. James J. Murphy, pp. 90–150. New York, 1972.

————. "Cicero's *Topica*: A Process View of Invention." In *Explorations in Rhetoric: Studies in Honor of Douglas Ehninger*, ed. Ray E. McKerrow, pp. 107–18. Glenview, 1982.

Psaty, Bruce M. "Cicero's Literal Metaphor and Propriety." *Central States Speech Journal*, 29 (1978), 107–17.

Sattler, William M. "Some Platonic Influences in the Rhetorical Works of Cicero." *Quarterly Journal of Speech*, 35 (1949), 164–69.

Street, Richard L., Jr. "Lexical Diversity as an Indicator of Audience Adaptation in Ciceronian Orations." *Central States Speech Journal*, 30 (1979), 286–88.

Thonssen, Lester, and Baird, A. Craig. "Cicero and Quintilian on Rhetoric." In *The Province of Rhetoric*, ed. Joseph Schwartz and John A. Rycenga, pp. 137–57. New York, 1965.

Threet, Douglas F. "Rhetorical Function of Ciceronian Probability." *Southern Speech Communication Journal*, 39 (1974), 309–21.

Volpe, Michael. "The Persuasive Force of Humor: Cicero's Defence of Caelius." *Quarterly Journal of Speech*, 63 (1977), 311–23.

————. "Cicero's 'Dust': Deception, Diversion, or Different Perspectives." *Central States Speech Journal*, 29 (1978), 118–26.

Wilkinson, L. P. "Cicero and the Relationship of Oratory to Literature." In *The Cambridge History of Classical Literature*, vol. 2: *Latin Literature*, ed. E. J. Kenney and W. V. Clausen. Cambridge, 1982.

Works on Rhetorical Theory

Connors, Robert J., Ede, Lisa S., and Lunsford, Andrea A., (eds.). *Essays on Classical Rhetoric and Modern Discourse*. Carbondale, 1984.

Corbett, Edward P. J. *Classical Rhetoric for the Modern Student*. New York, 1965.

Ehninger, Douglas. "On Systems of Rhetoric." *Philosophy and Rhetoric*, 1 (1968), 131–44.

Enos, Richard Leo. "The Classical Period." In *Historical Rhetoric: An Annotated Bibliography of Selected Sources in English*, ed. Winifred Bryan Horner. Boston, 1980.

————. "The Classical Period." In *The Present State of Scholarship in Historical and Contemporary Rhetoric*, ed. Winifred Bryan Horner. Columbia, 1983.

————. "The History of Rhetoric: The Reconstruction of Progress." In *Speech Communication in the 20th Century*, ed. Thomas W. Benson. Carbondale, 1985.

Farrell, Thomas B. "The Tradition of Rhetoric and the Philosophy of Communication." *Communication*, 7 (1983), 151–80.

Hinks, D. G. A. "Tisias and Corax and the Invention of Rhetoric." *Classical Quarterly*, 34 (1940), 61–69.

Howell, Wilbur Samuel. *Logic and Rhetoric in England, 1500–1700*. New York, 1961.

Leff, Michael C. "St. Augustine and Martianus Cappella: Continuity and Change in Fifth-Century Latin Rhetorical Theory." *Communication Quarterly*, 24 (1976), 2–9.

————. "The Topics of Argumentative Invention in Latin Rhetorical Theory from Cicero to Boethius." *Rhetorica*, 1 (1983), 23–44.

McKeon, Richard. "Rhetoric in the Middle Ages." *Speculum*, 17 (1942), 1–38.

Solmsen, Friedrich. "The Aristotelian Tradition in Ancient Rhetoric." *American Journal of Philology*, 62 (1941), 35–50, 169–90.

CICERO

ON

ORATORY AND ORATORS.

TRANSLATED OR EDITED

BY J. S. WATSON.

NEW YORK:

HARPER & BROTHERS, PUBLISHERS,

FRANKLIN SQUARE.

1878.

PREFACE.

A TRANSLATION of the Dialogues *De Oratore* was published in 1762 by George Barnes, a Barrister of the Inner Temple. Mr. Barnes's version was made with great care, and, though less known than Guthrie's, was far superior to it. If he occasionally mistook the sense of his author, he seems to have been always diligent in seeking for it. He added some notes, of which those deemed worth preserving are distinguished by the letter B.

Barnes's translation is the groundwork of the present; but every page of it has been carefully corrected, and many pages re-written. The text to which it is made conformable is that of Orellius, which differs but little from Ellendt's, the more recent editor and illustrator of the work, from whom some notes have been borrowed.

No labor has been spared to produce a faithful and readable translation of a treatise which must always be interesting to the orator and the student.

The translation of Cicero's " *Brutus ;* or, Remarks on Eminent Orators," is by E. Jones (first published in 1776), which has long had the well-deserved reputation of combining fidelity with elegance. It is therefore reprinted with but little variation.

J. S. W.

CICERO'S DIALOGUES

DE ORATORE;

OR,

ON THE CHARACTER OF THE ORATOR.

BOOK I.

THE ARGUMENT.

These Dialogues were written, or at least published, by Cicero in the year B.C. 55, when he was about fifty-two years old, in the second consulship of Pompey and Crassus. He composed them at the request of his brother Quintus, in order that he might set forth in better form, at a more advanced period of life, and after his long experience, those opinions on oratory which he had somewhat hastily and crudely advanced in his early years in his books on Invention. The Dialogues are supposed to have been held B.C. 91, when there were great contentions at Rome respecting the proposal of the tribune Marcus Livius Drusus to allow the senators, in common with the equites, to be judges on criminal trials.

The persons present at the dialogue related in the first book are Lucius Licinius Crassus, Marcus Antonius, his friend, the two most eminent orators of their day; Quintus Mucius Scævola, the father-in-law of Crassus, who was celebrated for his knowledge of the civil law, and from whom Cicero himself received instruction in his youth; and two young men, Caius Aurelius Cotta, and Publius Sulpicius Rufus, youths of much ability and promise, who were anxious to distinguish themselves in oratory, and for whose instruction the precepts and observations conveyed in the Dialogues are supposed to have been delivered. The scene of the conversations is the Tusculan villa of Crassus, to which he had retired from the tumults at Rome, and where he was joined by the rest of the party.

The object of Cicero, in these books, was to set before his reader all that was important in the rhetorical treatises of Aristotle, Isocrates, and other ancient writers on oratory, divested of technicalities, and presented in a pleasing form.

Crassus and Antonius, in the first book, discourse on all the qualifications of a perfect orator, Crassus being the exponent of the sentiments of Cicero himself, and maintaining that a complete orator must be acquainted with the whole circle of art and science. Antonius expresses his opinion that far less learning is required in the orator than

Crassus supposes, and that, as universal knowledge is unattainable, it will be well for him, not to attempt to acquire too much, as he will thus only distract his thoughts, and render himself less capable of attaining excellence in speaking, than if, contenting himself with moderate acquirements, he devoted his attention chiefly to the improvement of his natural talents and qualifications for oratory.

Cicero bestowed great consideration on the work, and had it long in hand. Ep. ad Att., iv., 12. See also Ad Att., iv., 16; xiii., 19; Ad Fam., i., 9.

I. As I frequently contemplate and call to mind the times of old, those in general seem to me, brother Quintus, to have been supremely happy, who, while they were distinguished with honors and the glory of their actions in the best days of the republic, were enabled to pursue such a course of life that they could continue either in employment without danger, or in retirement with dignity. To myself, also, there was a time[1] when I thought that a season for relaxation, and for turning my thoughts again to the noble studies once pursued by both of us, would be fairly allowable, and be conceded by almost every one; if the infinite labor of forensic business and the occupations of ambition should be brought to a stand, either by the completion of my course of honors,[2] or by the decline of age. Such expectations, with regard to my studies and designs, not only the severe calamities resulting from public occurrences, but a variety of our own private troubles,[3] have disappointed. For in that period,[4] which seemed likely to offer most quiet and tranquillity, the greatest pressures of trouble and the most turbulent storms arose. Nor to our wishes and earnest desires has the enjoyment of leisure been granted, to cultivate and revive between ourselves those studies to which we have from early youth been addicted. For at our first entrance into life we fell amidst the perturbation[5] of all ancient order; in my consulship we were involved in struggles

---

[1] After his consulship, A.U.C. 691, in the forty-fourth year of his age.

[2] There was a certain course of honors through which the Romans passed. After attaining the quæstorship, they aspired to the ædileship, and then to the prætorship and consulate. Cicero was augur, quæstor, ædile, prætor, consul, and proconsul of Asia. *Proust.*

[3] He refers to his exile and the proposed union between Cæsar and Pompey to make themselves masters of the whole commonwealth; a matter to which he was unwilling to allude more plainly. *Ellendt.*

[4] *Qui locus.* Quæ vitæ pars. *Proust.*

[5] The civil wars of Marius and Sylla. *Ellendt.*

and the hazard of every thing;[1] and all the time since that
consulship we have had to make opposition to those waves
which, prevented by my efforts from causing a general destruction, have abundantly recoiled upon myself. Yet, amidst the
difficulties of affairs, and the straitness of time, I shall endeavor to gratify my love of literature; and whatever leisure
the malice of enemies, the causes of friends, or the public
service will allow me, I shall chiefly devote to writing. As
to you, brother, I shall not fail to obey your exhortations and
entreaties; for no person can have more influence with me
than you have both by authority and affection.

II. Here the recollection of an old tradition must be revived in my mind, a recollection not indeed sufficiently distinct, but adapted, I think, so far to reply to what you ask,
that you may understand what opinions the most famous and
eloquent men entertained respecting the whole art of oratory.
For you wish, as you have often said to me (since what went
abroad rough and incomplete[2] from our own note-books, when
we were boys or young men, is scarcely worthy of my present
standing in life, and that experience which I have gained from
so many and such important causes as I have pleaded), that
something more polished and complete should be offered by
me on the same subjects; and you are at times inclined to
dissent from me in our disputations on this matter; inasmuch
as I consider eloquence to be the offspring of the accomplishments of the most learned men;[3] but you think it must be
regarded as independent of elegant learning, and attributable
to a peculiar kind of talent and practice.

Often, indeed, as I review in thought the greatest of mankind, and those endowed with the highest abilities, it has appeared to me worthy of inquiry what was the cause that a
greater number of persons have been admirable in every other pursuit than in speaking. For which way soever you direct your view in thought and contemplation, you will see
numbers excellent in every species, not only of the humble,
but even of the highest arts. Who, indeed, is there, that, if
he would measure the qualifications of illustrious men, either

---

[1] Alluding to the conspiracy of Catiline.
[2] The two books *De Inventione Rhetoricâ*.
[3] *Prudentissimorum*. Equivalent to *doctissimorum*. Pearce. Some
manuscripts have *eruditissimorum*.

by the usefulness or magnitude of their actions, would not prefer a general to an orator? Yet who doubts that we can produce, from this city alone, almost innumerable excellent commanders, while we can number scarcely a few eminent in speaking? There have been many also in our own memory, and more in that of our fathers, and even of our forefathers, who had abilities to rule and govern affairs of state by their counsel and wisdom; while for a long period no tolerable orators were found, or scarcely one in every age. But lest any one should think that the art of speaking may more justly be compared with other pursuits, which depend upon abstruse studies, and a varied field of learning, than with the merits of a general, or the wisdom of a prudent senator, let him turn his thoughts to those particular sciences themselves, and contemplate who and how many have flourished in them, as he will thus be best enabled to judge how great a scarcity of orators there is and has ever been.

III. It does not escape your observation that what the Greeks call PHILOSOPHY, is esteemed by the most learned men, the originator, as it were, and parent of all the arts which merit praise; philosophy, I say, in which it is difficult to enumerate how many distinguished men there have been, and of how great knowledge, variety, and comprehensiveness in their studies, men who have not confined their labors to one province separately, but have embraced whatever they could master either by scientific investigations, or by processes of reasoning. Who is ignorant in how great obscurity of matter, in how abstruse, manifold, and subtle an art they who are called mathematicians are engaged? Yet in that pursuit so many men have arrived at excellence, that not one seems to have applied himself to the science in earnest without attaining in it whatever he desired. Who has ever devoted himself wholly to music; who has ever given himself up to the learning which they profess who are called grammarians, without compassing, in knowledge and understanding, the whole substance and matter of those sciences, though almost boundless? Of all those who have engaged in the most liberal pursuits and departments of such sciences, I think I may truly say that a smaller number of eminent poets have arisen than of men distinguished in any other branch of literature; and in the whole multitude of the learned, among whom there rarely appears one of the highest excellence, there will be found, if you will but make a careful review of our own list and that of the Greeks, far fewer good orators than good poets. This ought to seem the more wonderful, as attainments in other sciences are drawn from recluse and hidden springs; but the whole art of speaking lies before us, and is concerned with common usage and the custom and language of all men; so that while in other things that is most excellent which is most remote from the knowledge and understanding of the illiterate, it is in speaking even the greatest of faults to vary from the ordinary kind of language, and the practice sanctioned by universal reason.

IV. Yet it can not be said with truth, either that more are devoted to the other arts, or that they are excited by greater pleasure, more abundant hope, or more ample rewards; for to say nothing of Greece, which was always desirous to hold the first place in eloquence, and Athens, that inventress of all literature, in which the utmost power of oratory was both discovered and brought to perfection, in this very city of ours, assuredly, no studies were ever pursued with more earnestness than those tending to the acquisition of eloquence. For when our empire over all nations was established, and after a period of peace had secured tranquillity, there was scarcely a youth ambitious of praise who did not think that he must strive, with all his endeavors, to attain the art of speaking. For a time, indeed, as being ignorant of all method, and as thinking there was no course of exercise for them, or any precepts of art, they attained what they could by the single force of genius and thought. But afterward, having heard the Greek orators, and gained an acquaintance with Greek literature, and procured instructors, our countrymen were inflamed with an incredible passion for eloquence. The magnitude, the variety, the multitude of all kind of causes, excited them to such a degree, that to that learning which each had acquired by his individual study, frequent practice, which was superior to the precepts of all masters, was at once added. There were then, as there are also now, the highest inducements offered for the cultivation of this study, in regard to public favor, wealth, and dignity. The abilities of our countrymen (as we may judge from many particulars) far excelled those of the men of every other nation. For which reasons, who would not justly won-

der that in the records of all ages, times, and states, so small
a number of orators should be found?

But the art of eloquence is something greater, and collected from more sciences and studies than people imagine.   V.
For who can suppose that, amid the greatest multitude of
students, the utmost abundance of masters, the most eminent
geniuses among men, the infinite variety of causes, the most
ample rewards offered to eloquence, there is any other reason
to be found for the small number of orators than the incredible magnitude and difficulty of the art?   A knowledge of a
vast number of things is necessary, without which volubility
of words is empty and ridiculous; speech itself is to be formed, not merely by choice, but by careful construction of words;
and all the emotions of the mind, which nature has given to
man, must be intimately known; for all the force and art of
speaking must be employed in allaying or exciting the feelings
of those who listen.   To this must be added a certain portion
of grace and wit, learning worthy of a well-bred man, and
quickness and brevity in replying as well as attacking, accompanied with a refined decorum and urbanity.   Besides, the
whole of antiquity and a multitude of examples is to be kept
in the memory; nor is the knowledge of laws in general, or
of the civil law in particular, to be neglected.   And why
need I add any remarks on delivery itself, which is to be ordered by action of body, by gesture, by look, and by modulation and variation of the voice, the great power of which,
alone and in itself, the comparatively trivial art of actors and
the stage proves, on which though all bestow their utmost labor to form their look, voice, and gesture, who knows not
how few there are, and have ever been, to whom we can attend with patience?   What can I say of that repository for
all things, the memory, which, unless it be made the keeper
of the matter and words that are the fruits of thought and
invention, all the talents of the orator, we see, though they be
of the highest degree of excellence, will be of no avail?   Let
us, then, cease to wonder what is the cause of the scarcity of
good speakers, since eloquence results from all those qualifications, in each of which singly it is a great merit to labor
successfully; and let us rather exhort our children, and others whose glory and honor is dear to us, to contemplate in
their minds the full magnitude of the object, and not to trust

that they can reach the height at which they aim, by the aid of the precepts, masters, and exercises, that they are all now following, but to understand that they must adopt others of a different character.

VI. In my opinion, indeed, no man can be an orator possessed of every praiseworthy accomplishment, unless he has attained the knowledge of every thing important, and of all liberal arts, for his language must be ornate and copious from knowledge, since, unless there be beneath the surface matter understood and felt by the speaker, oratory becomes an empty and almost puerile flow of words. Yet I will not lay so great a burden upon orators, especially our own, amid so many occupations of public and private life, as to think it allowable for them to be ignorant of nothing; although the qualifications of an orator, and his very profession of speaking well, seem to undertake and promise that he can discourse gracefully and copiously on whatever subject is proposed to him. But because this, I doubt not, will appear to most people an immense and infinite undertaking, and because I see that the Greeks, men amply endowed not only with genius and learning, but also with leisure and application, have made a kind of partition of the arts, and have not singly labored in the whole circle of oratory, but have separated from the other parts of rhetoric that department of eloquence which is used in the forum on trials or in deliberations, and have left this species only to the orator; I shall not embrace in these books more than has been attributed to this kind of speaking[1] by the almost unanimous consent of the greatest men, after much examination and discussion of the subject; and I shall repeat, not a series of precepts drawn from the infancy of our old and boyish learning, but matters which I have heard were formerly argued in a discussion among some of our countrymen who were of the highest eloquence, and of the first rank in every kind of dignity. Not that I contemn the instructions which the Greek rhetoricians and teachers have left us, but, as they are already public, and within the reach of all, and can neither be set forth more elegantly, nor explained more clearly by my interpretation, you will, I think, excuse me, my brother, if I prefer to the Greeks the authority of those to

[1] Deliberative and judicial oratory; omitting the epideictic or demonstrative kind.

whom the utmost merit in eloquence has been allowed by our own countrymen.

VII. At the time, then, when the consul Philippus was vehemently inveighing against the cause of the nobility, and the tribuneship of Drusus, undertaken to support the authority of the senate, seemed to be shaken and weakened, I was told, I remember, that Lucius Crassus, as if for the purpose of collecting his thoughts, betook himself, during the days of the Roman games, to his Tusculan country seat, whither also Quintus Mucius, who had been his father-in-law, is said to have come at the same time, as well as Marcus Antonius, a sharer in all the political proceedings of Crassus, and united in the closest friendship with him. There went out with Crassus himself two young men besides, great friends of Drusus, youths of whom our ancestors then entertained sanguine hopes that they would maintain the dignity of their order; Caius Cotta, who was then a candidate for the tribuneship of the people, and Publius Sulpicius, who was thought likely to stand for that office in due course. These, on the first day, conferred much together until very late in the evening, concerning the condition of those times, and the whole commonwealth, for which purpose they had met. Cotta repeated to me many things then prophetically lamented and noticed by the three of consular dignity in that conversation; so that no misfortune afterward happened to the state which they had not perceived to be hanging over it so long before; and he said that, when this conversation was finished, there was such politeness shown by Crassus, that after they had bathed and sat down to table, all the seriousness of the former discourse was banished; and there appeared so much pleasantry in him, and so much agreeableness in his humor, that though the early part of the day might seem to have been passed by them in the senate house, the banquet showed all the delights of the Tusculan villa.

But on the next day, when the older part of the company had taken sufficient repose, and were come to their walk, he told me that Scævola, after taking two or three turns, said, "Why should not we, Crassus, imitate Socrates in the Phædrus of Plato?[1] for this plane-tree of yours has put me in

----

[1] P. 229. Compare Ruhnken, ad Lex. Timæi, v. ἀμφιλαφές, and Manutius, ad Cic., Div., ii., 11, p. 254. Cicero aptly refers to that dia-

mind of it, which diffuses its spreading boughs to overshade this place, not less widely than that did whose covert Socrates sought, and which seems to me to have grown not so much from the rivulet which is described, as from the language of Plato: and what Socrates, with the hardest of feet, used to do, that is, to throw himself on the grass, while he delivered those sentiments which philosophers say were uttered divinely, may surely, with more justice, be allowed to my feet." Then Crassus rejoined, "Nay, we will yet farther consult your convenience;" and called for cushions; when they all, said Cotta, sat down on the seats that were under the plane-tree.

VIII. There (as Cotta used to relate), in order that the minds of them all might have some relaxation from their former discourse, Crassus introduced a conversation on the study of oratory. After he had commenced in this manner, That indeed Sulpicius and Cotta did not seem to need his exhortations, but rather both to deserve his praise, as they had already attained such powers as not only to excel their equals in age, but to be admitted to a comparison with their seniors; "Nor does any thing seem to me," he added, "more noble than to be able to fix the attention of assemblies of men by speaking, to fascinate their minds, to direct their passions to whatever object the orator pleases, and to dissuade them from whatsoever he desires. This particular art has constantly flourished above all others in every free state, and especially in those which have enjoyed peace and tranquillity, and has ever exercised great power. For what is so admirable as that, out of an infinite multitude of men, there should arise a single individual who can alone, or with only a few others, exert effectually that power which nature has granted to all? Or what is so pleasant to be heard and understood as an oration adorned and polished with wise thoughts and weighty expressions? Or what is so striking, so astonishing, as that the tumults of the people, the religious feelings of judges, the gravity of the senate, should be swayed by the speech of one man? Or what, moreover, is so kingly, so liberal, so munificent, as to give assistance to the suppliant, to raise the

logue of Plato, because much is said about eloquence in it. The plane-tree was greatly admired by the Romans for its wide-spreading shade. See I. H. Vossius, ad Virg., Georg., ii., 70; Plin., H. N., xii., 1; xvii., 15; Hor., Od., ii., 15, 5; Gronov., Obss., i., 5. *Ellendt.*

afflicted, to bestow security, to deliver from dangers, to maintain men in the rights of citizenship? What, also, is so necessary as to keep arms always ready, with which you may either
be protected yourself, or defy the malicious, or avenge yourself when provoked? Or consider (that you may not always
contemplate the forum, the benches, the rostra, and the senate) what can be more delightful in leisure, or more suited to
social intercourse, than elegant conversation, betraying no
want of intelligence on any subject? For it is by this one
gift that we are most distinguished from brute animals, that
we converse together, and can express our thoughts by speech.
Who, therefore, would not justly make this an object of admiration, and think it worthy of his utmost exertions, to surpass mankind themselves in that single excellence by which
they claim their superiority over brutes? But, that we may
notice the most important point of all, what other power could
either have assembled mankind, when dispersed, into one place,
or have brought them from wild and savage life to the present humane and civilized state of society; or, when cities were
established, have described for them laws, judicial institutions,
and rights? And that I may not mention more examples,
which are almost without number, I will conclude the subject
in one short sentence; for I consider, that by the judgment
and wisdom of the perfect orator, not only his own honor, but
that of many other individuals, and the welfare of the whole
state, are principally upheld. Go on, therefore, as you are
doing, young men, and apply earnestly to the study in which
you are engaged, that you may be an honor to yourselves, an
advantage to your friends, and a benefit to the republic."

IX. Scævola then observed with courtesy, as was always
his manner, "I agree with Crassus as to other points (that
I may not detract from the art or glory of Lælius, my father-
in-law, or of my son-in-law here),[1] but I am afraid, Crassus,
that I can not grant you these two points; one, that states
were, as you said, originally established, and have often been
preserved by orators; the other, that, setting aside the forum,
the assemblies of the people, the courts of judicature, and
the senate-house, the orator is, as you ʹpronounced, accomplished in every subject of conversation and learning. For
who will concede to you, either that mankind, dispersed

[1] Crassus.

originally in mountains and woods, inclosed themselves in towns and walls, not so much from being convinced by the counsels of the wise, as from being charmed by the speeches of the eloquent? Or that other advantages, arising either from the establishment or preservation of states, were settled, not by wise and brave men, but by fluent and elegant speakers? Does Romulus seem to you to have assembled the shepherds, and those that flocked to him from all parts, or to have formed marriages with the Sabines, or to have repelled the power of the neighboring people, by eloquence, and not by counsel and eminent wisdom? Is there any trace of eloquence apparent in Numa Pompilius, in Servius Tullius, or in the rest of our kings, from whom we have many excellent regulations for maintaining our government? After the kings were expelled (though we see that their expulsion was effected by the mind of Lucius Brutus, and not by his tongue), do we not perceive that all the subsequent transactions are full of wise counsel, but destitute of all mixture of eloquence? But if I should be inclined to adduce examples from our own and other states, I could cite more instances of mischief than of benefit done to public affairs by men of eminent eloquence; but, to omit others, I think, Crassus, that the most eloquent men I ever heard, except you two,[1] were the Sempronii, Tiberius and Caius, whose father, a prudent and grave man, but by no means eloquent, on several other occasions, but especially when censor, was of the utmost service to the republic; and he, not by any faultless flow of speech, but by a word and a nod, transferred the freedmen into the city tribes;[2] and, if he had not done so, we should now have no republic, which we still maintain with difficulty; but his sons, who were eloquent, and qualified for speaking by all the helps of nature and of learning, having found the state in a most flourishing condition, both through the counsels of their father, and the arms of their ancestors, brought their country, by means of their oratory, that most excellent ruler of states as you call it, to the verge of ruin.

[1] Crassus and Antonius.
[2] Livy, xlv., 15, says that the freedmen were previously dispersed among all the four city tribes, and that Gracchus included them all in the Esquiline tribe. The object was to allow the freedmen as little influence as possible in voting.

X. " Were our ancient laws, and the customs of our ancestors ; were the auspices, over which you, Crassus, and I
preside with great security to the republic ; were the religious rites and ceremonies ; were the civil laws, the knowledge
of which has long prevailed in our family (and without any
praise for eloquence), either invented, or understood, or in any
way ordered by the tribe of orators ?   I can remember that
Servius Galba, a man of godlike power in speaking, as well
as Marcus Æmilius Porcina, and Cneius Carbo himself, whom
you defeated when you were but a youth,[1] was ignorant of
the laws, at a loss in the practices of our ancestors, and unlearned in civil jurisprudence ; and, except you, Crassus, who,
rather from your own inclination to study, than because it
was any peculiar business of an orator, have learned the civil
law from us, as I am sometimes ashamed to say, this generation of ours is ignorant of law.

" But what you assumed, as by a law of your own, in
the last part of your speech, that an orator is able to speak
fluently on any subject, I would not, if I were not here in
your own domain, tolerate for a moment, but would head
a party who should either oppose you by an interdict,[2] or
summon you to contend with them at law, for having so
unceremoniously invaded the possessions of others.   In the
first place, all the Pythagoreans, and the followers of Democritus, would institute a suit against you, with the rest of the
natural philosophers, each in his own department, men who
are elegant and powerful speakers, with whom you could not
contend on equal terms.[3]   Whole troops of other philosophers
would assail you besides, even down from Socrates their ori-

[1] Caius Papirius Carbo, after having been a very seditious tribune,
went over in his consulship to the side of the patricians, and highly
extolled Lucius Opimius for killing Caius Gracchus.   But, at the expiration of his consulship, being impeached by Crassus, on what grounds
we do not know, he put himself to death.   Cic., Orat., iii., 20, 74 ;
Brut., 27, 103.   *Ellendt.*

[2] An edict of the prætor forbidding something to be done, in contra-
distinction to a *decree,* which ordered something to be done.   Ellendt
refers to Gaius, iv., 139, 160.

[3] *Justo sacramento.*   The *sacramentum* was a deposit of a certain sum
of money laid down by two parties who were going to law ; and when
the decision was made, the victorious party received his money back,
while that of the defeated party went into the public treasury.   Varro,
L. L., v., 180.

gin and head, and would convince you that you had learned nothing about good and evil in life, nothing about the passions of the mind, nothing about the moral conduct of mankind, nothing about the proper course of life; they would show you that you have made no due inquiry after knowledge, and that you know nothing; and, when they had made an attack upon you all together, then every sect would bring its separate action against you. The Academy would press you, and, whatever you asserted, force you to deny it. Our friends the Stoics would hold you entangled in the snares of their disputations and questions. The Peripatetics would prove that those very aids and ornaments to speaking, which you consider the peculiar property of the orators, must be sought from themselves; and they would show you that Aristotle and Theophrastus have written not only better, but also far more copiously, on these subjects, than all the masters of the art of speaking. I say nothing of the mathematicians, the grammarians, the musicians, with whose sciences this art of speaking of yours is not connected by the least affinity. I think, therefore, Crassus, that such great and numerous professions ought not to be made. What you can effect is sufficiently great, namely, that in judicial matters the cause which you plead shall seem the better and more probable; that in public assemblies, and in delivering opinions, your oratory shall have the most power to persuade; that, finally, you shall seem to the wise to speak with eloquence, and even to the simple to speak with truth. If you can do more than this, it will appear to me that it is not the orator, but Crassus himself that effects it by the force of talents peculiar to himself, and not common to other orators."

XI. Crassus then replied, "I am not ignorant, Scævola, that things of this sort are commonly asserted and maintained among the Greeks; for I was an auditor of their greatest men, when I came to Athens as quæstor from Macedonia,[1] and when the Academy was in a flourishing state, as it was represented in those days, for Charmadas, and Clitomachus, and Æschines were in possession of it. There was also Metrodorus, who, with the others, had been a diligent hearer of the famous Carneades himself, a man beyond all others, as

---

[1] Crassus was quæstor in Asia A.U.C. 645, and, on his return, at the expiration of his office, passed through Macedonia. *Ellendt.*

they told me, a most spirited and copious speaker. Mnesarchus, too, was in great esteem, a hearer of your friend Panætius, and Diodorus, a scholar of Critolaus the Peripatetic;
and there were many other famous men besides, highly distinguished in philosophy, by all of whom, with one voice as
it were, I observed that the orator was repelled from the government of states, excluded from all learning and knowledge
of great affairs, and degraded and thrust down into the courts
of justice and petty assemblies, as into a workshop. But I
neither assented to those men, nor to the originator of these
disputations, and by far the most eloquent of them all, the
eminently grave and oratorical Plato; whose Gorgias I then
diligently read over at Athens with Charmadas; from which
book I conceived the highest admiration of Plato, as he seemed to me to prove himself an eminent orator, even in ridiculing orators.   A controversy indeed on the word ORATOR has
long disturbed the minute Grecians, who are fonder of argument than of truth.   For if any one pronounces him to be an
orator who can speak fluently only on law in general, or on
judicial questions, or before the people, or in the senate, he
must yet necessarily grant and allow him a variety of talents;
for he can not treat even of these matters with sufficient skill
and accuracy without great attention to all public affairs, and
without a knowledge of laws, customs, and equity, nor without understanding the nature and manners of mankind; and
to him who knows these things, without which no one can
maintain even the most minute points in judicial pleadings,
how much is wanting of the knowledge even of the most important affairs?   But if you allow nothing to belong to the
orator but to speak aptly, ornately, and copiously, how can
he even attain these qualities without that knowledge which
you do not allow him? for there can be no true merit in
speaking, unless what is said is thoroughly understood by him
who says it.   If, therefore, the natural philosopher Democritus spoke with elegance, as he is reported to have spoken,
and as it appears to me that he did speak, the matter on which
he spoke belonged to the philosopher, but the graceful array
of words is to be ascribed to the orator.   And if Plato spoke
divinely upon subjects most remote from civil controversies,
as I grant that he did; if also Aristotle, and Theophrastus,
and Carneades, were eloquent, and spoke with sweetness and

grace on those matters which they discussed ; let the subjects on which they spoke belong to other studies, but their
speech itself, surely, is the peculiar offspring of that art of
which we are now discoursing and inquiring. For we see
that some have reasoned on the same subjects jejunely and
dryly, as Chrysippus, whom they celebrate as the acutest of
philosophers ; nor is he on this account to be thought to have
been deficient in philosophy, because he did not gain the talent of speaking from an art which is foreign to philosophy.

XII. "Where then lies the difference ? Or by what term
will you discriminate the fertility and copiousness of speech in
those whom I have named, from the barrenness of those who
use not this variety and elegance of phrase ? One thing there
will certainly be, which those who speak well will exhibit as
their own ; a graceful and elegant style, distinguished by a
peculiar artifice and polish. But this kind of diction, if there
be not matter beneath it clear and intelligible to the speaker,
must either amount to nothing, or be received with ridicule
by all who hear it. For what savors so much of madness,
as the empty sound of words, even the choicest and most elegant, when there is no sense or knowledge contained in them ?
Whatever be the subject of a speech, therefore, in whatever
art or branch of science, the orator, if he has made himself
master of it, as of his client's cause, will speak on it better
and more elegantly than even the very originator and author
of it can.[1] If, indeed, any one shall say that there are certain trains of thought and reasoning properly belonging to
orators, and a knowledge of certain things circumscribed within the limits of the forum, I will confess that our common
speech is employed about these matters chiefly ; but yet there
are many things, in these very topics, which those masters of
rhetoric, as they are called, neither teach nor understand.
For who is ignorant that the highest power of an orator consists in exciting the minds of men to anger, or to hatred, or
to grief, or in recalling them from these more violent emotions
to gentleness and compassion ? which power will never be able
to effect its object by eloquence, unless in him who has obtained a thorough insight into the nature of mankind, and all
the passions of humanity, and those causes by which our
minds are either impelled or restrained. But all these are

[1] See Quintilian, ii., 21.

thought to belong to the philosophers, nor will the orator, at least with my consent, ever deny that such is the case; but when he has conceded to them the knowledge of things, since they are willing to exhaust their labors on that alone, he will assume to himself the treatment of oratory, which without that knowledge is nothing. For the proper concern of an orator, as I have already often said, is language of power and elegance accommodated to the feelings and understandings of mankind.

XIII. " On these matters I confess that Aristotle and Theophrastus have written.[1] But consider, Scævola, whether this is not wholly in my favor. For I do not borrow from them what the orator possesses in common with them; but they allow that what they say on these subjects belongs to oratory. Their other treatises, accordingly, they distinguish by the name of the science on which each is written; their treatises on oratory they entitle and designate as books of rhetoric. For when, in their discussions (as often happens), such topics present themselves as require them to speak of the immortal gods, of piety, of concord, of friendship, of the common rights of their fellow-citizens, or those of all mankind, of the law of nations, of equity, of temperance, of greatness of mind, of every kind of virtue, all the academies and schools of philosophy, I imagine, will cry out that all these subjects are their property, and that no particle of them belongs to the orator. But when I have given them liberty to reason on all these subjects in corners to amuse their leisure, I shall give and assign to the orator his part, which is, to set forth with full power and attraction the very same topics which they discuss in such tame and bloodless phraseology. These points I then discussed with the philosophers in person at Athens, for Marcus Marcellus, our countryman, who is now curule ædile, obliged me to do so, and he would certainly have taken part in our present conversation, were he not now celebrating the public games; for he was then a youth marvelously given to these studies.

" Of the institution of laws, of war, of peace, of alliances, of tributes, of the civil law as relating to various ranks and ages respectively,[2] let the Greeks say, if they will, that Ly-

---

[1] Though they are philosophers, and not orators or rhetoricians.

[2] *De jure civili generatim in ordines ætatesque descripto.* Instead of

curgus or Solon (although I think that these should be enrolled
in the number of the eloquent) had more knowledge than Hy-
pereides or Demosthenes, men of the highest accomplishments
and refinement in oratory; or let our countrymen prefer, in
this sort of knowledge, the Decemviri who wrote the Twelve
Tables, and who must have been wise men, to Servius Galba,
and your father-in-law Lælius, who are allowed to have excelled in the glorious art of speaking.   I, indeed, shall never
deny that there are some sciences peculiarly well understood
by those who have applied their whole study to the knowledge and consideration of them; but the accomplished and
complete orator I shall call him who can speak on all subjects with variety and copiousness.   XIV. For often in those
causes which all acknowledge properly to belong to orators,
there is something to be drawn forth and adopted, not from
the routine of the Forum, which is the only knowledge that
you grant to the orator, but from some of the more obscure
sciences.   I ask whether a speech can be made for or against
a general, without an acquaintance with military affairs, or
often without a knowledge of certain inland and maritime
countries? whether a speech can be made to the people
about passing or rejecting laws, or in the senate on any kind
of public transactions, without the greatest knowledge and
judgment in political matters? whether a speech can be
adapted to excite or calm the thoughts and passions (which
alone is a great business of the orator) without a most diligent examination of all those doctrines which are set forth on
the nature and manners of men by the philosophers?   I do
not know whether I may not be less successful in maintaining what I am going to say; but I shall not hesitate to speak
that which I think.   Physics, and mathematics, and those
other things which you just now decided to belong to other
sciences, belong to the peculiar knowledge of those who profess them; but if any one would illustrate those arts by eloquence, he must have recourse to the power of oratory.   Nor,

civili, the old reading was *civium*, in accordance with which Lambinus
altered *descripto* into *descriptorum*.   *Civili* was an innovation of Ernesti,
which Ellendt condemns, and retains *civium*; observing that Cicero
means *jura civium* publica *singulis ordinibus et ætatibus assignata*.   "By
ordines," says Ernesti, "are meant patricians and plebeians, senators,
knights, and classes in the census; by *ætates*, younger and older persons."

if, as is said, Philo,[1] the famous architect, who built an arsenal
for the Athenians, gave that people an eloquent account of his
work, is it to be imagined that his eloquence proceeded from
the art of the architect, but from that of the orator.   Or, if
our friend Marcus Antonius had had to speak for Hermodorus[2]
on the subject of dock-building, he would have spoken, when
he had learned the case from Hermodorus, with elegance and
copiousness, drawn from an art quite unconnected with dock-
building.   And Asclepiades,[3] whom we knew as a physician
and a friend, did not, when he excelled others of his profession
in eloquence, employ, in his graceful elocution, the art of
physic, but that of oratory.   What Socrates used to say, that
all men are sufficiently eloquent in that which they understand, is
very plausible, but not true.   It would have been nearer truth
to say that no man can be eloquent on a subject that he does
not understand; and that, if he understands a subject ever
so well, but is ignorant how to form and polish his speech,
he can not express himself eloquently even about what he
does understand.

XV. " If, therefore, any one desires to define and comprehend the whole and peculiar power of an orator, that man, in
my opinion, will be an orator, worthy of so great a name,
who, whatever subject comes before him, and requires rhetorical elucidation, can speak on it judiciously, in set form, elegantly, and from memory, and with a certain dignity of action.
But if the phrase which I have used, " on whatever subject,'
is thought by any one too comprehensive, let him retrench
and curtail as much of it as he pleases; but this I will maintain, that though the orator be ignorant of what belongs to
other arts and pursuits, and understands only what concerns
the discussions and practice of the Forum, yet if he has to
speak on those arts, he will, when he has learned what per-
tains to any of them from persons who understand them, discourse upon them much better than the very persons of whom
those arts form the peculiar province.   Thus, if our friend
Sulpicius have to speak on military affairs, he will inquire

[1] He is frequently mentioned by the ancients; the passages relating
to him have been collected by Junius, de Picturâ in Catal. Artif.
Ernesti. See Plin., H. N.,vii., 38; Plut., Syll., c. 14; Val. Max.,vii.,12.
[2] A Roman ship-builder. See Turneb., Advers., xi., 2.
[3] See Plin., H. N., vii., 37. Celsus often refers to his authority as
the founder of a new party. *Ellendt.*

about them of my kinsman, Caius Marius,[1] and when he has received information, will speak upon them in such a manner, that he shall seem to Marius to understand them better than himself. Or if he has to speak on the civil law, he will consult with you, and will excel you, though eminently wise and learned in it, in speaking on those very points which he shall have learned from yourself.   Or if any subject presents itself, requiring him to speak on the nature and vices of men, on desire, on moderation, on continence, on grief, on death, perhaps, if he thinks proper (though the orator ought to have a knowledge of these things), he will consult with Sextus Pompeius,[2] a man learned in philosophy.   But this he will certainly accomplish, that, of whatever matter he gains a knowledge, or from whomsoever, he will speak upon it much more elegantly than the very person from whom he gained the knowledge. But, since philosophy is distinguished into three parts, inquiries into the obscurities of physics, the subtleties of logic, and the knowledge of life and manners, let us, if Sulpicius will listen to me, leave the two former, and consult our ease ; but unless we have a knowledge of the third, which has always been the province of the orator, we shall leave him nothing in which he can distinguish himself.   The part of philosophy, therefore, regarding life and manners, must be thoroughly mastered by the orator ; other subjects, even if he has not learned them, he will be able, whenever there is occasion, to adorn by his eloquence, if they are brought before him and made known to him.

XVI. "For it is allowed among the learned that Aratus, a man ignorant of astronomy, has treated of heaven and the constellations in extremely polished and excellent verses ; if Nicander,[3] of Colophon, a man totally unconnected with the

---

[1] The son of the great Caius Marius, seven times consul, had married Mucia, the daughter of the augur Scævola.   In Cicero's Oration for Balbus, also, c. 21, 49, where the merits of that eminent commander are celebrated, Crassus is called his *affinis*, relation by marriage. *Henrichsen.*

[2] The uncle of Cneius Pompey the Great, who had devoted excellent talents to the attainment of a thorough knowledge of civil law, geometry, and the doctrines of the Stoics.   See Cic., Brut., 47 ; Philipp., xii., 11 ; Beier, ad Off., i., 6, 19.   *Ellendt.*

[3] Nicander, a physician, grammarian, and poet, flourished in the time of Attalus, the second king of Pergamus, about fifty years before Christ. His Theriaca and Alexipharmaca are extant ; his Georgica, to which Cicero here alludes, has perished.   *Henrichsen.*

country, has written well on rural affairs, with the aid of poetical talent, and not from understanding husbandry, what reason is there why an orator should not speak most eloquently on those matters of which he shall have gained a knowledge for a certain purpose and occasion? For the poet is nearly allied to the orator; being somewhat more restricted in numbers, but less restrained in the choice of words, yet in many kinds of embellishment his rival and almost equal; in one respect, assuredly, nearly the same, that he circumscribes or bounds his jurisdiction by no limits, but reserves to himself full right to range wherever he pleases with the same ease and liberty. For why did you say, Scævola,[1] that you would not endure, unless you were in my domain, my assertion, that the orator ought to be accomplished in every style of speaking, and in every part of polite learning? I should certainly not have said this if I had thought myself to be the orator whom I conceive in my imagination. But, as Caius Lucilius used frequently to say (a man not very friendly to you,[2] and on that account less familiar with me than he could wish, but a man of learning and good breeding), I am of this opinion, that no one is to be numbered among orators who is not thoroughly accomplished in all branches of knowledge requisite for a man of good breeding; and though we may not put forward such knowledge in conversation, yet it is apparent, and indeed evident, whether we are destitute of it, or have acquired it; as those who play at tennis do not exhibit, in playing, the gestures of the palæstra, but their movements indicate whether they have learned those exercises or are unacquainted with them; and as those who shape out any thing, though they do not then exercise the art of painting, yet make it clear whether they can paint or not; so in orations to courts of justice, before the people, and in the senate, although other sciences have no peculiar place in them, yet is it easily proved whether he who speaks has only been exercised in the parade of declamation, or has devoted himself to oratory after having been instructed in all liberal knowledge."

[1] See c. x.

[2] It is Lucilius the Satirist that is meant. What cause there had been for unfriendliness between him and Scævola is unknown; perhaps he might have spoken too freely, or made some satirical remark on the accusation of Scævola by Albucius for bribery, on which there are some verses in b. iii., c. 43. *Ellendt.*

XVII. Then Scævola, smiling, said : " I will not struggle
with you any longer, Crassus; for you have, by some artifice,
made good what you asserted against me, so as to grant me
whatever I refused to allow to the orator, and yet so as to
wrest from me those very things again I know not how, and
to transfer them to the orator as his property.[1] When I went
as prætor to Rhodes, and communicated to Apollonius, that
famous instructor in this profession, what I had learned from
Panætius, Apollonius, as was his manner, ridiculed these matters,[2] threw contempt upon philosophy, and made many other
observations with less wisdom than wit; but your remarks
were of such a kind as not to express contempt for any arts
or sciences, but to admit that they are all attendants and
handmaids of the orator ; and if ever any one should comprehend them all, and the same person should add to that knowledge the powers of supremely elegant oratory, I can not but
say that he would be a man of high distinction and worthy
of the greatest admiration.   But if there should be such a
one, or indeed has ever been, or can possibly be, you alone
would be the person ; who, not only in my judgment, but in
that of all men, have hardly left to other orators (I speak it
with deference to this company) any glory to be acquired.
If, however, there is in yourself no deficiency of knowledge
pertaining to judicial and political affairs, and yet you have
not mastered all that additional learning which you assign to
the complete orator, let us consider whether you do not attribute to him more than possibility and truth itself will allow."
Here Crassus rejoined : " Remember that I have not been
speaking of my own talents, but of those of the true orator.
For what have I either learned or had a possibility of knowing, who entered upon pleading before I had any instruction ;

---

[1] You granted me all that I desired when you said that all arts and
sciences belong, as it were, respectively to those who have invented, or
profess, or study them ; . . . . but when you said that those arts and
sciences are necessary to the orator, and that he can speak upon them if
he wishes, with more elegance and effect than those who have made
them their peculiar study, you seemed to take them all from me again,
and to transfer them to the orator as his own property. *Proust.*

[2] Orellius reads *Hæc—irrisit*, where the reader will observe that the
pronoun is governed by the verb.   Ellendt and some others read *Quæ*
instead of *Hæc*.   Several alterations have been proposed, but none of
them bring the sentence into a satisfactory state.

whom the pressure of business overtasked amid the occupations of the forum, of canvassing, of public affairs, and the management of the causes of friends, before I could form any true notion of the importance of such great employments? But if there seem to you to be so much in me, to whom, though capacity, as you think, may not greatly have been wanting, yet to whom learning, leisure, and that keen application to study which is so necessary, have certainly been wanting, what do you think would be the case if those acquirements, which I have not gained, should be united to some greater genius than mine? How able, how great an orator, do you think, would he prove?"

XVIII. Antonius then observed : " You prove to me, Crassus, what you advance ; nor do I doubt that he will have a far greater fund of eloquence who shall have learned the reason and nature of every thing and of all sciences. But, in the first place, this is difficult to be achieved, especially in such a life as ours and such occupations ; and next, it is to be feared that we may, by such studies, be drawn away from our exercise and practice of speaking before the people and in the forum. The eloquence of those men whom you mentioned a little before, seems to me to be of a quite different sort, though they speak with grace and dignity, as well on the nature of things as on human life. Theirs is a neat and florid kind of language, but more adapted for parade and exercise in the schools, than for these tumults of the city and forum. For when I, who late in life, and then but lightly, touched upon Greek learning, was going as proconsul into Cilicia, and had arrived at Athens, I waited there several days on account of the difficulty of sailing ; and as I had every day with me the most learned men, nearly the same that you have just now named, and a report, I know not how, had spread among them that I, like you, was versed in causes of great importance, every one, according to his abilities, took occasion to discourse upon the office and art of an orator. Some of them, as Mnesarchus himself, said, that those whom we call orators were nothing but a set of mechanics with glib and well-practiced tongues, but that no one could be an orator but a man of true wisdom ; and that eloquence itself, as it consisted in the art of speaking well, was a kind of virtue,[1] and that he who pos-

---

[1] The Stoics called eloquence one of their virtues. See Quintilian, ii., 20.

sessed one virtue possessed all, and that virtues were in themselves equal and alike; and thus he who was eloquent possessed all virtues, and was a man of true wisdom.   But their
phraseology was intricate and dry, and quite unsuited to my
taste.   Charmadas indeed spoke much more diffusely on those
topics; not that he delivered his own opinion (for it is the
hereditary custom of every one in the Academy to take the
part of opponents to all in their disputations), but what he
chiefly signified was, that those who were called rhetoricians,
and laid down rules for the art of speaking, understood nothing; and that no man could attain any command of eloquence
who had not mastered the doctrines of the philosophers.

XIX. " Certain men of eloquence at Athens, versed in public affairs and judicial pleadings, disputed on the other side;
among whom was Menedemus, lately my guest at Rome; but
when he had observed that there is a sort of wisdom which is
employed in inquiring into the methods of settling and managing governments, he, though a ready speaker, was promptly
attacked by the other,[1] a man of abundant learning, and of an
almost incredible variety and copiousness of argument; who
maintained that every portion of such wisdom must be derived from philosophy, and that whatever was established in
a state concerning the immortal gods, the discipline of youth,
justice, patience, temperance, moderation in every thing, and
other matters, without which states would either not subsist
at all, or be corrupt in morals, was nowhere to be found in
the petty treatises of the rhetoricians.   For if those teachers
of rhetoric included in their art such a multitude of the most
important subjects, why, he asked, were their books crammed
with rules about proems and perorations, and such trifles (for
so he called them), while about the modeling of states, the
composition of laws, about equity, justice, integrity, about mas-
tering the appetites, and forming the morals of mankind, not
one single syllable was to be found in their pages?   Their precepts he ridiculed in such a manner, as to show that the teachers were not only destitute of the knowledge which they arro-
gated to themselves, but that they did not even know the proper art and method of speaking; for he thought that the principal business of an orator was, that he might appear to those
to whom he spoke to be such as he would wish to appear (that

---

[1] Charmadas.

this was to be attained by a life of good reputation, on which
those teachers of rhetoric had laid down nothing in their precepts) ; and that the minds of the audience should be affected
in such a manner as the orator would have them to be affected, an object, also, which could by no means be attained, unless the speaker understood by what methods, by what arguments, and by what sort of language the minds of men are
moved in any particular direction ; but that these matters
were involved and concealed in the profoundest doctrines of
philosophy, which these rhetoricians had not touched even
with the extremity of their lips. These assertions Menedemus endeavored to refute, but rather by *authorities* than by
arguments; for, repeating from memory many noble passages
from the orations of Demosthenes, he showed that the orator,
while he swayed the minds of judges or of the people by his
eloquence, was not ignorant by what means he attained his
end, which Charmadas denied that any one could know without philosophy.

XX. " To this Charmadas replied, that he did not deny
that Demosthenes was possessed of consummate ability and
the utmost energy of eloquence ; but whether he had these
powers from natural genius, or because he was, as was acknowledged, a diligent hearer of Plato, it was not what Demosthenes could do, but what the rhetoricians taught, that
was the subject of inquiry. Sometimes, too, he was carried
so far by the drift of his discourse as to maintain that there
was no art at all in speaking ; and having shown by various
arguments that we are so formed by nature as to be able to
flatter, and to insinuate ourselves, as suppliants, into the favor
of those from whom we wish to obtain any thing, as well as
to terrify our enemies by menaces, to relate matters of fact,
to confirm what we assert, to refute what is said against us,
and, finally, to use entreaty or lamentation ; particulars in
which the whole faculties of the orator are employed ; and
that practice and exercise sharpened the understanding, and
produced fluency of speech, he rested his cause, in conclusion,
on a multitude of examples that he adduced ; for first, as if
stating an indisputable fact,[1] he affirmed that no writer on

---

[1] *Quasi dedita opera.* As if Charmadas himself had collected all the
writers on the art of rhetoric, that he might be in a condition to prove
what he now asserted ; or, as if the writers on the art of rhetoric them-

the art of rhetoric was ever even moderately eloquent, going
back as far as I know not what Corax and Tisias,[1] who, he
said, appeared to be the inventors and first authors of rhetorical science; and then named a vast number of the most
eloquent men who had neither learned, nor cared to understand the rules of art, and among whom (whether in jest, or
because he thought, or had heard something to that effect) he
instanced me as one who had received none of their instructions, and yet, as he said, had some abilities as a speaker;
of which two observations I readily granted the truth of one,
that I had never been instructed, but thought that in the other he was either joking with me, or was under some mistake.
But he denied that there was any art, except such as lay in
things that were known and thoroughly understood, things
tending to the same object, and never misleading; but that
every thing treated by the orators was doubtful and uncertain;
as it was uttered by those who did not fully understand it,
and was heard by them to whom knowledge was not meant
to be communicated, but merely false, or at least obscure notions, intended to live in their minds only for a short time.
In short, he seemed bent on convincing me that there was no
art of speaking, and that no one could speak skillfully, or so
as fully to illustrate a subject, but one who had attained that
knowledge which is delivered by the most learned of the
philosophers.   On which occasions Charmadas used to say
with a passionate admiration of your genius, Crassus, that I
appeared to him very easy in listening, and you most pertinacious in disputation.

XXI. "Then it was that I, swayed by this opinion, remarked in a little treatise[2] which got abroad, and into people's hands, without my knowledge and against my will, that
I had known many good speakers, but never yet any one that
was truly eloquent; for I accounted him *a good speaker* who
could express his thoughts with accuracy and perspicuity, ac-

selves had purposely abstained from attempting to be eloquent.   But
Charmadas was very much in the wrong; for Gorgias, Isocrates, Protagoras, Theophrastus, and other teachers of rhetoric were eminent for eloquence. *Proust.*
   [1] Two Sicilians, said to have been the most ancient writers on rhetoric. See Quintilian, iii., 1.
   [2] See c. 47.—Cicero speaks of it as *exilis*, poor and dry, Brut., 44;
Orat., 5.

cording to the ordinary judgment of mankind, before an audience of moderate capacity; but I considered him alone *eloquent*, who could in a more admirable and noble manner amplify and adorn whatever subjects he chose, and who embraced in thought and memory all the principles of every thing relating to oratory. This, though it may be difficult to us, who, before we begin to speak in public, are overwhelmed by canvassings for office and by the business of the forum, is yet within the range of possibility and the powers of nature. For I, as far as I can divine by conjecture, and as far as I can estimate the abilities of our countrymen, do not despair that there may arise at some time or other a person, who, when, with a keener devotion to study than we feel, or have ever felt, with more leisure, with better and more mature talent for learning, and with superior labor and industry, he shall have given himself up to hearing, reading, and writing, may become such an orator as we desire to see—one who may justly be called not only a good speaker, but truly eloquent ; and such a character, in my opinion, is our friend Crassus, or some one, if such ever was, of equal genius, who, having heard, read, and written more than Crassus, shall be able to make some little addition to it."

Here Sulpicius observed : " That has happened by accident, Crassus, which neither Cotta nor I expected, but which we both earnestly desired—I mean, that you should insensibly glide into a discourse of this kind. For, as we were coming hither, we thought it would be a pleasure, if, while you were talking on other matters, we might gather something worthy to be remembered from your conversation ; but that you should go into a deep and full discussion on this very study, or art, or faculty, and penetrate into the heart of it, was what we could scarcely venture to hope. For I, who from my early youth have felt a strong affection for you both, and even a love for Crassus, having never left his company, could never yet elicit a word from him on the method and art of speaking, though I not only solicited him myself, but endeavored to move him by the agency of Drusus ; on which subject you, Antonius (I speak but the truth), never failed to answer my requests and interrogatories, and have very often told me what you used to notice in speaking.   And since each of you has opened a way to these subjects of our research, and since

Crassus was the first to commence this discourse, do us the favor to acquaint us fully and exactly what you think about the various kinds of eloquence. If we obtain this indulgence from you, I shall feel the greatest obligation to this school of yours, Crassus, and to your Tusculan villa, and shall prefer your suburban place of study to the famous Academy and Lyceum."

XXII. "Nay rather, Sulpicius," rejoined Crassus, "let us ask Antonius, who is both capable of doing what you desire, and, as I hear you say, has been accustomed to do so. As to myself, I acknowledge that I have ever avoided all such kind of discourse, and have often declined to comply with your requests and solicitations, as you just now observed. This I did, not from pride or want of politeness, nor because I was unwilling to aid your just and commendable aspirations, especially as I knew you to be eminently and above others formed and qualified by nature to become a speaker, but, in truth, from being unaccustomed to such kind of discussions, and from being ignorant of those principles which are laid down as institutes of the art." "Then," said Cotta, "since we have got over what we thought the greatest difficulty, to induce you, Crassus, to speak at all upon these subjects, for the rest, it will be our own fault if we let you go before you have explained all that we have to ask." "I believe I must answer," says Crassus, "as is usually written in the formulæ for entering on inheritances,[1] concerning such points AS I KNOW AND SHALL BE ABLE." "And which of us," rejoined Cotta, "can be so presuming as to desire to know or to be able to do any thing that you do not know or can not do?" "Well, then," returned Crassus, "on condition that I may say that I can not do what I can not do, and that I may own that I do not know what I do not know, you may put questions to me at your pleasure." "We shall, then, first ask of you," said Sulpicius, "what you think of what Antonius has advanced; whether you think that there is any art in speaking?" "What!" exclaimed Crassus, "do you put a trifling question to me, as to some idle and talkative, though

---

[1] *Cretionibus.* An heir was allowed a certain time to determine, *cernere*, whether he would enter upon an estate bequeathed to him, or not. See Cic., ad Att., xi., 12; xiii., 46; Gaius, Instit., ii., 164; Ulpian, Fragm., xxii., 27; Heinecc., Syntagm., ii., 14, 17.

perhaps studious and learned Greek, on which I may speak according to my humor? When do you imagine that I have ever regarded or thought upon such matters, or have not always rather ridiculed the impudence of those men who, seated in the schools, would demand if any one, in a numerous assembly of persons, wished to ask any question, and desire him to speak? This Gorgias the Leontine is said to have first done, who was thought to undertake and promise something vast, in pronouncing himself prepared to speak on all subjects on which any one should be inclined to hear him. But afterward those men made it a common practice, and continue it to this day; so that there is no topic of such importance, or so unexpected, or so new, on which they do not profess that they will say all that can be said. But if I had thought that you, Cotta, or you, Sulpicius, were desirous to hear such matters, I would have brought hither some Greek to amuse you with their manner of disputation; for there is with M. Piso[1] (a youth already addicted to this intellectual exercise, and one of superior talents, and of great affection for me) the peripatetic Staseas, a man with whom I am well acquainted, and who, as I perceive is agreed among the learned, is of the first eminence in his profession."

XXIII. "Why do you speak to me," says Scævola, "of this Staseas, this peripatetic? You must comply with the wishes of these young gentlemen, Crassus, who do not want the common, profitless talk of any Greek, or any empty declamations of the schools, but desire to know the opinions of a man in whose footsteps they long to tread—one who is the wisest and most eloquent of all men, who is not distinguished by petty books of precepts, but is the first, both in judgment and oratory, in causes of the greatest consequence, and in this seat of empire and glory. For my part, as I always thought you a god in eloquence, so I have never attributed to you greater praises for oratory than for politeness; which you ought to show on this occasion especially, and not to decline a discussion on which two young men of such excellent ability invite you to enter." "I am certainly," replied Crassus, "desirous to oblige them, nor shall I think it any trouble to speak

---

[1] Marcus Pupius Piso Calpurnianus, to whom Cicero was introduced by his father, that he might profit by his learning and experience. See Ascon., Ped. ad Pis., 26; Cic., Brut., 67; De Nat. De., i., 7, 16.

briefly, as is my manner, what I think upon any point of the subject. And to their first question (because I do not think it right for me to neglect your admonition, Scævola), I answer, that I think there is either no art of speaking at all, or but very little; but that all the disputation about it among the learned arises from a difference of opinion about the word. For if art is to be defined according to what Antonius just now asserted,[1] as lying in things thoroughly understood and fully known, such as are abstracted from the caprice of opinion and comprehended in the limits of science, there seems to me to be no art at all in oratory; since all the species of our forensic diction are various, and suited to the common understanding of the people. Yet if those things which have been observed in the practice and method of speaking have been noted and chronicled by ingenious and skillful men, have been set forth in words, illustrated in their several kinds, and distributed into parts (as I think may possibly be done), I do not understand why speaking may not be deemed an art, if not according to the exact definition of Antonius, at least according to common opinion. But whether it be an art, or merely the resemblance of an art, it is not, indeed, to be neglected; yet we must understand that there are other things of more consequence for the attainment of eloquence."

XXIV. Antonius then observed, that he was very strongly of opinion with Crassus; for he neither adopted such a definition of art as those preferred who attributed all the powers of eloquence to art, nor did he repudiate it entirely, as most of the philosophers had done. "But I imagine, Crassus," added he, "that you will gratify these two young men, if you will specify those particulars which you think may be more conducive to oratory than art itself." "I will indeed mention them," said he, "since I have engaged to do so, but must beg you not to publish my trifling remarks: though I will keep myself under such restraint as not to seem to speak like a master, or artist, but like one of the number of private citizens, moderately versed in the practice of the forum, and not altogether ignorant; not to have offered any thing from myself, but to have accidentally fallen in with the course of your conversation. Indeed, when I was a candidate for office, I used, at the time of canvassing, to send away Scævola from

¹ Cap. xx.

me, telling him I wanted to be foolish, that is, to solicit with flattery, a thing that can not be done to any purpose unless it be done foolishly; and that he was the only man in the world in whose presence I should least like to play the fool; and yet fortune has appointed him to be a witness and spectator of my folly.[1] For what is more foolish than to speak about speaking, when speaking itself is never otherwise than foolish, except it is absolutely necessary?" "Proceed, however, Crassus," said Scævola; "for I will take upon myself the blame which you fear."

XXV. "I am, then, of opinion," said Crassus, "that nature and genius in the first place contribute most aid to speaking; and that to those writers on the art, to whom Antonius just now alluded, it was not skill and method in speaking, but natural talent that was wanting; for there ought to be certain lively powers in the mind[2] and understanding, which may be acute to invent, fertile to explain and adorn, and strong and retentive to remember; and if any one imagines that these powers may be acquired by art (which is false, for it is very well if they can be animated and excited by art; but they certainly can not by art be ingrafted or instilled, since they are all the gifts of nature), what will he say of those qualities which are certainly born with the man himself, volubility of tongue, tone of voice, strength of lungs, and a peculiar conformation and aspect of the whole countenance and body? I do not say that art can not improve in these particulars (for I am not ignorant that what is good may be made better by education, and what is not very good may be in some degree polished and amended); but there are some persons so hesitating in their speech, so inharmonious in their tone of voice, or so unwieldy and rude in the air and movements of their bodies, that, whatever power they possess either from genius or art, they can never be reckoned in the number of accomplished speakers; while there are others so happily qualified in these respects, so eminently adorned with the gifts of nature, that they seem not to have been born like other men,

---

[1] See Val. Max., iv., 5, 4.

[2] *Animi atque ingenii celeres quidam motus.* This sense of *motus*, as Ellendt observes, is borrowed from the Greek κίνησις, by which the philosophers intimated an *active power*, as, without motion, all things would remain unchanged, and nothing be generated. See Matth., ad Cic. pro Sext., 67, 143.

but moulded by some divinity. It is, indeed, a great task and enterprise for a person to undertake and profess, that while every one else is silent, he alone must be heard on the most important subjects, and in a large assembly of men; for there is scarcely any one present who is not sharper and quicker to discover defects in the speaker than merits; and thus whatever offends the hearer effaces the recollection of what is worthy of praise. I do not make these observations for the purpose of altogether deterring young men from the study of oratory, even if they be deficient in some natural endowments. For who does not perceive that to C. Cælius, my contemporary, a new man, the mere mediocrity in speaking, which he was enabled to attain, was a great honor? Who does not know that Q. Varius, your equal in age, a clumsy, uncouth man, has obtained his great popularity by the cultivation of such faculties as he has?

XXVI. "But as our inquiry regards the COMPLETE ORATOR, we must imagine, in our discussion, an orator from whom every kind of fault is abstracted, and who is adorned with every kind of merit. For if the multitude of suits, if the variety of causes, if the rabble and barbarism of the forum afford room for even the most wretched speakers, we must not, for that reason, take our eyes from the object of our inquiry. In those arts, in which it is not indispensable usefulness that is sought, but liberal amusement for the mind, how nicely, how almost fastidiously, do we judge! For there are no suits or controversies which can force men, though they may tolerate indifferent orators in the forum, to endure also bad actors upon the stage. The orator therefore must take the most studious precaution not merely to satisfy those whom he necessarily must satisfy, but to seem worthy of admiration to those who are at liberty to judge disinterestedly. If you would know what I myself think, I will express to you, my intimate friends, what I have hitherto never mentioned, and thought that I never should mention. To me, those who speak best, and speak with the utmost ease and grace, appear, if they do not commence their speeches with some timidity, and show some confusion in the exordium, to have almost lost the sense of shame, though it is impossible that such should not be the case;[1] for the better qualified a man is to speak, the more he

---

[1] *Tametsi id accidere non potest.* "Quamvis id fieri non possit, ut qui optimè dicit, in exordio non perturbetur." *Proust.*

fears the difficulties of speaking, the uncertain success of a speech, and the expectation of the audience. But he who can produce and deliver nothing worthy of his subject, nothing worthy of the name of an orator, nothing worthy the attention of his audience, seems to me, though he be ever so confused while he is speaking, to be downright shameless ; for we ought to avoid a character for shamelessness, not by testifying shame, but by not doing that which does not become us. But the speaker who has no shame (as I see to be the case with many) I regard as deserving, not only of rebuke, but of personal castigation. Indeed, what I often observe in you I very frequently experience in myself, that I turn pale in the outset of my speech, and feel a tremor through my whole thoughts, as it were, and limbs. When I was a young man, I was on one occasion so timid in commencing an accusation, that I owed to Q. Maximus[1] the greatest of obligations for immediately dismissing the assembly, as soon as he saw me absolutely disheartened and incapacitated through fear." Here they all signified assent, looked significantly at one another, and began to talk together ; for there was a wonderful modesty in Crassus, which, however, was not only no disadvantage to his oratory, but even an assistance to it, by giving it the recommendation of probity.

XXVII. Antonius soon after said, " I have often observed, as you mention, Crassus, that both you and other most accomplished orators, although in my opinion none was ever equal to you, have felt some agitation in entering upon their speeches. When I inquired into the reason of this, and considered why a speaker, the more ability he possessed, felt the greater fear in speaking, I found that there were two causes of such timidity : one, that those whom experience and nature had formed for speaking, well knew that the event of a speech did not always satisfy expectation even in the greatest orators ; and thus, as often as they spoke, they feared, not without reason, that what sometimes happened might happen then ; the other (of which I am often in the habit of complaining) is, that men, tried and approved in other arts, if they ever do any thing with less success than usual, are thought either to

---

[1] He seems to be Quintus Fabius Maximus Eburnus, who was consul A.U.C. 638, and who, it is probable, presided as prætor on the occasion of which Crassus speaks. *Ellendt.*

have wanted inclination for it, or to have failed in performing
what they knew how to perform from ill health.   'Roscius,'
they say, 'would not act to-day,' or, 'he was indisposed.'
But if any deficiency is seen in the orator, it is thought to
proceed from want of sense; and want of sense admits of no
excuse, because nobody is supposed to have wanted sense because he 'was indisposed,' or because 'such was his inclination.'   Thus we undergo a severer judgment in oratory, and
judgment is pronounced upon us as often as we speak; if an
actor is once mistaken in an attitude, he is not immediately
considered to be ignorant of attitude in general; but if any
fault is found in a speaker, there prevails forever, or at least
for a very long time, a notion of his stupidity.

XXVIII.   "But in what you observed as to there being
many things in which, unless the orator has a full supply of
them from nature, he can not be much assisted by a master,
I agree with you entirely; and, in regard to that point, I
have always expressed the highest approbation of that eminent teacher, Apollonius of Alabanda,[1] who, though he taught
for pay, would not suffer such as he judged could never become
orators, to lose their labor with him; and he sent them away
with exhortations and encouragements to each of them to pursue that peculiar art for which he thought him naturally qualified.   To the acquirement of other arts it is sufficient for a
person to resemble a man, and to be able to comprehend in
his mind, and retain in his memory, what is instilled, or, if he
is very dull, inculcated into him; no volubility of tongue is
requisite, no quickness of utterance; none of those things
which we can not form for ourselves, aspect, countenance,
look, voice.   But in an orator, the acuteness of the logicians,
the wisdom of the philosophers, the language almost of poetry,
the memory of lawyers, the voice of tragedians, the gesture
almost of the best actors, is required.   Nothing, therefore, is
more rarely found among mankind than a consummate orator; for qualifications which professors of other arts are commended for acquiring in a moderate degree, each in his respective pursuit, will not be praised in the orator, unless they
are all combined in him in the highest possible excellence."

"Yet observe," said Crassus, "how much more diligence

[1] A town of Caria.   The Apollonius mentioned above, c. 17, was
Apollonius Molo, a native of Rhodes.   *Proust.*

is used in one of the light and trivial arts than in this, which is acknowledged to be of the greatest importance; for I often hear Roscius say that 'he could never yet find a scholar that he was thoroughly satisfied with; not that some of them were not worthy of approbation, but because, if they had any fault, he himself could not endure it.' Nothing, indeed, is so much noticed, or makes an impression of such lasting continuance on the memory, as that in which you give any sort of offense. To judge, therefore, of the accomplishments of the orator by comparison with this stage-player, do you not observe how every thing is done by him unexceptionably; every thing with the utmost grace; every thing in such a way as is becoming, and as moves and delights all? He has accordingly long attained such distinction, that in whatever pursuit a man excels, he is called a Roscius in his art. For my own part, while I desire this finish and perfection in an orator, of which I fall so far short myself, I act audaciously; for I wish indulgence to be granted to myself, while I grant none to others; for I think that he who has not abilities, who is faulty in action, who, in short, wants a graceful manner, should be sent off, as Apollonius advised, to that for which he has a capacity."

XXIX. "Would you then," said Sulpicius, "desire me, or our friend Cotta, to learn the civil law, or the military art?[1] for who can ever possibly arrive at that perfection of yours, that high excellence in every accomplishment?" "It was," replied Crassus, "because I knew that there was in both of you excellent and noble talents for oratory, that I have expressed myself fully on these matters; nor have I adapted my remarks more to deter those who had not abilities, than to encourage you who had; and though I perceive in you both consummate capacity and industry, yet I may say that the advantages of personal appearance, on which I have perhaps said more than the Greeks are wont to say, are in you, Sulpicius, even godlike. For any person better qualified for this profession by gracefulness of motion, by his very carriage and figure, or by the fullness and sweetness of his voice, I think that I have never heard speak; endowments which those, to whom they are granted by nature in an inferior de-

[1] The young Roman nobles were accustomed to pursue one of three studies, jurisprudence, eloquence, or war. *Proust.*

gree, may yet succeed in managing, in such measure as they possess them, with judgment and skill, and in such a manner as not to be *unbecoming;* for that is what is chiefly to be avoided, and concerning which it is most difficult to give any rules for instruction, not only for me, who talk of these matters like a private citizen, but even for Roscius himself, whom I often hear say 'that the most essential part of art is to be *becoming,*' which yet is the only thing that can not be taught by art. But, if it is agreeable, let us change the subject of conversation, and talk like ourselves a little, not like rhetoricians."

" By no means," said Cotta, "for we must now entreat you (since you retain us in this study, and do not dismiss us to any other pursuit) to tell us something of your own abilities, whatever they are, in speaking; for we are not inordinately ambitious; we are satisfied with that mediocrity of eloquence of yours; and what we inquire of you is (that we may not attain more than that humble degree of oratory at which you have arrived)[1] what you think, since you say that the endowments to be derived from nature are not very deficient in us, we ought to endeavor to acquire in addition."

XXX. Crassus, smiling, replied, "What do you think is wanting to you, Cotta, but a passionate inclination, and a sort of ardor like that of love, without which no man will ever attain any thing great in life, and especially such distinction as you desire? Yet I do not see that you need any encouragement to this pursuit; indeed, as you press rather hard even upon me, I consider that you burn with an extraordinarily fervent affection for it. But I am aware that a desire to reach any point avails nothing, unless you know what will lead and bring you to the mark at which you aim. Since, therefore, you lay but a light burden upon me, and do not question me about the whole art of the orator, but about my own ability, little as it is, I will set before you a course, not very obscure, or very difficult, or grand, or imposing, the course of my own practice, which I was accustomed to pursue when I had opportunity, in my youth, to apply to such studies."

" O day much wished for by us, Cotta !" exclaimed Sulpicius ; "for what I could never obtain, either by entreaty, or stratagem, or scrutiny (so that I was unable, not only to see

---

[1] Cotta speaks ironically.

what Crassus did, with a view to meditation or composition, but even to gain a notion of it from his secretary and reader, Diphilus), I hope we have now secured, and that we shall learn from himself all that we have long desired to know."

XXXI. " I conceive, however," proceeded Crassus, " that when you have heard me, you will not so much admire what I have said, as think that, when you desired to hear, there was no good reason for your desire ; for I shall say nothing abstruse, nothing to answer your expectation, nothing either previously unheard by you, or new to any one. In the first place, I will not deny that, as becomes a man well born and liberally educated, I learned those trite and common precepts of teachers in general ; first, that it is the business of an orator to speak in a manner adapted to persuade ; next, that every speech is either upon a question concerning a matter in general, without specification of persons or times, or concerning a matter referring to certain persons and times. But that, in either case, whatever falls under controversy, the question with regard to it is usually, whether such a thing has been done, or, if it has been done, of what nature it is, or by what name it should be called ; or, as some add, whether it seems to have been done rightly or not. That controversies arise also on the interpretation of writing, in which any thing has been expressed ambiguously, or contradictorily, or so that what is written is at variance with the writer's evident intention ; and that there are certain lines of argument adapted to all these cases. But that of such subjects as are distinct from general questions, part come under the head of judicial proceedings, part under that of deliberations ; and that there is a third kind which is employed in praising or censuring particular persons. That there are also certain commonplaces on which we may insist in judicial proceedings, in which equity is the object ; others, which we may adopt in deliberations, all which are to be directed to the advantage of those to whom we give counsel ; others in panegyric, in which all must be referred to the dignity of the persons commended. That, since all the business and art of an orator is divided into five parts,[1] he ought first to find out what he should say ; next, to dispose and arrange his matter, not only in a certain order,

[1] Invention, disposition, embellishment, memory, and delivery. See ii., 19. *Ellendt.*

but with a sort of power and judgment; then to clothe and deck his thoughts with language; then to secure them in his memory; and, lastly, to deliver them with dignity and grace. I had learned and understood also, that before we enter upon the main subject, the minds of the audience should be conciliated by an exordium; next, that the case should be clearly stated; then, that the point in controversy should be established; then, that what we maintain should be supported by proof, and that whatever was said on the other side should be refuted; and that, in the conclusion of our speech, whatever was in our favor should be amplified and enforced, and whatever made for our adversaries should be weakened and invalidated.

XXXII. "I had heard also what is taught about the costume of a speech; in regard to which it is first directed that we should speak correctly and in pure Latin; next, intelligibly and with perspicuity; then gracefully; then suitably to the dignity of the subject, and as it were becomingly; and I had made myself acquainted with the rules relating to every particular. Moreover, I had seen art applied to those things which are properly endowments of nature; for I had gone over some precepts concerning action, and some concerning artificial memory, which were short indeed, but requiring much exercise; matters on which almost all the learning of those artificial orators is employed; and if I should say that it is of no assistance, I should say what is not true; for it conveys some hints to admonish the orator, as it were, to what he should refer each part of his speech, and to what points he may direct his view, so as not to wander from the object which he has proposed to himself. But I consider that with regard to all precepts the case is this, not that orators by adhering to them have obtained distinction in eloquence, but that certain persons have noticed what men of eloquence practiced of their own accord, and formed rules accordingly;[1] so that eloquence has not sprung from art, but art from eloquence; not that, as I said before, I entirely reject art, for it is, though not essentially necessary to oratory, yet proper

[1] *Atque id egisse.* Most critics have supposed these words in some way faulty. Gesner conjectured *atque digessisse;* Lambinus, *atque in artem redegisse;* Ernesti, *ad artemque redegisse.* Ellendt supposes that *id egisse* may mean *ei rei operam dedisse.*

for a man of liberal education to learn. And by you, my young friends, some preliminary exercise must be undergone, though indeed you are already on the course; but those[1] who are to enter upon a race, and those who are preparing for what is to be done in the forum, as their field of battle, may alike previously learn, and try their powers by practicing in sport." "That sort of exercise," said Sulpicius, "is just what we wanted to understand; but we desire to hear more at large what you have briefly and cursorily delivered concerning art, though such matters are not strange even to us. Of that subject, however, we shall inquire hereafter; at present we wish to know your sentiments on exercise."

XXXIII. "I like that method," replied Crassus, "which you are accustomed to practice, namely, to lay down a case similar to those which are brought on in the forum, and to speak upon it, as nearly as possible, as if it were a real case.[2] But in such efforts the generality of students exercise only their voice (and not even that skillfully), and try their strength of lungs, and volubility of tongue, and please themselves with a torrent of their own words; in which exercise what they have heard deceives them, *that men by speaking succeed in becoming speakers.* For it is truly said also, *That men by speaking badly make sure of becoming bad speakers.* In those exercises, therefore, although it be useful even frequently to speak on the sudden, yet it is more advantageous, after taking time to consider, to speak with greater preparation and accuracy. But the chief point of all is that which (to say the truth) we hardly ever practice (for it requires great labor, which most of us avoid); I mean, to write as much as possible. *Writing* is said to be *the best and most excellent modeler and teacher of oratory;* and not without reason; for if what is meditated and considered easily surpasses sudden and extemporary speech, a constant and diligent habit of writing will surely be of more effect than meditation and consideration itself; since all the arguments relating to the subject on which we write, whether

---

[1] *Sed iis, qui ingrediuntur.* Orellius and Ellendt retain this reading, though Ernesti had long before observed that there is no verb on which *iis* can be considered as dependent, and that we must read *ii* or *hi* as a nominative to the following *possunt.*

[2] *Quàm maximè ad veritatem accommodatè,* "with as much adaptation as possible to truth."

they are suggested by art, or by a certain power of genius and understanding, will present themselves, and occur to us, while we examine and contemplate it in the full light of our intellect; and all the thoughts and words, which are the most expressive of their kind, must of necessity come under and submit to the keenness of our judgment while writing; and a fair arrangement and collocation of the words is effected by writing, in a certain rhythm and measure, not poetical, but oratorical. Such are the qualities which bring applause and admiration to good orators; nor will any man ever attain them unless after long and great practice in writing, however resolutely he may have exercised himself in extemporary speeches; and he who comes to speak after practice in writing brings this advantage with him, that though he speak at the call of the moment, yet what he says will bear a resemblance to something written; and if ever, when he comes to speak, he brings any thing with him in writing, the rest of his speech, when he departs from what is written, will flow on in a similar strain. As, when a boat has once been impelled forward, though the rowers suspend their efforts, the vessel herself still keeps her motion and course during the intermission of the impulse and force of the oars; so, in a continued stream of oratory, when written matter fails, the rest of the speech maintains a similar flow, being impelled by the resemblance and force acquired from what is written.

XXXIV. " But in my daily exercises I used, when a youth, to adopt chiefly that method which I knew that Caius Carbo, my adversary,[1] generally practiced; which was, that, having selected some nervous piece of poetry, or read over such a portion of a speech as I could retain in my memory, I used to declaim upon what I had been reading in other words, chosen with all the judgment that I possessed. But at length I perceived that in that method there was this inconvenience, that Ennius, if I exercised myself on his verses, or Gracchus, if I laid one of his orations before me, had forestalled such words as were peculiarly appropriate to the subject, and such as were the most elegant and altogether the best; so that, if I used the same words, it profited nothing; if others, it was even prejudicial to me, as I habituated myself to use such as were less eligible. Afterward I thought proper, and con-

[1] See c. x.

tinued the practice at a rather more advanced age,[1] to translate the orations of the best Greek orators;[2] by fixing upon
which I gained this advantage, that while I rendered into
Latin what I had read in Greek, I not only used the best
words, and yet such as were of common occurrence, but also
formed some words by imitation, which would be new to our
countrymen, taking care, however, that they were unobjection-
able.

  " As to the exertion and exercise of the voice, of the breath,
of the whole body, and of the tongue itself, they do not so
much require art as labor ; but in those matters we ought to
be particularly careful whom we imitate and whom we would
wish to resemble.   Not only orators are to be observed by
us, but even actors, lest by vicious habits we contract any
awkwardness or ungracefulness.   The memory is also to be
exercised by learning accurately by heart as many of our own
writings, and those of others, as we can.   In exercising the
memory, too, I shall not object if you accustom yourself to
adopt that plan of referring to places and figures which is
taught in treatises on the art.[3]   Your language must then be
brought forth from this domestic and retired exercise into
the midst of the field, into the dust and clamor, into the
camp and military array of the forum; you must acquire
practice in every thing; you must try the strength of your
understanding; and your retired lucubrations must be exposed to the light of reality.   The poets must also be studied;
an acquaintance must be formed with history; the writers
and teachers in all the liberal arts and sciences must be read,
and turned over, and must, for the sake of exercise, be praised,
interpreted, corrected, censured, refuted ; you must dispute
on both sides of every question ; and whatever may seem
maintainable on any point must be brought forward and illustrated.   The civil law must be thoroughly studied; laws
in general must be understood; all antiquity must be known ;
the usages of the senate, the nature of our government, the
rights of our allies, our treaties and conventions, and what-

  [1] *Adolescens.*   When he imitated the practice of Carbo, he was, he
says, *adolescentulus.*
  [2] A practice recommended by Quintilian, x., 5.
  [3] This is sufficiently explained in book ii., c. 87.   See also Quint.,
xi., 2.

ever concerns the interests of the state, must be learned. A certain intellectual grace must also be extracted from every kind of refinement, with which, as with salt, every oration must be seasoned. I have poured forth to you all I had to say, and perhaps any citizen whom you had laid hold of in any company whatever would have replied to your inquiries on these subjects equally well."

XXXV. When Crassus had uttered these words a silence ensued. But, though enough seemed to have been said, in the opinion of the company present, in 'reference to what had been proposed, yet they thought that he had concluded his speech more abruptly than they could have wished. Scævola then said, "What is the matter, Cotta? why are you silent? Does nothing more occur to you which you would wish to ask Crassus?" "Nay," rejoined he, "that is the very thing of which I am thinking; for the rapidity of his words was such, and his oration was winged with such speed, that, though I perceived its force and energy, I could scarcely see its track and course; and, as if I had come into some rich and well-furnished house, where the furniture[1] was not unpacked, nor the plate set-out, nor the pictures and statues placed in view, but a multitude of all these magnificent things laid up and heaped together; so just now, in the speech of Crassus, I saw his opulence and the riches of his genius through veils and curtains as it were, but when I desired to take a nearer view, there was scarcely opportunity for taking a glance at them; I can therefore neither say that I am wholly ignorant of what he possesses, nor that I have plainly ascertained and beheld it." "Then," said Scævola, "why do you not act in the same way as you would do if you had really come into a house or villa full of rich furniture? If every thing was put by as you describe, and you had a great curiosity to see it, you would not hesitate to ask the master to order it to be brought out, especially if he was your friend; in like manner you will now surely ask Crassus to bring forth into the light that profusion of splendid objects which are his property (and of which, piled together in one place, we have caught a glimpse, as it were through a lattice,[2] as we passed by), and set every thing in its

---

[1] *Veste.* Under this word is included tapestry, coverings of couches, and other things of that sort.

[2] An illustration, says Proust, borrowed from the practice of traders,

proper situation." "I rather ask you, Scævola," says Cotta, "to do that for me (for modesty forbids Sulpicius and myself to ask of one of the most eminent of mankind, who has ever held in contempt this kind of disputation, such things as he perhaps regards only as rudiments for children); but do you oblige us in this, Scævola, and prevail on Crassus to unfold and enlarge upon those matters which he has crowded together, and crammed into so small a space in his speech." "Indeed," said Scævola, "I desired that before, more upon your account than my own; nor did I feel so much longing for this discussion from Crassus, as I experience pleasure from his orations in pleading. But now, Crassus, I ask you also on my own account, that since we have so much more leisure than has been allowed us for a long time, you would not think it troublesome to complete the edifice which you have commenced; for I see a finer and better plan of the whole work than I could have imagined, and one of which I strongly approve."

XXXVI. "I can not sufficiently wonder," says Crassus, "that even you, Scævola, should require of me that which I do not understand like those who teach it, and.which is of such a nature that, if I understood it ever so well, it would be unworthy of your wisdom and attention." "Say you so?" replied Scævola. "If you think it scarcely worthy of my age to listen to those ordinary precepts, commonly known every where, can we possibly neglect those other matters which you said must be known by the orator, respecting the dispositions and manners of mankind, the means by which the minds of men are excited or calmed, history, antiquity, the administration of the republic, and, finally, of our own civil law itself? For I knew that all this science, this abundance of knowledge, was within the compass of your understanding, but had never seen such rich furniture among the equipments of the orator."

"Can you then," says Crassus "(to omit other things innumerable and without limit, and come to your study, the civil law), can you account them orators for whom Scævola,[1] who allow goods on which they set a high value to be seen only through lattice-work.

[1] Not Quintus Scævola the augur, the father-in-law of Crassus, in whose presence Crassus is speaking, but another Quintus Scævola, who was an eminent lawyer, and held the office of pontifex; but at the time to which Crassus alludes he was tribune of the people, B.C. 105. *Proust.*

though in haste to go to the Campus Martius, waited several hours, sometimes laughing and sometimes angry, while Hypsæus, in the loudest voice, and with a multitude of words, was trying to obtain of Marcus Crassus, the prætor, that the party whom he defended might be allowed to lose his suit; and Cneius Octavius, a man of consular dignity, in a speech of equal length, refused to consent that his adversary should lose his cause, and that the party for whom he was speaking should be released from the ignominious charge of having been unfaithful in his guardianship, and from all trouble, through the folly of his antagonist?"[1]   "I should have thought such men," replied Scævola "(for I remember Mucius[2] told me the story), not only unworthy of the name of orators, but unworthy even to appear to plead in the forum."   "Yet," rejoined Crassus, "those advocates neither wanted eloquence, nor method, nor abundance of words, but a knowledge of the civil law; for in this case one, in bringing his suit, sought to recover more damages than the law of the Twelve Tables allowed, and, if he had gained those damages, would have lost his cause: the other thought it unjust that he himself should be proceeded against for more than was allowed in that sort of action, and did not understand that his adversary, if he proceeded in that manner, would lose his suit.

[1] The cause was as follows: As Scævola the pontiff was going into the field of Mars, to the election of consuls, he passed, in his way, through the forum, where he found two orators in much litigation, and blundering grievously through ignorance of the civil law.   One of them was Hypsæus, the other Cneius Octavius, who had been consul B.C. 128. Hypsæus was accusing some guardian of maladministration of the fortunes of his ward.   This sort of cause was called *judicium tutelæ*.   Octavius defended the guardian.   The judge of this controversy was Marcus Crassus, then city prætor, B.C. 105.   He that was condemned on such a trial was decreed to pay damages to his ward to the amount of what his affairs had suffered through his means, and, in addition, by the law of the Twelve Tables, was to pay something by way of fine.   But if the ward, or his advocate, sought to recover more from the defendant than was due, he lost his cause.   Hypsæus proceeded in this manner, and therefore ought to have been nonsuited.   Octavius, an unskillful defender of his client, should have rejoiced at this, for if he had made the objection and proved it, he would have obtained his cause; but he refused to permit Hypsæus to proceed for more than was due, though such proceeding would, by the law, have been fatal to his suit. *Proust.*

[2] Quintus Mucius Scævola, mentioned in the last note but one.

XXXVII. " Within these few days,[1] while we were sitting at the tribunal of our friend Quintus Pompeius, the city prætor, did not a man who is ranked among the eloquent pray that the benefit of the ancient and usual exception, *of which sum there is time for payment,* might be allowed to a party from whom a sum of money was demanded ; an exception which he did not understand to be made for the benefit of the creditor; so that if the defendant[2] had proved to the judge that the action was brought for the money before it became due, the plaintiff,[3] on bringing a fresh action, would be precluded by the exception *that the matter had before come into judgment.* What more disgraceful, therefore, can possibly be said or done, than that he who has assumed the character of an advocate, ostensibly to defend the causes and interests of his. friends, to assist the distressed, to relieve such as are sick at heart, and to cheer the afflicted, should so err in the slightest and most trivial matters as to seem an object of pity to some, and of ridicule to others? I consider my relation, Publius Crassus, him who from his wealth had the surname of Dives,[4] to have

---

[1] The cause was this. One man owed another a sum of money, to be paid, for instance, in the beginning of January ; the plaintiff would not wait till that time, but brought his action in December; the ignorant lawyer who was for the defendant, instead of contesting with the plaintiff this point, that he demanded his money before it was due (which if he had proved the plaintiff would have lost his cause), only prayed the benefit of the exception, which forbade an action to be brought for money before the day of payment, and so only put off the cause for that time. This he did not perceive to be a clause inserted for the advantage of the plaintiff, that he might know when to bring his suit. Thus the plaintiff, when the money became due, was at liberty to bring a new action, as if this matter had never come to trial, which action he could never have brought if the first had been determined on the other point, namely, its having been brought before the money was due; for then the defendant might have pleaded a former judgment, and precluded the plaintiff from the second action. See Justin., Instit., iv., 13, 5, *de re judicatâ.* " Of which sum there is a time for payment," were words of form in the exception from whence it was nominated ; as, "That the matter had before come into judgment," were in the other exception *rei judicatæ.* Proust. *B.* See Gaius, Instit., iv., 131, and Heffter, Obs. on Gaius, iv., 23, p. 109, *seq.* *Ellendt.*

[2] *Infitiator.* The defendant or debtor.

[3] *Petitor.* The plaintiff or creditor.

[4] Publius Licinius Crassus Mucianus, son of Publius Mucius Scævola, who had been adopted into the Licinian family. He was consul with Lucius Valerius Flaccus, A.U.C. 623. . . . . But the name of Dives had

been, in many other respects, a man of taste and elegance, but especially worthy of praise and commendation on this account, that (as he was the brother of Publius Scævola)[1] he was accustomed to observe to him *that neither could he*[2] *have satisfied the claims of the civil law if he had not added the power of speaking* (which his son here, who was my colleague in the consulate, has fully attained); *nor had he himself*[3] *begun to practice, and plead the causes of his friends, before he had gained a knowledge of the civil law.* What sort of character was the illustrious Marcus Cato? Was he not possessed of as great a share of eloquence as those times and that age[4] would admit in this city, and at the same time the most learned of all men in the civil law? I have been speaking for some time the more timidly on this point, because there is with us a man[5] eminent in speaking, whom I admire as an orator beyond all others, but who has ever held the civil law in contempt. But, as you desired to learn my sentiments and opinions, I will conceal nothing from you, but, as far as I am able, will communicate to you my thoughts upon every subject.

XXXVIII. "The almost incredible, unparalleled, and divine power of genius in Antonius appears to me, although wanting in legal knowledge, to be able easily to sustain and defend itself with the aid of other weapons of reason ; let him therefore be an exception ; but I shall not hesitate to condemn others, by my sentence, of want of industry in the first place, and of want of modesty in the next. For to flutter about the forum, to loiter in courts of justice and at the tribunals of the prætors, to undertake private suits in matters of the greatest concern, in which the question is often not about fact, but about equity and law, to swagger in causes heard be-

previously been in the family of the Crassi, for Publius Crassus, who was consul with Publius Africanus, A.U.C. 549, was so called. *Ellendt.*

[1] By birth. He had his name of Crassus from adoption, as stated in the preceding note.

[2] Publius Scævola, his brother. In the phrase, *neque illum in jure civili satis illi arti facere posse*, the words *illi arti* are regarded by Ernesti and Orellius as spurious, but Ellendt thinks them genuine, explaining *in jure civili* by *quod ad jus civile attinet.* I have followed Orellius and Ernesti in my translation. [3] Publius Crassus.

[4] *Illa tempora atque illa ætas.* By *tempora* is meant the state of the times as to political affairs ; by *ætas*, the period of advancement in learning and civilization which Rome had reached. [5] Antonius.

fore the centumviri,[1] in which the laws of prescriptive rights, of guardianship, of kindred,[2] of agnation,[3] of alluvions, circumluvions,[4] of bonds, of transferring property, of party walls, lights, *stillicidia*,[5] of wills, transgressed or established, and innumerable other matters are debated, when a man is utterly ignorant what is properly his own and what his neighbor's, why any person is considered a citizen or a foreigner, a slave or a freeman, is a proof of extraordinary impudence. It is ridiculous arrogance for a man to confess himself unskillful in navigating smaller vessels, and yet say that he has learned to pilot galleys with five banks of oars, or even larger ships. You who are deceived by a quibble of your adversary in a private company, you who set your seal to a deed for your client, in which that is written by which he is overreached, can I think that any cause of greater consequence ought to be intrusted to you? Sooner assuredly shall he who oversets a two-oared boat in the harbor steer the vessel of the Argonauts in the Euxine Sea.

"But what if the causes are not trivial, but often of the utmost importance, in which disputes arise concerning points of civil law? What front must that advocate have who dares to appear in causes of such a nature without any knowledge of that law? What cause, for instance, could be of more consequence than that of the soldier, of whose death a false report having been brought home from the army, and his father,

[1] A body of inferior *judices*, chosen three out of each tribe, so that the full number was a hundred and five. They took cognizance of such minor causes as the prætor intrusted to their decision.

[2] *Gentilitatum.* Kindred or family. Persons of the same family or descent had certain peculiar rights, *e. g.*, in entering upon an inheritance, in undertaking guardianship. In such rights slaves, freedmen, and *capite deminuti* had no participation. See Cic., Top., 6, 29. *Proust.*

[3] The *agnati*, as a brother by the same father, a brother's son or grandson, an uncle's son or grandson, had their peculiar rights. See Gaius, i., 156.

[4] About these, various controversies might arise; as, when the force of a river has detached a portion from your land, and added it to that of your neighbor, to whom does that portion belong? Or if trees have been carried away from your land to that of your neighbor, and have taken root there, etc. *Proust.*

[5] When a person was obliged to let the water, which dropped from his house, run into the garden or area of his neighbor, or to receive the water that fell from his neighbor's house into his area. Adam's Roman Antiquities, p. 49.

through giving credit to that report, having altered his will, and appointed another person, whom he thought proper, to be his heir, and having then died himself, the affair, when the soldier returned home, and instituted a suit for his paternal inheritance, came on to be heard before the centumviri? The point assuredly in that case was a question of civil law, whether a son could be disinherited of his father's possessions, whom the father neither appointed his heir by will, nor disinherited by name?[1]

XXXIX. "On the point, too, which the centumviri decided between the Marcelli and the Claudii, two patrician families, when the Marcelli said that an estate, which had belonged to the son of a freedman, reverted to them by right of *stirps*, and the Claudii alleged that the property of the man reverted to them by right of *gens*, was it not necessary for the pleaders in that cause to speak upon all the rights of *stirps* and *gens*?[2] As to that other matter also, which we have heard was contested at law before the centumviri, when an exile came to Rome (who had the privilege of living in exile at Rome if he attached himself to any citizen as a patron) and died intestate, was not, in a cause of that nature, the law of *attachment*,[3] obscure and indeed unknown, expounded and il-

---

[1] For he who had a son under his power should have taken care to institute him his heir, or to disinherit him by name ; since if a father pretermitted or passed over his son in silence, the testament was of no effect. Just., Inst., ii., 13. And if the parents disinherited their children without cause, the civil law was, that they might complain that such testaments were invalid, under color that their parents were not of sound mind when they made them. Just., Inst., ii., 18. *B.*

[2] The son of a freedman of the Claudian family had died without making a will, and his property fell by law to the Claudii; but there were two families of them—the Claudii Pulchri, who were patricians, and the Claudii Marcelli, who were plebeians; and these two families went to law about the possession of the dead man's property. The patrician Claudii (whose family was the eldest of the name) claimed the inheritance by right of *gens*, on the ground that the freedman was of the *gens Claudia*, of which their family was the chief; . . . . while the Claudii Marcelli, or plebeian Claudii, claimed it by right of *stirps*, on the ground that the freedman was more nearly related to them than to the Pulchri. *Pearce.* The term *gens* was used in reference to patricians ; that of *stirps* to plebeians. *Proust.*

[3] *Jus applicationis.* This was a right which a Roman *quasi-patronus* had to the estate of a foreign client dying intestate. He was called *quasi-patronus*, because none but Roman citizens could have patrons.

lustrated by the pleader? When I myself lately defended the cause of Sergius Aurata, on a private suit against our friend Antonius, did not my whole defense turn upon a point of law? For when Marius Gratidianus had sold a house to Aurata, and had not specified, in the deed of sale, that any part of the building owed service,[1] we argued that, for whatever encumbrance attended the thing sold, if the seller knew of it, and did not make it known, he ought to indemnify the purchaser.[2] In this kind of action our friend Marcus Bucculeius, a man not a fool in my opinion, and very wise in his own, and one who has no aversion to the study of law, made a mistake lately in an affair of a somewhat similar nature. For when he sold a house to Lucius Fufius, he engaged, in the act of conveyance, that the window-lights should remain as they then were. But Fufius, as soon as a building began to rise in some part of the city, which could but just be seen from that house, brought an action against Bucculeius, on the ground that whatever portion of the sky was intercepted, at however great a distance, the window-light underwent a change.[3] Amid

The difficulty in this cause proceeded from the obscurity of the law on which this kind of right was founded.

[1] The services of city estates are those which appertain to buildings. It is required by city services that neighbors should bear the burdens of neighbors; and, by such services, one neighbor may be permitted to place a beam upon the wall of another; may be compelled to receive the droppings and currents from the gutter-pipes of another man's house upon his own house, area, or sewer; or may be exempted from receiving them; or may be restrained from raising his house in height, lest he should darken the habitation of his neighbor. Harris's Justinian, ii., 3. *B.*

[2] There is a more particular statement of this cause between Gratidianus and Aurata in Cicero's Offices, iii., 16. The Roman law, in that particular founded on the law of nature, ordained, to avoid deceit in bargain and sale, that the seller should give notice of all the bad qualities in the thing sold which he knew of, or pay damages to the purchaser for his silence; to which law Horace alludes, Sat., iii., 2:

> Mentem nisi litigiosus
> Exciperet dominus cum venderet.

But if he told the faults, or they were such as must be seen by a person using common care, the buyer suffered for his negligence, as Horace again indicates, Epist., ii., 2:

> Ille feret pretium pœnæ securus opinor:
> Prudens emisti vitiosum. Dicta tibi est Lex.

See also Grotius, ii., 12, and Puffendorf, v. 3, s. 4, 5. *B.*

[3] The mistake of Bucculeius seems to have consisted in this: he meant to restrain Fufius from raising the house in height, which might

what a concourse of people too, and with what universal interest, was the famous cause between Manius Curius and Marcus Coponius lately conducted before the centumviri!   On
which occasion Quintus Scævola, my equal in age, and my
colleague,[1] a man of all others the most learned in the practice
of the civil law, and of the most acute genius and discernment,
a speaker most polished and refined in his language, and indeed, as I am accustomed to remark, the best orator among
the lawyers, and the best lawyer among the orators, argued
the law from the letter of the will, and maintained that he who
was appointed second heir, after a posthumous son should be
born and die, could not possibly inherit, unless such posthumous son had actually been born, and had died before he came
out of tutelage : I, on the other side, argued that he who made
the will had this intention, that if there was no son at all who
could come of tutelage, Manius Curius should be his heir.
Did either of us, in that cause, fail to exert ourselves in citing
authorities, and precedents, and forms of wills, that is, to dispute on the profoundest points of civil law?[2]

XL. "I forbear to mention many examples of causes of
the greatest consequence, which are indeed without number.
It may often happen that even capital cases may turn upon
a point of law ; for, as an example, Publius Rutilius, the son
of Marcus, when tribune of the people, ordered Caius Mancinus, a most noble and excellent man, and of consular
dignity, to be put out of the senate ; on the occasion when
the chief herald had given him up to the Numantines, according to a decree of the senate, passed on account of the odium
which he had incurred by his treaty with that people, and
they would not receive him,[3] and he had then returned home,
and had not hesitated to take his place in the senate ; the
tribune, I say, ordered him to be put out of the house, main-

darken, or making any new windows which might overlook, some neighboring habitation which belonged to him ; but by the use of words adapted by law for another purpose, he restrained himself from building within the prospect of those windows already made in the house which Fufius
purchased. B.   [1] In the consulship.
  [2] This celebrated cause is so clearly stated by Cicero as to require no
explanation.   It was gained by Crassus, the evident intention of the
testator prevailing over the letter of the will.   It is quoted as a prece-
dent by Cicero, pro Cæcinâ, c. 18.
  [3] See Florus, ii., 18 ; Vell. Pat., ii., 1.

taining that he was not a citizen ; because it was a received tradition, *That he whom his own father, or the people, had sold, or the chief herald had given up, had no* postliminium,[1] *or right of return.* What more important cause or argument can we find, among all the variety of civil transactions, than one concerning the rank, the citizenship, the liberty, the condition of a man of consular dignity, especially as the case depended, not on any charge which he might deny, but on the interpretation of the civil law? In a like case, but concerning a person of inferior degree, it was inquired among our ancestors whether, if a person belonging to a state in alliance with Rome had been in servitude among us, and gained his freedom, and afterward returned home, he returned by the right of *postliminium*, and lost the citizenship of this city. May not a dispute arise on a point of civil law respecting liberty, than which no cause can be of more importance, when the question is, for example, whether he who is enrolled as a citizen, by his master's consent, is free at once, or when the lustrum is completed? As to the case, also, that happened in the memory of our fathers, when the father of a family, who had come from Spain to Rome, and had left a wife pregnant in that province, and married another at Rome, without sending any notice of divorce to the former, and died intestate, after a son had been born of each wife, did a small matter come into controversy when the question was concerning the rights of two citizens, I mean concerning the boy who was born of the latter wife and his mother, who, if it were adjudged that a divorce was effected from a former wife by a certain set of words, and not by a second marriage, would be deemed a concubine? For a man, then, who is ignorant of these and other similar laws of his own country, to wander about the forum with a great crowd at his heels, erect and haughty, looking hither and thither with a gay and assured face and air, offering and tendering protection to his clients, assistance to his friends, and the light of his genius and counsel to almost all his fellow-citizens, is it not to be thought in the highest degree scandalous?

XLI. " Since I have spoken of the audacity, let me also censure the indolence and inertness of mankind. For if the study of the law were illimitable and arduous, yet the great-

---

[1] See Cic., Topic., c. 8; Gaius, i., 129; Aul. Gell., vii., 18.

ness of the advantage ought to impel men to undergo the labor of learning it; but, O ye immortal gods, I would not say this in the hearing of Scævola, unless he himself were accustomed to say it, namely, that *the attainment of no science seems to him more easy.* It is, indeed, for certain reasons, thought otherwise by most people, first, because those of old, who were at the head of this science, would not, for the sake of securing and extending their own influence, allow their art to be made public; in the next place, when it was published, the forms of actions at law being first set forth by Cneius Flavius, there were none who could compose a general system of those matters arranged under regular heads. For nothing can be reduced into a science unless he who understands the matters of which he would form a science has previously gained such knowledge as to enable him to constitute a science out of subjects in which there has never yet been any science. I perceive that, from desire to express this briefly, I have expressed it rather obscurely; but I will make an effort to explain myself, if possible, with more perspicuity.

XLII. "All things which are now comprised in sciences were formerly unconnected, and in a state, as it were, of dispersion; as in music, numbers, sounds, and measures; in geometry, lines, figures, spaces, magnitudes; in astronomy, the revolution of the heavens, the rising, setting, and other motions of the stars; in grammar, the study of the poets, the knowledge of history, the interpretation of words, the peculiar tone of pronunciation; and, finally, in this very art of oratory, invention, embellishment, arrangement, memory, delivery, seemed of old not to be fully understood by any, and to be wholly unconnected. A certain extrinsic art was therefore applied, adopted from another department of knowledge,[1] which the philosophers wholly claim to themselves, an art which might serve to cement things previously separate and uncombined, and unite them in a kind of system.

"Let, then, the end proposed in civil law be the preservation of legitimate and practical equity in the affairs and causes of the citizens. The general heads of it are then to be noted, and reduced to a certain number, as few as may be. A general head is that which comprehends two or more particulars, similar to one another by having something in com-

---

[1] From philosophy.

mon, but differing in species. Particulars are included under the general heads from which they spring. All names, which are given either to general heads, or particulars, must be limited by definitions, showing what exact meaning they have. A definition is a short and precise specification of whatever properly belongs to the thing which we would define. I should add examples on these points, were I not sensible to whom my discourse is addressed. I will now comprise what I proposed in a short space. For if I should have leisure to do what I have long meditated, or if any other person should undertake the task while I am occupied, or accomplish it after my death (I mean, to digest, first of all, the whole civil law under general heads, which are very few; next, to branch out those general heads, as it were, into members; then to explain the peculiar nature of each by a definition), you will have a complete system of civil law, large and full indeed, but neither difficult nor obscure. In the mean time, while what is unconnected is being combined, a person may, even by gathering here and there, and collecting from all parts, be furnished with a competent knowledge of the civil law.

XLIII. "Do you not observe that Caius Aculeo,[1] a Roman knight, a man of the most acute genius in the world, but of little learning in other sciences, who now lives, and has always lived with me, understands the civil law so well, that none even of the most skillful, if you except my friend Scævola here, can be preferred to him? Every thing in it, indeed, is set plainly before our eyes, connected with our daily habits, with our intercourse among men, and with the forum, and is not contained in a vast quantity of writing, or many large volumes; for the elements that were at first published by several writers are the same; and the same things, with the change of a few words, have been repeatedly written by the same authors. Added to this, that the civil law may be more readily learned and understood, there is (what most people little imagine) a wonderful pleasure and delight in

---

[1] This Aculeo married Cicero's aunt by the mother's side, as he tells us in the beginning of the second book of this treatise, c. 1, and his sons by that marriage, cousins to Cicero and his brother Quintus, were all bred up together with them, in a method approved by L. Crassus, the chief character in this dialogue, and by those very masters under whom Crassus himself had been. *B.*

acquiring a knowledge of it.   For, whether any person is attracted by the study of antiquity,[1] there is, in every part of the civil law, in the pontifical books, and in the Twelve Tables, abundance of instruction as to ancient matters, since not only the original sense of words is thence understood, but certain kinds of law proceedings illustrate the customs and lives of our ancestors ; or if he has a view to the science of government (which Scævola judges not to belong to the orator, but to science of another sort), he will find it all comprised in the Twelve Tables, every advantage of civil government, and every part of it being there described; or if authoritative and vaunting philosophy delight him (I will speak very boldly), he will find there the sources of all the philosophers' disputations, which lie in civil laws and enactments ; for from these we perceive that virtue is above all things desirable, since honest, just, and conscientious industry is ennobled with honors, rewards, and distinctions ; but the vices and frauds of mankind are punished by fines, ignominy, imprisonment, stripes, banishment, and death ; and we are taught, not by disputations endless and full of discord, but by the authority and mandate of the laws, to hold our appetites in subjection, to restrain all our passions, to defend our own property, and to keep our thoughts, eyes, and hands, from that of others.

XLIV. " Though all the world exclaim against me, I will say what I think : that single little book of the Twelve Tables, if any one look to the fountains and sources of laws, seems to me, assuredly, to surpass the libraries of all the philosophers, both in weight of authority and in plenitude of utility. And if our country has our love, as it ought to have in the highest degree—our country, I say, of which the force and natural attraction is so strong, that one of the wisest of mankind preferred his Ithaca, fixed, like a little nest, among the roughest of rocks, to immortality itself—with what affection

[1] Orellius retains *hæc aliena studia* in his text, but acknowledges *aliena* to be corrupt.   Wyttenbach conjectured *antiqua studia* for *antiquitatis studia*.   Ellendt observes that Madvig proposed *Æliana*, from Lucius Ælius Stilo, the master of Varro, extolled by Cicero, Brut., 56 ; Acad., i., 2, 8 ; Legg., ii., 23.   See Suetonius, de Ill. Gramm., c. 3 ; and Aul. Gell., x., 21.   This conjecture, says Henrichsen, will suit very well with the word *hæc*, which Crassus may be supposed to have used, because Ælius Stilo was then alive, and engaged in those studies.

ought we to be warmed toward such a country as ours, which, pre-eminently above all other countries, is the seat of virtue, empire, and dignity? Its spirit, customs, and discipline ought to be our first objects of study, both because our country is the parent of us all, and because as much wisdom must be thought to have been employed in framing such laws, as in establishing so vast and powerful an empire. You will receive also this pleasure and delight from the study of the law, that you will then most readily comprehend how far our ancestors excelled other nations in wisdom, if you compare our laws with those of their Lycurgus, Draco, and Solon. It is indeed incredible how undigested and almost ridiculous is all civil law except our own; on which subject I am accustomed to say much in my daily conversation, when I am praising the wisdom of our countrymen above that of all other men, and especially of the Greeks. For these reasons have I declared, Scævola, that the knowledge of the civil law is indispensable to those who would become accomplished orators.

XLV. "And who does not know what an accession of honor, popularity, and dignity such knowledge, even of itself, brings with it to those who are eminent in it? As, therefore, among the Greeks, men of the lowest rank, induced by a trifling reward, offer themselves as assistants to the pleaders on trials (men who are by them called *pragmatici*),[1] so in our city, on the contrary, every personage of the most eminent rank and

---

[1] It appears from Quintilian and Juvenal that this was a Roman custom as well as a Grecian, under the emperors; they are also mentioned by Ulpian. But in Cicero's time the *Patroni causarum*, or advocates, though they studied nothing but oratory, and were in general ignorant of the law, yet did not make use of any of these low people called *Pragmatici*, as the Greeks did at that time, but upon any doubts on the law, applied themselves to men of the greatest reputation in that science, such as the Scævolæ. But under the emperors there was not the same encouragement for these great men to study that science; the orators, therefore, fell of necessity into the Grecian custom. Quint., xii., 3: "Neque ego sum nostri moris ignarus, oblitusve eorum, qui velut ad Arculas sedent, et tela agentibus subministrant, neque idem Græcos nescio factitare, unde nomen his Pragmaticorum datum est." Juv., Sat., vii., 123:

Si quater egisti, si contigit aureus unus,
Inde cadunt partes ex fœdere Pragmaticorum. *B.*

character, such as that Ælius Sextus,[1] who, for his knowledge in the civil law, was called by our great poet,

" 'A man of thought and prudence, nobly wise,

and many besides, who, after arriving at distinction by means of their ability, attained such influence, that, in answering questions on points of law,[2] they found their authority of more weight than even their ability. For ennobling and dignifying old age, indeed, what can be a more honorable resource than the interpretation of the law? For myself, I have, even from my youth, been securing this resource, not merely with a view to benefit in pleadings in the forum, but also for an honor and ornament to the decline of life; so that, when my strength begins to fail me (for which the time is even now almost approaching), I may, by that means, preserve my house from solitude. For what is more noble than for an old man, who has held the highest honors and offices of the state, to be able justly to say for himself that which the Pythian Apollo says in Ennius, that he is the person from whom, if not nations and kings, yet all his fellow-citizens, solicit advice,

" 'Uncertain how to act; whom, by my aid,
I send away undoubting, full of counsel,
No more with rashness things perplex'd to sway;'

for without doubt the house of an eminent lawyer is the oracle of the whole city. Of this fact the gate and vestibule of our friend Quintus Mucius is a proof, which, even in his very

[1] As the collection of forms published by Flavius, and from him called *Jus civile Flavianum*, soon grew defective, as new contracts arose every day, another was afterward compiled, or rather only made public, by Sextus Ælius, for the forms seem to have been composed as the different emergencies arose, by such of the patricians as understood the law, and to have been by them secreted to extend their own influence; however, this collection, wherein were many new forms adapted to the cases and circumstances which had happened since the time of Flavius, went under the title of *Jus Ælianum*, from the Ælius here praised by Ennius. *B.*

[2] The custom *Respondendi de Jure*, and the interpretations and decisions of the learned, were so universally approved, that, although they were unwritten, they became a new species of law, and were called *Auctoritas*, or *Responsa Prudentum*. This custom continued to the time of Augustus without interruption, who selected particular lawyers, and gave them the sanction of a patent; but then grew into desuetude, till Hadrian renewed this office or grant, which made so considerable a branch of the Roman law. *B.*

infirm state of health and advanced age, is daily frequented
by a vast crowd of citizens, and by persons of the highest rank
and splendor.

XLVI. " It requires no very long explanation to show why
I think the public laws[1] also, which concern the state and
government, as well as the records of history, and the precedents of antiquity, ought to be known to the orator; for, as in
causes and trials relative to private affairs, his language is
often to be borrowed from the civil law, and therefore, as we
said before, the knowledge of the civil law is necessary to the
orator; so in regard to causes affecting public matters, before
our courts, in assemblies of the people, and in the senate, all
the history of these and of past times, the authority of public
law, the system and science of governing the state, ought to
be at the command of orators occupied with affairs of government, as the very groundwork of their speeches.[2] For
we are not contemplating, in this discourse, the character of
an every-day pleader, bawler, or barrator, but that of a man
who, in the first place, may be, as it were, the high-priest of
this profession, for which, though nature herself has given
rich endowments to man, yet it was thought to be a god that
gave it, so that the very thing which is the distinguishing
property of man might not seem to have been acquired by
ourselves, but bestowed upon us by some divinity; who, in
the next place, can move with safety even amid the weapons
of his adversaries, distinguished not so much by a herald's
caduceus[3] as by his title of orator ; who, likewise, is able, by
means of his eloquence, to expose guilt and deceit to the hatred of his countrymen, and to restrain them by penalties;
who can also, with the shield of his genius, protect innocence

---

[1] *Jura publica.*   Dr. Taylor, in his History of the Roman Law, p. 62,
has given us the heads of the Roman *Jus publicum*, which were, religion
and divine worship—peace and war—legislation—exchequer and *res
fisci*, escheats—the prerogative—law of treasons—taxes and imposts—
coinage—jurisdiction—magistracies— regalia—embassies—honors and
titles—colleges, schools, corporations—castles and fortifications—fairs,
mercats, staple—forests—naturalization.   *B.*

[2] *Tanquam aliqua materies.*   Ernesti's text, says Orellius, has *alia* by
mistake.   *Aliqua* is not very satisfactory.   Nobbe, the editor of Tauch-
nitz's text, retains Ernesti's *alia.*

[3] The herald's caduceus, or wand, renders his person inviolable.
Pearce.

from punishment; who can rouse a spiritless and desponding people to glory, or reclaim them from infatuation, or inflame their rage against the guilty, or mitigate it, if incited against the virtuous; who, finally, whatever feeling in the minds of men his object and cause require, can either excite or calm it by his eloquence. If any one supposes that this power has either been sufficiently set forth by those who have written on the art of speaking, or can be set forth by me in so brief a space, he is greatly mistaken, and understands neither my inability nor the magnitude of the subject. For my own part, since it was your desire, I thought that the fountains ought to be shown you from which you might draw, and the roads which you might pursue, not so that I should become your guide (which would be an endless and unnecessary labor), but so that I might point out to you the way, and, as the practice is, might hold out my finger toward the spring."[1]

XLVII. "To me," remarked Scævola, "enough appears to have been said by you, and more than enough, to stimulate the efforts of these young men, if they are but studiously inclined; for as they say that the illustrious Socrates used to observe that his object was attained if any one was by his exhortations sufficiently incited to desire to know and understand virtue (since to those who were persuaded to desire nothing so much as to become good men, what remained to be learned was easy); so I consider that if you wish to penetrate into those subjects which Crassus has set before you in his remarks, you will, with the greatest ease, arrive at your object, after this course and gate has been opened to you."
"To us," said Sulpicius, "these instructions are exceedingly pleasant and delightful; but there are a few things more which we still desire to hear, especially those which were touched upon so briefly by you, Crassus, in reference to oratory as an art, when you confessed that you did not despise them, but had learned them. If you will speak somewhat more at length on those points, you will satisfy all the eagerness of our long desire. For we have now heard to what objects we must direct our efforts, a point which is of great importance; but we long to be instructed in the ways and means of pursuing those objects."

---

[1] *Ut fieri solet.* Ernesti conjectures *ut dici solet.* Ellendt thinks the common reading right, requiring only that we should understand *à commonstrantibus.*

"Then," said Crassus " (since I, to detain you at my house with less difficulty, have rather complied with your desires than my own habit or inclination), what if we ask Antonius to tell us something of what he still keeps in reserve, and has not yet made known to us (on which subjects he complained, a while ago, that a book has already dropped from his pen), and to reveal to us his mysteries in the art of speaking?" "As you please," said Sulpicius; "for, if Antonius speaks, we shall still learn what you think." "I request of you, then, Antonius," said Crassus, "since this task is put upon men of our time of life by the studious inclinations of these youths, to deliver your sentiments upon these subjects which, you see, are required from you."

XLVIII. "I see plainly, and understand indeed," replied Antonius, "that I am caught, not only because those things are required from me in which I am ignorant and unpracticed, but because these young men do not permit me to avoid, on the present occasion, what I always carefully avoid in my public pleadings, namely, not to speak after you, Crassus. But I will enter upon what you desire the more boldly, as I hope the same thing will happen to me in this discussion as usually happens to me at the bar, that no flowers of rhetoric will be expected from me. For I am not going to speak about *art*, which I never learned, but about my own practice; and those very particulars which I have entered in my commonplace book are of this kind,[1] not expressed with any thing like learning, but just as they are treated in business and pleadings; and if they do not meet with approbation from men of your extensive knowledge, you must blame your own unreasonableness in requiring from me what I do not know; and you must praise my complaisance, since I make no difficulty in answering your questions, being induced, not by my own judgment, but your earnest desire." "Go on, Antonius," rejoined Crassus, "for there is no danger that you will say any thing otherwise than so discreetly that no one here will repent of having prompted you to speak."

"I will go on, then," said Antonius, "and will do what I think ought to be done in all discussions at the commencement; I mean, that the subject, whatever it may be, on which

---

[1] Not recorded with any elegance, but in the plain style in which I am now going to express myself. *Ernesti.*

the discussion is held, should be defined; so that the discourse may not be forced to wander and stray from its course, from the disputants not having the same notion of the matter under debate. If, for instance, it were inquired, 'What is the art of a general?' I should think that we ought to settle, at the outset, what a general is; and when he was defined to be *a commander for conducting a war*, we might then proceed to speak of troops, of encampments, of marching in battle array, of engagements, of besieging towns, of provisions, of laying and avoiding ambuscades, and other matters relative to the management of a war; and those who had the capacity and knowledge to direct such affairs I should call generals; and should adduce the examples of the Africani and Maximi, and speak of Epaminondas, and Hannibal, and men of such character. But if we should inquire what sort of character he is, who should contribute his experience, and knowledge, and zeal to the management of the state, I should give this sort of definition, that *he who understands by what means the interests of the republic are secured and promoted, and employs those means, is worthy to be esteemed a director in affairs of government, and a leader in public councils;* and I should mention Publius Lentulus, the chief of the senate,[1] and Tiberius Gracchus the father, and Quintus Metellus, and Publius Africanus, and Caius Lælius, and others without number, as well of our own city as of foreign states. But if it should be asked 'Who truly deserved the name of a lawyer?' I should say that he deserves it *who is learned in the laws, and that general usage*[2] *which private persons observe in their intercourse in the community, who can give an answer on any point, can plead, and can take precautions for the interests of his client;* and I should name Sextus Ælius, Manius Manilius, Publius Mucius, as distinguished in those respects. XLIX. In like manner, to notice sciences of a less important character, if a musician, if a grammarian, if a poet were the subject of consideration, I could state that which each of them possesses, and than which nothing more is to be expected from each. Even of the philosopher himself, who alone, from his abilities and wisdom, professes almost every thing, there is a sort of definition, signifying that *he who studies to learn the powers, nature, and causes of*

---

[1] *Principem illum.* Nempe *senatûs.* He was consul with Cneius Domitius, A.U.C. 592. *Ellendt.*   [2] The unwritten law.

all things, divine and human, and to understand and explain the whole science of living virtuously, may justly deserve this appellation.

" The orator, however, since it is about him that we are considering, I do not conceive to be exactly the same character that Crassus makes him, who seemed to me to include all knowledge of all matters and sciences under the single profession and name of an orator; but I regard him as *one who can use words agreeable to hear, and thoughts adapted to prove, not only in causes that are pleaded in the forum, but in causes in general.* Him I call an orator, and would have him, besides, accomplished in delivery and action, and with a certain degree of wit. But our friend Crassus seemed to me to define the faculty of an orator, not by the proper limits of his art, but by the almost immense limits of his own genius; for, by his definition, he delivered the helm of civil government into the hands of his orator; a point which it appeared very strange to me, Scævola, that you should grant him; when the senate has often given its assent on affairs of the utmost consequence to yourself, though you have spoken briefly and without ornament. And M. Scaurus, who I hear is in the country, at his villa not far off, a man eminently skilled in affairs of government, if he should hear that the authority which his gravity and counsels bear with them is claimed by you, Crassus, as you say that it is the property of the orator, he would, I believe, come hither without delay, and frighten us out of our talk by his very countenance and aspect; who, though he is no contemptible speaker, yet depends more upon his judgment in affairs of consequence than upon his ability in speaking; and, if any one has abilities in both these ways, he who is of authority in the public councils, and a good senator, is not on those accounts an orator; and if he that is an eloquent and powerful speaker be also eminent in civil administration, he did not acquire his political knowledge[1] through oratory. Those talents differ very much in their nature, and are quite separate and distinct from each other; nor did Marcus Cato, Publius Africanus, Quintus Metellus,

---

[1] *Aliquam scientiam.* For *aliquam* Manutius conjectured *illam*, which Lambinus, Ernesti, and Müller approve. Wyttenbach suggested *alienam*, which has been adopted by Schutz and Orellius. I have followed Manutius.

Caius Lælius, who were all eloquent, give lustre to their own orations, and to the dignity of the republic, by the same art and method.

L. "It is not enjoined, let me observe, by the nature of things, or by any law or custom, that one man must not know more than one art; and therefore, though Pericles was the best orator in Athens, and was also for many years director of the public counsels in that city, the talent for both those characters must not be thought to belong to the same art because it existed in the same man; nor if Publius Crassus was both an orator and a lawyer, is the knowledge of the civil law for that reason included in the power of speaking. For if any man, who, while excelling in any art or science, has acquired another art or science in addition, shall represent that his additional knowledge is a part of that in which he previously excelled,[1] we may, by such a mode of argument, pretend that to play well at tennis or counters[2] is a part of the knowledge of civil law, because Publius Mucius was skilled in both; and, by parity of reasoning, those whom the Greeks call φυσικοί, 'natural philosophers,' may be regarded as poets, because Empedocles the natural philosopher wrote an excellent poem. But not even the philosophers themselves, who would have every thing, as their own right, to be theirs, and in their possession, have the confidence to say that geometry or music is a part of philosophy, because all acknowledge Plato to have been eminently excellent in those sciences. And if it be still your pleasure to attribute all sciences to the orator, it will be better for us, rather, to express ourselves to this effect, that since eloquence must not be bald and unadorned, but marked and distinguished by a certain pleasing variety of manifold qualities, it is necessary for a good orator to have heard and seen much, to have gone over many subjects in thought and reflection, and many also in reading; though not so as to have taken possession of them as his own property, but to have tasted of them as things be-

---

[1] *Sciet—excellet.* The commentators say nothing against these futures.

[2] *Duodecim scriptis.* This was a game played with counters on a board, moved according to throws of the dice, but different from our backgammon. The reader may find all that is known of it in Adam's Roman Antiquities, p. 423, and Smith's Dict. of Gr. and Rom. Ant., art. Latrunculi.

longing to others.   For I confess that the orator should be a
knowing man, not quite a tyro or novice in any subject, not
utterly ignorant or inexperienced in any business of life.

LI. "Nor am I discomposed, Crassus, by those tragic arguments of yours,[1] on which the philosophers dwell most of all;
I mean, when you said, *That no man can, by speaking, excite the
passions of his audience, or calm them when excited (in which
efforts it is that the power and greatness of an orator are chiefly
seen), unless one who has gained a thorough insight into the nature
of all things, and the dispositions and motives of mankind; on
which account philosophy must of necessity be studied by the orator;*
a study in which we see that the whole lives of men of the
greatest talent and leisure are spent; the copiousness and
magnitude of whose learning and knowledge I not only do not
despise, but greatly admire; but, for us who are engaged in
so busy a state, and such occupations in the forum, it is sufficient to know and say just so much about the manners of
mankind as is not inconsistent with human nature.   For
what great and powerful orator, whose object was to make a
judge angry with his adversary, ever hesitated, because he
was ignorant what anger was, whether 'a heat of temper,' or
'a desire of vengeance for pain received?'[2]   Who, when he
wished to stir up and inflame other passions in the minds of
the judges or people by his eloquence, ever uttered such things
as are said by the philosophers? part of whom deny that any
passions whatever should be excited in the mind, and say that
they who rouse them in the breasts of the judges are guilty of
a heinous crime, and part, who are inclined to be more toler-
ant, and to accommodate themselves more to the realities of
life, say that such emotions ought to be but very moderate
and gentle.   But the orator, by his eloquence, represents all
those things which, in the common affairs of life, are considered evil and troublesome, and to be avoided, as heavier and
more grievous than they really are; and at the same time
amplifies and embellishes, by power of language, those things
which to the generality of mankind seem inviting and desirable; nor does he wish to appear so very wise among fools as

---

[1] *Istis tragœdiis tuis.*   Persons are said *tragœdias in nugis agere* who
make a small matter great by clamoring over it, as is done by actors in
tragedies. *Proust.* See b. ii., c. 51; Quint., vi., 1, 36.
[2] See Aristotle, Rhetor., ii., 2; Cic., Tusc. Quæst., iv.

that his audience should think him impertinent or a pedantic
Greek, or, though they very much approve his understanding,
and admire his wisdom, yet should feel uneasy that they themselves are but idiots to him ; but he so effectually penetrates
the minds of men, so works upon their senses and feelings,
that he has no occasion for the definitions of philosophers, or
to consider in the course of his speech 'whether the chief
good lies in the mind or in the body;' 'whether it is to be
defined as consisting in virtue or in pleasure ;' ' whether these
two can be united and coupled together;' or ' whether,' as
some think, 'nothing certain can be known, nothing clearly
perceived and understood;' questions in which I acknowledge
that a vast multiplicity of learning, and a great abundance of
varied reasoning is involved ; but we seek something of a far
different character; we want a man of superior intelligence,
sagacious by nature and from experience, who can acutely divine what his fellow-citizens, and all those whom he wishes
to convince on any subject by his eloquence, think, feel, imagine, or hope.   LII. He must penetrate the inmost recesses of
the mind of every class, age, and rank, and must ascertain
the sentiments and notions of those before whom he is pleading,[1] or intends to plead ; but his books of philosophy he must
reserve to himself, for the leisure and tranquillity of such a
Tusculan villa as this, and must not, when he is to speak on
justice and honesty, borrow from Plato ; who, when he
thought that such subjects were to be illustrated in writing,
imagined in his pages a new kind of commonwealth ; so much
was that which he thought necessary to be said of justice at
variance with ordinary life and the general customs of the
world.   But if such notions were received in existing communities and nations, who would have permitted you, Crassus,
though a man of the highest character, and the chief leader in
the city, to utter what you addressed to a vast assembly of
your fellow-citizens ?[2]   DELIVER US FROM THESE MISERIES.

[1] Most copies have *aget ;* Pearce, with the minority, prefers *agit.*
[2] These words are taken from a speech which Crassus had a short
time before delivered in an assembly of the people, and in which he had
made severe complaints of the Roman knights, who exercised their judicial powers with severity and injustice, and gave great trouble to the
senate.   Crassus took the part of the senate, and addressed the exhortation in the text to the people.   *Proust.*   Crassus was supporting the
Servilian law.   *Manutius.*

DELIVER US FROM THE JAWS OF THOSE WHOSE CRUELTY CAN
NOT BE SATIATED EVEN WITH BLOOD; SUFFER US NOT TO BE
SLAVES TO ANY BUT YOURSELVES AS A PEOPLE, WHOM WE
BOTH CAN AND OUGHT TO SERVE. I say nothing about the
word MISERIES, in which, as the philosophers say,[1] a man of
fortitude can not be; I say nothing of the JAWS from which
you desire to be delivered, that your blood may not be drunk
by an unjust sentence; a thing which they say can not happen to a wise man; but how durst you say that not only
yourself, but the whole senate, whose cause you were then
pleading, were SLAVES?   Can virtue, Crassus, possibly be EN-
SLAVED, according to those whose precepts you make necessary
to the science of an orator; virtue which is ever and alone
free, and which, though our bodies be captured in war, or
bound with fetters, yet ought to maintain its rights and liberty inviolate in all circumstances?[2]   And as to what you added, that the senate not only CAN, but OUGHT to be SLAVES to
the people, what philosopher is so effeminate, so languid, so
enervated, so eager to refer every thing to bodily pleasure or
pain, as to allow that the senate should be the SLAVES of the
people, to whom the people themselves have delivered the
power, like certain reins as it were, to guide and govern
them?

LIII. " Accordingly, when I regarded these words of yours
as the divinest eloquence, Publius Rutilius Rufus,[3] a man of
learning, and devoted to philosophy, observed that what you
had said was not only injudicious, but base and dishonorable.
The same Rutilius used severely to censure Servius Galba,
whom he said he very well remembered, because, when Lucius
Scribonius brought an accusation against him, and Marcus
Cato, a bitter and implacable enemy to Galba, had spoken
with rancor and vehemence against him before the assembled
people of Rome (in a speech which he published in his Ori-
gines[4]), Rutilius, I say, censured Galba for holding up, almost

---

[1] *Ut illi aiunt.*   The philosophers, especially the Stoics, who affirmed
that the wise man alone is happy.   *Ellendt.*

[2] See the paradox of Cicero on the words *Omnes sapientes liberi, omnes
stulti servi.*

[3] Mentioned by Cic., Brut., c. 30.   *Proust.*   He was a perfect Stoic.
Ellendt.

[4] A work on the origin of the people and cities of Italy, and other
matters, now lost.   Cic., Brut., c. 85; Corn. Nep., Life of Cato, c. 3.

upon his shoulders, Quintus, the orphan son of Caius Sulpicius
Gallus, his near relation, that he might, through the memory
of his most illustrious father, draw tears from the people, and
for recommending two little sons of his own to the guardianship of the public, and saying that he himself (as if he was
making his will in the ranks before a battle,[1] without balance
o. writing-tables[2]) appointed the people of Rome protectors of
their orphan condition.   As Galba, therefore, labored under
the ill opinion and dislike of the people, Rutilius said that he
owed his deliverance to such tragic tricks as these ; and I see it
is also recorded in Cato's book, that *if he had not employed children and tears, he would have suffered.*   Such proceedings Rutilius severely condemned, and said banishment, or even death,
was more eligible than such meanness.   Nor did he merely
say this, but thought and acted accordingly ; for being a man,
as you know, of exemplary integrity, a man to whom no person in the city was superior in honesty and integrity, he not
only refused to supplicate his judges, but would not allow his
cause to be pleaded with more ornament or freedom of language than the simple plainness of truth carried with it.[3]
Small was the part of it he assigned to Cotta here, his sister's
son, and a youth of great eloquence ; and Quintus Mucius also
took some share in his defense, speaking in his usual manner,
without ostentation, but simply and with perspicuity.   But if
you, Crassus, had then spoken—you, who just now said that
the orator must seek assistance from those disputations in
which the philosophers indulge, to supply himself with matter
for his speeches—if you had been at liberty to speak for Publius Rutilius, not after the manner of philosophers, but in your
own way, although his accusers had been, as they really were,
abandoned and mischievous citizens, and worthy of the se-
verest punishment, yet the force of your eloquence would
have rooted all their unwarrantable cruelty from the bottom
of their hearts.   But, as it was, a man of such character was
lost, because his cause was pleaded in such a manner as if the

[1] When a soldier, in the hearing of three or more of his comrades,
named some one his heir in case he should fall in the engagement.

[2] When a person, in the presence of five witnesses and a *libripens*,
assigned his property to somebody as his heir. Gaius, ii., 101 ; Aul.
Gell., xv., 27.

[3] He was falsely accused of extortion in his province of Asia, and, being condemned, was sent into exile. Cic., Brut., c. 30. *Proust.*

whole affair had been transacted in the imaginary commonwealth of Plato.   Not a single individual uttered a groan;
not one of the advocates gave vent to an exclamation; no one
showed any appearance of grief; no one complained; no one
supplicated, no one implored the mercy of the public.   In
short, no one even stamped a foot on the trial, for fear, I suppose, of renouncing the doctrine of the Stoics.

LIV.   " Thus a Roman, of consular dignity, imitated the
illustrious Socrates of old, who, as he was a man of the greatest wisdom, and had lived in the utmost integrity, spoke for
himself, when on trial for his life, in such a manner as not to
seem a suppliant or prisoner, but the lord and master of his
judges.   Even when Lysias, a most eloquent orator, brought
him a written speech, which, if he pleased, he might learn by
heart, and repeat at his trial, he willingly read it over, and
said it was written in a manner very well suited to the occasion; but, said he, if you had brought me Sicyonian shoes,[1] I
should not wear them, though they might be easy and suit
my feet, because they would be effeminate; so that speech
seems to me to be eloquent and becoming an orator, but not
fearless and manly.   In consequence, he also was condemned,
not only by the first votes, by which the judges only decided
whether they should acquit or condemn, but also by those
which, in conformity with the laws, they were obliged to give
afterward.   For at Athens, if the accused person was found
guilty, and if his crime was not capital, there was a sort of
estimation of punishment; and when sentence was to be finally given by the judges, the criminal was asked what degree
of punishment he acknowledged himself, at most, to deserve;
and when this question was put to Socrates, he answered
that he deserved to be distinguished with the noblest honors
and rewards, and to be daily maintained at the public expense
in the Prytaneum; an honor which, among the Greeks, is accounted the very highest.   By which answer his judges were
so exasperated that they condemned the most innocent of
men to death.   But had he been acquitted (which, indeed,
though it is of no concern to us, yet I could wish to have been
the case, because of the greatness of his genius), how could
we have patience with those philosophers who now, though

[1] Shoes made at Sicyon, and worn only by the effeminate and luxuri-
ous.   Lucret., iv., 1121.

Socrates was condemned for no other crime but want of skill in speaking, maintain that the precepts of oratory should be learned from themselves, who are disciples of Socrates? With these men I have no dispute as to which of the two sciences is superior, or carries more truth in it; I only say that the one is distinct from the other, and that oratory may exist in the highest perfection without philosophy.

LV. "In bestowing such warm approbation on the civil law, Crassus, I see what was your motive; when you were speaking, I did not see it.[1] In the first place, you were willing to oblige Scævola, whom we ought all to esteem most deservedly for his singularly excellent disposition; and seeing his science undowried and unadorned, you have enriched it with your eloquence as with a portion, and decorated it with a profusion of ornaments. In the next, as you had spent much pains and labor in the acquisition of it (since you had in your own house one[2] who encouraged and instructed you in that study), you were afraid that you might lose the fruit of your industry if you did not magnify the science by your eloquence. But I have no controversy with the science; let it be of as much consequence as you represent it; for without doubt it is of great and extensive concern, having relation to multitudes of people, and has always been held in the highest honor; and our most eminent citizens have ever been, and are still, at the head of the profession of it; but take care, Crassus, lest, while you strive to adorn the knowledge of the civil law with new and foreign ornaments, you spoil and denude her of what is granted and accorded to her as her own. For if you were to say that he who is a lawyer is also an orator, and that he who is an orator is also a lawyer, you would make two excellent branches of knowledge, each equal to the other, and sharers of the same dignity; but now you allow that a man may be a lawyer without the eloquence which we are considering, and that there have been many such; and you deny that a man can be an orator who has not acquired a knowledge of law. Thus the lawyer is, of himself, nothing with you but a sort of wary and acute legalist, an instructor

---

[1] *Tum, quum dicebas, non videbam.* Many copies omit the negative; an omission approved by Ernesti, Henrichsen, and Ellendt.

[2] Either Scævola, the father-in-law of Crassus, or Lucius Cœlius Antipater, whom Cicero mentions in his Brutus. *Proust.*

in actions,[1] a repeater of forms, a catcher at syllables; but because the orator has frequent occasion for the aid of the law in his pleadings, you have of necessity joined legal knowledge to eloquence as a handmaid and attendant.

LVI. "But as to your wonder at the effrontery of those advocates who, though they were ignorant of small things, profess great ones, or who ventured, in the management of causes, to treat of the most important points in the civil law, though they neither understood nor had ever learned them, the defense on both charges is easy and ready. For it is not at all surprising that he who is ignorant in what form of words a contract of marriage is made, should be able to defend the cause of a woman who has formed such a contract; nor, though the same skill in steering is requisite for a small as for a large vessel, is he therefore, who is ignorant of the form of words by which an estate is to be divided, incapable of pleading a cause relative to the division of an estate.[2] For though you appealed to causes of great consequence, pleaded before the centumviri, that turned upon points of law, what cause was there among them all which could not have been ably pleaded by an eloquent man unacquainted with law? in all which causes, as in the cause of Manius Curius, which was lately pleaded by you,[3] and that of Caius Hostilius Mancinus,[4] and that of the boy who was born of a second wife, without

---

[1] *Præco actionum.* One who informs those who are ignorant of law when the courts will be open; by what kind of suit any person must prosecute his claims on any other person; and acts in law proceedings as another sort of *præco* acts at auctions. *Strebæus.*

[2] *Herctum cieri—herciscundæ familiæ.* Co-heirs, when an estate descended among them, were, by the Roman law, bound to each other by the action *familiæ herciscundæ;* that is, to divide the whole family inheritance, and settle all the accounts which related to it. Just., Inst., iii., 28, 4. The word *herctum,* says Festus, signifies whole or undivided, and *cio,* to divide; so, *familiam herctam ciere* was to divide the inheritance of the family, which two words, *herctum ciere,* were afterward contracted into *herciscere:* hence this law-term used here, *familiam herciscere.* Servius has, therefore, from Donatus, thus illustrated a passage in Virgil, at the end of the VIIIth Æneid,

Citæ Metium in diversa quadrigæ
Distulerant.

Citæ, says he, is a law-term, and signifies divided, as *hercto non cito,* the inheritance being undivided. *Citæ quadrigæ,* therefore, in that passage, does not mean *quick* or *swift,* as is generally imagined, but *drawing different ways.* B.   [3] See c. 39.   [4] C. 40.

any notice of divorce having been sent to the first,[1] there was the greatest disagreement among the most skillful lawyers on points of law. I ask, then, how in these causes a knowledge of the law could have aided the orator, when that lawyer must have had the superiority, who was supported, not by his own, but a foreign art, not by knowledge of the law, but by eloquence? I have often heard that, when Publius Crassus was a candidate for the ædileship, and Servius Galba, though older than he, and even of consular dignity, attended upon him to promote his interest (having betrothed Crassus's daughter to his son Caius), there came a countryman to Crassus to consult him on some matter of law ; and when he had taken Crassus aside, and laid the affair before him, and received from him such an answer as was rather right than suited to his wishes, Galba, seeing him look dejected, called him by his name, and asked him on what matter he had consulted Crassus ; when, having heard his case, and seeing the man in great trouble, ' I perceive,' said he, ' that Crassus gave you an answer while his mind was anxious, and preoccupied with other affairs.' He then took Crassus by the hand, and said, ' Hark you, how came it into your head to give this man such an answer ?' Crassus, who was a man of great legal knowledge, confidently repeated that the matter was exactly as he had stated in his answer, and that there could be no doubt. But Galba, referring to a variety and multiplicity of matters, adduced abundance of similar cases, and used many arguments for equity against the strict letter of law; while Crassus, as he could not maintain his ground in the debate (for, though he was numbered among the eloquent, he was by no means equal to Galba), had recourse to authorities, and showed what he had asserted in the books of his brother Publius Mucius,[2] and in the commentaries of Sextus Ælius ; though he allowed, at the same time, that Galba's arguments had appeared to him plausible, and almost true.

LVII. " But causes which are of such a kind that there can be no doubt of the law relative to them do not usually come to be tried at all. Does any one claim an inheritance under a will, which the father of a family made before he had

[1] C. 40.
[2] The Crassus here mentioned was Publius Crassus Dives, brother of Publius Mucius, Pontifex Maximus. See c. 37. *Ellendt.*

a son born? Nobody; because it is clear that by the birth of
a son the will is canceled.[1]   Upon such points of law, therefore, there are no questions to be tried.   The orator, accordingly, may be ignorant of all this part of the law relative to
controversies,[2] which is, without doubt, the far greater part;
but on those points which are disputed, even among the most
skillful lawyers, it will not be difficult for the orator to find
some writer of authority on that side, whichsoever it be, that
he is to defend, from whom, when he has received his javelins
ready for throwing, he will hurl them with the arm and
strength of an orator.   Unless we are to suppose, indeed (I
would wish to make the observation without offending this
excellent man Scævola), that you, Crassus, defended the cause
of Manius Curius out of the writings and rules of your father-
in-law.   Did you not, on the contrary, undertake the defense
of equity, the support of wills, and the intention of the dead?
Indeed, in my opinion (for I was frequently present and heard
you), you won the far greater number of votes by your wit,
humor, and happy raillery, when you joked upon the extraordinary acuteness, and expressed admiration of the genius, of
Scævola, who had discovered that *a man must be born before
he can die;* and when you adduced many cases, both from the
laws and decrees of the senate, as well as from common life
and intercourse, not only acutely, but facetiously and sarcas-
tically, in which, if we attended to the letter, and not the spirit, nothing would result.   The trial, therefore, was attended
with abundance of mirth and pleasantry; but of what service
your knowledge of the civil law was to you upon it, I do not
understand; your great power in speaking, united with the
utmost humor and grace, certainly was of great service.   Even
Mucius himself, the defender of the father's right, who fought
as it were for his own patrimony, what argument did he advance in the cause, when he spoke against you, that appeared
to be drawn from the civil law?   What particular law did he
recite?   What did he explain in his speech that was unintel-

---

[1] Cicero pro Cæcinâ, c. 25; Gaius, ii., 138.
[2] *Omnem hanc partem juris in controversiis.*   For *in controversiis* Lambinus and Ernesti would read, from a correction in an old copy, *incon-
troversi;* but as there is no authority for this word, Ellendt, with Bakius,
prefers *non controversi.*   With this alteration, the sense will be, "all this
uncontroverted part of the law."

ligible to the unlearned? The whole of his oration was employed upon one point ; that is, in maintaining that what was
written ought to be valid. But every boy is exercised on
such subjects by his master, when he is instructed to support,
in such cases as these, sometimes the written letter, sometimes
equity. In that cause of the soldier, I presume, if you had
defended either him or the heir, you would have had recourse
to the cases of Hostilius,[1] and not to your own power and talent as an orator. Nay, rather, if you had defended the will,
you would have argued in such a manner that the entire va-
lidity of all wills whatsoever would have seemed to depend
upon that single trial ; or, if you had pleaded the cause of the
soldier, you would have raised his father, with your usual eloquence, from the dead ; you would have placed him before the
eyes of the audience ; he would have embraced his son, and
with tears have recommended him to the Centumviri ; you
would have forced the very stones to weep and lament, so that
all that clause, AS THE TONGUE HAD DECLARED, would seem
not to have been written in the Twelve Tables, which you
prefer to all libraries, but in some mere formula of a teacher.

LVIII. "As to the indolence of which you accuse our
youth, for not learning that science, because, in the first place,
it is very easy (how easy it is, let them consider who strut
about before us, presuming on their knowledge of the science,
as if it were extremely difficult ; and do you yourself also consider that point, who say, that it is an easy science, which
you admit as yet to be no science at all, but say that if somebody shall ever learn some other science, so as to be able to
make this a science, it will then be a science) ; and because,
in the next place, it is full of pleasure (but as to that matter,
every one is willing to leave the pleasure to yourself, and is
content to be without it, for there is not one of the young
men who would not rather, if he must get any thing by heart,
learn the Teucer of Pacuvius than the Manilian laws[2] on emp-
tion and vendition) ; and, in the third place, because you think

---

[1] Certain legal formulæ, of which some lawyer named Hostilius was
the author. *Ernesti.*
[2] *Manilianas—leges.* They were formulæ which those who wished
not to be deceived might use in buying and selling ; they are called
actiones by Varro, R. R., ii., 5, 11. . . . . . The author was Manius Manilius, an eminent lawyer, who was consul A.U.C. 603. *Ernesti.*

that, from love to our country, we ought to acquire a knowledge of the practices of our ancestors ; do .you not perceive that the old laws are either grown out of date from their very antiquity, or are set aside by such as are new ?[1] As to your opinion, that men are rendered good by learning the civil law, because, by laws, rewards are appointed for virtue, and punishment for vice ; I, for my part, imagined that virtue was instilled into mankind (if it can be instilled by any means) by instruction and persuasion, not by menaces, and force, and terror. As to the maxim that we should avoid evil, we can understand how good a thing it is to do so without a knowledge of the law. And as to myself, to whom alone you allow the power of managing causes satisfactorily, without any knowledge of law, I make you, Crassus, this answer : that I never learned the civil law, nor was ever at a loss for the want of knowledge in it, in those causes which I was able to defend in the courts.[2] It is one thing to be a master in any pursuit or art, and another to be neither stupid nor ignorant in common life, and the ordinary customs of mankind. May not every one of us go over our farms, or inspect our country affairs, for the sake of profit or delight at least ?[3] No man lives without using his eyes and understanding, so far as to be entirely ignorant what sowing and reaping is ; or what pruning vines and other trees means ; or at what season of the year, and in what manner, those things are done. If, therefore, any one of us has to look at his grounds, or give any directions about agriculture to his steward, or any orders to his bailiff, must we study the books of Mago the Carthaginian,[4] or may we be content with our ordinary knowledge? Why, then, with regard to the civil law, may we not also, especially as we are worn out in causes and public business, and in the

[1] There is no proper grammatical construction in this sentence. Ernesti observes that it is, perhaps, in some way unsound.

[2] *In jure.* "Apud tribunal prætoris." *Ernesti.*

[3] I translate the conclusion of the sentence in conformity with the text of Orellius, who puts *tamen* at the end of it, instead of letting it stand at the beginning of the next sentence, as is the case in other editions. His interpretation is, *invisere saltem.* "Though we be much occupied, yet we can visit our farms."

He wrote eight-and-twenty books on country affairs in the Punic language, which were translated into Latin, by order of the senate, by Cassius Dionysius of Utica. See Varro, R. R., i., 1; and Columella, who calls him the father of farming. *Proust.*

forum, be sufficiently instructed, to such a degree at least as not to appear foreigners and strangers in our own country? Or, if any cause, a little more obscure than ordinary, should be brought to us, it would, I presume, be difficult to communicate with our friend Scævola here; although indeed the parties, whose concern it is, bring nothing to us that has not been thoroughly considered and investigated. If there is a question about the nature of a thing itself under consideration; if about boundaries (as we do not go in person to view the property itself[1]); if about writings and bonds,[2] we of necessity have to study matters that are intricate and often difficult; and if we have to consider laws, or the opinions of men skilled in law, need we fear that we shall not be able to understand them, if we have not studied the civil law from our youth?

LIX. "Is the knowledge of the civil law, then, of no advantage to the orator? I can not deny that every kind of knowledge is of advantage, especially to him whose eloquence ought to be adorned with variety of matter; but the things which are absolutely necessary to an orator are numerous, important, and difficult, so that I would not distract his industry among too many studies. Who can deny that the gesture and grace of Roscius are necessary in the orator's action and deportment? Yet nobody would advise youths that are studying oratory to labor in forming their attitudes like players. What is so necessary to an orator as the voice? Yet, by my recommendation, no student in eloquence will be a slave to his voice like the Greeks and tragedians,[3] who pass whole years in sedentary declamation, and daily, before they venture upon delivery, raise their voice by degrees as they sit, and, when they have finished pleading, sit down again, and lower and recover it, as it were, through a scale, from the

[1] *Quum in rem præsentem non venimus.* We do not go *ad locum, unde præsentes rem et fines inspicere possimus.* Ellendt.

[2] *Perscriptionibus. Perscriptio* is considered by Ellendt to signify a draft or check to be presented to a banker.

[3] *Græcorum more et tragœdorum.* Lambinus would strike out *et*, on the authority of three manuscripts; and Pearce thinks that the conjunction ought to be absent. Ernesti thinks that some substantive belonging to *Græcorum* has dropped out of the text. A Leipsic edition, he observes, has *Græcorum more sophistarum et tragœdorum*, but on what authority he does not know.

highest to the deepest tone. If we should do this, they whose
causes we undertake would be condemned before we had repeated the *pæan* and the *munio*[1] as often as is prescribed.
But if we must not employ ourselves upon gesture, which is
of great service to the orator, or upon the culture of the voice,
which alone is a great recommendation and support of eloquence; and if we can only improve in either in proportion
to the leisure afforded us in this field of daily business, how
much less must we apply to the occupation of learning the
civil law? of which we may learn the chief points without
regular study, and which is also unlike those other matters in
this respect, that power of voice and gesture can not be got
suddenly, or caught up from another person; but a knowledge of the law, as far as it is useful in any cause, may be
gained on the shortest possible notice, either from learned men
or from books.   Those eminent Greek orators, therefore, as
they are unskilled in the law themselves, have, in their causes,
men acquainted with the law to assist them, who are, as you
before observed, called *pragmatici.*   In this respect our countrymen act far better, as they would have the laws and judicial decisions supported by the authority of men of the highest rank.   But the Greeks would not have neglected, if they
had thought it necessary, to instruct the orator in the civil
law, instead of allowing him a *pragmaticus* for an assistant.

LX. "As to your remark that age is preserved from solitude by the science of the civil law, we may perhaps also say
that it is preserved from solitude by a large fortune.   But
we are inquiring, not what is advantageous to ourselves, but
what is necessary for the orator.   Although (since we take
so many points of comparison with the orator from one sort
of artist) Roscius, whom we mentioned before, is accustomed
to say that, as age advances upon him, he will make the measures of the flute-player slower, and the notes softer.   But if
he who is restricted to a certain modulation of numbers and
feet, meditates, notwithstanding, something for his ease in the
decline of life, how much more easily can we, I will not say
lower our tones, but alter them entirely?   For it is no secret

---

[1] *Pæanem aut munionem.*   The word *munionem* is corrupt.   Many editions have *nomium,* which is left equally unexplained.   The best conjec-
tural emendation, as Orellius observes, is *nomum,* proposed by a critic of
Jena.

to you, Crassus, how many and how various are the modes of
speaking; a variety which I know not whether you yourself
have not been the first to exhibit to us, since you have for
some time spoken more softly and gently than you used to do ;
nor is this mildness in your eloquence, which carries so high
authority with it, less approved than your former vast energy
and exertion ; and there have been many orators, as we hear
of Scipio and Lælius, who always spoke in a tone only a little
raised above that of ordinary conversation, but never exerted
their lungs or throats like Servius Galba.   But if you shall
ever be unable or unwilling to speak in this manner, are you
afraid that your house, the house of such a man and such a
citizen, will, if it be not frequented by the litigious, be deserted by the rest of mankind?   For my part, I am so far from
having any similar feeling with regard to my own house, that
I not only do not think that comfort for my old age is to be
expected from a multitude of clients, but look for that solitude
which you dread as for a safe harbor ; for I esteem repose to
be the most agreeable solace in the last stage of life.

"Those other branches of knowledge (though they certainly assist the orator) — I mean general history, and jurisprudence, and the course of things in old times, and variety of
precedents—I will, if ever I have occasion for them, borrow
from my friend Longinus,[1] an excellent man, and one of the
greatest erudition in such matters.   Nor will I dissuade these
youths from reading every thing, hearing every thing, and acquainting themselves with every liberal study, and all polite
learning, as you just now recommended ; but, upon my word,
they do not seem likely to have too much time, if they are inclined to pursue and practice all that you, Crassus, have dic-
tated ; for you seemed to me to impose upon their youth obligations almost too severe (though almost necessary, I admit,
for the attainment of their desires), since extemporary exercises upon stated cases, and accurate and studied meditations,
and practice in writing, which you truly called the modeler
and finisher of the art of speaking, are tasks of much difficulty ;
and that comparison of their own composition with the writings of others, and extemporal discussion on the work of another by way of praise or censure, confirmation or refutation,

---

[1] Ernesti supposes him to be Caius Cassius Longinus, who is mentioned by Cicero, pro Plânco, c. 24.

demand no ordinary exertion, either of memory or powers of imitation.

LXI. "But what you added was appalling, and indeed will have, I fear, a greater tendency to deter than to encourage. You would have every one of us a Roscius in our profession ; and you said that what was excellent did not so much attract approbation, as what was faulty produced settled disgust; but I do not think that want of perfection is so disparagingly regarded in us as in the players; and I observe, accordingly, that we are often heard with the utmost attention, even when we are hoarse, for the interest of the subject itself and of the cause detains the audience; while Æsopus, if he has the least hoarseness, is hissed; for at those from whom nothing is expected but to please the ear, offense is taken whenever the least diminution of that pleasure occurs. But in eloquence there are many qualities that captivate; and, if they are not all of the highest excellence, and yet most of them are praise- worthy, those that are of the highest excellence must necessarily excite admiration.

"To return, therefore, to our first consideration, let the orator be, as Crassus described him, *one who can speak in a manner adapted to persuade ;* and let him strictly devote himself to those things which are of common practice in civil communities, and in the forum, and, laying aside all other studies, however high and noble they may be, let him apply himself day and night, if I may say so, to this one pursuit, and imitate him to whom doubtless the highest excellence in oratory is conceded, Demosthenes the Athenian, in whom there is said to have been so much ardor and perseverance, that he overcame, first of all, the impediments of nature by pains and diligence ; and, though his voice was so inarticulate that he was unable to pronounce the first letter of the very art which he was so eager to acquire, he accomplished so much by practice that no one is thought to have spoken more distinctly; and, though his breath was short, he effected such improvement by holding it in while he spoke, that in one sequence of words (as his writings show) two risings and two fallings of his voice were included ;[1] and he also (as is related), after putting peb-

---

[1] In one period or sentence he twice raised and twice lowered his voice; he raised it in the former members of the period, and lowered it in the latter; and this he did in one breath. *Proust.* This seems not

bles into his mouth, used to pronounce several verses at the highest pitch of his voice without taking breath, not standing in one place, but walking forward, and mounting a steep ascent. With such encouragements as these, I sincerely agree with you, Crassus, that youths should be incited to study and industry ; other accomplishments which you have collected from various and distinct arts and sciences, though you have mastered them all yourself, I regard as unconnected with the proper business and duty of an orator."

LXII. When Antonius had concluded these observations, Sulpicius and Cotta appeared to be in doubt whose discourse of the two seemed to approach nearer to the truth. Crassus then said, "You make our orator a mere mechanic, Antonius, but I am not certain whether you are not really of another opinion, and whether you are not practicing upon us your wonderful skill in refutation, in which no one was ever your superior ; a talent of which the exercise belongs properly to orators, but has now become common among philosophers, especially those who are accustomed to speak fully and fluently on both sides of any question proposed. But I did not think, especially in the hearing of these young men, that merely such an orator was to be described by me as would pass his whole life in courts of justice, and would carry thither nothing more than the necessity of his causes required ; but I contemplated something greater when I expressed my opinion that the orator, especially in such a republic as ours, ought to be deficient in nothing that could adorn his profession. But you, since you have circumscribed the whole business of an orator within such narrow limits, will explain to us with the less difficulty what you have settled as to oratorical[1] duties and rules ; I think, however, that this may be done to-morrow, for we have talked enough for to-day. And Scævola, since he has appointed to go to his own Tusculan seat,[2] will

quite correct. Cicero appears to mean, that of the two members the voice was once raised and once lowered in each.

[1] Orellius's text has *præceptis oratoris ;* but we must undoubtedly read *oratoriis* with Pearce.

[2] Atticus was exceedingly pleased with this treatise, and commended it extremely, but objected to the dismission of Scævola from the disputation after he had been introduced into the first dialogue. Cicero defends himself by the example of their "god Plato," as he calls him, in his book *De Republicâ;* where the scene being laid in the house of an

now repose a little till the heat is abated; and let us also, as the day is so far advanced, consult our health."[1] The proposal pleased the whole company. Scævola then said, "Indeed, I could wish that I had not made an appointment with Lælius to go to that part of the Tusculan territory to-day. I would willingly hear Antonius;" and, as he rose from his seat, he smiled and added, "for he did not offend me so much when he pulled our civil law to pieces, as he amused me when he professed himself ignorant of it."

BOOK II.

THE ARGUMENT.

In this book Antonius gives instructions respecting invention in oratory, and the arrangements of the different parts of a speech; departments in which he was thought to have attained great excellence, though his language was not always highly studied or elegant. See Cic., de Clar. Orat., c. 37. As humor in speaking was considered as a part of invention, Caius Julius Cæsar, who was called the most facetious man of his time, speaks copiously on that subject, c. 54–71.

I. THERE was, if you remember, brother Quintus, a strong persuasion in us when we were boys, that Lucius Crassus had acquired no more learning than he had been enabled to gain from instruction in his youth, and that Marcus Antonius was entirely destitute and ignorant of all erudition whatsoever; and there were many who, though they did not believe that such was really the case, yet, that they might more easily deter us from the pursuit of learning, when we were inflamed with a desire of attaining it, took a pleasure in reporting what

old gentleman, Cephalus, the old man, after bearing a part in the first conversation, excuses himself, saying that he must go to prayers, and returns no more, Plato not thinking it suitable to his age to be detained in the company through so long a discourse. With greater reason, therefore, he says that he had used the same caution in the case of Scævola, since it was not to be supposed that a person of his dignity, extreme age, and infirm health, would spend several successive days in another man's house: that the first day's dialogue related to his particular profession, but the other two chiefly to the rules and precepts of the art, at which it was not proper for one of Scævola's temper and character to be present only as a hearer. Ad Attic., iv., 16. B.

[1] Retire from the heat, like Scævola, and take rest.

I have said of these orators; so that, if men of no learning had acquired the greatest wisdom, and an incredible degree of eloquence, all our industry might seem vain, and the earnest perseverance of our father, one of the best and most sensible of men, in educating us, might appear to be folly. These reasoners we, as boys, used at that time to refute with the aid of witnesses whom we had at home, our father, Caius Aculeo our relative, and Lucius Cicero our uncle; for our father, Aculeo (who married our mother's sister, and whom Crassus esteemed the most of all his friends), and our own uncle (who went with Antonius into Cilicia, and quitted it at the same time with him), often told us many particulars about Crassus, relative to his studies and learning; and as we, with our cousins, Aculeo's sons, learned what Crassus approved, and were instructed by the masters whom he engaged, we had also frequent opportunities of observing (since, though boys,[1] we could understand this) that he spoke Greek so well that he might have been thought not to know any other language, and he put such questions to our masters, and discoursed upon such subjects in his conversation with them, that nothing appeared to be new or strange to him. But with regard to Antonius, although we had frequently heard from our uncle, a person of the greatest learning, how he had devoted himself, both at Athens and at Rhodes, to the conversation of the most learned men, yet I myself also, when quite a youth, often asked him many questions on the subject, as far as the bashfulness of my early years would permit. What I am writing will certainly not be new to you (for at that very time you heard it from me), namely, that from many and various conversations, he appeared to me neither ignorant nor unaccomplished in any thing in those branches of knowledge of which I could form any opinion. But there was such peculiarity in each, that Crassus desired not so much to be thought unlearned as to hold learning in contempt, and to prefer, on every subject, the understanding of our countrymen to that of the Greeks; while Antonius thought that his oratory would be better received by the Roman people if he were believed to have had no learning at all; and thus the one imagined that he should have more authority if he appeared

---

[1] The words *cùm essemus ejusmodi* in this parenthesis, which all commentators regard as corrupt, are left untranslated.

to despise the Greeks, and the other if he seemed to know nothing of them.

But what their object was is certainly nothing to our present purpose. It is pertinent, however, to the treatise which I have commenced, and to this portion of it, to remark, that no man could ever excel and reach eminence in eloquence without learning, not only the art of oratory, but every branch of useful knowledge. II. For almost all other arts can support themselves independently, and by their own resources; but to speak well, that is, to speak with learning, and skill, and elegance, has no definite province within the limits of which it is inclosed and restricted. Every thing that can possibly fall under discussion among mankind must be effectively treated by him who professes that he can practice this art, or he must relinquish all title to eloquence. For my own part, therefore, though I confess that both in our own country and in Greece itself, which always held this art in the highest estimation, there have arisen many men of extraordinary powers, and of the highest excellence in speaking,[1] without this absolute knowledge of every thing; yet I affirm that such a degree of eloquence as was in Crassus and Antonius could not exist without a knowledge of all subjects that contribute to form that wisdom and that force of oratory which were seen in them. On this account, I had the greater satisfaction in committing to writing that dialogue which they formerly held on these subjects; both that the notion which had always prevailed, that the one had no great learning, and that the other was wholly unlearned, might be eradicated, and that I might preserve, in the records of literature, the opinions which I thought divinely delivered by those consummate orators concerning eloquence, if I could by any means learn and fully register them; and also, indeed, that I might, as far as I should be able, rescue their fame, now upon the decline, from silence and oblivion. If they could have been known from writings of their own, I should, perhaps, have thought it less necessary for me to be thus elaborate; but as one left but

---

[1] *Multos et ingeniis et magnâ laude dicendi.* This passage, as Ellendt observes, is manifestly corrupt. He proposes *ingeniis magnos et laude dicendi;* but this seems hardly Ciceronian. Aldus Manutius noticed that an adjective was apparently wanting to *ingeniis,* but other editors have passed the passage in silence.

little in writing (at least, there is little extant), and that he
wrote in his youth,[1] the other almost nothing, I thought it
due from me to men of such genius, while we still retain a
lively remembrance of them, to render their fame, if I could,
imperishable. I enter upon this undertaking with the greater hopes of effecting my object,[2] because I am not writing of
the eloquence of Servius Galba or Caius Carbo, concerning
which I should be at liberty to invent whatever I pleased, as
no one now living could confute me; but I publish an account
to be read by those who have frequently heard the men themselves of whom I am speaking, that I may commend those
two illustrious men to such as have never seen either of them,
from the recollection, as a testimony, of those to whom both
those orators were known, and who are now alive and present
among us.

III. Nor do I now aim at instructing you, dearest and best
of brothers, by means of rhetorical treatises, which you regard
as unpolished (for what can be more refined or graceful than
your own language ?) ; but though, whether it be, as you used
to say, from judgment, or, as Isocrates, the father of eloquence,
has written of himself, from a sort of bashfulness and ingenuous timidity, that you have shrunk from speaking in public,
or whether, as you sometimes jocosely remark, you thought
one orator sufficient, not only for one family, but almost for a
whole community, I yet think that these books will not appear
to you of that kind which may deservedly be ridiculed on account of the deficiency in elegant learning in those who have
discussed the art of speaking; for nothing seems to me to be
wanting in the conversation of Crassus and Antonius that
any one could imagine possible to be known or understood by
men of the greatest genius, the keenest application, the most
consummate learning, and the utmost experience ; as you will
very easily be able to judge, who have been pleased to acquire
the knowledge and theory of oratory through your own exertions, and to observe the practice of it in mine. But that
we may the sooner accomplish the task which we have undertaken, and which is no ordinary one, let us leave our exordium, and proceed to the conversation and arguments of the
characters whom I have offered to your notice.

[1] See Brut., c. 43, 44.
[2] *Spe aggredior majore ad probandum.* That *ad probandum* is to be
joined with *spe*, not with *aggredior*, is shown by Ellendt on b. i., c. 4.

The next day, then, after the former conversation had taken place, about the second hour,[1] while Crassus was yet in bed, and Sulpicius sitting by him, and Antonius walking with Cotta in the portico, on a sudden Quintus Catulus[2] the elder, with his brother Caius Julius,[3] arrived there; and when Crassus heard of their coming, he arose in some haste, and they were all in a state of wonder, suspecting that the occasion of their arrival was of more than common importance. The parties having greeted each other with most friendly salutations, as their intimacy required, "What has brought you hither at last?" said Crassus; "is it any thing new?" "Nothing, indeed," said Catulus; "for you know it is the time of the public games. But (you may think us, if you please," added he, "either foolish or impertinent) when Cæsar came yesterday in the evening to my Tusculan villa from his own, he told me that he had met Scævola going from hence; from whom he said that he had heard a wonderful account, namely, that you, whom I could never entice into such conversation, though I endeavored to prevail on you in every way, had held long dissertations with Antonius on eloquence, and had disputed, as in the schools, almost in the manner of the Greeks; and my brother, therefore, entreated me, not being of myself, indeed, averse to hear you, but, at the same time, afraid we might make a troublesome visit to you, to come hither with him; for he said that Scævola had told him that a great part of the discourse was postponed till to-day. If you think we have acted too forwardly, you will lay the blame upon Cæsar; if too familiarly, upon both of us; for we are rejoiced to have come, if we do not give you trouble by our visit." IV. Crassus replied, "Whatever object had brought you hither, I should rejoice to see at my house men for whom I have so much affection and friendship; but yet (to say the truth) I had rather

[1] The second hour of the morning, answering to our eight o'clock.

[2] The same that was consul with Caius Marius, when they obtained, in conjunction, the famous victory over the Cimbri.

[3] He was the brother of Quintus Catulus by the mother's side, and about twenty years his junior. The mother's name was Popilia. *Ellendt.* See c. 11. He was remarkable for wit, but his oratory is said to have wanted nerve. Brut., c. 48. Cicero, with great propriety, makes Sulpicius sit with Crassus, and Cotta walk with Antonius; for Sulpicius wished to resemble Crassus in his style of oratory; Cotta preferred the manner of Antonius. Brutus, c. 55.

it had been any other object than that which you mention. For I (to speak as I think) was never less satisfied with myself than yesterday; though this happened more through my own good-nature than any other fault of mine; for, while I complied with the request of these youths, I forgot that I was an old man, and did that which I had never done even when young; I spoke on subjects that depended on a certain degree of learning. But it has happened very fortunately for me, that, as my part is finished, you have come to hear Antonius." "For my part, Crassus," returned Cæsar, "I am indeed desirous to hear you in that kind of fuller and continuous discussion, yet so that, if I can not have that happiness, I can be contented with your ordinary conversation. I will therefore endeavor that neither my friend Sulpicius, nor Cotta, may seem to have more influence with you than myself, and will certainly entreat you to show some of your good-nature even to Catulus and me. But if you are not so inclined I will not press you, nor cause you, while you are afraid of appearing impertinent yourself, to think me impertinent." "Indeed, Cæsar," replied Crassus, "I have always thought of all Latin words there was the greatest significance in that which you have just used; for he whom we call *impertinent* seems to me to bear an appellation derived from *not being pertinent;* and that appellation, according to our mode of speaking, is of very extensive meaning; for whoever either does not discern what occasion requires, or talks too much, or is ostentatious of himself, or is forgetful either of the dignity or convenience of those in whose presence he is, or is in any respect awkward or presuming, is called *impertinent.* With this fault that most learned nation of the Greeks abounds; and, consequently, because the Greeks do not feel the influence of this evil, they have not even found a name for the foible; for, though you make the most diligent inquiry, you will not find out how the Greeks designate an *impertinent* person. But of all their other impertinences, which are innumerable, I do not know whether there be any greater than their custom of raising the most subtile disputations on the most difficult or unnecessary points, in whatever place, and before whatever persons they think proper. This we were compelled to do by these youths yesterday, though against our will, and though we at first declined."

V. "The Greeks, however, Crassus," rejoined Catulus, "who were eminent and illustrious in their respective states, as you are, and as we all desire to be, in our own republic, bore no resemblance to those Greeks who force themselves on our ears; yet they did not in their leisure avoid this kind of discourse and disputation. And if they seem to you, as they ought to seem, impertinent, who have no regard to times, places, or persons, does this place, I pray, seem ill adapted to our purpose, in which the very portico where we are walking, and this field of exercise, and the seats in so many directions, revive in some degree the remembrance of the Greek gymnasia and disputations? Or is the time unseasonable, during so much leisure as is seldom afforded us, and is now afforded at a season when it is most desirable? Or are the company unsuited to this kind of discussion, when we are all of such a character as to think that life is nothing without these studies?" "I contemplate all these things," said Crassus, "in a quite different light; for I think that even the Greeks themselves originally contrived their palæstræ, and seats, and porticoes for exercise and amusement, not for disputation; since their gymnasia were invented many generations before the philosophers began to prate in them; and at this very day, when the philosophers occupy all the gymnasia, their audience would still rather hear the discus than a philosopher; and as soon as it begins to sound, they all desert the philosopher in the middle of his discourse, though discussing matters of the utmost weight and consequence, to anoint themselves for exercise; thus preferring the lightest amusement to what the philosophers represent to be of the utmost utility. As to the leisure which you say we have, I agree with you; but the enjoyment of leisure is not exertion of mind, but relaxation. VI. I have often heard from my father-in-law, in conversation, that his father-in-law Lælius was almost always accustomed to go into the country with Scipio, and that they used to grow incredibly boyish again when they had escaped out of town, as if from a prison, into the open fields. I scarcely dare to say it of such eminent persons, yet Scævola is in the habit of relating that they used to gather shells and pebbles at Caieta and Laurentum, and to descend to every sort of pastime and amusement. For such is the case, that as we see birds form and build nests for the sake of procreation and

their own convenience, and, when they have completed any
part, fly abroad in freedom, disengaged from their toils, in order to alleviate their anxiety, so our minds, wearied with
legal business and the labors of the city, exult and long to
flutter about, as it were, relieved from care and solicitude.
In what I said to Scævola, therefore, in pleading for Curius,[1]
I said only what I thought.   'For if,' said I, 'Scævola, no
will shall be properly made but what is of your writing, all
of us citizens will come to you with our tablets, and you alone
shall write all our wills; but then,' continued I, 'when will
you attend to public business? when to that of your friends?
when to your own? when, in a word, will you do nothing?'
adding, 'for he does not seem to me to be a free man who
does not sometimes *do nothing;*' of which opinion, Catulus, I
still continue; and, when I come hither, the mere privilege of
doing nothing, and of being fairly idle, delights me.   As to the
third remark which you added, that you are of such a disposition as to think life insipid without these studies, that observation not only does not encourage me to any discussion,
but even deters me from it.   For as Caius Lucilius, a man of
great learning and wit, used to say, that what he wrote he
would neither wish to have read by the most illiterate persons,
nor by those of the greatest learning, since the one sort understood nothing, and the other perhaps more than himself; to
which purpose he also wrote, *I do not care to read Persius*[2] (for
he was, as we know, about the most learned of all our countrymen); *but I wish to read Lælius Decimus* (with whom we
were also acquainted, a man of worth and of some learning,
but nothing to Persius); so I, if I am now to discuss these
studies of ours, should not wish to do so before peasants, but
much less before you; for I had rather that my talk should
not be understood than be censured."

VII. "Indeed, Catulus," rejoined Cæsar, "I think I have
already gained some profit[3] by coming hither; for these reasons for declining a discussion have been to me a very agree-

---

[1] In the speech which he made on behalf of Curius, on the occasion
mentioned in book i., c. 39. *Proust.*

[2] A learned orator, who wrote in the time of the Gracchi, and who is
mentioned by Cicero, Brut., c. 26. *Proust.* Of Decimus Lælius nothing is known. *Ellendt.*

[3] *Navâsse operam;* that is, *bene collocâsse.* Ernesti.

able discussion. But why do we delay Antonius, whose part is, I hear, to give a dissertation upon eloquence in general, and for whom Cotta and Sulpicius have been some time waiting?" "But I," interposed Crassus, "will neither allow Antonius to speak a word, nor will I utter a syllable myself, unless I first obtain one favor from you." "What is it?" said Catulus. "That you spend the day here." Then, while Catulus hesitated, because he had promised to go to his brother's house, "I," said Julius, "will answer for both. We will do so; and you would detain me even in case you were not to say a single word." Here Catulus smiled, and said, "My hesitation, then, is brought to an end; for I had left no orders at home, and he at whose house I was to have been has thus readily engaged us to you, without waiting for my assent."

They then all turned their eyes upon Antonius, who cried out, "Be attentive, I say, be attentive, for you shall hear a man from the schools, a man from the professor's chair, deeply versed in Greek learning;[1] and I shall, on this account, speak with the greater confidence, that Catulus is added to the audience, to whom not only we of the Latin tongue, but even the Greeks themselves, are wont to allow refinement and elegance in the Greek language. But since the whole process of speaking, whether it be an art or a business, can be of no avail without the addition of assurance, I will teach you, my scholars, that which I have not learned myself, what I think of *every kind of speaking*." When they all laughed, "It is a matter that seems to me," proceeded he, "to depend very greatly on talent, but only moderately on art; for art lies in things which are known; but all the pleading of an orator depends not on knowledge, but on opinion; for we both address ourselves to those who are ignorant, and speak of what we do not know ourselves; and, consequently, our hearers think and judge differently at different times concerning the same subjects, and we often take contrary sides, not only so that Crassus sometimes speaks against me, or I against Crassus, when one of us must of necessity advance what is false, but even that each of us, at different times, maintains different opinions on the same question, when more than one of those opinions can not possibly be right. I will speak, therefore, as on a subject which is of a character to defend false-

_____
[1] Ironically spoken.

hood, which rarely arrives at knowledge,[1] and which is ready
to take advantage of the opinions and even errors of mankind,
if you think that there is still reason why you should listen
to me."

VIII. " We think, indeed, that there is very great reason,"
said Catulus, " and the more so, as you seem resolved to use
no ostentation ; for you have commenced, not boastfully, but
rather, as you think, with truth, than with any fanciful notion
of the dignity of your subject." " As I have acknowledged,
then," continued Antonius, " that it is not one of the greatest
of arts, so I allow, at the same time, that certain artful directions may be given for moving the feelings and gaining the
favor of mankind. If any one thinks proper to say that the
knowledge how to do this is a great art, I shall not contradict him ; for as many speakers speak upon causes in the forum without due consideration or method, while others, from
study, or a certain degree of practice, do their business with
more address, there is no doubt that, if any one sets himself
to observe what is the cause why some speak better than others, he may discover that cause ; and, consequently, he who
shall extend such observation over the whole field of eloquence, will find in it, if not an art absolutely, yet something
resembling an art. And I could wish that, as I seem to see
matters as they occur in the forum, and in pleadings, so I
could now set them before you just as they are conducted !

" But I must consider my own powers. I now assert only
that of which I am convinced, that although oratory is not
an art, no excellence is superior to that of a consummate orator. For, to say nothing of the advantages of eloquence,
which has the highest influence in every well-ordered and free
state, there is such delight attendant on the very power of eloquent speaking, that nothing more pleasing can be received
into the ears or understanding of man. What music can be
found more sweet than the pronunciation of a well-ordered
oration ? What poem more agreeable than the skillful structure of prose ? What actor has ever given greater pleasure
in imitating, than an orator gives in supporting, truth ? What
penetrates the mind more keenly than an acute and quick suc-

---

[1] *Quæ ad scientiam non sæpe perveniat.* Ellendt incloses these words
in brackets as spurious, regarding them as a gloss on the preceding
phrase that has crept into the text. Their absence is desirable.

cession of arguments? What is more admirable than thoughts illumined by brilliancy of expression? What nearer to perfection than a speech replete with every variety of matter? for there is no subject susceptible of being treated with elegance and effect that may not fall under the province of the orator. IX. It is his, in giving counsel on important affairs, to deliver his opinion with clearness and dignity; it is his to rouse a people when they are languid, and to calm them when immoderately excited. By the same power of language, the wickedness of mankind is brought to destruction, and virtue to security. Who can exhort to virtue more ardently than the orator? Who reclaim from vice with greater energy? Who can reprove the bad with more asperity, or praise the good with better grace? Who can break the force of unlawful desire by more effective reprehension? Who can alleviate grief with more soothing consolation? By what other voice, too, than that of the orator, is history, the evidence of time, the light of truth, the life of memory, the directress of life, the herald of antiquity, committed to immortality? For if there be any other art which professes skill in inventing or selecting words; if any one, besides the orator, is said to form a discourse, and to vary and adorn it with certain distinctions, as it were, of words and thoughts; or if any method of argument, or expression of thought, or distribution and arrangement of matter, is taught, except by this one art, let us confess that either that, of which this art makes profession, is foreign to it, or possessed in common with some other art. But if such method and teaching be confined to this alone, it is not, though professors of other arts may have spoken well, the less on that account the property of this art; but as an orator can speak best of all men on subjects that belong to other arts, if he makes himself acquainted with them (as Crassus observed yesterday), so the professors of other arts speak more eloquently on their own subjects, if they have acquired any instruction from this art; for if any person versed in agriculture has spoken or written with eloquence on rural affairs, or a physician, as many have done, on diseases, or a painter upon painting, his eloquence is not, on that account, to be considered as belonging to any of those arts; although in eloquence, indeed, such is the force of human genius, many men of every class and profession[1] attain some proficiency even without instruction ; but, though you may judge what is peculiar to each art when you have observed what they severally teach, yet nothing can be more certain than that all other arts can discharge their duties without eloquence, but that an orator can not even acquire his name without it ; so that other men, if they are eloquent, borrow something from him ; while he, if he is not supplied from his own stores, can not obtain the power of speaking from any other art."

X. Catulus then said, " Although, Antonius, the course of your remarks ought by no means to be retarded by interruption, yet ·you will bear with me and grant me pardon ; *for I can not help crying out*, as he in the Trinummus[2] says, so ably do you seem to me to have described the powers of the orator, and so copiously to have extolled them, as the eloquent man, indeed, must necessarily do ; he must extol eloquence best of all men ; for to praise it he has to employ the very eloquence which he praises.   But proceed, for I agree with you, that to speak eloquently is all your own ; and that, if any one does so on any other art, he employs an accomplishment borrowed from something else, not peculiar to him or his own."   " The night," added Crassus, "has made you polite to us, Antonius, and humanized you ; for in yesterday's address to us,[3] you described the orator as a man that can do only one thing, like *a waterman or a porter*, as Cæcilius[4] says ; a fellow void of all learning and politeness."   " Why yesterday," rejoined Antonius, " I had made it my object, if I refuted you, to take your scholars from you ;[5] but now, as Catulus and Cæsar make part of the audience, I think I ought not so much to argue against you as to declare what I myself think.   It follows, then, that, as the orator of whom we speak is to be placed in the forum, and in the view of the public, we must consider what employment we are to give him, and to what duties we should wish him to be appointed.   For Crassus[6] yesterday, when you,

---

[1] The reader will observe that the construction in the text is *multi omnium generum atque artium*, as Ellendt observes, referring to Matthiæ.

[2] iii., 2, 7.   [3] See b. i., c. 62.

[4] The writer of Comedies, *Vincere Cæcilius gravitate, Terentius arte.* Hor.

[5] I wished to refute you yesterday, that I might draw Scævola and Cotta from you. This is spoken in jest. *Proust.*   [6] B. i., c. 31.

Catulus and Cæsar, were not present, made, in a few words, the same statement in regard to the division of the art that most of the Greeks have made; not expressing what he himself thought, but what was said by them; that there are two principal sorts of questions about which eloquence is employed—one indefinite, the other definite. He seemed to me to call that indefinite in which the subject of inquiry is general, as, *Whether eloquence is desirable; whether honors should be sought;* and that definite in which there is an inquiry with respect to particular persons, or any settled and defined point; of which sort are the questions agitated in the forum, and in the causes and disputes of private citizens. These appear to me to consist either in judicial pleadings, or in giving counsel; for that third kind, which was noticed by Crassus, and which, I hear, Aristotle[1] himself, who has fully illustrated these subjects, added, is, though it be useful, less necessary." "What kind do you mean?" said Catulus; "is it panegyric? for I observe that that is introduced as a third kind."

XI. "It is so," says Antonius; "and as to this kind of oratory, I know that I myself, and all who were present, were extremely delighted when your mother Popilia[2] was honored with a panegyric by you; the first woman, I think, to whom such honor was ever paid in this city. But it does not seem to me that all subjects on which we speak are to be included in art, and made subject to rules; for from those fountains, whence all the ornaments of speech are drawn, we may also take the ornaments of panegyric, without requiring elementary instructions; for who is ignorant, though no one teach him, what qualities are to be commended in any person? For if we but look to those things which Crassus has mentioned in the beginning of the speech which he delivered when censor in opposition to his colleague,[3] *That in those things which are bestowed on mankind by nature or fortune, he could contentedly allow himself to be excelled; but that in whatever men could procure for themselves, he could not suffer himself to be excelled,* he who would pronounce the panegyric of any person will understand that he must expatiate on the blessings of fortune; and these are advantages of birth, wealth, re-

---

[1] Rhet., i., 3, 1.   [2] See note on c. 3.
[3] Domitius Ahenobarbus. Plin., H. N., xvii., I.

lationship, friends, resources, health, beauty, strength, talent, and such other qualities as are either personal, or dependent on circumstances; and, if he possessed these, he must show that he made a proper use of them; if not, that he managed wisely without them; if he lost them, that he bore the loss with resignation; he must then state what he whom he praises did or suffered with wisdom, or with liberality, or with forti- tude, or with justice, or with honor, or with piety, or with gratitude, or with humanity, or, in a word, under the influence of any virtue. These particulars, and whatever others are of similar kind, he will easily observe who is inclined to praise any person; and he who is inclined to blame him the con- trary." "Why, then, do you hesitate," said Catulus, "to make this a third kind, since it is so in the nature of things? for if it is more easy than others, it is not, on that account, to be excluded from the number." "Because I am unwill- ing," replied Antonius, "to treat of all that falls under the province of an orator, as if nothing, however small it may be, could be uttered without regard to stated rules. Evidence, for instance, is often to be given, and sometimes with great exactness, as I was obliged to give mine against Sextus Ti- tius,[1] a seditious and turbulent member of the commonwealth; when, in delivering my evidence, I explained all the proceed- ings of my consulate, in which I, on behalf of the common- wealth, opposed him as tribune of the people, and exposed all that I thought he had done contrary to the interest of the state; I was detained long, I listened to much, I answered many objections; but would you therefore wish, when you give precepts on eloquence, to add any instructions on giving evidence as a portion of the art of oratory?"

XII. "There is, indeed," said Catulus, "no necessity." "Or if (as often happens to the greatest men) communications are to be delivered, either in the senate from a commander in chief, or to such a commander, or from the senate to any king or people, does it appear to you that because, on such subjects, we must use a more accurate sort of language than ordinary, this kind of speaking should be counted as a department of

---

[1] A tribune of the people, A.U.C. 655, whom Antonius opposed about the Agrarian law. He is mentioned also in c. 66, and appears to be the same that is said to have played vigorously at ball, ii., 62; iii., 23. *Ellendt.* See also Cic., Brut., c. 62.

eloquence, and be furnished with peculiar precepts?" "By no means," replied Catulus; "for an eloquent man, in speaking on subjects of that sort, will not be at a loss for that talent which he has acquired by practice on other matters and topics." "'Those other kinds of subjects, therefore," continued Antonius, "which often require to be treated with eloquence, and which, as I said just now (when I was praising eloquence), belong to the orator, have neither any place in the division of the parts of oratory, nor fall under any peculiar kind of rules, and yet must be handled as eloquently as arguments in pleadings; such are reproof, exhortation, consolation, all which demand the finest graces of language; yet these matters need no rules from art." "I am decidedly of that opinion," said Catulus. "Well, then, to proceed," said Antonius, "what sort of orator, or how great a master of language, do you think it requires to write history?" "If to write it as the Greeks have written, a man of the highest powers," said Catulus; "if as our own countrymen, there is no need of an orator; it is sufficient for the writer to tell the truth." "But," rejoined Antonius, "that you may not despise those of our own country, the Greeks themselves too wrote at first just like our Cato, and Pictor, and Piso. For history was nothing else but a compilation of annals; and accordingly, for the sake of preserving the memory of public events, the pontifex maximus used to commit to writing the occurrences of every year, from the earliest period of Roman affairs to the time of the pontifex Publius Mucius, and had them engrossed on white tablets, which he set forth as a register in his own house, so that all the people had liberty to inspect it; and these records are yet called the Great Annals. This mode of writing many have adopted, and, without any ornaments of style, have left behind them simple chronicles of times, persons, places, and events. Such, therefore, as were Pherecydes, Hellanicus, Acusilas,[1] and many others among the Greeks, are Cato, and Pictor, and Piso with us, who neither understand how composition is to be adorned (for ornaments of style have been but recently introduced among us), and, provided what they related can be understood, think brevity of expression the only merit. Antipater,[2] an excellent man, the friend of Crassus,

---

[1] Of these, Acusilas or Acusilaus, a native of Argos, was the most ancient, according to Suidas. *Ellendt.* The others are better known.

[2] Lucius Cælius Antipater published a history of the Punic Wars, as

raised himself a little, and gave history a higher tone; the others were not embellishers of facts, but mere narrators."

XIII. "It is," rejoined Catulus, "as you say; but Antipater himself neither diversified his narrative by variety of thoughts, nor polished his style by an apt arrangement of words, or a smooth and equal flow of language, but rough-hewed it as he could, being a man of no learning, and not extremely well qualified for an orator; yet he excelled, as you say, his predecessors." "It is far from being wonderful," said Antonius, "if history has not yet made a figure in our language; for none of our countrymen study eloquence, unless that it may be displayed in causes and in the forum; whereas among the Greeks, the most eloquent men, wholly unconnected with public pleading, applied themselves as well to other honorable studies as to writing history; for of Herodotus himself, who first embellished this kind of writing, we hear that he was never engaged in pleading; yet his eloquence is so great as to delight me extremely, as far as I can understand Greek writing. After him, in my opinion, Thucydides has certainly surpassed all historians in the art of composition; for he is so abundant in matter, that he almost equals the number of his words by the number of his thoughts; and he is so happy and judicious in his expressions,[1] that you are at a loss to decide whether his facts are set off by his style, or his style by his thoughts; and of him, too, we do not hear, though he was engaged in public affairs, that he was of the number of those who pleaded causes, and he is said to have written his books at a time when he was removed from all civil employments, and, as usually happened to every eminent man at Athens, was driven into banishment. He was followed by Philistus[2] of Syracuse, who, living in great familiarity with the tyrant Dionysius, spent his leisure in writing history, and, as I think, principally imitated Thucydides. But afterward, two men of great genius, Theopompus and Ephorus, coming from what we may call the noblest school of rhetoric,

Cicero says in his Orator, and was the master of Crassus, the speaker in these dialogues, as appears from Cic., Brut., c. 26.   *Proust.*

[1] *Aptus et pressus.* A *scriptor*, or *orator aptus*, will be one "structâ et rotundâ compositione verborum utens;" and *pressus* will be "in verborum circuitione nec superfluens nec claudicans."   *Ellendt.*

[2] He is called *Pusillus Thucydides* by Cicero, Ep. ad Q. Fratr., xii.

applied themselves to history by the persuasion of their master Isocrates, and never attended to pleading at all. XIV. At
last historians arose also among the philosophers; first Xenophon, the follower of Socrates, and afterward Callisthenes,
the pupil of Aristotle and companion of Alexander. The
latter wrote in an almost rhetorical manner; the former
used a milder strain of language, which has not the animation of oratory, but, though perhaps less energetic, is, as it
seems to me, much more pleasing. Timæus, the last of all
these, but, as far as I can judge, by far the most learned,
and abounding most with richness of matter and variety of
thought, and not unpolished in style, brought a large store of
eloquence·to this kind of writing, but no experience in pleading causes."

When Antonius had spoken thus, "What is this, Catulus?"
said Cæsar. "Where are they who say that Antonius is ignorant of Greek? how many historians has he named! and
how learnedly and judiciously has he spoken of each!" "On
my word," said Catulus, "while I wonder at this, I cease to
wonder at what I regarded with much greater wonder before,
namely, that he, being unacquainted with these matters, should
have such power as a speaker." "But, Catulus," said Antonius, "my custom is to read these books, and some others,
when I have leisure, not to hunt for any thing that may improve me in speaking, but for my own amusement. What
profit is there from it, then? I own that there is not much;
yet there is some; for as, when I walk in the sun, though I
may walk for another purpose, yet it naturally happens that
I gain a deeper color; so, when I have read those books attentively at Misenum[1] (for at Rome I have scarcely opportunity to do so), I can perceive that my language acquires a complexion,[2] as it were, from my intercourse with them. But,
that you may not take what I say in too wide a sense, I only
understand such of the Greek writings as their authors wished to be understood by the generality of people. If I ever

---

[1] A promontory of Campania, where Antonius had a country house.

[2] Ruhnken, in a note on Timæus's Lex., p. 78, expresses a suspicion
that Cicero, when he wrote this, was thinking of a passage in Plato's
Letters, Ep. vii., p. 718, F. *Greenwood.* Orellius very judiciously in-
serts *tactu*, the conjecture of Ernesti, in his text, instead of the old reading *cantu*, which, though Ellendt retains and attempts to defend it, can
not be made to give any satisfactory sense.

fall in with the philosophers, deluded by the titles to their
books, as they generally profess to be written on well-known
and plain subjects, as virtue, justice, probity, pleasure, I do
not understand a single word of them, so restricted are they
to close and exact disputations. The poets, as speaking in a
different language, I never attempt to touch at all; but amuse
myself, as I said, with those who have written history, or their
own speeches,[1] or who have adopted such a style that they
seem to wish to be familiar to us who are not of the deepest
erudition. XV. But I return to my subject. Do you see
how far the study of history is the business of the orator? I
know not whether it is not his most important business, for
flow and variety of diction; yet I do not find it any where
treated separately under the rules of the rhetoricians. Indeed, all rules respecting it are obvious to common view; for
who is ignorant that it is the first law in writing history that
the historian must not dare to tell any falsehood, and the next,
that he must be bold enough to tell the whole truth? Also,
that there must be no suspicion of partiality in his writings,
or of personal animosity? These fundamental rules are doubtless universally known. The superstructure depends on facts
and style. The course of facts requires attention to order of
time and descriptions of countries; and since, in great affairs,
and such as are worthy of remembrance, first the designs, then
the actions, and afterward the results, are expected, it demands also that it should be shown, in regard to the designs,
what the writer approves, and that it should be told, in regard
to the actions, not only what was done or said, but in what
manner; and when the result is stated, that all the causes
contributing to it should be set forth, whether arising from
accident, wisdom, or temerity; and of the characters concerned, not only their acts, but, at least of those eminent in reputation and dignity, the life and manners of each. The sort of
language and character of style to be observed must be regular and continuous, flowing with a kind of equable smoothness, without the roughness of judicial pleadings, and the sharp-
pointed sentences used at the bar. Concerning all these numerous and important points, there are no rules, do you observe, to be found in the treatises of the rhetoricians.

---

[1] Cicero means orators. The speeches which historians have written
are not given as their own, but put into the mouths of others. *Ellendt.*

" In the same silence have lain many other duties of the orator ; exhortation, consolation, precept, admonition, all of which are subjects for the highest eloquence, and yet have no place in those treatises on the art which are in circulation. Under this head, too, there is an infinite field of matter ; for (as Crassus observed) most writers assign to the orator two kinds of subjects on which he may speak ; the one *concerning stated and defined questions*, such as are treated in judicial pleadings or political debates, to which he that will may add panegyrics ; the other, what all authors term (though none give any explanation) *questions unlimited in their kind, without reference to time or person*. When they speak of this sort of subjects, they do not appear to know the nature and extent of it ; for if it is the business of an orator to be able to speak on whatever subject is proposed *without limitation*, he will have to speak on the magnitude of the sun, and on the shape of the earth ; nor will be able, when he has undertaken such a task, to refuse to speak on mathematical and musical subjects. In short, for him who professes it to be his business to speak not only on those questions which are confined to certain times and persons (that is, on all judicial questions), but also on such as are unlimited in their kinds, there can be no subject for oratory to which he can take exception.

XVI. " But if we are disposed to assign to the orator that sort of questions, also, which are undefined, unsettled, and of extreme latitude, so as to suppose that he must speak of good and evil, of things to be desired or avoided, honorable or dishonorable, profitable or unprofitable ; of virtue, justice, temperance, prudence, magnanimity, liberality, piety, friendship, fidelity, duty, and of other virtues and their opposite vices, as well as on state affairs, on government, on military matters, on civil polity, on morality ; let us take upon us that sort of subjects also, but so that it be circumscribed by moderate limits. I think, indeed, that all matters relative to intercourse between fellow-citizens, and the transactions of mankind in general, every thing that concerns habits of life, administration of public affairs, civil society, the common sense of mankind, the law of nature, and moral duties, falls within the province of an orator, if not to such an extent that he may answer on every subject separately, like the philosophers, yet so at least that he may interweave them judiciously into his pleadings, and may speak upon such topics as those who established laws, statutes, and commonwealths have spoken upon them, with simplicity and perspicuity, without any strict order of discussion, or jejune contention about words. That it may not seem wonderful that no rules on so many topics of such importance are here laid down by me, I give this as my reason: As in other arts, when the most difficult parts of each have been taught, other particulars, as being easier, or similar, are not necessary to be taught; for example, in painting, he who has learned to paint the figure of a man can paint one of any shape or age without special instruction; and as there is no danger that he who excels in painting a lion or a bull will be unable to succeed in painting other quadrupeds (for there is indeed no art whatever in which every thing capable of being effected by it is taught by the master; but they who have learned the general principles regarding the chief and fixed points, accomplish the rest of themselves without any trouble), so I conceive that in oratory, whether it be an art, or an attainment from practice only, he who has acquired such ability that he can, at his pleasure, influence the understandings of those who listen to him with some power of deciding, on questions concerning public matters, or his own private affairs, or concerning those for or against whom he speaks, will, on every other kind of oratorical subject, be no more at a loss what to say than the famous Polycletus, when he formed his Hercules, was at a loss how to execute the lion's skin, or the hydra, although he had never been taught to form them separately."

XVII. Catulus then observed, "You seem to me, Antonius, to have set clearly before us what he who designs to be an orator ought to learn, and what he may assume from that which he has learned without particular instruction; for you have reduced his whole business to two kinds of causes only, and have left particulars, which are innumerable, to practice and comparison. But take care lest the hydra and lion's skin be included in those two kinds, and the Hercules and other greater works be left among the matters which you omit. For it does not seem to me to be less difficult to speak on the nature of things in general, than on the causes of particular persons, and it seems even much more difficult to discourse on the nature of the gods, than on matters that are litigated among men." "It is not so," replied Antonius; "for to you, Catulus, I will speak, not so much like a person of learning, as, what is more, one of experience. To speak on all other subjects is, believe me, mere play to a man who does not want parts or practice, and is not destitute of common literature or polite instruction ; but in contested causes, the business is of great difficulty ; I know not whether it be not the greatest by far of all human efforts, where the abilities of the orator are, by the unlearned, estimated according to the result and success ; where an adversary presents himself armed at all points, who is to be at once attacked and repelled ; where he, who is to decide the question, is averse, or offended, or even friendly to your adversary, and hostile to yourself; when he is either to be instructed or undeceived, restrained or incited, or managed in every way, by force of argument, according to the cause and occasion ; when his benevolence is often to be turned to hostility, and his hostility to benevolence ; when he is to be moved, as by some machinery, to severity or to indulgence, to sorrow or to merriment——you must exert your whole power of thought and your whole force of language ; with which must be joined a delivery varied, energetic, full of life, full of spirit, full of feeling, full of nature. If any one, in such efforts as these, shall have mastered the art to such a degree that, like Phidias, he can make a statue of Minerva, he will, like that great artist, find no difficulty in learning how to execute the smaller figures upon the shield."

XVIII. "The greater and more wonderful you represent such performances," said Catulus, "the greater longing possesses me to know by what methods or precepts such power in oratory may be acquired ; not that it any longer concerns me personally (for my age does not stand in need of it, and we used to pursue a different plan of speaking, as we never extorted decisions from the judges by force of eloquence, but rather received them from their hands, after conciliating their good-will only so far as they themselves would permit), yet I wish to learn your thoughts, not for any advantage to myself, as I say, but from a desire for knowledge. Nor have I occasion for any Greek master to repeat his hackneyed precepts, when he himself never saw the forum, or was present at a trial ; presumption similar to what is told of Phormio the Peripatetic ; for when Hannibal, driven from Carthage, came to

Ephesus as an exile to seek the protection of Antiochus, and, as his name was held in great honor among all men, was invited by those who entertained him to hear the philosopher whom I mentioned, if he were inclined; and when he had signified that he was not unwilling, that copious speaker is said to have harangued some hours upon the duties of a general, and the whole military art; and when the rest of the audience, who were extremely delighted, inquired of Hannibal what he thought of the philosopher, the Carthaginian is reported to have answered, not in very good Greek, but with very good sense, that 'he had seen many doting old men, but had never seen any one deeper in his dotage than Phormio.' Nor did he say so, indeed, without reason; for what could have been a greater proof of arrogance, or impertinent loquacity, than for a Greek, who had never seen an enemy or a camp, or had the least concern in any public employment, to deliver instructions on the military art to Hannibal, who had contended so many years for empire with the Romans, the conquerors of all nations? In this manner all those seem to me to act who give rules on the art of speaking, for they teach others that of which they have no experience themselves. But they are perhaps less in error in this respect that they do not attempt to instruct you, Antonius, as he did Hannibal, but boys only, or youths."

XIX. "You are wrong, Catulus," said Antonius, "for I myself have met with many Phormios. Who, indeed, is there among those Greeks that seems to think any of us understand any thing? To me, however, they are not so very troublesome; I easily bear with and endure them all; for they either produce something which diverts me, or make me repent less of not having learned from them. I dismiss them less contumeliously than Hannibal dismissed the philosopher, and on that account, perhaps, have more trouble with them; but certainly all their teaching, as far as I can judge, is extremely ridiculous. For they divide the whole matter of oratory into two parts, the controversy about the cause and about the question. The cause they call the matter relating to the dispute or litigation affecting the persons concerned;[1] the ques-

---

[1] *Reorum.* This reading is very properly adopted by Orellius and Ellendt in place of the old *rerum.* Ellendt refers to c. 43 and 79 for the sense of *reus.*

tion, a matter of infinite doubt. Respecting the cause they give some precepts; on the other part of pleading they are wonderfully silent. They then make five parts, as it were, of oratory ; to invent what you are to say, to arrange what you have invented, to clothe it in proper language, then to commit it to memory, and at last to deliver it with due action and elocution ; a task, surely, requiring no very abstruse study. For who would not understand without assistance that nobody can make a speech unless he has settled what to say, and in what words, and in what order, and remembers it ? Not that I find any fault with these rules, but I say that they are obvious to all, as are likewise those four, five, six, or even seven partitions (since they are differently divided by different teachers) into which every oration is by them distributed ; for they bid us adopt such an exordium as to make the hearer favorable to us, and willing to be informed and attentive ; then to state our case in such a manner that the detail may be probable, clear, and concise; next, to divide or propound the question ; to confirm what makes for us by arguments and reasoning, and refute what makes for the adversary ; after this some place the conclusion of the speech, and peroration as it were ; others direct you, before you come to the peroration, to make a digression by way of embellishment or amplification, then to sum up and conclude. Nor do I altogether condemn these divisions; for they are made with some nicety, though without sufficient judgment, as must of necessity be the case with men who had no experience in real pleading. For the precepts which they confine to the exordium and statement of facts are to be observed through the whole speech ; since I can more easily make a judge favorable to me in the progress of my speech, than when no part of the cause has been heard ; and desirous of information, not when I promise that I will prove something, but when I actually prove and explain ; and I can best make him attentive, not by the first statement, but by working on his mind through the whole course of the pleading. As to their direction that the statement of facts should be probable, and clear, and concise, they direct rightly ; but in supposing that these qualities belong more peculiarly to the statement of facts than to the whole of the speech, they seem to me to be greatly in error ; and their whole mistake lies assuredly in this, that they think oratory an art or science, not unlike other sciences, such as Crassus said yesterday might be formed from the civil law itself; so that the general heads of the subject must first be enumerated, when it is a fault if any head be omitted; next, the particulars under each general head, when it is a fault if any particular be either deficient or redundant; then the definitions of all the terms, in which there ought to be nothing either wanting or superfluous.

XX. "But if the more learned can attain this exactness in the civil law, as well as in other studies of a small or moderate extent, the same can not, I think, be done in an affair of this compass and magnitude. If, however, any are of opinion that it can be done, they must be introduced to those who profess to teach these things as a science; they will find every thing ready set forth and complete; for there are books without number on these subjects, neither concealed nor obscure. But let them consider what they mean to do; whether they will take up arms for sport or for real warfare; for with us a regular engagement and field of battle require one thing, the parade and school of exercise another. Yet preparatory exercise in arms is of some use both to the gladiator and the soldier; but it is a bold and ready mind, acute and quick at expedients, that renders men invincible, and certainly not less effectively if art be united with it.

"I will now, therefore, form an orator for you, if I can, commencing so as to ascertain, first of all, what he is able to do. Let him have a tincture of learning; let him have heard and read something; let him have received those very instructions in rhetoric to which I have alluded. I will try what becomes him; what he can accomplish with his voice, his lungs, his breath, and his tongue. If I conceive that he may reach the level of eminent speakers, I will not only exhort him to persevere in labor, but, if he seem to me to be a good man,[1] will entreat him; so much honor to the whole community do I think that there is in an excellent orator, who is at the same

---

[1] Cato defined an orator *vir bonus dicendi peritus*. Cicero in this passage, under the character of Antonius, and in his own person, De Inv., i., 3, 4, signifies that, though he thinks a good character of great importance in an orator, he does not deny that much eloquence may at times be found in a man of bad character. Cato and Cicero spoke each according to the character of his own age. Quintilian, xii., 1, goes back to the opinion of Cato. Aristotle had previously required good morals in an orator, Rhet., i., 2, 4; ii., 1, 5. *Ellendt.*

time a good man. But if he shall appear likely, after he has done his utmost in every way, to be numbered only among tolerable speakers, I will allow him to act as he pleases, and not be very troublesome to him. But if he shall be altogether unfit for the profession, and wanting in sense, I will advise him to make no attempts, or to turn himself to some other pursuit. For neither is he, who can do excellently, to be left destitute of encouragement from us, nor is he, who can do some little, to be deterred; because one seems to be the part of a sort of divinity; the other, either to refrain from what you can not do extremely well, or to do what you can perform not contemptibly, is the part of a reasonable human being; but the conduct of the third character, to declaim in spite of decency and natural deficiency, is that of a man who, as you said, Catulus, of a certain haranguer, collects as many witnesses as possible of his folly by a proclamation from himself. Of him, then, who shall prove such as to merit our exhortation and encouragement, let me speak so as to communicate to him only what experience has taught myself, that, under my guidance, he may arrive at that point which I have reached without any guide; for I can give him no better instructions.

XXI. "To commence, then, Catulus, by taking an example from our friend Sulpicius here; I first heard him, when he was but a youth, in a cause of small importance; he was possessed of a voice, figure, deportment, and other qualifications suited for the profession which we are considering. His mode of speaking was quick and hurried, which was owing to his genius; his style animated and somewhat too redundant, which was owing to his youth. I was very far from entertaining a slight opinion of him, since I like fertility to show itself in a young man; for, as in vines, those branches which have spread too luxuriantly are more easily pruned than new shoots are produced by culture if the stem is defective, so I would wish there to be that in a youth from which I may take something away. The sap can not be enduring in that which attains maturity too soon. I immediately saw his ability; nor did I lose any time, but exhorted him to consider the forum as his school for improving himself, and to choose whom he pleased for a master; if he would take my advice, Lucius Crassus. To this advice he eagerly listened, and assured me that he would act accordingly; and added also, as a compliment, that I too should be a master to him. Scarce a year had passed from the time of this conversation and recommendation of mine when he accused Caius Norbanus,[1] and I defended him. It is incredible what a difference there appeared to me between him as he was then and as he had been a year before; nature herself led him irresistibly into the magnificent and noble style of Crassus; but he could never have arrived at a satisfactory degree of excellence in it if he had not directed his efforts, by study and imitation, in the same course in which nature led him, so as intently to contemplate Crassus with his whole mind and faculties.

XXII. " Let this, then, be the first of my precepts, to point out to the student whom he should imitate, and in such a manner that he may most carefully copy the chief excellencies of him whom he takes for his model. Let practice then follow, by which he may represent in his imitation the exact resemblance of him whom he chose as his pattern; not as I have known many imitators do, who endeavor to acquire by imitation what is easy, or what is remarkable, or almost faulty; for nothing is easier than to imitate any person's dress, or attitude, or carriage; or if there is any thing offensive in a character, it is no very difficult matter to adopt it, and be offensive in the same way; in like manner as that Fusius, who even now, though he has lost his voice, rants on public topics, could never attain that nervous style of speaking which Caius Fimbria had, though he succeeds in imitating his distortion of features and broad prounciation ; but he neither knew how to choose a pattern whom he would chiefly resemble, and in him that he did choose he preferred copying the blemishes. But he who shall act as he ought must first of all be very careful in making this choice, and must use the utmost diligence to attain the chief excellencies of him whom he has approved.

" What, let me ask, do you conceive to be the reason why almost every age has produced a peculiar style of speaking? a matter on which we can not so easily form a judgment in regard to the orators of our own country (because they have, to say the truth, left but few writings from which such judgment might be formed), as those of the Greeks, from whose writings it may be understood what was the character and

[1] See c. 47.

tendency of eloquence in each particular age. The most ancient, of whom there are any works extant, are Pericles[1] and
Alcibiades,[2] and, in the same age, Thucydides, writers perspi-
cacious, pointed, concise, abounding more in thoughts than in
words. It could not possibly have happened that they should
all have the same character, unless they had proposed to themselves some one example for imitation. These were followed
in order of time by Critias, Theramenes, and Lysias. There
are extant many writings of Lysias, some of Critias;[3] of
Theramenes[4] we only hear. They all still retained the vigorous style of Pericles, but had somewhat more exuberance.
Then behold Isocrates arose, from whose school,[5] as from the
Trojan horse, none but real heroes proceeded; but some of
them were desirous to be distinguished on parade, some in
the field of battle. XXIII. Accordingly, those Theopompi,
Ephori, Philisti,[6] Naucratæ,[7] and many others, differ in gen-

---

[1] Cicero, Brut., c. 7, says that some compositions were in circulation
under the name of Pericles; and Quintilian, iii., 1, 12, looking to that
observation of Cicero, tacitly assents to those who denied the genuine-
ness of those compositions. See also Quint., x., 2, 22; 10, 49. *Ellendt.*

[2] That Alcibiades left nothing in writing, though he had great reputation as a speaker, seems to be rightly inferred by Ruhnken from De-
mosth., De Cor., c. 40. Thucydides is here mentioned among orators
on account of the orations which he inserted in his history. *Ellendt.*

[3] He wrote not only orations, which are mentioned by Dionys. Hali-
carn., de Lysiâ jud., c. 2; cf. de Isæo, c. 2; by Phrynichus, ap. Phot.,
Cod. 158, and by others, but also tragedies, elegies, and other works.
That he was eloquent and learned we are told by Cicero, De Or., iii.,
34; Brut., c. 7. *Henrichsen.* The remains of his writings were collected by Bach, 1827. *Ellendt.*

[4] The eloquence of Theramenes is mentioned by Cicero, iii., 16;
Brut., c. 7. The writings which Suidas enumerates as being his were
doubtless spurious. See Ruhnken, Hist. Crit. Or. Gr., p. xl. *Ellendt.*

[5] The words *magister istorum omnium* which, though retained by
Orellius, are pronounced spurious by Lambinus, Ernesti, Ruhnken,
Schutz, and Ellendt, are left untranslated. "They can not be Cicero's
words," says Ellendt, "even though they are found quoted by Nonius,
p. 344."

[6] Henrichsen and Ellendt read *Philisci.* Philistus, apparently, from
the way in which he is mentioned in c. 13, has, as Ellendt observes, no
place here. "Philiscus of Miletus, a disciple of Isocrates (see Anon.
Vit. Isocr.), and master of Timæus the historian (see Suidas, under
Philiscus and Timæus), wrote a treatise on rhetoric, orations, and a life
of Lycurgus, noticed by Olympiodorus in Comment. ad Plat. Gorg., and
other works. See Ruhnken, Hist. Crit. Or. Gr., p. lxxxiii. Goell., de
Situ et Orig. Syracus., p. 114." *Henrichsen.*

[7] Naucrates, a native of Erythræ, called Ἰσοκράτους ἑταῖρος by Dio-

rus, but in their manner bear a strong resemblance both to each other and to their master; and those who applied themselves to causes, as Demosthenes, Hyperides, Æschines, Lycurgus, Dinarchus, and a multitude of others, although they were dissimilar in abilities one to another, yet were all engaged in imitating the same kind of natural excellence; and as long as the imitation of their manner lasted, so long did that character and system of eloquence prevail. Afterward, when these were dead, and all recollection of them grew gradually obscure, and at last vanished, more lax and remiss modes of speaking prevailed. Subsequently Demochares, who, they say, was the son of Demosthenes' sister and the famous Demetrius Phalereus, the most polished of all that class, in my opinion, and others of like talents, arose; and if we choose to pursue the list down to the present times, we shall understand that, as at this day all Asia imitates the famous Menecles of Alabanda, and his brother Hierocles, to both of whom we have listened, so there has always been some one whom the generality desired to resemble.

"Whoever, then, shall seek to attain such resemblance, let him endeavor to acquire it by frequent and laborious exercise, and especially by composition; and if our friend Sulpicius would practice this, his language would be more compact; for there is now in it at times, as farmers say of their corn when in the blade, amid the greatest fertility, a sort of luxuriance which ought to be, as it were, eaten down[1] by the use of the pen." Here Sulpicius observed, "You advise me rightly, and I am obliged to you; but I think that even you, An-

nysius Halicarnassensis, Rhet., vi., 1, was distinguished for the composition of funeral orations. He seems also to have written on rhetoric. See Cicero, De Orat., iii., 44; Brut., 51; Quintil., iii., 6, 3; also Taylor, Lect. Lys., c. 3, p. 232; Ruhnken, Hist. Crit. Or. Gr., p. lxxxiv. *Henrichsen.*

[1] This is one of Virgil's directions to the farmer in the first Georgic, where he gives the reason for it:

Quid, qui ne gravidis procumbat culmus aristis,
Luxuriem segetum tenerâ depascit in herbâ,
Cum primum sulcos æquant sata?—Georg., i., 114.

And Pliny, l. 18: "Luxuries segetum castigatur dente pecoris, in herba duntaxat, et depastæ quidem vel sæpius nullam in spica injuriam sentiunt: ita juvenilis ubertas et luxuries orationis stylo et assiduitate scribendi quasi absumitur et reprimitur."—B.

tonius, have never written much." " As if," rejoined Antonius, " I could not direct others in matters in which I am deficient myself; but, indeed, I am supposed not to write even
my own accounts.   But in this particular a judgment may be
formed from my circumstances, and in the other from my ability in speaking, however small it be, what I do in either way.
We see, however, that there are many who imitate nobody,
but attain what they desire by their own natural powers, without resembling any one ; a fact of which an instance may be
seen in you, Cæsar and Cotta ; for one of you has acquired a
kind of pleasing humor and wit unusual in the orators of our
country ; the other an extremely keen and subtle species of
oratory.   Nor does Curio, who is about your age, and the son
of a father who was, in my opinion, very eloquent for his time,
seem to me to imitate any one much ; but by a certain force,
elegance, and copiousness of expression, has formed a sort of
style and character of eloquence of his own ; of which I was
chiefly enabled to judge in that cause which he pleaded against
me before the Centumviri in behalf of the brothers Cossi, and
in which no quality was wanting in him that an orator, not
merely of fluency, but of judgment, ought to possess.

XXIV. " But to conduct, at length, him whom we are
forming to the management of causes, and those in which there
is considerable trouble, judicial trials, and contested suits (somebody will perhaps laugh at the precept which I am going to
give, for it is not so much sagacious as necessary, and seems
rather to proceed from a monitor who is not quite a fool than
from a master of profound learning), our first precept for him
shall be, That, whatever causes he undertakes to plead, he must
acquire a minute and thorough knowledge of them.   This is
not a precept laid down in the schools ; for easy causes are
given to boys.   'The law forbids a stranger to ascend the
wall ; he ascends it ; he beats back the enemy ; he is accused.'
It is no trouble to understand such a cause as this.   They are
right, therefore, in giving no precepts about learning the cause ;
for such is generally the form of causes in the schools.   But
in the forum, wills, evidence, contracts, covenants, stipulations,
relationship by blood, by affinity, decrees, opinions of lawyers,
and even the lives and characters of those concerned in the
cause. are all to be investigated ; and by negligence in these
particulars we see many causes lost, especially those relative

to private concerns, as they are often of greater intricacy. Thus some, while they would have their business thought very extensive, that they may seem to fly about the whole forum, and to go from one cause to another, speak upon causes which they have not mastered, whence they incur much censure; censure for negligence if they voluntarily undertake the business, or for perfidiousness if they undertake it under any engagement;[1] but such censure is assuredly of worse consequence than they imagine, since nobody can possibly speak on a subject which he does not understand otherwise than to his own disgrace; and thus, while they despise the imputation of ignorance, which is in reality the greater fault, they incur that of stupidity also, which they more anxiously avoid.

"It is my custom to use my endeavor that every one of my clients may give me instructions in his own affairs himself, and that nobody else be present, so that he may speak with the greater freedom.[2] I am accustomed also to plead to him the cause of his adversary, in order to engage him to plead his own, and state boldly what he thinks of his own case. When he is gone, I conceive myself in three characters—my own, that of the adversary, and that of the judge. Whatever circumstance is such as to promise more support or assistance than obstruction, I resolve to speak upon it; wherever I find more harm than good, I set aside and totally reject that part entirely; and thus I gain this advantage, that I consider at one time what I shall say, and say it at another; two things which most speakers, relying upon their genius, do at one and the same time; but certainly those very persons would speak considerably better if they would but resolve to take one time for premeditation, and another for speaking.

"When I have acquired a thorough understanding of the business and the cause, it immediately becomes my consider-

[1] *Magna offensio vel negligentiæ, susceptis rebus, vel perfidiæ, receptis.* *Recipere* is used with a reference to others, by whom we allow some duty to be laid upon us; *suscipere* regards only ourselves. *Ellendt.*

[2] *Inertia.* This passage puzzled Lambinus and others, who did not see how the reproach of *inertia* in an orator could be greater than that of *tarditas*, or stupidity. But *inertia* here signifies *artis ignorantia*, ignorance of his art, which is doubtless the greatest fault in an orator. *Verburg.*

ation what ground there may be for doubt. For of all points that are disputed among mankind, whether the case is of a criminal nature, as concerning an act of violence ; or controversial, as concerning an inheritance ; or deliberative, as on going to war ; or personal, as in panegyric ; or argumentative, as on modes of life, there is nothing in which the inquiry is not either what has been done, or is being done, or will be done, or of what nature a thing is, or how it should be designated.

XXV. " Our causes, such at least as concern criminal matters, are generally defended by the plea of not guilty ; for in charges of extortion of money, which are the most important, the facts are almost all to be denied ; and in those of bribery to procure offices, it is seldom in our power to distinguish munificence and liberality from corruption and criminal largess. In accusations of stabbing, or poisoning, or embezzlement of the public money, we necessarily deny the charge. On trials, therefore, the first kind of causes is that which arises from dispute as to the fact. In deliberations, the discussion generally springs from a question as to what is to be done, rarely about any thing present or already done. But oftentimes the question is not whether a thing is a fact or not, but of what nature it is ; as when the consul, Caius Carbo, in my hearing, defended the cause of Opimius before the people, he denied no circumstance in the death of Caius Gracchus, but maintained that it was a lawful act for the good of his country ; or, as when Publius Africanus replied to the same Carbo (then tribune of the people, engaging in political affairs with very different views,[1] and asking a question about the death of Tiberius Gracchus) ' that he seemed to have been lawfully put to death.' ˙But every thing may be asserted to have been done lawfully, which is of such a kind that it may be said that it ought to have been done, or was properly and necessarily done, or done unawares, or by accident. Then the question ' what a thing should be called' arises when there is a dispute by what term an act should be designated, as was the great point of dispute between myself and our friend Sulpicius in Norbanus's cause ; for though I admitted most of the charges made by him on the other side, I still denied that treason had been committed by Norbanus ; on the signification of

[1] Because he was then attached to the party of the Gracchi. *Proust.*

which word, by the Apuleian law,[1] the whole cause depended. And in this species of causes some lay it down as a rule that both parties should define clearly and briefly the term that gives rise to the question. This seems to me extremely puerile; for it is quite a different thing from defining words when any dispute arises among the learned about matters relating to science, as when it is inquired, what is an art, what is a law, what is a state? On which occasions reason and learning direct, that the whole force of the thing which you define should be expressed in such a manner that there be nothing omitted or superfluous; but this neither Sulpicius did in that cause, nor did I attempt to do it; for each of us, to the best of our abilities, enlarged with the utmost copiousness of language upon what it was to commit treason. Since, in the first place, a definition, if one word is objectionable, or may be added or taken away, is often wrested out of our hands; and, in the next, the very practice itself savors of school learning and almost puerile exercise; and besides, it can not penetrate into the mind and understanding of the judge, for it glides off before it has made any impression.

XXVI. "But in that kind of causes in which it is disputed of what nature any thing is, the contest often arises from the interpretation of writing, when there can be no controversy but about something that is doubtful. For even the case, in which the written letter differs from the intention, involves a species of doubt, which is cleared up when the words which are wanting are supplied; and such addition being made, it is maintained that the intention of the writing was clear; and if any doubt arises from contradictory writings, it is not a new kind of controversy that arises, but a cause of the former sort is doubled;[2] and this can either never be determined, or must be so determined that, by supplying the missing words, the writing which we defend, whichsoever of the two it is, may be rendered complete. Thus, of those causes which arise from a controversy about a writing, when any thing is ex-

---

[1] A law of Lucius Apuleius Saturninus, tribune of the people, A.U.C. 652. It is also mentioned in c. 49. But neither the cause nor subject of it is at all known. *Ellendt.*

[2] *Superioris generis causa duplicatur.* Ellendt explains these words thus: "in the same cause, the allegations of the two parties are judged as two separate questions of the same kind.

pressed ambiguously, there exists but one kind. But as there are many sorts of ambiguities (which they who are called logicians seem to me to understand better than other men; while those of our profession, who ought to know them full as well, seem to be ignorant of them), so that is the most frequent in occurrence, either in discourse or writing, when a question arises from a word or words being left out. They make another mistake when they distinguish this kind of causes, which consist in the interpretation of writing, from those in which it is disputed of what nature a thing is; for there is nowhere so much dispute respecting the exact nature of a thing as in regard to writing, which is totally separated from controversy concerning fact. There are in all, therefore, three sorts of matters which may possibly fall under doubt and discussion—what is now done, what has been done, or what is to be done; what the nature of a thing is, or how it should be designated; for as to the question which some Greeks add, whether a thing be rightly done, it is wholly included in the inquiry what the nature of the thing is.

XXVII. "But to return to my own method. When, after hearing and understanding the nature of a cause, I proceed to examine the subject-matter of it, I settle nothing until I have ascertained to what point my whole speech, bearing immediately on the question and case, must be directed. I then very diligently consider two other points; the one, how to recommend myself, or those for whom I plead; the other, how to sway the minds of those before whom I speak to that which I desire. Thus the whole business of speaking rests upon three things for success in persuasion: that we prove what we maintain to be true; that we conciliate those who hear; that we produce in their minds whatever feeling our cause may require. For the purpose of proof, two kinds of matter present themselves to the orator; one, consisting of such things as are not invented by him, but, as appertaining to the cause, are judiciously treated by him, as deeds, testimonies, covenants, contracts, examinations, laws, acts of the senate, precedents, decrees, opinions of lawyers, and whatever else is not found out by the orator, but brought under his notice by the cause and by his clients; the other, consisting entirely in the orator's own reasoning and arguments: so that, as to the former head, he has only to handle the arguments with which he is furnished; as to the latter, to invent arguments likewise. Those who profess to teach eloquence, after dividing causes into several kinds, suggest a number of arguments for each kind, which method, though it may be better adapted to the instruction of youth, in order that when a case is proposed to them they may have something to which they may refer, and from whence they may draw forth arguments ready prepared ; yet it shows a slowness of mind to pursue the rivulets, instead of seeking for the fountain-head ; and it becomes our age and experience to derive what we want to know from the source, and to ascertain the spring from which every thing proceeds.

"But that first kind of matters which are brought before the orator ought to be the constant subject of our contemplation for general practice in affairs of that nature.   For in support of deeds and against them, for and against evidence, for and against examinations by torture, and in other subjects of that sort, we usually speak either of each kind in general and abstractedly, or as confined to particular occasions, persons, and causes ; and such commonplaces (I speak to you, Cotta and Sulpicius) you ought to keep ready and prepared with much study and meditation.   It would occupy too much time at present to show by what means we should confirm or invalidate testimony, deeds, and examinations.   These matters are all to be attained with a moderate share of capacity, though with very great practice ; and they require art and instruction only so far as they should be illustrated with certain embellishments of language.   So also those which are of the other kind, and which proceed wholly from the orator, are not difficult of invention, but require perspicuous and correct exposition.   As these two things, therefore, are the objects of our inquiry in causes, first, what we shall say, and, next, how we shall say it, the former, which seems to be wholly concerned with art, though it does indeed require some art, is yet an affair of but ordinary understanding, namely, to see what ought to be said; the latter is the department in which the divine power and excellence of the orator is seen ; I mean in delivering what is to be said with elegance, copiousness, and variety of language.

XXVIII. "The former part,[1] then, since you have once

---

[1] Which shows what a speaker ought to say, and what is effective in persuading an audience. *Proust.*

declared it to be your pleasure, I will not refuse to finish off
and complete (how far I shall succeed you will best judge),
and shall show from what topics a speech must be furnished
in order to effect these three objects which alone have power
to persuade; namely, that the minds of the audience be *conciliated*, *informed*, and *moved*, for these are the three; but how
they should be illustrated, there is one present who can instruct us all; one who first introduced this excellence into our
practice, who principally improved it, who alone has brought
it to perfection.   For I think, Catulus (and I will say this
without any dread of a suspicion of flattery), that there is no
orator, at all more eminent than ordinary, either Grecian or
Roman, that our age has produced, whom I have not heard
often and attentively; and, therefore, if there is any ability in
me (as I may now presume to hope, since you, men of such
talents, take so much trouble in giving me audience), it arises
from this, that no orator ever delivered any thing in my hearing which did not sink deeply into my memory; and I, such
as I am, and as far as I have capacity to form a judgment,
having heard all orators, without any hesitation decide and
pronounce this, That none of them all had so many and such
excellent accomplishments in speaking as are in Crassus.   On
which account, if you also are of the same opinion, it will not,
as I think, be an unjust partition, if, when I shall have given
birth, and education, and strength to this orator whom I am
forming, as is my design, I deliver him to Crassus to be furnished with apparel and ornaments."

Crassus then said, " Do you rather, Antonius, go on as you
have commenced; for it is not the part of a good or liberal
parent not to clothe and adorn him whom he has engendered
and brought up, especially as you can not deny that you are
wealthy enough.   For what grace, what power, what spirit,
what dignity was wanting to that orator, who, at the close of
a speech, did not hesitate to call forth his accused client, though
of consular rank, and to tear open his garment, and to expose
to the judges the scars on the breast of the old commander?[1]

[1] Manius Aquilius, who, after the termination of the servile war in
Sicily, was brought to trial on a charge of extortion.   As he was unwilling to entreat the pity of the judges, Antonius, who pleaded for him,
tore open his tunic in front, and showed the scars of the honorable wounds
which he had received in battle.   He was acquitted.   Livy, Epit. *Proust.*

who also, when he defended a seditious madman,[1] Sulpicius
here being the accuser, did not hesitate to speak in favor of
sedition itself, and to demonstrate, with the utmost power of
language, that many popular insurrections are just, for which
nobody could be accountable? adding that many seditions had
occurred to the benefit of the commonwealth, as when the
kings were expelled, and when the power of the tribunes was
established; and that the sedition of Norbanus, proceeding
from the grief of the citizens, and their hatred to Cæpio, who
had lost the army, could not possibly be restrained, and was
blown up into a flame by a just indignation. Could this, so
hazardous a topic, so unprecedented, so delicate, so new, be
handled without an incredible force and power of eloquence?
What shall I say of the compassion excited for Cneius Manlius,[2] or that in favor of Quintus Rex?[3] What of other innumerable instances, in which it was not that extraordinary
acuteness, which every body allows you, that was most conspicuous, but it was those very qualities which you now ascribe to me, that were always eminent and excellent in you."

XXIX. "For my part," said Catulus, "what I am accustomed most to admire in you both is, that while you are totally unlike each other in your manner of speaking, yet each of
you speaks so well, that nothing seems either to have been denied you by nature, or not to have been bestowed on you by
learning. You, therefore, Crassus, from your obliging disposition, will neither withhold from us the illustration of whatever may have been inadvertently or purposely omitted by
Antonius ; nor if you, Antonius, do not speak on every point,
we shall think, not that you could not speak on it, but that
you preferred that it should be treated by Crassus." Here
Crassus said, "Do you rather, Antonius, omit those particulars which you have proposed to treat, and which no one here
needs, namely, from what topics the statements made in pleadings are to be derived, which, though they would be treated
by you in a new and excellent way, are in their nature very

---

[1] Norbanus the tribune. See note on c. 47. *Ellendt.*

[2] He was consul with Publius Rutilius, A.U.C. 649; and having refused to unite his troops with those of Quintus Cæpio, the proconsul, was
defeated by the Cimbri, and lost his army. Livy, Ep. lxvii. For this
miscarriage he was, with Cæpio, brought to trial, and must have been
defended by Antonius. *Ellendt.*

[3] Of the trial of Quintus Marcius Rex nothing is known. *Ellendt.*

easy, and commonly set forth in books of rules; but show us those resources whence you draw that eloquence which you frequently exert, and always divinely." "I will indeed show you them," said Antonius; "and that I may the more easily obtain from you what I require, I will refuse you nothing that you ask. The supports of my whole eloquence, and that power of speaking which Crassus just now extolled to the skies, are, as I observed before, three processes; the first, that of conciliating my hearers; the second, that of instructing them; and the third, that of moving them. The first of these divisions requires mildness of address; the second penetration; the third energy; for it is impossible but that he, who is to determine a cause in our favor, must either lean to our side from propensity of feeling, or be swayed by the arguments of our defense, or be forced by action upon his mind. But since that part, in which the opening of the case itself and the defense lie, seems to comprehend all that is laid down as doctrine on this head, I shall speak on that first, and say but few words; for I seem to have but few observations gained from experience, and imprinted as it were on my memory.

XXX. "We shall willingly consent to your judicious proposal, Crassus, to omit those defenses for every sort of causes which the masters of rhetoric are accustomed to teach boys, and to open those sources whence all arguments for every cause and speech are derived. For neither, as often as we have occasion to write any word, need the letters of that word be so often collected in our thoughts; nor, as often as we are to plead a cause, need we turn to the separate arguments for that cause; but we should have certain commonplaces which, like letters for forming a word, immediately occur to us to aid in stating a cause. But these commonplaces can be of advantage only to that orator who is conversant in business, and has that experience which age at length brings with it; or one who has so much attention and power of thought as to anticipate age by study and diligence. For if you bring to me a man of ever so deep erudition, of ever so acute and subtile an intellect, or ever so ready an elocution, if he be a stranger to the customs of civil communities, to the examples, to the institutions, to the manners and inclinations of his fellow-citizens, the commonplaces from which arguments are drawn will be of little benefit to him. I must have a well-cultivated genius, like a field not once plowed only, but again and again, with renewed and repeated tillage, that it may produce better and larger crops; and the cultivation here required is experience, attentive hearing of other orators, reading, and writing.

" First, then, let him examine the nature of his cause, which is never obscure so far as the inquiry ' whether a thing has been done or not;' or ' of what nature it is;' or ' what name it should receive;' and when this is ascertained, it immediately occurs, with the aid of natural good sense, and not of those artifices which teachers of rhetoric inculcate, ' what constitutes the cause,' that is, the point without which there would be no controversy; then, ' what is the matter for trial,' which they direct you to ascertain in this manner: Opimius slew Gracchus: what constitutes the cause? ' That he slew him for the good of the republic, when he had called the people to arms, in consequence of a decree of the senate.' Set this point aside, and there will be no question for trial. But Decius denies that such a deed could be authorized contrary to the laws. The point therefore to be tried will be ' whether Opimius had authority to do so from the decree of the senate, for the good of the commonwealth.' These matters are indeed clear, and may be settled by common sense; but it remains to be considered what arguments, relative to the point for trial, ought to be advanced, as well by the accuser as by him who has undertaken the defense.

XXXI. " Here we must notice a capital error in those masters to whom we send our children; not that it has much to do with speaking, but that you may see how stupid and unpolished a set of men they are who imagine themselves learned. For, in distinguishing the different kinds of speaking, they make two species of causes. One they call ' that in which the question is about a general proposition, without reference to persons and times;' the other, ' that which is confined to certain persons and times;' being ignorant that all controversies must have relation to the force and nature of the general position; for in that very cause which I mentioned, the person of Opimius or Decius has nothing to do with the common arguments of the orator; since the inquiry has unrestricted reference to the question in general, ' whether he seems deserving of punishment who has slain a citizen under a decree

of the senate for the preservation of his country, when such a
deed was not permitted by the laws.' There is, indeed, no
cause in which the point that falls under dispute is considered
with reference to the parties to the suit, and not from arguments relating to such questions in general. But even in
those very cases where the dispute is about a fact, as 'whether
Publius Decius[1] has taken money contrary to law,' the arguments both for the accusation and for the defense must have
reference to the general question, and the general nature of
the case; as, to show that the defendant is expensive, the
arguments must refer to luxury; that he is covetous of another's property, to avarice; that he is seditious, to turbulent
and ill-designing citizens in general; that he is convicted by
many proofs, to the general nature of evidence: and, on the
other side, whatever is said for the defendant must of necessity be abstracted from the occasion and individual, and referred to the general notions of things and questions of the
kind. These, perhaps, to a man who can not readily comprehend in his mind all that is in the nature of things, may
seem extremely numerous to come under consideration when
the question is about a single fact; but it is the number of
charges, and not of modes of defense, or topics for them, that
is infinite.[2]

XXXII. "But when there is no contest about facts, the
questions on the nature of facts, if you reckon them from the
number of the parties accused, are innumerable and intricate;
if from the facts themselves, very few and clear. For if we
consider the case of Mancinus[3] so as referring to Mancinus
alone, then, whenever a person whom the chief herald has surrendered to the enemy is not readmitted into his country, a
new case will arise. But if what gives rise to the controversy be the general question, 'whether to him whom the
chief herald has surrendered, if he has not been readmitted
into his country, there seems to be a right of return,' the name
of Mancinus has nothing to do with the mode of speaking upon

[1] He was accused of having been bribed to bring Opimius to trial for
having caused the death of Caius Gracchus. See Smith's Dict. of
Biog. and Mythol., art. Decius, n. 4.
[2] Innumerable accusations may be brought against a person, as against
Verres by Cicero; but the *loci*, common topics or grounds, on which the
attack or defense will rest (respecting, for instance, avarice, luxury, violence, treason), will be but few. *Ellendt.*   [3] See i., 40.

it, or the arguments for the defense. And if the merit or de-
merit of the person give rise to any discussion, it is wholly
beside the question; and the part of the speech referring to
the question must, of necessity, be adapted to such arguments
in general. I do not reason upon these subjects for the purpose of confuting learned teachers; although those merit reproof who, in their general definition, describe this sort of
causes as relating to persons and times. For, although times
and persons are incident to them, yet it should be understood
that the causes depend not upon them, but upon the general
question. But this is not my business; for we ought to have
no contest with that sort of people; it is sufficient that this
only should be known, that they have not even attained a
point which they might have effected amid so much leisure,
even without any experience in affairs of the forum; that is,
they might have distinguished the general natures of cases,
and explained them a little more accurately. But this, as I
said, is not my business; it is mine, and much more yours,
my friends Cotta and Sulpicius, to know, that as their artificial rules now stand, the multitude of causes is to be dreaded; for it is infinite if they are referred to persons; so many
men, so many causes; but, if they are referred to general
questions, they are so limited and few, that studious orators
of good memory and judgment ought to have them digested in
their minds, and, I may almost say, learned by heart; unless,
perhaps, you imagine that Lucius Crassus took his notion of
that famous cause[1] from Manius Curius personally, and thus
brought many arguments to show why, though no posthumous
s n was born, yet Curius ought to be the heir of Coponius.
The name of Coponius or of Curius had no influence at all on
the array of arguments advanced, or on the force and nature
of the question; the whole controversy had regard to all affairs and events of that kind in general, not to particular occasions or names; since the writing was thus, *If a son is born
to me, and he die before, etc., then let him be my heir;* and if a
son was not born, the question was whether he ought to be
heir who was appointed heir on the death of the son.

XXXIII. "A question regarding unvarying equity, and of
a general nature, requires no names of persons, but merely
skill in speaking, and sources of proper argument. In this

[1] See i., 39.

respect even the lawyers themselves are an impediment to us, and hinder us from learning; for I perceive it to be generally reported in the books of Cato and of Brutus what answers they gave on points of law to any particular man or woman by name, that we might imagine, I suppose, some cause for consultation or doubt to have arisen from the persons, not from the thing; so that, since persons are innumerable, we might be deterred from the study of the law, and lay aside all inclination to learn it, at the same time with all hope of ever attaining a thorough knowledge of it.

" But Crassus will some day make all these points clear to us, and set them forth arranged under general heads ; for you must know, Catulus, that he promised us yesterday that he would reduce the civil law, which is now in a state of confusion and dispersion, under certain general heads, and digest it into an easy system." "And, indeed," said Catulus, "that is by no means a difficult undertaking for Crassus, who has all of law that can be learned, and he will supply that which was wanting in those who taught him ; for he will be able to define exactly, and to illustrate eloquently, every point comprehended in the law." "We shall then," said Antonius, "learn all these things from Crassus, when he shall have betaken himself, as he intends, from the tumult of public business and the benches of the forum to a quiet retreat and to his throne."[1] "I have indeed often," observed Catulus, " heard him say ' that he was resolved to retire from pleading and the courts of justice;' but, as I frequently tell him, it will never be in his power; for neither will he permit his assistance to be repeatedly implored in vain by persons of character, nor will the public endure his retirement patiently, as they will think that if they lose the eloquence of Lucius Crassus, they will lose one of the principal ornaments of the city." "Indeed, then," remarked Antonius, "if what Catulus says is true, Crassus, you must still live on in the same workshop with me, and we must give up that yawning and sleepy science to the tranquillity of the Scævolæ and other such happy people." Here Crassus smiled a little, and said, " Finish weaving, Antonius, the web which you have begun ; yet that yawning science, as you term it, when I have sheltered myself under it, will vindicate my right to liberty."

[1] See i., 45; also iii., 33; ii., 55; and De Legg., i., 3.

XXXIV. "This is indeed the end," continued Antonius, "of that part on which I just now entered; for it is now understood that all matters which admit of doubt are to be decided, not with reference to individuals, who are innumerable, or to occasions, which are infinitely various, but to general considerations and the nature of things ; that general considerations are not only limited in number, but very few ; that those who are studious of speaking should embrace in their minds the subjects peculiar to the several departments of eloquence, arranged under general heads, as well as arrayed and adorned, I mean with thoughts and illustrations. These will, by their own force, beget words, which always seem to me to be elegant enough, if they are such that the subject seems to have suggested them. And if you ask the truth (as far, that is, as it is apparent to me, for I can affirm nothing more than my own notions and opinions), we ought to carry this preparatory stock of general questions and commonplaces into the forum with us, and not, when any cause is brought before us, begin then to seek for topics from which we may draw our arguments ; topics which, indeed, by all who have made them the subjects of but moderate consideration, may be thoroughly prepared by means of study and practice ; but the thoughts must still revert to those general heads and commonplaces to which I have so often alluded, and from which all arguments are drawn for every species of oratory. All that is required, whether it result from art, or observation, or practice, is but to know those parts of the field in which you may hunt for, and trace out, what you wish to find ; for when you have embraced in your thoughts the whole of any topic, if you are but well practiced in the treatment of subjects, nothing will escape you, and every circumstance material to the question will occur and suggest itself to you.

XXXV. "Since, then, in speaking, three things are requisite for finding argument—genius, method (which, if we please, we may call art), and diligence, I can not but assign the chief place to genius ; yet diligence can raise even genius itself out of dullness ; diligence, I say, which, as it avails in all things, is also of the utmost moment in pleading causes. Diligence is to be particularly cultivated by us ; it is to be constantly exerted ; it is capable of effecting almost every thing. That a cause is thoroughly understood, as I said at

first, is owing to diligence ; that we listen to our adversary
attentively, and possess ourselves, not only of his thoughts,
but even of his every word ; that we observe all the motions
of his countenance, which generally indicate the workings of
the mind, is owing to diligence [but to do this covertly, that
he may not seem to derive any advantage to himself, is the
part of prudence] ;[1] that the mind ruminates on those topics
which I shall soon mention, that it insinuates itself thoroughly into the cause, that it fixes itself on it with care and attention, is owing to diligence ; that it applies the memory like a
light, to all these matters, as well as the tone of voice and
power of delivery, is owing to diligence.   Betwixt genius and
diligence there is very little room left for art ; art only shows
you where to look, and where that lies which you want to
find ; all the rest depends on care, attention, consideration,
vigilance, assiduity, industry ; all which I include in that one
word which I have so often repeated, diligence ; a single virtue, in which all other virtues are comprehended.   For we
see how the philosophers abound in copiousness of language,
who, as I think (but you, Catulus, know these matters better),
lay down no precepts of eloquence, and yet do not, on that account, the less undertake to speak with fullness and fluency
on whatever subject is proposed to them."

XXXVI. Catulus then observed, " It is as you say, Antonius, that most philosophers deliver no precepts of eloquence,
and yet are prepared with something to say on any subject.
But Aristotle, he whom I admire more than any of them, has
set forth certain topics from which every line of argument
may be deduced, not only for the disputations of philosophy,
but even for the reasoning which we use in pleading causes ;
from whose notions your discourse, Antonius, has for some
time past not varied ; whether you, from a resemblance to
that divine genius, hit upon his track, or whether you have
read and made yourself master of his writings—a supposition,
indeed, which seems to be more probable than the other, for
I see that you have paid more attention to the Greek writers
than we had imagined."   " You shall hear from myself," said
he, " Catulus, what is really the case : I always thought that
an orator would be more agreeable to the Roman people, and

---

[1] The words in brackets are regarded by all the best critics as the
production of some interpolator.

better approved, who should give, above all, as little indication as possible of artifice, and none at all of having studied Grecian literature. At the same time, when the Greeks undertook, professed, and executed such great things, when they offered to teach mankind how to penetrate the most obscure subjects, to live virtuously and to speak eloquently, I thought it the part of an irrational animal rather than a man not to pay them some degree of attention, and, if we can not venture to hear them openly, for fear of diminishing our authority with our own fellow-citizens, to catch their words at least by listening privately, and hearkening at a distance to what they stated; and thus I have acted, Catulus, and have gained a general notion of the arguments and subjects of all their writers."

XXXVII. "Really and truly," said Catulus, "you have steered your bark to the coasts of philosophy with the utmost caution, as if you had been approaching some rock of unlawful desire,[1] though this country has never despised philosophy. For Italy was formerly full of Pythagoreans, at the time when part of this country was called Great Greece[2] (whence some report that Numa Pompilius, one of our kings, was a Pythagorean, though he lived many years before the time of Pythagoras; for which reason he is to be accounted the greater man, as he had the wisdom and knowledge to regulate our state almost two centuries before the Greeks knew that it had arisen in the world); and certainly this country never produced men more renowned for glorious actions, or of greater gravity and authority, or possessed of more polite learning than Publius Africanus, Caius Lælius, and Lucius Furius, who always had about them publicly the most learned men from Greece. I have often heard them say that the Athenians had done what was very pleasing to them, and to many of the leading men in the city, in sending, when they dispatched embassadors to the senate about important concerns of their own, the three most illustrious philosophers of that age, Car-

---

[1] That the allusion is to the islands of the Sirens, who tried to allure Ulysses to listen to their song, the commentators have already observed. *Ellendt.*

[2] *Quum erat in hac gente Magna illa Græcia,* "when Great Greece was in (or among) this people." *In hac gente,* i. e., in Italis, among the Italians, or in Italy. *Ellendt.*

neades, Critolaus, and Diogenes; who, during their stay at Rome, were frequently heard lecturing by them and others. And when you had such authorities as these, Antonius, I wonder why you should, like Zethus in Pacuvius's play,[1] almost declare war against philosophy." "I have not by any means done so," replied Antonius, "for I have determined rather to philosophize, like Ennius's Neoptolemus, *a little, since to be absolutely a philosopher is not agreeable to me.* But my opinion, which I think I have clearly laid down, is this: I do not disapprove of such studies if they be but moderately pursued; but I think that the reputation of that kind of learning, and all suspicion of artifice, is prejudicial to the orator with those who have the decision of affairs; for it diminishes the authority of the speaker and the credit of his speech."

XXXVIII. " But that our conversation may return to the point from which it digressed, do you observe that of those three illustrious philosophers, who, as you said, came to Rome, one was Diogenes, who professed to teach the art of reasoning well, and distinguishing truth from falsehood, which he called by the Greek name διαλεκτική, or logic? In this art, if it be an art, there are no directions how truth may be discovered, but only how it may be judged. For every thing of which we speak we either affirm to be or not to be;[2] and if it be expressed absolutely, the logicians take it in hand to judge whether it be true or false; or, if it be expressed conditionally, and qualifications are added, they determine whether such qualifications are rightly added, and whether the conclusion of each syllogism is true; and at last they torment themselves with their own subtilties, and, after much disquisition, find out not only what they themselves can not resolve, but

---

[1] In one of the tragedies of Pacuvius were represented two brothers, Amphion and Zethus, the former fond of philosophy, music, and the refined arts, the other of a rougher disposition, addicted to war and despising science. To this story Horace also alludes, Ep. i., 18, 41:

Gratia sic fratrum geminorum Amphionis atque
Zethi, dissiluit, donec suspecta severo
Conticuit lyra. Fraternis cessisse putatur
Moribus Amphion. *B.*

[2] In this passage I adopt the correction, or rather restoration, of Ellendt, *Nam et omne, quod eloquimur, fit, ut id aut esse dicamus aut non esse.* All other modern editions for *fit* have *sic.*

even arguments, by which what they had before begun to resolve, or rather had almost made clear, is again involved in
obscurity. Here, then, that Stoic[1] can be of no assistance to
me, because he does not teach me how to find out what to
say; he is rather even an impediment to me; for he finds
many difficulties which he says can by no means be cleared,
and unites with them a kind of language that is not clear,
easy, and fluent, but poor, dry, succinct, and concise; and if
any one shall approve of such a style, he will approve it with
the acknowledgment that it is not suited to the orator. For
our mode of speaking is to be adapted to the ear of the multitude, to fascinate and excite their minds, and to prove matters that are not weighed in the scales of the goldsmith, but
in the balance, as it were, of popular opinion; we may therefore entirely dismiss an art which is too silent about the invention of arguments, and too full of words in pronouncing
judgment on them. That Critolaus, whom you mention as
having come hither with Diogenes, might, I fancy, have been
of more assistance to our studies, for he was out of the school
of that Aristotle from whose method I seem to you not greatly to differ. Between this Aristotle (of whom I have read,
as well that book in which he explains the rhetorical systems
of all who went before him, as those in which he gives us
some notions of his own on the art), between him, I say, and
the professed teachers of the art, there appeared to me to be
this difference: that he, with the same acuteness of intellect
with which he had penetrated the qualities and nature of
things throughout the universe, saw into every thing that per-
tained to the art of rhetoric, which he thought beneath him;
but they, who thought this art alone worthy of cultivation,
passed their whole lives in contemplating this one subject, not
with as much ability as he, but with constant practice in their
single pursuit, and greater devotion to it. As to Carneades,
that extraordinary force and variety of eloquence which he
possessed would be extremely desirable for us; a man who
never took up any argument in his disputations which he did
not prove; never attacked any argument that he did not overthrow. But this is too arduous an accomplishment to be expected from those who profess and teach rhetoric.

XXXIX. "If it were my desire that a person totally il-

---

[1] Diogenes, and other Stoics like him. *Proust.*

literate should be instructed in the art of speaking, I would willingly send him to these perpetual workers at the same employment, who hammer day and night on the same anvil, and who would put his literary food into his mouth, in the smallest pieces, minced as fine as possible, as nurses put theirs into the mouths of children. But if he were one who had had a liberal education, and some degree of practice, and seemed to have some acuteness of genius, I would instantly conduct him, not where a little brook of water was confined by itself, but to the source whence a whole flood gushed forth; to an instructor who would show him the seats and abodes, as it were, of every sort of arguments, and would illustrate them briefly, and define them in proper terms. For what point is there in which he can hesitate, who shall see that whatever is assumed in speaking, either to prove or to refute, is either derived from the peculiar force and nature of the subject itself, or borrowed from something foreign to it? From its own peculiar force: as when it is inquired, 'what the nature of a whole thing is,' or 'a part of it,' or 'what name it has,' or whatever belongs to the whole matter. From what is foreign to it: as when circumstances which are extrinsic, and not inherent in the nature of the thing, are enumerated in combination. If the inquiry regard the whole, its whole force is to be explained by a definition, thus: 'If the majesty of a state be its greatness and dignity, he is a traitor to its majesty who delivers up an army to the enemies of the Roman people, not he who delivers up him who has violated it into the power of the Roman people.' But if the question respect only a part, the matter must be managed by partition in this manner: 'Either the senate should have been obeyed concerning the safety of the republic, or some other authority should have been constituted, or he should have acted on his own judgment: to constitute another authority had been haughty; to act on his own judgment had been arrogant; he had therefore to obey the direction of the senate.' If we argue from a name, we may express ourselves like Carbo: 'If he be a consul who consults the good of his country, what else has Opimius done?' But if we argue from what is intimately connected with the subject, there are many sources of arguments and commonplaces; for we shall look to adjuncts, to general views, to particulars falling under general views, to things similar and dissimilar, contrary, consequential; to such as agree with the case, and are, as it were, forerunners of it, and such as are at variance with it; we shall investigate the causes of circumstances, and whatever has arisen from those causes; and shall notice cases that are stronger, or similar, or weaker.

XL. " From things closely relating to the subject arguments are drawn thus: 'If the utmost praise is to be attributed to filial duty, you ought to be moved when you see Quintus Metellus mourn so tenderly.' From general considerations, thus: 'If magistrates ought to be under the power of the Roman people, of what do you accuse Norbanus, whose tribuneship was subservient to the will of the state?' From particulars that fall under the general consideration, thus: 'If all who consult the interest of the public ought to be dear to us, certainly military commanders should be peculiarly dear, by whose conduct, courage, and exposure to danger we preserve our own safety and the dignity of the empire.' From similarity, thus: 'If wild beasts love their offspring, what affection ought we to feel for our children?' From dissimilarity, thus: 'If it be the character of barbarians to live as it were for a short season, our plans ought to have respect to perpetuity.' In both modes of comparison, from similarity as well as dissimilarity, examples are taken from the acts, sayings, and successes of others; and fictitious narratives may often be introduced. From contraries, arguments are drawn thus: 'If Gracchus acted in a detestable, Opimius has acted in a glorious manner.' From subsequent circumstances, thus: 'If he be slain with a weapon, and you, his enemy, are found on the very spot with a bloody sword, and nobody but you is seen there, and no one else had any reason to commit the act, and you were always of a daring character, what ground is there on which we can possibly doubt of your guilt?' From concurrent, antecedent, and repugnant circumstances, thus, as Crassus argued when he was quite a young man: 'Although, Carbo, you defended Opimius, this audience will not on that account esteem you a good citizen; for it is clear that you dissembled and had other views, because you often, in your harangues, deplored the fate of Tiberius Gracchus, because you were an accomplice in the death of Publius Africanus, because you proposed a law of such a nature in your tribuneship, because you have always dissented from good members of the state.' From the causes of things, thus : ' If you would abolish avarice, you must abolish the parent of it, luxury.' From whatever arises from those causes, thus : ' If we use the money in the treasury as well for the services of war as the ornaments of peace, let us take care of the public revenues.' Stronger, weaker, and parallel instances, we shall compare thus : from a stronger we shall argue in this way : ' If a good name be preferable to riches, and money is pursued with so much industry, with how much more exertion is glory to be sought?' From a weaker, thus :

> " Since merely for a small acquaintance' sake
> He takes this woman's death so nearly, what
> If he himself had loved? what would he feel
> For me, his father ? " [1]

" From a parallel case, thus : ' It is natural to the same character to be rapacious of the public money, and to be profuse of it to the public prejudice.' But instances borrowed from extraneous circumstances are such as are not supported by their own strength, but somewhat foreign : as, ' This is true; for Quintus Lutatius has affirmed it :' ' This is false; for an examination has been made :' ' This must of necessity follow; for I shall read the writings ;' on which head I spoke fully a little while ago. XLI. I have been as brief in the exemplification of these matters as their nature would permit. For as, if I wished to make known to any one a quantity of gold, that was buried in separate heaps, it ought to be sufficient if I told him the signs and marks of the places, with the knowledge of which he might dig for himself, and find what he wished with very little trouble, and without any mistake; so I wished to specify such marks, as it were, of arguments, as would let him who seeks them know where they are ; [2] what remains is to be brought out by industry and thought. What kind of arguments is most suitable to any particular kind of cause it requires no exquisite skill to prescribe, but

---

[1] Terence, Andr., i., 1, 83, Colman's translation.

[2] I follow Ellendt's text : *Sic has ego argumentorum volui notas quærenti demonstrare ubi sint.* Orellius and most other editors have *Sic has ego argumentorum novi notas, quæ illa mihi quærenti demonstrant,* "sententiâ perineptâ," as Ellendt observes ; for it was not what Antonius himself knew that was to be specified, but how he wished learners to be assisted.

merely moderate capacity to determine. For it is not now my design to set forth any system of rhetoric, but to communicate to men of eminent learning some hints drawn from my own experience. These commonplaces, therefore, being fixed in the mind and memory, and called forth on every subject proposed to be discussed, there will be nothing that can escape the orator, not merely in matters litigated in the forum, but in any department of eloquence whatever. But if he shall attain such success as to seem to be what he would wish to seem, and to affect the minds of those before whom he pleads in such a manner as to lead or rather force them in whatever direction he pleases, he will assuredly require nothing else to render him accomplished in oratory.

"We now see that it is by no means sufficient to find out what to say, unless we can handle it skillfully when we have found it. This treatment ought to be diversified, that he who listens may neither discover any artifice, nor be tired and satiated with uniformity. Whatever you advance should be laid down as a proposition, and you should show why it is so; and, from the same premises, you should sometimes form a conclusion, and sometimes leave it to be formed by the hearer, and make a transition to something else. Frequently, however, you need make no proposition, but show, by the reasoning which you shall use, what proposition might have been made. If you produce a comparison to any thing, you should first confirm what you offer as a comparison, and then apply to it the point in question. In general, you should shade the distinctive points of your arguments so that none of your hearers may count them; and that, while they appear clear as to matter, they may seem blended in your mode of speaking on them.

XLII. "I run over these matters cursorily, as addressing men of learning, and, being myself but half-learned, that we may at length arrive at matters of greater consequence. For there is nothing, Catulus, of more importance in speaking than that the hearer should be favorable to the speaker, and be himself so strongly moved that he may be influenced more by impulse and excitement of mind than by judgment or reflection. For mankind make far more determinations through hatred, or love, or desire, or anger, or grief, or joy, or hope, or fear, or error, or some other affection of mind, than from re-

gard to truth, or any settled maxim, or principle of right, or
judicial form, or adherence to the laws. Unless any thing
else, therefore, be agreeable to you, let us proceed to consider
these points."

"There seems," observed Catulus, "to be still some little
wanting to those matters which you have discussed, Antonius,
something that requires to be explained before you proceed to
what you propose." "What is it?" asked Antonius. "What
order," replied Catulus, "and arrangement of arguments, has
your approbation; for in that department you always seem a
god to me." "You may see how much of a god I am in that
respect, Catulus," rejoined Antonius, "for I assure you the
matter would never have come into my thoughts if I had not
been reminded of it; so that you may suppose I am generally
led by mere practice in speaking, or rather perhaps by chance,
to fix on that arrangement of matter by which I seem at times
to produce some effect. However, that very point which I,
because I had no thought of it, passed by as I should by a person unknown to me, is of such efficacy in oratory that nothing
is more conducive to victory; but yet you seem to me to have
required from me prematurely an account of the order and
disposition of the orator's material; for if I had placed all
his power in argumentation, and in proving his case from its
own inherent merits, it might be time to say something on the
order and arrangement of his arguments; but as three heads
were specified by me, and I have spoken on only one, it will
be proper, after I have attended to the other two, to consider,
last of all, about the general arrangement of a speech.

XLIII. "It contributes much to success in speaking that
the morals, principles, conduct, and lives of those who plead
causes, and of those for whom they plead, should be such as
to merit esteem, and that those of their adversaries should be
such as to deserve censure; and also that the minds of those
before whom the cause is pleaded should be moved as much as
possible to a favorable feeling, as well toward the speaker as
toward him for whom he speaks. The feelings of the hearers
are conciliated by a person's dignity, by his actions, by the
character of his life; particulars which can more easily be
adorned by eloquence if they really exist, than be invented
if they have no existence. But the qualities that attract
favor to the orator are a soft tone of voice, a countenance

expressive of modesty, a mild manner of speaking; so that if
he attacks any one with severity, he may seem to do so
unwillingly and from compulsion.   It is of peculiar advantage
that indications of good-nature, of liberality, of gentleness, of
piety, of grateful feelings, free from selfishness and avarice,
should appear in him; and every thing that characterizes men
of probity and humility, not acrimonious, nor pertinacious,
nor litigious, nor harsh, very much conciliates benevolence,
and alienates the affections from those in whom such qualities
are not apparent.   The contrary qualities to these, therefore,
are to be imputed to your opponents.   This mode of address
is extremely excellent in those causes in which the mind of
the judge can not well be inflamed by ardent and vehement
incitation; for energetic oratory is not always desirable, but
often smooth, submissive, gentle language, which gains much
favor for *rei*, or defendants, a term by which I designate
not only such as are accused, but all persons about whose
affairs there is any litigation; for in that sense people formerly
used the word.   To describe the character of your clients in
your speeches, therefore, as just, full of integrity, religious,
unpresuming, and patient of injuries, has an extraordinary
effect; and such a description, either in the commencement, or
in your statement of facts, or in the peroration, has so much
influence, if it is agreeably and judiciously managed, that it
often prevails more than the merits of the cause.   Such
influence, indeed, is produced by a certain feeling and art in
speaking, that the speech seems to represent, as it were, the
character of the speaker; for, by adopting a peculiar mode of
thought and expression, united with action that is gentle and
indicative of amiableness, such an effect is produced that the
speaker seems to be a man of probity, integrity, and virtue.

XLIV. "To this mode of speaking we may subjoin the
opposite method, which moves the minds of the judges by
very different means, and impels them to hate, or love, or
envy, or benevolence, or fear, or hope, or desire, or abhorrence, or joy, or grief, or pity, or severity; or leads them to
whatever feelings resemble and are allied to these and
similar emotions of mind.   It is desirable, too, for the orator,
that the judges may voluntarily bring to the hearing of the
cause some feelings in their breasts favorable to the object
of the speaker.   For it is easier, as they say, to increase the

speed of him that is already running, than to excite to motion him that is torpid. But if such shall not be the case, or be somewhat doubtful, then, as a careful physician, before he proceeds to administer any medicine to a patient, must not only understand the disease of him whom he would cure, but also his habit and constitution of body when in health, so I, for my part, when I undertake a cause of such doubt and importance as is likely to excite the feelings of the judges, employ all my sagacity on the care and consideration of ascertaining, as skillfully as I can, what their sentiments and opinions are, what they expect, to which side they incline, and to what conclusion they are likely to be led, with the least difficulty, by the force of oratory. If they yield themselves up, and, as I said before, voluntarily incline and preponderate to the side to which I would impel them, I embrace what is offered, and turn my sails to that quarter from whence any breath of wind is perceived to blow. But if the judge is unbiased, and free from all passion, it is a work of greater difficulty; for every feeling must then be moved by the power of oratory, without any assistance from nature. But so great are the powers of that which was rightly termed by a good poet,[1]

"Incliner of the soul, and queen of all things,"

Eloquence, that it can not only make him upright who is biased, or bias him who is steadfast, but can, like an able and resolute commander, lead even him captive who resists and opposes.

XLV. "These are the points about which Crassus just now jocosely questioned me when he said that I treated them divinely, and praised what I did as being meritoriously done in the causes of Manius Aquilius,[2] Caius Norbanus,[3] and some others; but really, Crassus, when such arts are adopted by you in pleading, I used to feel terrified; such power of mind, such impetuosity, such passion, is expressed in your eyes, your countenance, your gesture, and even in your very finger;[4] such a torrent is there of the most emphatic and best chosen words,

[1] Pacuvius in his Hermione, as appears from Nonius v. *flexanima.* The thought is borrowed from Euripides, Hec., 816. *Ellendt.*
[2] See note on c. 28.   [3] See note on c. 47.
[4] The forefinger, which Crassus is said to have pointed with wonderful effect. See Quintilian, xi., 3, 94.

such noble thoughts, so just, so new, so free from all disguise or puerile embellishment, that you seem not only to me to fire the judge, but to be yourself on fire. Nor is it possible that the judge should feel concern, or hate, or envy, or fear in any degree, or that he should be moved to compassion and tears, unless all these sensations which the orator would awaken in the judge shall appear to be deeply felt and experienced by the orator himself. For if a counterfeit passion were to be assumed, and if there were nothing in a speech of that kind but what was false and simulated, still greater art would perhaps be necessary. What is the case with you, however, Crassus, or with others, I do not know; as to myself, there is no reason why I should say what is false to men of your great good sense and friendship for me—I never yet, upon my honor, tried to excite sorrow, or compassion, or envy, or hatred, when speaking before a court of judicature, but I myself, in rousing the judges, was affected with the very same sensations that I wished to produce in them. For it is not easy to cause the judge to be angry with him with whom you desire him to be angry, if you yourself appear to take the matter coolly; or to make him hate him whom you wish him to hate, unless he first see you burning with hatred; nor will he be moved to pity unless you give him plain indications of your own acute feelings by your expressions, sentiments, tone of voice, look, and, finally, by sympathetic tears; for as no fuel is so combustible as to kindle without the application of fire, so no disposition of mind is so susceptible of the impressions of the orator as to be animated to strong feeling unless he himself approach it full of inflammation and ardor.

XLVI. "And that it may not appear to you extraordinary and astonishing that a man should so often be angry, so often grieve, and be so often excited by every passion of the mind, especially in other men's concerns, there is such force, let me assure you, in those thoughts and sentiments which you apply, handle, and discuss in speaking, that there is no occasion for simulation or deceit; for the very nature of the language which is adopted to move the passions of others moves the orator himself in a greater degree than any one of those who listen to him. That we may not be surprised, too, that this happens in causes, in criminal trials, in the danger of our friends, and before a multitude in the city and in the forum,

where not only our reputation for ability is at stake (for that
might be a slight consideration; although, when you have professed to accomplish what few can do, it is not wholly to be
neglected), but where other things of greater importance are
concerned, fidelity, duty to our clients, and earnestness in dis-
charging that duty; we are so much moved by such considerations, that even while we defend the merest strangers we can
not regard them as strangers, if we wish to be thought honest
men ourselves.   But, as I said, that this may not appear surprising in us, what can be more fictitious than poetry, than
theatrical representations, than the argument of a play?   Yet
on the stage I myself have often observed the eyes of the actor,
through his mask, appear inflamed with fury while he was repeating these verses,[1]

> "Have you, then, dared to separate him from you,
>   Or enter Salamis without your brother?
>   And dreaded not your father's countenance?"

He never uttered the word ' countenance' but Telamon seemed to me to be distracted with rage and grief for his son.   And
how, lowering his voice to a tone of sorrow, did he appear to
weep and bewail, as he exclaimed,

> "Whom childless now in the decline of life
>   You have afflicted, and bereaved, and killed;
>   Regardless of your brother's death, regardless
>   Of his young son intrusted to your keeping!"

And if even the player who pronounced these verses every day
could not yet pronounce them efficiently without a feeling of
real grief, can you suppose that Pacuvius, when he wrote
them, was in a cool and tranquil state of mind?   Such could
not be the case; for I have often heard that no man can be a
good poet (as they say is left recorded in the writings of both
Democritus and Plato) without ardor of imagination, and the
excitement of something similar to phrensy.

XLVII.   "Do not therefore imagine that I, who had no
desire to imitate or represent the calamities or fictitious sorrows of the heroes of antiquity in my speech, and was no actor
of a foreign and personated part, but a supporter of my own,

---

[1] *Spondalia.* For this word I have given " verses."   " That it is corrupt," says Ellendt, " all the commentators agree." Hermann, Opusc.,
i., p. 304, conjectures *è spondâ illâ,* " from that couch," on which he supposes Telamon may have been reclining.

when Manius Aquilius, by my efforts, was to be maintained
in his rights as a citizen, did that which I did in the peroration of that cause, without a strong feeling. For when I saw
him whom I remembered to have been consul, and, as a general honored by the senate, to have marched up to the Capitol with the pomp of an ovation, afflicted, dejected, sorrow-
ful, reduced to the last extremity of danger, I no sooner attempted to excite compassion in others than I was myself
moved with compassion. I observed, indeed, that the judges
were wonderfully moved when I brought forward the sorrow-
ful old man habited in mourning, and did what you, Crassus,
commend, not with art (of which I know not what to say),
but with great concern and emotion of mind, so that I tore
open his garment and showed his scars ; when Caius Marius,
who was present and sat by, heightened the sorrow expressed
in my speech by his tears ; and when I, frequently calling
upon him, recommended his colleague to his protection, and
invoked him as an advocate to defend the common fortune of
commanders. This excitement of compassion, this adjuration
of all gods and men, of citizens and allies, was not unaccom-
panied by my tears and extreme commiseration on my part ;
and if, from all the expressions which I then used, real concern of my own had been absent, my speech would not only
have failed to excite commiseration, but would have even deserved ridicule. I therefore instruct you in these particulars,
Sulpicius, I that am, forsooth, so skillful and so learned a master, showing you how, in speaking, you may be angry, and sor-
rowful, and weep.

"Though why, indeed, should I teach you this, who, in accusing my quæstor and companion in office,[1] raised so fierce

[1] Quintus Servilius Cæpio, in his consulship, says Henrichsen, had
embezzled a large portion of the gold taken at the capture of Toulouse,
A.U.C. 648. In the following year, when, through the disagreement between him and the consul Manlius, the Romans were defeated in two
battles by the Cimbri, his property was confiscated, and his command
taken from him. Some years afterward, A.U.C. 659, when Crassus and
Scævola were consuls, Caius Norbanus, then tribune of the people,
brought Cæpio to trial, as it appears, for the embezzlement of the gold
at Toulouse, and for exciting sedition in the city. The senate, to whom
Cæpio, in his consulship, had tried to restore the judicial power, exerted
themselves strongly in his behalf; but Norbanus, after exciting a great
tumult, carried his point by force, and Cæpio went into banishment at
Smyrna.

a flame, not only by your speech, but much more by your vehemence, passion, and fiery spirit, that I could scarce venture
to approach to extinguish it? For you had in that cause every thing in your favor; you brought before the judges violence, flight, pelting with stones, the cruel exercise of the tribu-
nitian power in the grievous and miserable calamity of Cæpio;
it also appeared that Marcus Æmilius, the first man, not only
in the senate, but in the city, had been struck with one of the
stones; and nobody could deny that Lucius Cotta and Titus
Didius, when they would have interposed their negative upon
the passing of the law, had been driven in a tumultuous manner from the temple.

XLVIII. There was also this circumstance in your favor,
that you, being merely a youth, were thought to make these
complaints on behalf of the commonwealth with the utmost
propriety; I, a man of censorian rank, was thought hardly in
a condition to appear with any honor in defense of a seditious
citizen, a man who had been unrelenting at the calamity of
a consular person. The judges were citizens of the highest
character; the forum was crowded with respectable people,
so that scarcely even a slight excuse was allowed me, although
I was to speak in defense of one who had been my quæstor.
In these circumstances why need I say that I had recourse
to some degree of art? I will state how I acted, and, if you
please, you may place my defense under some head of art. I
noticed, in connection, the natures, ill effects, and dangers of
every kind of sedition. I brought down my discourse on that
subject through all the changes of circumstances in our commonwealth; and I concluded by observing that, though all
seditions had ever been attended with troubles, yet that some
had been supported by justice, and almost by necessity. I
then dwelt on those topics which Crassus just now mentioned,
that neither could kings have been expelled from this city, nor
tribunes of the people have been created, nor the consular
power have so often been dismissed by votes of the common-
alty, nor the right of appeal, that patroness of the state and
guardian of our liberty, have been granted to the Roman people, without disagreement with the nobility; and if those seditions had been of advantage to the republic, it should not
immediately, if any commotion had been raised among the
people, be laid to the charge of Caius Norbanus as a heinous

crime or capital misdemeanor; but that, if it had ever been allowed to the people of Rome to appear justly provoked (and I showed that it had been often allowed), no occasion was ever more just than that of which I was speaking. I then gave another turn to my speech, and directed it to the condemnation of Cæpio's flight, and lamentation for the loss of the army. By this diversion I made the grief of those to flow afresh who were mourning for their friends, and re-excited the minds of the Roman knights before whom, as judges, the cause was being pleaded, to hatred toward Quintus Cæpio, from whom they were alienated on account of the right of judicature.[1]

XLIX. " But as soon as I perceived that I was in possession of the favor of the court, and that I had secured ground for defense, because I had both conciliated the good feeling of the people, whose rights I had maintained even in conjunction with sedition, and had brought over the whole feeling of the judges to our side of the question, either from their concern for the calamity of the public, or from grief or regret for their relations, or from their own individual aversion to Cæpio, I then began to intermix with this vehement and ardent style of oratory that other species of which I discoursed before, full of lenity and mildness; saying that I was contending for my companion in office, who, according to the custom of our ancestors, ought to stand in relation to me as one of my children, and for almost my whole reputation and fortunes; that nothing could possibly happen more dishonorable to my character, or more bitterly adapted to give pain to me, than if I, who was reputed to have been oftentimes the preservation of those who were entire strangers to me, but yet my fellow-citizens, should not be able to assist an officer of my own. I requested of the judges to make this concession to my age, to the honors which I had attained, to the actions which I had performed, if they saw that I was affected with a just and tender sorrow, and especially if they were sensible that in other causes I had asked every thing for my friends in peril, but never any thing for myself. Thus, in the whole of that defense and cause, the part which seemed to depend on art, the speaking on the Apuleian law, and explaining what it was to commit

---

[1] As Cæpio had tried to take it out of the hands of the knights, and to restore it to the senate.

treason, I skimmed and touched upon as briefly as possible.
But by the aid of these two parts of eloquence, to one of which
belongs the excitement of the passions, to the other recommendation to favor (parts not at all fully treated in the rules
in books on the art), was the whole of that cause conducted
by me; so that, in reviving the popular displeasure against
Cæpio, I appeared to be a person of the keenest acrimony;
and, in speaking of my behavior toward my friends, to be of
the most humane disposition. In this manner, rather by exciting the passions of the judges than by informing their understandings, was your accusation, Sulpicius, at that time overthrown by me."

L. "In good truth, Antonius," interposed Sulpicius, "you
recall these circumstances to my memory with justice, since
I never saw any thing slip out of any person's hands as that
cause then slipped out of mine. For whereas, as you observed, I had given you not a cause to plead, but a flame to
extinguish; what a commencement was it (immortal gods!)
that you made! What timidity was there! What distrust!
What a degree of hesitation and slowness of speech! But, as
soon as you had gained that by your exordium, which was
the only thing that the assembly allowed you as an excuse,
namely, that you were pleading for a man intimately connected with you, and your own quæstor, how quickly did you
secure your way to a fair audience! But lo! when I thought
that you had reaped no other benefit than that the hearers
would think they ought to excuse you for defending a pernicious citizen, on account of the ties of union betwixt you,
you began to proceed gradually and tacitly, while others had
as yet no suspicion of your designs, though I myself felt some
apprehension, to maintain in your defense that what had happened was not sedition in Norbanus, but resentment on the
part of the Roman people, resentment not excited unjustly,
but deservedly, and in conformity with their duty. In the
next place, what argument did you omit against Cæpio?
How did you confound all the circumstances of the case by
allusions to hatred, ill-will, and compassion? Nor was this
the case only in your defense, but even in regard to Scaurus
and my other witnesses, whose evidence you did not confute
by disproving it, but by having recourse to the same impetuosity of the people. When those circumstances were men-

tioned by you just now, I felt no desire for any rules of instruction; for the very demonstration of your methods of defense, as stated by yourself, I regard as no ordinary instruction." "But if you are so disposed," said Antonius, "I will tell you what maxims I adopt in speaking, and what I keep principally in view; for a long life and experience in important affairs have taught me to discern by what means the minds of men are to be moved.

LI. "The first thing I generally consider is whether the cause requires that the minds of the audience should be excited; for such fiery oratory is not to be exerted on trivial subjects, nor when the minds of men are so affected that we can do nothing by eloquence to influence their opinions, lest we be thought to deserve ridicule or dislike, if we either act tragedies about trifles or endeavor to pluck up what can not be moved.   For as the feelings on which we have to work in the minds of the judges, or whoever they may be before whom we may plead, are *love, hatred, anger, envy, pity, hope, joy, fear, anxiety,* we are sensible that *love* may be gained if you seem to advocate what is advantageous to the persons before whom you are speaking; or if you appear to exert yourself in behalf of good men, or at least for such as are good and serviceable to them; for the latter case more engages favor, the former, the defense of virtue, esteem; and if a hope of future advantage is proposed, it has a greater effect than the mention of past benefits.   You must endeavor to show that in the cause which you defend, either your dignity or advantage is concerned; and you should signify that he for whom you solicit their love has referred nothing to his own private benefit, and done nothing at all for his own sake; for dislike is felt for the selfish gains of individuals, while favor is shown to their desires to serve others.   But we must take care, while we are on this topic, not to appear to extol the merit and glory of those whom we would wish to be esteemed for their good deeds, too highly, as these qualities are usually the greatest objects of envy.   From these considerations, too, we shall learn how to draw *hatred* on our adversaries, and to avert it from ourselves and our friends.   The same means are to be used, also, either to excite or allay *anger;* for if you exaggerate every fact that is hurtful or disadvantageous to the audience, their hatred is excited; but if any thing of the kind is thrown out against men of worth, or against characters on whom no one ought to cast any reflection, or against the public, there is then produced, if not so violent a degree of hatred, at least an unfavorable feeling, or displeasure near akin to hatred. *Fear* is also inculcated either from people's own dangers or those of the public. Personal fear affects men more deeply; but that which is common to all is to be treated by the orator as having similar influence.[1]

LII. "Similar, or rather the same, is the case with regard to *hope, joy,* and *anxiety ;* but I know not whether the feeling of *envy* is not by far the most violent of all emotions ; nor does it require less power to suppress than to excite it. Men envy chiefly their equals or inferiors when they perceive themselves left behind, and are mortified that the others have outstripped them ; but there is often a strong unfavorable feeling toward superiors, which is the stronger if they are intolerably arrogant, and transgress the fair bounds of common justice through super-eminence in dignity or fortune. If such advantages are to be made instruments to kindle dislike,[2] the chief thing to be said is, 'that they are not the acquisitions of virtue, that they have been gained perhaps by vice and crime ; and that, however honorable or imposing they may appear, no merit was ever carried so high as the insolence of mankind and their contumelious disdain.' To allay envy, it may be observed, 'that such advantages have been gained by extreme toil and imminent perils ; that they have not been applied to the individual's own private benefit, but that of others ; that he himself, if he appear to have gained any glory, although it might not be an undue reward for danger, was not elated with it, but wholly set it aside and undervalued it ;' and such an effect must by all means be produced (since most men are envious, and it is a most common and prevalent vice, and envy is felt toward all super-eminent and flourishing fortune), that the opinion entertained of such characters be lowered, and that their fortunes, so excellent in people's imaginations, may appear mingled with labor and trouble.

"*Pity* is excited if he who hears can be induced to apply to

---

[1] Since public or common fear must affect individuals.
[2] *Quæ si inflammanda sunt.* An elegant mode of expression, for "si ad animos invidiâ inflammandos adhibenda sunt tanquam faces." *Ernesti.*

his own circumstances those unhappy particulars which are lamented in the case of others, particulars which they have either suffered or fear to suffer; and while he looks at another, to glance frequently at himself. Thus, as all the circumstances incident to human suffering are heard with concern, if they are pathetically represented, so virtue in affliction and humiliation is the most powerful of all objects of contemplation; and as that other department of eloquence which, by its recommendation of goodness, ought to give the picture of a virtuous man, should be in a gentle and (as I have often observed) a submissive strain, so this, which is adopted by the orator to effect a change in the minds of the audience, and to work upon them in every way, should be vehement and energetic.

LIII. "But there is a certain resemblance in these two kinds (one of which we would have to be gentle, the other vehement) that makes it difficult to distinguish them. For something of that lenity with which we conciliate the affections of an audience ought to mingle with the ardor with which we awaken their passions; and something of this ardor should occasionally communicate a warmth to our gentleness of language; nor is there any species of eloquence better tempered than that in which the asperity of contention in the orator is mitigated by his humanity, or in which the relaxed tone of lenity is sustained by a becoming gravity and energy. But in both modes of speaking, as well that in which spirit and force are required as that which is brought down to ordinary life and manners, the beginning should be slow, but the sequel full and diffuse.[1] For you must not spring at once into the pathetic portion of your speech, as it forms no part of the question, and men are first desirous to learn the very point that is to come under their judgment; nor, when you have entered upon that track, are you suddenly to diverge from it; for you are not to suppose that as an argument is understood as soon as it is stated, and a second and a third are then desired, so you can with the same ease move compassion, or envy, or anger, as soon as you make the attempt.[2] Reason itself confirms

[1] *Exitus spissi et producti esse debent.* "Non abrupti, sed lenti." *Ellendt.* "Vehementes et longiores." *Proust.*
[2] *Simul atque intuleris.* Rem sc. "As soon as you have introduced the subject."

an argument which fixes itself in the mind as soon as it is delivered ; but that sort of eloquence does not aim at instructing the judge, but rather at agitating his mind by excessive emotion, which no one can produce unless by fullness and variety, and even copiousness of language, and a proportionate energy of delivery. Those, therefore, who speak either with brevity, or in a low, submissive strain, may indeed inform the judge, but can never move him, an effect on which success altogether depends.

"It is clear that the ability of arguing on every subject on both sides of the question is drawn from the same considerations. But we must resist the force of an argument, either by refuting those things which are assumed in support of it, or by showing that the conclusion which our opponents would draw can not be deduced from the premises, or possibly follow from them ; or, if you can not refute an argument in this manner, you must bring something against it of greater or equal weight. But whatever is delivered with gentleness to conciliate favor, or with vehemence to excite emotion, is to be obviated[1] by moving contrary feelings, so that benevolence may be eradicated by hatred, and compassion be dispelled by jealousy.

LIV. "A jocose manner, too, and strokes of wit, give pleasure to an audience, and are often of great advantage to the speaker; qualities which, even if every thing else can be taught by art, are certainly peculiar gifts of nature, and require no aid from instruction. In that department you, Cæsar, in my opinion, far excel all other men ; on which account you can better bear me testimony, either that there is no art in wit, or, if there be any, you will best instruct us in it." "I indeed," says Cæsar, "think that a man who is not destitute of polite learning can discourse upon any subject more wittily than upon wit itself. Accordingly, when I met with some Greek books entitled ' On Jests,' I conceived some hope that I might learn something from them. I found, it is true, many laughable and witty sayings of the Greeks ; for those of Sicily excel in that way, as well as the Rhodians and Byzantines, but, above all, the people of Attica. But they who have at-

---

[1] Orellius's text has *inferenda ;* many others, *efferenda.* There have been various conjectures offered, as *infirmanda, evertenda, elevanda, infringenda.* The reader may take his choice.

tempted to deliver rules and principles on that subject, have
shown themselves so extremely foolish, that nothing else in
them has excited laughter but their folly.   This talent, therefore, appears to me incapable of being communicated by teaching.   As there are two kinds of wit, one running regularly
through a whole speech, the other pointed and concise; the
ancients denominated the former humor,[1] the latter jesting.
Each sort has but a light name, and justly;[2] for it is altogether but a light thing to raise a laugh.   However, as you
observe, Antonius, I have seen advantageous effects produced
in pleadings by the aid of wit and humor; but, as in the former kind, I mean humor that runs through a speech, no aid
from art is required (for Nature forms and produces men to
be facetious mimics or story-tellers; their look, and voice, and
mode of expression assisting their conceptions); so likewise
in the other, that of occasional facetiousness, what room is
there for art, when the joke ought to be uttered, and fixed in
the mind of the hearer, before it appears possible to have been
conceived?   For what assistance could my brother here receive from art, when, being asked by Philippus why he barked
so, he replied, *Because he saw a thief*?   Or what aid could
Crassus have received in that whole speech which he delivered before the centumviri, in opposition to Scævola, or when
he pleaded for Cneius Plancus against the accusation of Brutus?   For that talent which you, Antonius, attribute to me,
must be allowed to Crassus by the confession of all mankind;
since hardly any person can be found besides him eminent in
both these kinds of wit, that which runs through a continued
discourse, and that which consists in smartness and occasional
jokes.   His whole defense in the cause of Curius, in opposition to Scævola, was redundant with a certain pleasantry and
humor; but of those sharp short jests it had none; for he
was tender of the dignity of his opponent, and in that respect
maintained his own; though it is extremely difficult for men
of wit and facetiousness to preserve a regard to persons and
times, and to suppress what occurs to them when it may be
expressed with most pungent effect.   Accordingly, some jesters put a humorous interpretation upon the well-known words

---

[1] *Cavillatio.*   Ironical or satirical humor seems to be meant.
[2] *Quippe; leve enim,* etc.   *Quippe* is equivalent to the Greek εἰκότως.
Ellendt.

of Ennius; for he said, as they observe, *That a wise man can more easily keep in flame while his mouth is on fire, than withhold ' bona dicta,' good words;* and they say that *good words* mean *witty sayings;* for sayings are called *dicta* by an appropriate term.

LV. " But as Crassus forbore from such jests in his speech against Scævola, and sported throughout that cause and discussion with that other species of humor in which there are no stings of sarcasm; so in that against Brutus, whom he hated, and thought deserving of insult, he fought with both kinds of wit.   How many severe things did he say about the baths which Brutus had lately sold? how many on the loss of his paternal estate?   And they were concise; as when Brutus, speaking of himself, said *that he sweated without cause.   ' No wonder that you sweat,'* said Crassus, *'for you are just turned out of the baths.'*   There were innumerable things of this kind in the speech, but his continuous vein of pleasantry was not less amusing; for when Brutus had called up two readers, and had given to one the speech of Crassus upon the colony of Narbonne, to the other that on the Servilian law, to read, and had compared together the contradictory sections on public affairs contained in each, our friend very facetiously gave the three books of Brutus's father, written on the civil law, to three different persons to read.   Out of the first book was read this sentence, ' It happened by chance that we were on my estate at Privernum.'   On which clause Crassus made this observation, *' Brutus, your father testifies that he left you an estate at Privernum.'*   Again, out of the second book, ' My son Marcus and I were at my Alban villa;' when Crassus remarked, *' This wise man, who was justly ranked among the wisest in our city, had evidently some foreknowledge of this spendthrift's character, and was afraid that, when he came to have nothing, it might be imagined that nothing was left him.'*   Afterward out of the third book, with which the author concluded his work (for that number of books, as I have heard Scævola say, are the genuine compositions of Brutus), ' It chanced that my son Marcus and myself were sitting in my villa near Tibur;' when Crassus exclaimed, *' Where are those estates now, Brutus, that your father left you, as recorded in his public commentaries?   But if he had not seen you arrived at the age of puberty, he would have composed a fourth book, and left it in*

writing that he talked with his son in his own baths.' Who does
not acknowledge, now, that Brutus was not less confuted by
this humor, these comic jests, than by that tragic tone which
the same orator adopted, when by accident, during the hearing of the same cause, the funeral procession of the old lady
Junia passed by? Ye immortal gods! what force and energy
was that with which he spoke! how unexpected! how sudden! when, casting his eyes that way, with his whole gesture
directed toward Brutus, with the utmost gravity and rapidity
of expression, he exclaimed, ' *Brutus, why do you sit still?
What would you have that old lady communicate to your father?
What to all those whose statues you see carried by? What to
your other ancestors? What to Lucius Brutus, who freed this
people from legal tyranny? What shall she say that you are doing? What business, what glory, what virtue shall she say that
you are pursuing? That you are engaged in increasing your patrimony? But that is no characteristic of nobility. Yet suppose
it were; you have none left to increase; your extravagance has
squandered the whole of it. That you are studying the civil law?
That was your father's pursuit; but she will relate that when you
sold your house, you did not even among the movables[1] reserve the
chair from which your father answered his clients. That you are
applying to the military art? You who have never seen a camp.
Or to eloquence? But no portion of eloquence dwells in you;
and such power of voice and tongue as you have, you have devoted
to the infamous trade of a common informer. Dare you even behold the light? Or look this assembly in the face? Dare you
present yourself in the forum, in the city, in the public assembly of
the citizens? Do you not fear even that dead corpse, and those
very images of your ancestors, you who have not only left yourself
no room for the imitation of their virtues, but none in which you
can place their statues?'*

LVI. "This is in a tragic and sublime strain of language;
but you all recollect instances without number of facetiousness and polite humor in one speech; for never was there
a more vehement dispute on any occasion, or an oration of
greater power delivered before the people, than that of Cras-

---

[1] *Ne in rutis quidem et cœsis. Ruta* were such things as could be removed from houses and other premises without pulling down or dama-
ging any portion of them; *cœsa*, as Proust remarks, refers to the cutting
down of trees.

sus lately in his censorship, in opposition to his colleague, nor one better seasoned with wit and humor. I agree with you, therefore, Antonius, in both points, that jesting is often of great advantage in speaking, and that it can not be taught by any rules of art. But I am astonished that you should attribute so much power to me in that way, and not assign to Crassus the palm of pre-eminence in this as in other departments of eloquence." "I should have done so," said Antonius, "if I had not sometimes envied Crassus a little in this respect; for to be ever so facetious and witty is not of itself an extraordinary subject of envy; but, when you are the most graceful and polite of speakers, to be, and to be thought, at the same time, the most grave and dignified of men, a distinction which has been granted to Crassus alone, seems to me almost unendurable." Crassus having smiled at this, Antonius said, "But, Julius, while you denied that art had any thing to do with facetiousness, you brought to our notice something that seemed worthy of precept; for you said that regard ought to be paid to persons, times, and circumstances, that jesting might not detract from dignity; a rule which is particularly observed by Crassus. But this rule only directs that jokes should be suppressed when there is no fair occasion for them; what we desire to know is, how we may use them when there is occasion; as against an adversary, especially if his folly be open to attack, or against a foolish, covetous, trifling witness, if the audience seem disposed to listen patiently. Those sayings are more likely to be approved which we utter on provocation, than those which we utter when we begin an attack; for the quickness of wit, which is shown in answering, is more remarkable, and to reply is thought allowable, as being natural to the human temper; since it is presumed that we should have remained quiet if we had not been attacked; as in that very speech to which you alluded scarcely any thing was said by our friend Crassus here, any thing at least that was at all humorous, which he did not utter in reply, and on provocation. For there was so much gravity and authority in Domitius,[1] that the objections which came from him seem-

---

[1] Cneius Domitius Ahenobarbus, in his tribuneship, A.U.C. 651, was hostile to the pontifices, because they had not chosen him in the place of his father, and proposed a law that those who were chosen by the pontifices into their body should not be appointed till their choice was

ed more likely to be enfeebled by jests than broken by arguments."

LVII. Sulpicius soon after said, "Shall we, then, suffer Cæsar, who, though he allows wit to Crassus, is yet himself far more intent on acquiring a character for it, to exempt himself from explaining to us the whole subject of humor, what is the nature of it, and from whence derived; especially as he owns that there is so much efficacy and advantage in wit and jesting?" "What if I agree with Antonius," rejoined Cæsar, "in thinking that art has no concern with wit?" As Sulpicius made no remark, "As if," said Crassus, "art could at all assist in acquiring those talents of which Antonius has been so long speaking. There is a certain observation to be paid, as he remarked, to those particulars which are most effective in oratory; but if such observation could make men eloquent, who would not be so? For who could not learn these particulars, if not with ease, at least in some way? But I think that of such precepts, the use and advantage is, not that we may be directed by art to find out what we are to say, but that we may either feel certain as to what we attain by natural parts, by study, or by exercise, that it is right, or understand that it is wrong, having been instructed to what rule the several particulars are to be referred. I, therefore, also join in the petition to you, Cæsar, that you would, if it is agreeable to you, tell us what you think on jocoseness in general, lest, by accident, any part of eloquence, since that is your object, should appear to have been passed over in so learned an assembly and such a studied conversation." "Well, then, Crassus," replied Cæsar, "since you require payment from a guest, I will, by refusing it, furnish you with a pretext for refusing to entertain us again; though I am often astonished at the impudence of those who act upon the stage while Roscius is a spectator of their attitudes; for who can make the least motion without Roscius seeing his imperfections? So I shall now have to speak first on wit in the hearing of Crassus, and to teach like a swine,[1] as they say, that orator of whom Catulus said, when he heard him lately, *That other speakers ought*

sanctioned by the people. Vell. Pat., ii., 12; Suet., Ner., 2; Cic., Rull., ii., 7. He had some ability in speaking, but was not numbered among eminent orators. Cic., Brut., 45. *Henrichsen.*

[1] An allusion to the proverb *Sus Minervam.*

to be fed upon hay."[1] "Ah !" said Crassus, "Catulus was joking, especially as he speaks himself in such a manner that he seems to deserve to be fed on ambrosia. But let us hear you, Cæsar, that we may afterward return to the remainder of the discourse of Antonius." "There is little remaining for me to say," replied Antonius; "but as I am wearied with the labor and the length of what I have said, I shall repose during the discourse of Cæsar as in some opportune place of entertainment." LVIII. "But," said Cæsar, "you will not pronounce my entertainment very liberal; for as soon as you have tasted a little I shall thrust you out, and turn you into the road again. However, not to detain you any longer, I will deliver my sentiments very briefly on this department of eloquence in general.

"Concerning laughter, there are five things which are subjects of consideration : one, 'What it is ;' another, 'Whence it originates ;' a third, 'Whether it becomes the orator to wish to excite laughter ;' a fourth, 'To what degree ;' a fifth, 'What are the several kinds of the *ridiculous ?*' As to the first, 'What laughter itself is,' by what means it is excited, where it lies, how it arises, and bursts forth so suddenly that we are unable, though we desire, to restrain it, and how it affects at once the sides, the face, the veins, the countenance, the eyes, let Democritus consider; for all this has nothing to do with my remarks, and if it had to do with them, I should not be ashamed to say that I am ignorant of that which not even they understand who profess to explain it. But the seat and as it were province of what is laughed at (for that is the next point of inquiry), lies in a certain offensiveness and deformity ; for those sayings are laughed at solely or chiefly which point out and designate something offensive in an inoffensive manner. But, to come to the third point, it certainly becomes the orator to excite laughter ; either because mirth itself attracts favor to him by whom it is raised ; or because all admire wit, which is often comprised in a single word, especially in him who replies, and sometimes in him who attacks ; or because it overthrows the adversary, or hampers him, or makes light of him, or discourages, or refutes him ; or because it proves the orator himself to be a man of taste, or learning, or polish ; but

---

[1] He signified that other pleaders were mere brute animals in comparison with Crassus, and therefore to be fed upon hay. *Turnebus.*

chiefly because it mitigates and relaxes gravity and severity, and often, by a joke or a laugh, breaks the force of offensive remarks, which can not easily be overthrown by arguments. But to what degree the laughable should be carried by the orator requires very diligent consideration; a point which we placed as the fourth subject of inquiry; for neither great vice, such as is united with crime, nor great misery, is a subject for ridicule and laughter; since people will have those guilty of enormous crimes attacked with more forcible weapons than ridicule; and do not like the miserable to be derided, unless perhaps when they are insolent; and you must be considerate, too, of the feelings of mankind, lest you rashly speak against those who are personally beloved.

LIX. "Such is the caution that must be principally observed in joking. Those subjects accordingly are most readily jested upon which are neither provocative of violent aversion nor of extreme compassion. All matter for ridicule is therefore found to lie in such defects as are to be observed in the characters of men not in universal esteem, nor in calamitous circumstances, and who do not appear deserving to be dragged to punishment for their crimes; such topics nicely managed create laughter. In deformity, also, and bodily defects, is found fair enough matter for ridicule; but we have to ask the same question here as is asked on other points, 'How far the ridicule may be carried?' In this respect it is not only directed that the orator should say nothing impertinently, but also that, even if he can say any thing very ridiculously, he should avoid both errors, lest his jokes become either buffoonery or mimicry; qualities of which we shall better understand the nature when we come to consider the different species of *the ridiculous.*

"There are two sorts of jokes, one of which is excited by things, the other by words. By things, whenever any matter is told in the way of a story; as you, Crassus, formerly stated in a speech against Memmius,[1] *That he had eaten a piece of Largius's arm,* because he had had a quarrel with him at Tarracina about a courtesan; it was a witty story, but wholly of your own invention. You added this particular, that throughout Tarracina these letters were inscribed on every wall, **M M,**

---

[1] The same that is mentioned by Sallust as having accused Calpurnius Bestia.

L L L; and that when you inquired what they meant, an old man of the town replied, *Mordacious Memmius Lacerates Largius's Limb.*[1] You perceive clearly how facetious this mode of joking may be, how elegant, how suitable to an orator; whether you have any true story to tell (which, however, must be interspersed with fictitious circumstances), or whether you merely invent. The excellence of such jesting is, that you can describe things as occurring in such a way, that the manners, the language, and every look of the person of whom you speak, may be represented, so that the occurrence may seem to the audience to pass and take place at the very time when you address them. Another kind of jest taken from things is that which is derived from a depraved sort of imitation, or mimicry; as when Crassus also exclaimed, *By your nobility, by your family*, what else was there at which the assembly could laugh but that mimicry of look and tone? But when he said, *by your statues*, and added something of gesture by extending his arm, we all laughed immoderately.[2] Of this species is Roscius's imitation of an old man; when he says,

"'For you, my Antipho, I plant these trees,'[3]

it is old age itself that seems to speak while I listen to him. But all this department of ridicule is of such a nature that it must be attempted with the greatest caution. For if the imitation is too extravagant, it becomes, like indecency, the part of players in pantomine and farce; the orator should be moderate in imitation, that the audience may conceive more than they can see represented by him; he ought also to give proof of ingenuousness and modesty, by avoiding every thing offensive or unbecoming in word or act.

LX. "These, therefore, are the two kinds of the ridiculous which is drawn from things; and they suit well with continuous pieces of humor, in which the manners of mankind are so described and expressed that, either by means of some nar-

---

[1] *Lacerat Lacertum Largi Mordax Memmius.* The writer of the article "Memmius" in Dr. Smith's Biog. Dict. thinks that Memmius had from some cause the nickname of *Mordax*. The story of his having eaten or bitten Largius's arm appears, from what Cicero says, to have been a mere invention of Crassus. We do not half understand the joke.

[2] This jest is from a speech of Crassus against Domitius. The *gens Domitia*, a family of great nobility, had produced many patricians remarkable as well for other vices as for vanity. *Ellendt.*

[3] These words are from some play now lost.

rative, their character is exactly understood, or, by throwing
in a little mimicry, they may be convicted of some impro-
priety remarkable enough for ridicule. But in *words*, the
ridiculous is that which is excited by the point of a particular
expression or thought; but as, in the former kind, both in
narration and imitation, all resemblance to the players of pantomime should be avoided, so, in this, all scurrilous buffoonery
is to be studiously shunned by the orator. How, then, shall
we distinguish from Crassus, from Catulus, and from others,
your acquaintance Granius, or my friend Vargula? No proper distinction really occurs to me; for they are both witty;
no man has more of verbal witticism than Granius. The first
point to be observed, however, is, I think, that we should not
fancy ourselves obliged to utter a jest whenever one may be
uttered. A very little witness was produced. *May I question him?* says Philippus. The judge who presided,[1] being in
a hurry, replied, *Yes, if he is short. You shall have no fault
to find,* said Philippus, *for I shall question him very short.*
This was ridiculous enough; but Lucius Aurifex was sitting
as judge in the cause, who was shorter than the witness himself; so that all the laughter was turned upon the judge, and
hence the joke appeared scurrilous. Those good things, therefore, which hit those whom you do not mean to hit, however
witty they are, are yet in their nature scurrilous; as when Appius, who would be thought witty—and indeed is so, but
sometimes slides into this fault of scurrility—said to Caius
Sextius, an acquaintance of mine, who is blind of an eye, *I
will sup with you to-night, for I see that there is a vacancy for one.*
This was a scurrilous joke, both because he attacked Sextius
without provocation, and said what was equally applicable to
all one-eyed persons. Such jokes, as they are thought premeditated, excite less laughter; but the reply of Sextius was
excellent and extempore: *Wash your hands,*[2] said he, *and
come to supper.* A regard, therefore, to proper times, moderation and forbearance in jesting, and a limitation in the number of jokes, will distinguish the orator from the buffoon; and

---

[1] *Quæsitor.* The magistrate who presided at a *quæstio capitalis*,
whether the prætor or any other. See Cic., Verr., i., 10; Vatin., 14;
Sall., Jug., 40. *Henrichsen.*

[2] Whether the joke was directed against him as being unclean, or as
being dishonest, is uncertain. *Ellendt.*

the circumstance, besides, that we joke with an object, not that we may appear to be jesters, but that we may gain some advantage, while they joke all day without any purpose whatever. For what did Vargula gain by saying, when Aulus Sempronius, then a candidate for office, and his brother Marcus, saluted him, *Boy, drive away the flies ?* His aim was to raise a laugh, which is, in my opinion, a very poor effect of wit. The proper season, then, for jesting, we must determine by our own prudence and judgment; in the exercise of which I wish that we had some body of rules to direct us; but nature is the sovereign guide.

LXI. "Let us now consider briefly the sorts of jests that chiefly excite laughter. Let this, then, be our first division, that whatever is expressed wittily, consists sometimes in a thought, sometimes in the mere language, but that men are most delighted with a joke when the laugh is raised by the thought and the language in conjunction. But remember this, that whatever topics I shall touch upon, from which ridicule may be drawn, from almost the same topics serious thoughts may be derived : there is only this difference, that seriousness is used on dignified subjects with gravity, joking on such as are in some degree unbecoming, and as it were grotesque; for instance, we may with the very same words commend a thrifty servant, and jest upon one that is extravagant. That old saying of Nero[1] about a thieving servant is humorous enough, *That he was the only one from whom nothing in the house was sealed or locked up;* a thing which is not only said of a good servant, but in the very same words. From the same sources spring all kinds of sayings. What his mother said to Spurius Carvilius, who halted grievously from a wound received in the public service, and was on that account ashamed to go out of doors, *Go, my Spurius, that as often as you take a step you may be reminded of your merits,* was a noble and serious thought; but what Glaucia said to Calvinus, when he limped, *Where is the old proverb—does he claudicate ? no; but he clodicates,*[2] is ridiculous; and yet both are derived

---

[1] Probably taken from the apophthegms of Cato, and probably, also, a saying of Caius Claudius Nero, who was consul with Marcus Livius, A.U.C. 547, and defeated Hannibal at Sena. Liv., xxvii., 34. *Ellendt.*

[2] The original is, *Num claudicat? at hic clodicat.* "What, is he lame ? No; but he favors Clodius." The reader easily sees that the

from what may be observed with regard to lameness. *What is more ignave than this Nœvius?*[1] said Scipio, with severity; but Philippus, with some humor, to one who had a strong smell, *I perceive that I am circumvented by you;*[2] yet it is the resemblance of words, with the change only of a letter, that constitutes both jokes.

"Those smart sayings which spring from some ambiguity are thought extremely ingenious; but they are not always employed to express jests, but often even grave thoughts. What Publius Licinus Varus said to Africanus the elder, when he was endeavoring to fit a chaplet to his head at an entertainment, and it broke several times, *Do not wonder if it does not fit you, for you have a great head,* was a fine and noble thought; but *He is bald enough, for he says but little,*[3] is of the same sort. Not to be tedious, there is no subject for jest from which serious and grave reflections may not be drawn. It is also to be observed that every thing which is ridiculous is not witty; for what can be so ridiculous as a buffoon?[4] But it

force of the pun, which is bad enough at the first hand, is entirely lost by a literal translation. I have been forced to coin two English words from the Latin to convey some idea of it. Had Clodius lived in this country, and his name been Greville, I had been as happy as Glaucia; for then I could have said, " Where is the old proverb, What, is he *gravelled?* No; but he is *Grevilled.* B. *Num claudicat* is thought by Strebæus to have been a common question with regard to a man suspected of want of judgment or honesty.

[1] *Quid hoc Nœvio ignavius?* It is thought to have been a joke of Publius Africanus Major, who, according to some, was accused by the Petilii, tribunes of the people, or, according to others, by a certain Marcus Nævius. See Liv., xxxviii., 50, 56; Val. Max., iii., 7; A. Gell., iv., 18. But it might have been said by Africanus the younger in reference to some other man. *Ellendt.*

[2] *Video me à te circumveniri.* Toup, in his Appendix to Theocritus, suggests that we should read *Video me à te non circum, sed hircumveniri,* referring to a similar joke of Aristophanes, Acharn., 850.

[3] *Calvus satis est, quod dicit parum.* The meaning is by no means clear, and no change in the punctuation elucidates it. . . . . Pearce supposes that it is said of a bad orator: "If he were to say more, he would give less satisfaction; what he has said is so far satisfactory, as it is brief." . . . . Henrichsen thinks that *calvus* might be used metaphorically, as *calva oratio* for *jejuna;* and that the joke is on the ambiguity of the word. To me the passage seems inexplicable. *Ellendt.* Whether *calvus* in the text be a proper name or not, is a matter of uncertainty; Turnebus thinks it is not.

[4] *Sannio.* The *sanniones* were so called from *sanna,* a grimace, and personated ridiculous characters, like the *Arlecchini* or *Pulcinelli* of the Italians. *Ellendt.*

is by his face, his appearance, his look, his mimicry, his voice, and, in fine, by his whole figure, that he excites laughter. I might, indeed, call him witty, but not in such a way that I would have an orator, but an actor in pantomime, to be witty.

LXII. "This kind of jesting, above all, then, though it powerfully excites laughter, is not suited to us; it represents the morose, the superstitious, the suspicious, the vainglorious, the foolish; habits of mind which are in themselves ridiculous; and such kind of characters we are to expose, not to assume. There is another kind of jesting which is extremely ludicrous, namely, mimicry; but it is allowable only in us to attempt it cautiously, if ever we do attempt it, and but for a moment, otherwise it is far from becoming to a man of education. A third is distortion of features, utterly unworthy of us. A fourth is indecency in language, a disgrace not only to the forum, but to any company of well-bred people. So many things, then, being deducted from this part of oratory, the kinds of jesting which remain are (as I distinguished them before) such as consist in thought or in expression. That which, in whatever terms you express it, is still wit, consists in the thought; that which by a change of words loses its spirit, has no wit but what depends on expression.

"Plays on ambiguous words are extremely ingenious, but depend wholly on the expression, not on the matter. They seldom, however, excite much laughter, but are rather commended as jests of elegance and scholarship; as that about Titus, whom, being a great tennis-player, and at the same time suspected of having broken the sacred images by night, Terentius Vespa excused, when his companions inquired for him, as he did not come to the Campus Martius, by saying that *he had broken an arm.* Or as that of Africanus, which is in Lucilius,

" ' *Quid? Decius, nuculam an confixum vis facere? inquit.*"[1]

Or, as your friend Granius, Crassus, said of somebody, *That*

---

[1] This verse of Lucilius would be unintelligible to us, even if we were certain that the reading of it is sound. Heusinger thinks that Lucilius referred to the game played with nuts, which the author of the elegy entitled "Nux" mentions: *Quas puer aut rectus certo dilaminat ictu.* Others think that *confixum facere* signifies merely *configere.* Ernesti supposes that a sort of dish, made of pieces of flesh, *fricassee,* is meant. Schutz suggests that, if this be the meaning of *confixum,* some kind of eatable must be intended by *nucula.* But this profits us nothing. *Ellendt.*

he was not worth the sixth part of an as.[1]   And if you were to
ask me, I should say that he who is called a jester excels
chiefly in jokes of this kind, but that other jests excite laughter in a greater degree.   The ambiguous gains great admiration, as I observed before, from its nature, for it appears the
part of a wit to be able to turn the force of a word to quite
another sense than that in which other people take it; but it
excites surprise rather than laughter, unless when it happens
to be joined with some other sorts of jesting.

LXIII.   "Some of these sorts of jesting I will now run
over: but you are aware that that is the most common kind
of joke, when we expect one thing and another is said; in
which case our own disappointed expectation makes us laugh.
But if something of the ambiguous is thrown in with it, the
wit is heightened; as in Nævius, a man seems to be moved
with compassion who, seeing another, that was sentenced for
debt, being led away, inquires, *For how much is he adjudged?*
He is answered, *A thousand sestertii.*   If he had then added
only, *You may take him away,* it would have been a species of
joke that takes you by surprise; but as he said, *I add no more;
you may take him away* (thus introducing the ambiguous, another kind of jest), the repartee, as it seems to me, is rendered
witty in the highest degree.   Such equivocation is most happy
when, in any dispute, a word is caught from your adversary,
and thence something severe is turned upon the very person
who gave the provocation, as by Catulus upon Philippus.[2]
But as there are several sorts of ambiguity, with regard to
which accurate study is necessary, we should be attentive and
on the watch for words; and thus, though we may avoid frigid
witticisms (for we must be cautious that a jest is not thought
far-fetched), we shall hit upon many acute sayings.   Another
kind is that which consists in a slight change in a word, which,
when produced by the alteration of a letter, the Greeks call
παρονομασία, as Cato called *Nobilior*[3] *Mobilior;* or as, when he

---

[1] *Non esse sextantis.*   A phrase applied either to any thing worth more
than a *sextans,* and therefore perhaps of great value, or to any thing
worth less than a *sextans,* or of no value at all.   *Turnebus.*

[2] See c. 54.

[3] Marcus Fulvius Nobilior.   Cato had accused him of having taken
poets with him into his province, and called him *Mobilior,* to denote his
levity, which, among the Romans, who were fond of gravity and steadi-
ness, was a great crime.   *Turnebus.*   See Cic., Tusc. Quæst., i., 2.   He

had said to a certain person, *Eamus deambulatum*, and the other asked, *Quid opus fuit* DE? Cato rejoined, *Imò verò, quid opus fuit* TE?[1] Or that repartee of the same Cato, *If you are both adverse and averse in your shameless practices.* The interpretation of a name also has wit in it, when you assign a ridiculous reason why a person is so called; as I lately said of Nummius, who distributed money[2] at elections, that he had found a name in the Campus Martius as Neoptolemus found one at Troy.

LXIV. " All such jokes lie in a single word. Often too a verse is humorously introduced, either just as it is, or with some little alteration; or some part of a verse, as Statius said to Scaurus when in a violent passion (whence some say, Crassus, that your law[3] on citizenship had its rise):

> "'Hush! Silence! what is all this noise? Have you,
> Who neither have a father nor a mother,
> Such confidence? Away with all that pride.'

In the case of Cælius, that joke of yours, Antonius, was assuredly of advantage to your cause; when, appearing as a witness, he had admitted that a great deal of money had gone from him, and as he had a son who was a man of pleasure, you, as he was going away, said,

> "'See you the old man, touch'd for thirty minæ?'

To the same purpose proverbs may be applied; as in the joke of Scipio, when Asellus was boasting that while he had served in the army, he had marched through all the provinces, *Drive an ass*, etc.[4] Such jokes, as they can not, if any change is made in the words of them, retain the same grace, are necessarily considered as turning, not on the matter, but on the mere expression.

" There is also a kind of joke, not at all absurd, which lies

had also built a temple to the Muses. Cic., ib., et Arch., c. 11; Brut., c. 20; Plin., H. N., xxxv., 36. *Ellendt.*

[1] This appears to us moderns a very poor joke. No translation can make it intelligible to those who do not understand the original.

[2] *Divisorem. Divisores* were those who distributed money among the tribes, in the name of the candidates, as bribes for their votes. See Cic., Verr., i., 8; Planc., 19. *Ellendt.*

[3] The *Lex Licinia Mucia de civibus regendis*, A.U.C. 659, by which it was provided that no one should be accounted a citizen who was not really a citizen. Cic., Off., iii., 11. *Ellendt.*

[4] Turnebus thinks that the reference is to the Greek proverb, Εἰ μὴ

in expression, when you seem to understand a thing literally,
and not in its obvious meaning; in which kind it was that
Tutor,[1] the old mimic, an exceedingly laughable actor, ex-
clusively distinguished himself.   But I have nothing to do
with actors; I only wished this kind of jesting to be illustrated by some notable example.   Of this kind was your answer lately, Crassus, to one who asked you *whether he should
be troublesome if he came to you some time before it was light;*
and you said, *You will not be troublesome:* when he rejoined,
You will order yourself to be waked then? to which you replied,
Surely I said that you would not be troublesome.   Of the same
sort was that old joke which they say that Marcus Scipio
Maluginensis made, when he had to report from his century
that Acidinus was voted consul, and the officer cried out, *Declare as to Lucius Manlius,* he said, *I declare him to be a worthy
man, and an excellent member of the commonwealth.*   The answer of Lucius [Porcius][2] Nasica to Cato the censor was humorous enough, when Cato said to him, *Are you truly satisfied
that you have taken a wife?   No, indeed,* replied Nasica, *I am
not truly satisfied.*[3]   Such jests are insipid, or witty only when
another answer is expected ; for our surprise (as I before[4] observed) naturally amuses us ; and thus, when we are deceived,
as it were, in our expectation, we laugh.

LXV.   "Those jests also lie in words, which spring from
some allegorical phraseology, or from a metaphorical use of
some one word, or from using words ironically.   From allegorical phraseology : as when Rusca, in old times, proposed
the law to fix the ages of candidates for offices, and Marcus
Servilius, who opposed the law, said to him : *Tell me, Marcus
Pinarius Rusca, if I speak against you, will you speak ill of me*

δύναιο βοῦν, ἔλαυνε ὄνον, "If you can not drive an ox, drive an ass" (see
Apostol., Prov., vii., 53; Zenob., iii., 54); but that proverb seems inap-
plicable to this passage.   Talæus and Lambinus suppose, with more
probability, that something like this must be understood : *Agas asellum,
cursum non docebitur.*   Asellus is again mentioned in c. 66.   *Ellendt.*

[1] Nothing is recorded of that actor in pantomime.   *Ellendt.*
[2] This passage is corrupt, but as no emendation of it can be trusted,
it will be sufficient to inclose *Porcius* in brackets.   *Orellius.*
[3] *Ex tui animi sententiâ tu uxorem habes?*   The words *ex animi sententiâ* had two significations : they were used by the censors in putting questions in the sense of "truly, sincerely;" but they were used in common
conversation in the sense of "to a person's satisfaction."   From the
ambiguity of the phrase proceeds the joke.   [4] C. 63.

as you have spoken of others? As you shall sow, replied he, *so you shall reap.* From the use of a single word in a metaphorical sense: as when the elder Scipio said to the Corinthians, who offered to put up a statue of him in the place where those of other commanders were, *That he did not like such comrades.* From the ironical use of words: as when Crassus spoke for Aculeo before Marcus Perperna as judge, and Lucius Ælius Lama appeared for Gratidianus against Aculeo, and Lama, who was deformed, as you know, offered impertinent interruptions, Crassus said, *Let us hear this beautiful youth.* When a laugh followed, *I could not form my own shape,* said Lama, *but I could form my understanding.* *Then,* said Crassus, *let us hear this able orator;* when a greater laugh than before ensued. Such jests are agreeable as well in grave as in humorous speeches. For I observed, a little while ago,[1] that the subjects for jest and for gravity are distinct; but that the same form of expression will serve for grave remarks as for jokes. Words antithetically used[2] are a great ornament to language; and the same mode of using them is often also humorous; thus, when the well-known Servius Galba carried to Lucius Scribonius the tribune a list of his own intimates to be appointed as judges, and Libo said, *What, Galba, will you never go out of your own dining-room?* *Yes,* replied Galba, *when you go out of other men's bed-chambers.* To this kind of joke the saying of Glaucia to Metellus is not very dissimilar: *You have your villa at Tibur, but your court on Mount Palatine.*[3]

LXVI. "Such kinds of jokes as lie in words I think that I have now sufficiently discussed; but such as relate to things are more numerous, and excite more laughter, as I observed before.[4] Among them is narrative, a matter of exceeding difficulty; for such things are to be described and set before the eyes, as may seem to be probable, which is the excellence of narration, and such also as are grotesque, which is the peculiar province of the ridiculous; for an example, as the shortest that I recollect, let that serve which I mentioned before,

---

[1] C. 61.

[2] *Verba relata contrarie.* Which the Greeks call ἀντίθετα, when *contrariis opponuntur contraria.* Cic., Or., 50.

[3] *Villam in Tiburte habes, cortem in Palatio.* Cors or chors meant a coop, pen, or movable sheepfold. Schutz and Strebæus, therefore, suppose that Glaucia intended to designate the companions of Metellus as *cattle,* for which he had a *pen* on the Palatine.   [4] C. 61.

the story of Crassus about Memmius.[1]   To this head we may
assign the narratives given in fables.   Allusions are also
drawn from history; as when Sextus Titius[2] said he was a
Cassandra, *I can name*, said Antonius, *many of your Ajaces
Oilei.*[3]   Such jests are also derived from *similitudes*, which include either *comparison* or something of bodily *representation*.
A *comparison*, as when Gallus, that was once a witness against
Piso, said that a countless sum of money had been given to
Magius[4] the governor, and Scaurus tried to refute him, by alleging the poverty of Magius, *You mistake me, Scaurus*, said he,
*for I do not say that Magius has saved it, but that, like a man
gathering nuts without his clothes, he has put it into his belly.*   Or,
as when Marcus Cicero[5] the elder, the father of that excellent
man our friend, said, *That the men of our times were like the
Syrian slaves; the more Greek they knew, the greater knaves they
were.*   Representations also create much laughter, and these
commonly bear upon some deformity, or bodily defect, with a
comparison to something still more deformed : as my own
saying on Helvius Mancia, *I will now show*, said I, *what sort
of man you are;* when he exclaimed, *Show us, I pray you;* and
I pointed with my finger to a Gaul represented upon the Cim-
brian shield of Marius under the new shops[6] in the forum,
with his body distorted, his tongue lolling out, and his cheeks
flabby.   A general laugh ensued ; for nothing was ever seen
to resemble Mancia so much.   Or as I said to the witness
Titus Pinarius, who twisted his chin about while he was speaking, *That he might speak, if he pleased, if he had done cracking
his nut.*   There are jokes, too, from things being extenuated
or exaggerated hyperbolically, and to astonish; as you, Crassus, said in a speech to the people, that *Memmius fancied himself so great a man, that as he came into the forum he stooped his
head at the arch of Fabius.*   Of which kind is the saying also,
that Scipio is reported to have uttered at Numantia when

---

[1] C. 59.   [2] C. 11.
[3] Antonius impudicos hominis mores insectatur, cùm Cassandræ ab
Ajace post expugnatam Trojam vim illatam fuisse constet.   *Ellendt.*
[4] Of Magius nothing is known.   *Ellendt.*
[5] The grandfather of the orator, as is clearly shown by Corradus in ·
Quæst.   *Ernesti.*
[6] *Sub Novis.*   Understand *Tabernis argentariis.*   See P. Fabr. ad
Quæst.   Acad., iv., 22 ; Drakenborch ad Liv., xxvi., 27 ; xliv., 17.
Ernesti.

he was angry with Metellus, that *If his mother were to produce a fifth, she would bring forth an ass.*[1]   There is also frequently acuteness shown, when something obscure and not commonly known is illustrated by a slight circumstance, and often by a single word, as when Publius Cornelius, a man, as was suspected, of a covetous and rapacious disposition, but of great courage and an able commander, thanked Caius Fabricius for having, though he was his enemy, made him consul, especially during a difficult and important war, *You have no reason to thank me,* returned Fabricius, *if I had rather be pillaged than sold for a slave.*   Or, as Africanus said to Asellus, who objected to him that unfortunate lustration in his censorship, *Do not wonder ; for he who restored you to the rights of a citizen, compelled the lustration and sacrificed the bull.*   There was a tacit suspicion that Mummius seemed to have laid the state under the necessity of expiation by removing the mark of ignominy from Asellus.

LXVII. " Ironical dissimulation has also an agreeable effect, when you say something different from what you think ; not after the manner to which I alluded before, when you say the exact reverse of what you mean, as Crassus said to Lama, but when through the whole course of a speech you are seriously jocose, your thoughts being different from your words ; as our friend Scævola said to that Septumuleius of Anagnia (to whom its weight in gold was paid for the head of Caius Gracchus), when he petitioned that he would take him as his lieutenant general into Asia, *What would you have, foolish man ? there is such a multitude of bad citizens that, I warrant you, if you stay at Rome, you will in a few years make a vast fortune.* Fannius, in his Annals, says that Africanus the younger, he that was named Æmilianus, was remarkable for this kind of jests ; and calls him by a Greek term είρων, an ironical jester ; but, according to what those say who know these matters better than myself, I conceive that Socrates, for irony and dissimulation, far excelled all other men in the wit and genius which he displayed.   It is an elegant kind of humor, satirical with a mixture of gravity, and adapted to oratory as well as to polite conversation.   Indeed, all the kinds of humor of

---

[1] Quintus Metellus Macedonicus, as Plutarch relates in his treatise *De Fortunâ Romanorum,* had four sons, whose abilities were in proportion to their ages, the youngest being the least gifted. *Proust.*

which I have spoken, are seasonings not more appropriate to
law-pleadings in the forum, than to any other kind of discourse.
For that which is mentioned by Cato (who has reported many
apophthegms, several of which have been produced by me as
examples), seems to me a very happy saying, *that Caius Publius used to observe that Publius Mummius was a man for all occasions;* so it certainly is with regard to our present subject,
that there is no time of life in which wit and polite humor
may not very properly be exercised.

"But I will pursue the remainder of my subject.   It is a
kind of joking similar to a sort of dissimulation, when any
thing disgraceful is designated by an honorable term ; as when
Africanus the censor removed from his tribe that centurion
who absented himself from the battle in which Paulus commanded, alleging that he had remained in the camp to guard
it, and inquiring why he had such a mark of ignominy set
upon him, *I do not like,* replied Africanus, *over vigilant people.*
It is an excellent joke, too, when you take any part of another
person's words in a different sense from that which he intended ; as Fabius Maximus did with Livius Salinator,[1] when, on
Tarentum being lost, Livius had still preserved the citadel,
and had made many successful sallies from it, and Fabius,
some years afterward, having retaken the town, Livius begged
him to remember that it was owing to him that Tarentum
was retaken.   *How can I do otherwise than remember,* said Fabius, *for I should never have retaken it if you had not lost it.*
Such jokes as the following, too, are, though rather absurd,
often on that very account extremely amusing, and very apposite, not only to characters in plays, but also to us orators :

" 'The foolish man !
As soon as he had come to wealth, he died.'
        " 'That woman, what is she to you ?
My wife.   Like you, by Hercules !'[2]

---

[1] The same anecdote is noticed by Cicero, De Senect., c. 4 ; and Livy
speaks of the occurrence at some length, xxvi., 25.   But that the Marcus
Livius there mentioned had not the cognomen of Salinator, but of
Macatus, is shown by P. Wesseling, Obss. ii., 5 ; and there seems little
doubt that Cicero made a mistake here, as in some other places.
Ellendt.

[2] We may suppose, says Strebæus, the woman to have been deformed,
and some one to have asked the man, " What relation is that woman to
you ? your sister ?"   When the man answered, " My wife," the ques-

" ' As long as he was living at the waters
He never¹ died.'

LXVIII. " This kind of jokes is rather trifling, and, as I
said, fit for actors in farces ; but sometimes it finds a proper
place with us, as even one who is not a fool may express himself like a fool in a humorous way, as Mancia congratulated
you, Antonius, when he heard that you were accused by Marcus Duronius of bribery in your censorship : *At length*, said
he, *you will have an opportunity of attending to your own business.*
Such jests excite great laughter, and, in truth, all sayings that
are uttered by men of sense with a degree of absurdity and
sarcasm, under the pretense of not understanding what is said
to them.   A joke of this kind is not to seem to comprehend
what you comprehend very well; as when Pontidius, being
asked, *What do you think of him who is taken in adultery?* replied, *That he is slow.*   Or such as was my reply to Metellus,
when, at a time of levying troops, he would not excuse me
from serving for the weakness of my eyes, and said to me,
What! can you see nothing ?   Yes truly, answered I, *I can see
your villa from the Esquiline Gate.*² Or as the repartee of Nasica, who, having called at the house of the poet Ennius, and
the maid-servant having told him, on his inquiring at the
door, that Ennius was not at home, saw that she had said so
by her master's order, and that he was really within; and
when, a few days afterward, Ennius called at Nasica's house,
and inquired for him at the gate, Nasica cried out, *That he
was not at home.   What?* says Ennius, *do I not know your
voice ?   You are an impudent fellow*, rejoined Nasica ; *when I
inquired for you, I believed your servant when she told me that
you were not at home, and will not you believe me when I tell you
that I am not at home?*   It is a very happy stroke, too, when
he who has uttered a sarcasm is jested upon in the same strain
in which he has attacked another ; as when Quintus Opimius,
a man of consular dignity, who had the report of having been
licentious in his youth, said to Egilius, a man of wit, who

---

tioner would exclaim, "And yet, how like you she is ! I should have
taken her for your sister ;" wittily indicating the deformity of the man.
   ¹ The joke, says Schutz, is in the word *never*, as if it were possible
that a man might die several times.
   ² A reflection, says Turnebus, on the extraordinary size and magnificence of the building.

seemed to be an effeminate person, but was in reality not so, *How do you do, my Egilia? when will you pay me a visit with your distaff and spindle?* and Egilius replied, *I certainly dare not; for my mother forbade me to visit women of bad character.*

LXIX. "There are witty sayings also which carry a concealed suspicion of ridicule; of which sort is that of the Sicilian, who, when a friend of his made lamentation to him, saying, that his wife had hanged herself upon a fig-tree, said, *I beseech you give me some shoots of that tree, that I may plant them.* Of the same sort is what Catulus said to a certain bad orator, who, when he imagined that he had excited compassion at the close of a speech, asked our friend here, after he had sat down, whether he appeared to have raised pity in the audience : *Very great pity,* replied Crassus, *for I believe there is no one here so hard-hearted but that your speech seemed pitiable to him.* Those jests amuse me extremely, which are expressed in passion and as it were with moroseness; not when they are uttered by a person really morose, for in that case it is not the wit, but the natural temper that is laughed at. Of this kind of jest there is a very humorous example, as it appears to me, in Nævius :

"'Why mourn you, father?
Strange that I do not sing! I am condemn'd.'

Contrasted with this there is a patient and cool species of the humorous : as when Cato received a stroke from a man carrying a trunk, who afterward called to him to *take care,* he asked him, *whether he carried any thing else besides the trunk?* There is also a witty mode of exposing folly; as when the Sicilian to whom Scipio, when prætor, assigned his host for an advocate in some cause, a man of rank but extremely stupid, said, *I beseech you, prætor, give this advocate to my adversary, and give me none.* Explanations of things, too, are amusing, which are given from conjecture in a sense far different from that which they are intended to convey, but with ingenuity and aptness. As when Scaurus accused Rutilius of bribery (at the time when he himself was made consul, and Rutilius suffered a disappointment), and showed these letters in Rutilius's books,[1] A. F. P. R., and said that they signified, *Actum Fide Publii Rutilii,* 'transacted on the faith of Publius Rutilius;' while Rutilius declared that they meant, *Ante Fac-*

---

[1] Which Scaurus required to be produced on the trial.

tum Post Relatum, 'done before, entered after;' but Caius Canius, being on the side of Rufus, observed that neither of those senses was intended by the letters : *What, then, is the meaning?* inquired Scaurus. *Æmilius fecit, plectitur Rutilius,* replied Canius ; '*Æmilius is guilty, Rutilius is punished.*'

LXX. "A union of discordant particulars is laughable : as, *What is wanting to him, except fortune and virtue?* A familiar reproof of a person, as if he were in error, is also amusing ; as when Albucius taunted Granius, because, when something appeared to be proved by Albucius from Granius's writing, Granius rejoiced extremely that Scævola[1] was acquitted, and did not understand that judgment was given against the credit of his own writing. Similar to this is friendly admonition by way of giving advice : as when Granius persuaded a bad pleader, who had made himself hoarse with speaking, to drink a cold mixture of honey and wine as soon as he got home : *I shall ruin my voice,* said he, *if I do so. It will be better,* said Granius, *than to ruin your clients.* It is a happy hit, too, when something is said that is peculiarly applicable to the character of some particular person ; as when Scaurus had incurred some unpopularity for having taken possession of the effects of Phrygio Pompeius, a rich man who died without a will, and was sitting as counsel for Bestia, then under impeachment, Caius Memmius the accuser, as a funeral procession passed by, said, *Look, Scaurus, a dead body is going by, if you can but get possession!* But of all jokes none create greater laughter than something said contrary to expectation ; of which there are examples without number. Such was the saying of Appius the elder,[2] who, when the matter about the public lands, and the law of Thorius, was in agitation in the senate, and Lucilius was hard pressed by those who asserted that the public pastures were grazed by his cattle, said, *They are not the cattle of Lucilius ; you mistake* (he seemed to be going to defend Lucilius) ; *I look upon them*

---

[1] Texts vary greatly in this passage. I adhere strictly to that of Orellius. "It appears," says Pearce, "that Scævola was accused of extortion, as Cicero says in his Brutus, and in the first book De Finibus, and that Albucius, to prove the accusation, brought forward some writing of Granius, who, when judgment was given in favor of Scævola, did not understand that it was at the same time given against his own writing."

[2] He is called the elder, because he had a brother of the same name, the father of Publius Clodius, the enemy of Cicero. *Proust.*

as free, for they feed where they please. That saying also of the Scipio who slew Tiberius Gracchus amuses me. When, after many charges were made against him, Marcus Flaccus proposed Publius Mucius as one of his judges, *I except against him,* said he, *he is unjust;* and when this occasioned a general murmur, *Ah!* said he, *I do not except against him, Conscript Fathers, as unjust to me, but to every body.* But nothing could be more witty than the joke of our friend Crassus. When Silus, a witness, was injuring the cause of Piso, by something that he said he had heard against him, *It is possible,* said he, *Silus, that the person from whom you heard this said it in anger.* Silus assented. *It is possible, too, that you did not rightly understand him.* To this also he assented with the lowest of bows, expressing entire agreement with Crassus. *It is also possible,* continued Crassus, *that what you say you have heard you never heard at all.* This was so different from what was expected, that the witness was overwhelmed by a general laugh. Nævius is full of this kind of humor, and it is a familiar joke, *Wise man, if you are cold you will shake;* and there are many other such sayings.

LXXI. "You may often also humorously grant to your adversary what he wishes to detract from you; as Caius Lælius, when a man of disreputable family told him that he was unworthy of his ancestors, replied, *But, by Hercules, you are worthy of yours.* Jokes, too, are frequently uttered in a sententious manner; as Marcus Cincius, on the day when he proposed his law about gifts and presents, and Caius Cento stood forth and asked him with some scorn, *What are you proposing, little Cincius?* replied, *That you, Caius, may pay for what you wish to use.* [1] Things also which are impossible are

---

[1] A species of ridicule expressed in a pithy sentence. The example produced requires that we should explain the Cincian law. This can not be done better than in the words of Dr. Middleton. The business of pleading, says he, though a profession of all others the most laborious, yet was not among the Romans mercenary, or undertaken for any pay; for it was illegal to take money, or to accept even a present for it; but the richest, the greatest, and the noblest of Rome freely offered their talents to the service of their citizens, as the common guardians and protectors of the innocent and distressed. This was an institution as old as Romulus, who assigned the patronage of the people to the patricians or senators, without fee or reward; but in succeeding ages, when, through the avarice of the nobles, it had become a custom for all clients to make annual presents to their patrons, by which the body of the citi-

often wished for with much wit; as Marcus Lepidus, when
he lay down upon the grass, while others were taking their
exercise in the Campus Martius, exclaimed, *I wish this were
labor.*[1] It is an excellent joke also to give inquisitive people
who teaze you, as it were, a calm answer, of such a nature as
they do not expect; as Lepidus the censor, when he deprived
Antistius of Pyrgi of his horse;[2] and his friends called out to
him, and inquired what reason Antistius could give his father
why his horse was taken from him, when he was[3] an excellent, industrious, modest, frugal member of the colony, rejoined, *That I believe not a word of it.* Some other sorts of jests
are enumerated by the Greeks, as execrations, expressions of
admiration, threats. But I think that I have divided these
matters into too many heads already; for such as lie in the
force and meaning of a word, are commonly easy to settle and
define; but in general, as I observed before, they are heard
rather with approbation than laughter. Jokes, however,
which lie in the subject and thought, are, though infinite in

zens was made tributary as it were to the senate, M. Cincius, a tribune,
published a law prohibiting all senators to take money or gifts on any
account, and especially for pleading causes. This Cincian law was
made in the year of Rome 549; and recommended to the people, as
Cicero tells us (De Senect. 4), by Quintus Fabius Maximus, in the extremity of his age. Caius Cento was one of the orators who opposed it.
Livy, xxxiv., 4, gives us the reason for passing this law, " Quid legem
Cinciam de donis et muneribus, nisi quia vectigalis jam et stipendiaria
plebs esse senatui cæperat?" It is also mentioned by Tacitus, Annal.,
xi., 5: "Consurgunt patres legemque Cinciam flagitant, qua cavetur
antiquitus ne quis ob causam orandam pecuniam donumve accipiat."
We also find from the same author (xi., 7), that this law was not well
observed in Cicero's time: "prompta sibi exempla quantis mercedibus
P. Clodius aut C. Curio concionari soliti sint;" so the Emperor Claudius confined the fees to be allowed not to exceed a certain sum, which
amounted to £80 14s. 7d. of our money, "Capiendis pecuniis posuit
modum usque ad dena sestertia, quem egressi repetundarum tenerentur."
The Cincian law, says Dr. Taylor, has been well commented upon by
several of the moderns, as Ranchinus, ii.; Var., vii.; Burgius, i.; Elect.,
xviii.; and Brummerus. *B.* Turnebus understands the sense of the
repartee to be, that patrons were not to expect thenceforward to live
upon gifts from their clients, but must buy whatever they wished to
have.

[1] He wishes that labor were as easy as ease.
[2] Excluding him from the number of the knights, to whom a horse
was given at the public expense.
[3] That is, says Proust, was so reported by those who wished to favor
him.

their varieties, reducible under a very few general heads ; for it is by deceiving expectation, by satirizing the tempers of others, by playing humorously on our own, by comparing a thing with something worse, by dissembling, by uttering apparent absurdities, and by reproving folly, that laughter is excited ; and he who would be a facetious speaker, must be endowed with a natural genius for such kinds of wit, as well as with personal qualifications, so that his very look may adapt itself to every species of the ridiculous ; and the graver and more serious such a person is, as is the case with you, Crassus, so much more humorous do the sayings which fall from him generally appear.

"But now I think that you, Antonius, who said[1] that you would repose during my discourse, as in some place of refreshment, will, as if you had stopped in the Pomptine Marsh, neither a pleasant nor a wholesome region, consider that you have rested long enough, and will proceed to complete the remainder of your journey." "I will," said Antonius, "having been very pleasantly entertained by you, and having also acquired instruction, as well as encouragement, to indulge in jesting ; for I am no longer afraid lest any one should charge me with levity in that respect, since you have produced such authorities as the Fabricii, the Africani, the Maximi, the Catos, and the Lepidi, in its favor. But you have heard what you desired from me, at least such points as it was necessary to consider and detail with particular accuracy ; the rest are more easy, and arise wholly from what has been already said.

LXXII.[2] "For when I have entered upon a cause, and traced out all its bearings in my mind, as far as I could possibly do so; when I have ascertained and contemplated the proper arguments for the case, and those particulars by which the feelings of the judges may be conciliated or excited, I then consider what strong or weak points the cause contains; for hardly any subject can be called into question and controversy in pleading, which has not both ; but *to what degree* is the chief concern. In pleading, my usual method is, to fix on whatever strong points a cause has, and to illustrate and make the most of them, dwelling on them, insisting on them,

---

[1] C. 57.
[2] Antonius returns to the point from which he had digressed at c. 57.

clinging to them; but to hold back from the weak and defective points in such a way that I may not appear to shun them, but that their whole force may be dissembled and overwhelmed[1] by the ornament and amplification of the strong parts. If the cause turn upon arguments, I maintain chiefly such as are the strongest, whether they are several or whether there be but one; but if the cause depend on the conciliation or excitement of the feelings of the judges, I apply myself chiefly to that part which is best adapted to move men's minds. Finally, the principal point for consideration on this head is, that if my speech can be made more effective by refuting my adversary, than by supporting my own side of the question, I employ all my weapons against him; but if my own case can be more easily supported, than that on the other side can be confuted, I endeavor to withdraw the attention of the judges from the opposite party's defense, and to fix it on my own. In conclusion, I adopt, on my own responsibility, two courses which appear to me most easy (since I can not attempt what is more difficult): one, that I make, sometimes, no reply at all to a troublesome or difficult argument or point (and at such forbearance perhaps somebody may reasonably laugh; for who is there that can not practice it? but I am now speaking of my own abilities, not those of others; and I confess that, if any particular press very hard upon me, I usually retreat from it, but in such a manner as not only not to appear to flee with my shield thrown away, but even with it thrown over my shoulders; adopting, at the same time, a certain pomp and parade of language, and a mode of flight that resembles fighting; and keeping upon my guard in such a way, that I seem to have retired, not to avoid my enemy, but to choose more advantageous ground); the other is one which I think most of all worthy of the orator's precaution and foresight, and which generally occasions me very great anxiety: I am accustomed to study not so much to benefit the causes which I undertake, as not to injure them; not but that an orator must aim at both objects; but it is, however, a much greater disgrace to him to be thought to have damaged a cause than not to have profited it.

LXXIII. "But what are you saying among yourselves on

---

[1] *Dissimulatum . . . obruatur.* The word *ante*, which is retained by Orellius, but is wanting in several manuscripts, I leave untranslated.

this subject, Catulus? Do you slight what I say, as indeed it deserves to be slighted?" "By no means," rejoined Catulus; "but Cæsar seemed desirous to say something on the point." "Let him say it, then, with all my heart," continued Antonius, "whether he wish to confute, or to question me." "Indeed, Antonius," said Cæsar, "I have always been the man to say of you as an orator, that you appeared to me in your speeches the most guarded of all men, and that it was your peculiar merit, that nothing was ever spoken by you that could injure him for whom you spoke. And I well remember, that, on entering into a conversation with Crassus here concerning you, in the hearing of a large company, and Crassus having largely extolled your eloquence, I said, that among your other merits this was even the principal, that you not only said all that ought to be said, but also never said any thing that ought not to be said; and I recollect that he then observed to me, that your other qualities deserved the highest degree of praise, but that to speak what was not to the purpose, and to injure one's own client, was the conduct of an unprincipled and perfidious person; and, consequently, that he did not appear to him to be a good pleader, who avoided doing so, though he who did so was certainly dishonest. Now, if you please, Antonius, I would wish you to show why you think it a matter of such importance, to do no harm to a cause; so much so, that nothing in an orator appears to you of greater consequence."

LXXIV. "I will readily tell you, Cæsar," replied Antonius, "what I mean; but do you, and all who are here, remember this, that I am not speaking of the divine power of the complete orator, but of my own humble efforts and practice. The remark of Crassus is indeed that of an excellent and singular genius; to whom it appeared something like a prodigy, that any orator could possibly be found, who could do any mischief in speaking, and injure him whom he had to defend. For he judges from himself; as his force of intellect is such, that he thinks no man speaks what makes against himself, unless on purpose; but I am not alluding to any supereminent and illustrious power, but to common and almost universal sense. Among the Greeks, Themistocles the Athenian is reported to have possessed an incredible compass of understanding and genius; and a certain person of learning and singular accomplishments is said to have gone to him, and offered to teach him the *art of memory*, an art then first made public. When he inquired what that art could do for him, the professor replied, that it would enable him to remember every thing; when Themistocles rejoined, that he would oblige him much more if he could instruct him how to forget, rather than to remember, what he chose. Do you conceive what force and vigor of genius, how powerful and extensive a capacity, there was in that great man? who answered in such a manner that we may understand that nothing, which had once entered his mind, could ever slip out of it; and to whom it was much more desirable to be enabled to forget what he did not wish to remember, than to remember whatever he had once heard or seen. But neither on account of this answer of Themistocles are we to forbear to cultivate our memory, nor is my precaution and timidity in pleading causes to be slighted on account of the excellent understanding of Crassus; for neither the one nor the other of them has given me any additional ability, but has merely signified his own. There are numbers of points[1] in causes that call for circumspection in every part of your speech, that you may not stumble, that you may not fall over any thing. Oftentimes some witness either does no mischief, or does less, if he be not provoked; my client entreats me, the advocates press me, to inveigh against him, to abuse him, or, finally, to plague him with questions; I am not moved, I do not comply, I will not gratify them; yet I gain no commendations;

[1] Antonius mentions seven ways by which the indiscretion of the orator may be of prejudice to the cause, to illustrate his last observation: 1. By irritating a witness, who would not have injured his client without provocation. 2. By not giving way when the arguments press too hard upon him, he may lose his cause. 3. By extolling those qualities in his client which ought to be extenuated, he may do mischief. 4. By throwing invectives upon those who are entitled to the esteem and favor of the judges. 5. By upbraiding his adversary with the same defects that are in some of the judges; of which Philip's derision of a dwarfish evidence, before Lucius Aurifex, who was still lower in stature, was an instance mentioned before. 6. He may plead his own cause rather than that of his client; which blame Cicero seems to have incurred in his oration for Publius Sextius, a cause in which he was warmly and specially interested. Whoever has any inclination to read the history of that trial, may find it in Dr. Middleton's Life of Cicero, vol. ii., p. 45, etc. 7. By the use of false or repugnant arguments, or such as are foreign to the usage of the bar and judicial proceedings. *B.*

for ignorant people can more easily blame what you say in-
judiciously, than praise you for what you discreetly leave unnoticed.   In such a case how much harm may be done if you
offend a witness who is passionate, or one who is a man of
sense, or of influential character? for he has the will to do
you mischief from his passion, the power in his understanding, and the means in his reputation; nor, if Crassus never
commits this offense, is that a reason that many are not guilty
of it, and often; on which account nothing ever appears to
me more ignominious, than when from any observation, or
reply, or question, of a pleader, such remarks as this follow:
*He has ruined—Whom? his adversary? No truly, but himself
and his client.*

LXXV. "This Crassus thinks can never happen but
through perfidiousness; but I very frequently observe that
persons by no means dishonest do mischief in causes.   In regard to that particular which I mentioned before, that I am
used to retreat, or, to speak more plainly, to flee from those
points which would press hard on my side of the question,
how much harm do others do when they neglect this, saunter
in the enemy's camp, and dismiss their own guards?   Do
they occasion but slight detriment to their causes when they
either strengthen the supports of their adversaries or inflame
the wounds which they can not heal?   What harm do they
cause when they pay no regard to the characters of those
whom they defend?   If they do not mitigate by extenuation
those qualities in them that excite ill-will, but make them
more obnoxious to it by commending and extolling them, how
much mischief is caused by such management?   Or what if,
without any precautionary language, you throw bitter and
contumelious invectives upon popular persons, in favor with
the judges, do you not alienate their feelings from you?   Or
what if there be vices or bad qualities in one or more of the
judges, and you, in upbraiding your adversaries with such
demerits, are not aware that you are attacking the judges, is
it a small error which you then commit?   Or what if, while
you are speaking for another, you make his cause your own,
or, taking affront, are carried away from the question by passion, and start aside from the subject, do you occasion no
harm?   In this respect I am esteemed too patient and for-
bearing, not because I willingly hear myself abused, but be-

cause I am unwilling to lose sight of the cause; as, for instance, when I reproved you yourself, Sulpicius, for attacking
an agent, not me your adversary.[1] From such conduct, however, I acquire this advantage, that if any one does abuse me,
he is thought to be either ill-tempered or out of his wits.
Or if in your arguments you shall state any thing either
manifestly false, or contradictory to what you have said or
are going to say, or foreign in its nature to the practice of
trials and of the forum, do you occasion no damage to your
cause? Why need I say more on this head? My whole care
is constantly devoted to this object (for I will repeat it frequently), to effect, if I can, some good by speaking; but if
not, to do at least no harm.

LXXVI. "I now return therefore to that point, Catulus,
on which you a little while ago accorded me praise; the order
and arrangement of facts and topics of argument. On this
head, two methods may be observed; one, which the nature
of causes dictates; the other, which is suggested by the orator's judgment and prudence. For, to premise something before we come to the main point; then to explain the matter
in question; then to support it by strengthening our own arguments, and refuting those on the other side; next, to sum
up, and come to the peroration, is a mode of speaking that nature herself prescribes. But to determine how we should arrange the particulars that are to be advanced in order to prove,
to inform, to persuade, more peculiarly belongs to the orator's
discretion. For many arguments occur to him; many, that
seem likely to be of service to his pleading; but some of them
are so trifling as to be utterly contemptible; some, if they are
of any assistance at all, are sometimes of such a nature, that
there is some defect inherent in them; while that which appears to be advantageous, is not of such import that it need be
advanced in conjunction with any thing prejudicial. And as
to those arguments which are to the purpose, and deserving of
trust, if they are (as it often happens) very numerous, I think
that such of them as are of least weight, or as are of the same

[1] *Quod ministratorem peteres, non adversarium.* The *ministrator* was a
witness, from whose evidence Antonius had drawn arguments. *Ellendt.*
Whether by *adversarius* is meant Antonius or not, is, as Henrichsen
says, uncertain. Ellendt thinks that Antonius is not meant. I have,
however, differed from him, as the context seems to indicate that Antonius is meant.

tendency with others of greater force, ought to be set aside, and excluded altogether from our pleading. I myself, indeed, in collecting proofs, make it a practice rather to weigh than to count them.

LXXVII. " Since, too, as I have often observed, we bring over people in general to our opinions by three methods, by instructing their understandings, conciliating their benevolence, or exciting their passions, one only of these three methods is to be professed by us, so that we may appear to desire nothing else but to instruct ; the other two, like blood throughout the body, ought to be diffused through the whole of our pleading ; for both the beginning, and the other parts of a speech, on which we will by-and-by say a few words, ought to have this power in a great degree, so that they may penetrate the minds of those before whom we plead, in order to excite them. But in those parts of the speech which, though they do not convince by argument, yet by solicitation and excitement produce great effect, though their proper place is chiefly in the exordium and the peroration, still, to make a digression from what you have proposed-and are discussing, for the sake of exciting the passions, is often advantageous. Since, after the statement of the case has been made, an opportunity often presents itself of making a digression to rouse the feelings of the audience ; or this may be properly done after the confirmation of our own arguments, or the refutation of those on the other side, or in either place, or in all, if the cause has sufficient copiousness and importance ; and those causes are the most considerable, and most pregnant with matter for amplification and embellishment, which afford the most frequent opportunities for that kind of digression in which you may descant on those points by which the passions of the audience are either excited or calmed. In touching on this matter, I can not but blame those who place the arguments to which they trust least in the front ; and, in like manner, I think that they commit an error who, if ever they employ several advocates (a practice which never had my approbation), will have him to speak first in whom they confide least, and rank the others also according to their abilities.[1] For a cause requires

---

[1] *Ut in quoque eorum minimum putant esse, ita eum primum volunt dicere.* " As in each of them they think that there is least, so they wish him to speak first."

that the expectations of the audience should be met with all possible expedition; and if nothing to satisfy them be offered in the commencement, much more labor is necessary in the sequel; for that case is in a bad condition which does not at the commencement of the pleading at once appear to be the better. For this reason, as, in regard to pleaders,[1] he who is the most able should speak first, so in regard to a speech, let the arguments of most weight be put foremost; yet so that this rule be observed with respect to both, that some of superior efficiency be reserved for the peroration; if any are but of moderate strength (for to the weak no place should be given at all), they may be thrown into the main body and into the midst of the group. All these things being duly considered, it is then my custom to think last of that which is to be spoken first, namely, what exordium I shall adopt. For whenever I have felt inclined to think of that first, nothing occurs to me but what is jejune, or nugatory, or vulgar and ordinary.

LXXVIII. "The beginnings of speeches ought always to be accurate and judicious, well furnished with thoughts, and happy in expression, as well as peculiarly suited to their respective causes; for our earliest acquaintance with a speech, as it were, and the first recommendation of it to our notice, is at the commencement, which ought at once to propitiate and attract the audience. In regard to this point, I can not but feel astonished, not indeed at such as have paid no attention to the art, but at a man of singular eloquence and erudition, I mean Philippus, who generally rises to speak with so little preparation, that he knows not what word he shall utter first; and he says, that when he has warmed his arm, then it is his custom to begin to fight; but he does not consider that those from whom he takes this simile hurl their first lances gently, so as to preserve the utmost grace in their action, and at the same time to husband their strength. Nor is there any doubt, but that the beginning of a speech ought very seldom to be vehement and pugnacious; but if even in the combat of gladiators for life, which is decided by the sword, many passes are made previous to the actual encounter, which appear to be intended, not for mischief, but for display, how much more natu-

---

[1] *Ut in oratore.* Schutz conjectures *in oratoribus,* but he had better, as Ellendt observes, have conjectured *ex oratoribus.* But the text may be correct.

rally is such prelude to be expected in a speech, in which an
exhibition of force is not more required than gratification?
Besides, there is nothing in the whole nature of things that is
all produced at once, and that springs entire into being in an
instant; and nature herself has introduced every thing that
is done and accomplished most energetically with a moderate
beginning. Nor is the exordium of a speech to be sought
from without, or from any thing unconnected with the subject,
but to be derived from the very essence of the cause. It is,
therefore, after the whole cause has been considered and examined, and after every argument has been excogitated and
prepared, that you must determine what sort of exordium to
adopt; for thus it will easily be settled,[1] as it will be drawn
from those points which are most fertile in arguments, or in
those matters on which I said[2] you ought often to make digressions. Thus our exordia will give additional weight,
when they are drawn from the most intimate parts of our defense; and it will be shown that they are not only not common, and can not be transferred to other causes, but that they
have wholly grown out of the cause under consideration.

LXXIX. "But every exordium ought either to convey an
intimation of the whole matter in hand, or some introduction
and support to the cause, or something of ornament and dignity. But, like vestibules and approaches to houses and temples, so the introductions that we prefix to causes should be
suited to the importance of the subjects. In small and unimportant[3] causes, therefore, it is often more advisable to
commence with the subject-matter itself without any preface.
But, when we are to use an exordium (as will generally be
the case), our matter for it may be derived either from the
suitor, from the adversary, from the subject, or from those
before whom we plead. From the suitor (I call all those
suitors whom a suit concerns) we may deduce such particulars as characterize a worthy, generous, or unfortunate man,
or one deserving of compassion; or such particulars as avail
against a false accusation. From the adversary we may de-

---

[1] *Reperientur . . . sumentur.* These words are plural in Orellius's text,
but Ellendt and others seem rightly to determine that they should be
singular. [2] C. 77.
[3] *Infrequentibus causis. Infrequens causa* is a cause at the pleading of
which few auditors are likely to attend. *Ernesti.*

duce almost the contrary particulars from the same points. From the subject, if the matter under consideration be cruel, or heinous, or beyond expectation, or undeserved, or pitiable, or savoring of ingratitude or indignity, or unprecedented, or not admitting restitution or satisfaction. From those before whom we plead we may draw such considerations as to procure their benevolence and good opinion; an object better attained in the course of pleading than by direct entreaty. This object indeed is to be kept in view throughout the whole oration, and especially in the conclusion; but many exordia, however, are wholly based upon it; for the Greeks recommend us to make the judge, at the very commencement, attentive and desirous of information; and such hints are useful, but not more proper for the exordium than for other parts; but they are indeed easier[1] to be observed in the beginning, because the audience are then most attentive, when they are in expectation of the whole affair, and they may also, in the commencement, be more easily informed, as the particulars stated in the outset are generally of greater perspicuity than those which are spoken by way of argument, or refutation, in the body of the pleading. But we shall derive the greatest abundance and variety of matter for exordia, either to conciliate or to arouse the judge, from those points in the cause which are adapted to create emotion in the mind; yet the whole of these ought not to be brought forward in the exordium; the judge should only receive a slight impulse at the outset, so that the rest of our speech may come with full force upon him when he is already impressed in our favor.

LXXX. "Let the exordium, also, be so connected with the sequel of the speech, that it may not appear, like a musician's prelude, to be something attached merely from imagination, but a coherent member of the whole body; for some speakers, when they have delivered their premeditated exordium, make such a transition to what is to follow, that they seem positively unwilling to have an audience. But a prolusion of that kind ought not to be like that of gladiators,[2] who brandish spears before the fight, of which they make no use in the en-

---

[1] *Faciliora etiam in principiis.* Ellendt justly observes that *etiam* must be corrupt, and that *autem* should probably be substituted for it.
[2] *Samnitium.* A kind of gladiators so called, that fought with Samnite arms. They had their origin among the Campanians. Liv., ix., 40.

counter; but should be such, that speakers may even use as weapons the thoughts which they advanced in the prelude.

"But as to the directions which they give to consult brevity in the narration, if that is to be called brevity where there is no word redundant, the language of Lucius Crassus is distinguished by brevity; but if that kind of brevity is intended when only just so many words are used as are absolutely necessary, such conciseness is indeed sometimes proper; but it is often prejudicial, especially in narration; not only as it produces obscurity, but also because it destroys that which is the chief excellence of narration, that it be pleasing and adapted to persuade. For instance, the narrative,

"For he, as soon as he became of age," etc.,[1]

how long is it! The manners of the youth himself, the inquiries of the servant, the death of Chrysis, the look, figure, and affliction of the sister, and the other circumstances, are told with the utmost variety and agreeableness. But if he had been studious of such brevity as this,

"She's carried forth; we go; we reach the place
Of sepulture; she's laid upon the pile,"

he might have comprised the whole in ten lines: although 'She's carried forth, we go,' is only so far concise, as to consult, not absolute brevity, but elegance; for if there had been nothing expressed but 'she's laid upon the pile,' the whole matter would have been easily comprehended. But a narration referring to various characters, and intersected by dialogue, affords much gratification; and that becomes more probable which you report to have been done, when you describe the manner in which it was done; and it is much more clearly understood if you sometimes pause for that purpose, and do not hurry over it with affected brevity. For the narrative parts of a speech, as well as the other parts, ought to be perspicuous, and we ought to take the more pains with that part, because it is more difficult not to be obscure in stating a case, than either in an exordium, in argumentation, in refuting of an accusation, or in a peroration: and obscurity in this part of a speech is attended with greater danger than in other parts; both because, if any thing be obscurely expressed in any other part, only that is lost which is so ex-

[1] Terence, Andr., Act I., Sc. 1.

pressed; but obscurity in the narrative part spreads darkness
over the whole speech; and because, as to other parts, if you
have expressed any thing obscurely in one place, you may explain it more clearly in another; while for the narrative part
of a speech there is but one place.   But your narrative will
be clear if it be given in ordinary language, with adherence to
the order of time and without interruption.

LXXXI. "But when we ought to introduce a statement
of facts, and when we ought not, requires judicious consideration.   For we ought to make no such statement, either if
the matter is notorious, or if the circumstances are free from
doubt, or if the adversary has related them, unless, indeed,
we wish to confute his statement ; and whenever we do make
a statement of facts, let us not insist too eagerly upon points
which may create suspicion and ill-feeling, and make against
us, but let us extenuate such points as much as possible ; lest
that should happen which, whenever it occurs, Crassus thinks
is done through treachery, not through folly, namely, that we
damage our own cause; for it concerns the fortune of the
whole cause, whether the case is stated with caution or otherwise, because the statement of the case is the foundation of
all the rest of the speech.

"What follows is, that the matter in question be laid down,
when we must settle what is the point that comes under dispute; then the chief grounds of the cause are to be laid down
conjunctively, so as to weaken your adversary's supports, and
to strengthen your own; for there is in causes but one method
for that part of your speech, which is of efficacy to prove your
arguments; and that needs both confirmation and refutation ;
but because what is alleged on the other side can not be refuted unless you confirm your own statements, and your own
statements can not be confirmed unless you refute the allegations on the opposite side, these matters are in consequence
united both by their nature, by their object, and by their mode
of treatment.   The whole speech is then generally brought to
a conclusion by some amplification on the different points, or
by exciting or mollifying the judge ; and every particular, not
only in the former parts of the speech, but more especially
toward the conclusion, is to be adapted to excite as much as
possible the feelings of the judges, and to incline them in our
favor.

"Nor does there now appear to be any reason, indeed, why we should make a distinct head of those precepts which are given concerning suasory or panegyrical speeches ; for most of them are common to all kinds of oratory ; yet, to speak in favor of any important matter, or against it, seems to me to belong only to the most dignified character ; for it is the part of a wise man to deliver his opinion on momentous affairs, and that of a man of integrity and eloquence, to be able to provide for others by his prudence, to confirm by his authority, and to persuade by his language.

LXXXII. "Speeches are to be made in the senate with less display ; for it is an assembly of wise men ;[1] and opportunity is to be left for many others to speak. All suspicion, too, of ostentation of ability is to be avoided. A speech to the people, on the other hand, requires all the force, weight, and various coloring of eloquence. For persuading, then, nothing is more desirable than worth ; for he who thinks that expediency is more desirable, does not consider what the counselor chiefly wishes, but what he prefers upon occasion to follow ; and there is no man, especially in so noble a state as this, who does not think that worth ought chiefly to be regarded ; but expediency commonly prevails, there being a concealed fear, that even worth can not be supported if expediency be disregarded. But the difference between the opinions of men lies either in this question, ' which of two things is of the greater utility ?' or, if that point is agreed, it is disputed ' whether honor or expediency ought rather to be consulted.' As these seem often to oppose each other, he who is an advocate for expediency, will enumerate the benefits of peace, of plenty, of power, of riches, of settled revenues, of troops in garrison, and of other things, the enjoyment of which we estimate by their utility ; and he will specify the disadvantages of a contrary state of things. He who exhorts his audience to regard honor, will collect examples from our ancestors, which may be imitated with glory, though attended with danger ; he will expatiate on immortal fame among posterity ; he will maintain that advantage arises from the observance of honor, and that it is always united with worth. But what is possible or impossible, and what is necessary or unneces-

---

[1] *Sapiens enim est consilium.* These words I regard as a scholium that has crept into the text. *Ernesti.*

sary, are questions of the greatest moment in regard to both; for all debate is at an end, if it is understood that a thing is impossible, or if any necessity for it appears; and he who shows what the case is, when others have overlooked it, sees farthest of all. But for giving counsel in civil affairs the chief qualification is a knowledge of the constitution; and, to speak on such matters so as to be approved, an acquaintance with the manners of the people is required; and, as these frequently vary, the fashion of speaking must often be varied; and, although the power of eloquence is mostly the same, yet, as the highest dignity is in the people, as the concerns of the republic are of the utmost importance, and as the commotions of the multitude are of extraordinary violence, a more grand and imposing manner of addressing them seems necessary to be adopted; and the greatest part of a speech is to be devoted to the excitement of the feelings, either by exhortation, or the commemoration of some illustrious action, or by moving the people to hope, or to fear, or to ambition, or desire of glory; and often also to dissuade them from temerity, from rage, from ardent expectation, from injustice, from envy, from cruelty.

LXXXIII. "But it happens that, because a popular assembly appears to the orator to be his most enlarged scene of action,[1] he is naturally excited in it to a more magnificent species of eloquence; for a multitude has such influence, that, as the flute-player can not play without his flutes, so the orator can not be eloquent without a numerous audience. And, as the inclinations of popular assemblies take many and various turns, an unfavorable expression of feeling from the whole people must not be incurred; an expression which may be excited by some fault in the speech, if any thing appears to have been spoken with harshness, with arrogance, in a base or mean manner, or with any improper feeling whatever; or it may proceed from some offense taken, or ill-will conceived, at some particular individuals, which is either just, or arising from some calumny or bad report; or it may happen if the subject be displeasing; or if the multitude be swayed by any impulse from their own hopes or fears. To these four causes as many remedies may be applied: the severity of rebuke, if

---

[1] *Quia maxima quasi oratori scena videtur concionis.* "Because the greatest stage, as it were, for an orator, appears [to be that] of a public assembly."

you have sufficient authority for it; admonition, which is a milder kind of rebuke; an assurance, that if they will give you a hearing, they will approve what you say; and entreaty, which is the most condescending method, but sometimes very advantageous. But on no occasion is facetiousness and ready wit[1] of more effect, and any smart saying that is consistent with dignity and true jocularity; for nothing is so easily diverted from gloom, and often from rancor, as a multitude, even by a single expression uttered opportunely, quickly, smartly, and with good humor.

LXXXIV. "I have now stated to you generally, to the best of my abilities, what it is in my practice, in both kinds of causes, to pursue, what to avoid, what to keep in view, and to what method I ordinarily adhere in my pleadings. Nor is that third kind, panegyric, which I in the commencement excluded, as it were, from my rules, attended with any difficulty; but it was because there are many departments of oratory both of greater importance and power, concerning which hardly any author has given particular rules, and because we of this country are not accustomed to deal much in panegyric, that I set this topic entirely apart. For the Greek authors themselves, who are the most worthy of being read, wrote their panegyrics either for amusement, or to compliment some particular person, rather than with any desire to promote forensic eloquence; and books of their composition are extant, in which Themistocles, Aristides, Agesilaus, Epaminondas, Philip, Alexander, and others, are the subjects of praise. Our laudatory speeches, which we deliver in the forum, have either the simple and unadorned brevity of testimony, or are written as funeral orations, which are by no means suitable for the pomp of panegyric. But as we must sometimes attempt that department, and must occasionally write panegyrics, Caius Lælius wrote one for Publius Tubero, when he wished to praise his uncle Africanus, and in order that we ourselves may be enabled to praise, after the manner of the Greeks, such persons as we may be inclined to praise, let that subject also form part of our discourse. It is clear, then, that some qualities in mankind are desirable, and some praiseworthy. Birth, beauty, strength, power, riches, and

---

[1] *Celeritas.* The same word is used in c. 54: *hoc quod in celeritate atque dicto est.* Schütz conjectured *hilaritas.*

other things which fortune bestows, either amid external circumstances, or as personal endowments, carry with them no real praise, which is thought to be due to virtue alone; but, as virtue itself becomes chiefly conspicuous in the use and management of such things, these endowments of nature and of fortune are also to be considered in panegyrics; in which it is mentioned as the highest praise for a person not to have been haughty in power, or insolent in wealth, or to have assumed a pre-eminence over others from the abundance of the blessings of fortune; so that his riches and plenty seem to have afforded means and opportunities, not for the indulgence of pride and vicious appetites, but for the cultivation of goodness and moderation. Virtue, too, which is of itself praiseworthy, and without which nothing can be deserving of praise, is distinguished, however, into several species, some of which are more adapted to panegyric than others; for there are some virtues which are conspicuous in the manners of men, and consist in some degree in affability and beneficence; and there are others which depend on some peculiar natural genius, or superior greatness and strength of mind. Clemency, justice, benignity, fidelity, fortitude in common dangers, are subjects agreeable to the audience in panegyric (for all such virtues are thought beneficial, not so much to the persons who possess them, as to mankind in general); while wisdom, and that greatness of soul by which all human affairs are regarded as mean and inconsiderable, eminent power of thought, and eloquence itself, excite indeed no less admiration, but not equal delight; for they appear to be an ornament and support rather to the persons themselves whom we commend, than to those before whom we commend them; yet, in panegyric, these two kinds of virtues must be united; for the ears of men tolerate the praises not only of those parts of virtue which are delightful and agreeable, but of those which excite admiration.

LXXXV. "Since, also, there are certain offices and duties belonging to every kind of virtue, and since to each virtue its peculiar praise is due, it will be necessary to specify, in a panegyric on justice, what he who is praised performed with fidelity, or equanimity, or in accordance with any other moral duty. In other points, too, the praise of actions must be adapted to the nature, power, and name of the virtue under which they fall. The praise of those acts is heard with the greatest pleasure, which appear to have been undertaken by men of spirit, without advantage or reward; but those which have been also attended with toil and danger to themselves afford the largest scope for panegyric, because they may be set forth with the greatest ornaments of eloquence, and the account of them may be heard with the utmost satisfaction; for that appears the highest virtue in a man of eminence, which is beneficial to others, but attended with danger or toil, or at least without advantage, to himself. It is commonly regarded, too, as a great and admirable merit, to have borne adversity with wisdom, not to have been vanquished by fortune, and to have maintained dignity in the worst of circumstances. It is also an honor to a man that distinctions have been bestowed upon him, rewards decreed to his merit, and that his achievements have been approved by the judgment of mankind; and, on such subjects, to attribute success itself to the judgment of the immortal gods, is a part of panegyric. But such actions should be selected for praise as are either of extraordinary greatness, or unprecedented novelty, or singular in their kind; for such as are trivial, or common, or ordinary, generally appear to deserve no admiration or even commendation. A comparison also with other great men has a noble effect in panegyric.

"On this species of eloquence I have felt inclined to say something more than I had proposed, not so much for the improvement of pleading in the forum, which has been kept in view by me through this whole discourse, as that you might see that, if panegyric be a part of the orator's business—and nobody denies that it is—a knowledge of all the virtues, without which panegyric can not be composed, is necessary to the orator. As to the rules for censuring, it is clear that they are to be deduced from the vices contrary to these virtues; and it is also obvious, that neither can a good man be praised with propriety and copiousness of matter, without a knowledge of the several virtues, nor a bad man be stigmatized and branded with sufficient distinction and asperity, without a knowledge of the opposite vices. On these topics of panegyric and satire we must often touch in all kinds of causes.

"You have now heard what I think about the invention and arrangement of matter. I shall add some observations on memory, with a view to lighten the labor of Crassus, and to leave nothing for him to discuss but the art of embellishing those departments of eloquence which I have specified."

LXXXVI. "Proceed," said Crassus; "for I feel pleasure in seeing you appear as a professed artist, stripped of the disguises of dissimulation, and fairly exposed to view; and, in leaving nothing for me to do or but little, you consult my convenience, and confer a favor upon me." "How much I leave you to do," said Antonius, "will be in your own power; for if you are inclined to act fairly, I leave you every thing to do; but if you wish to shrink from any portion of your undertaking, you must consider how you can give this company satisfaction. But to return to the point; I am not," he continued, "possessed of such intellectual power as Themistocles had, that I had rather know the art of forgetfulness than that of memory; and I am grateful to the famous Simonides of Ceos, who, as people say, first invented an art of memory. For they relate, that when Simonides was at Crannon in Thessaly, at an entertainment given by Scopas, a man of rank and fortune, and had recited a poem which he had composed in his praise, in which, for the sake of embellishment, after the manner of the poets, there were many particulars introduced concerning Castor and Pollux, Scopas told Simonides, with extraordinary meanness, that he would pay him half the sum which he had agreed to give for the poem, and that he might ask the remainder, if he thought proper, from his Tyndaridæ, to whom he had given an equal share of praise. A short time after, they say that a message was brought in to Simonides, to desire him to go out, as two youths were waiting at the gate who earnestly wished him to come forth to them; when he arose, went forth, and found nobody. In the mean time the apartment in which Scopas was feasting fell down, and he himself, and his company, were overwhelmed and buried in the ruins; and when their friends were desirous to inter their remains, but could not possibly distinguish one from another, so much crushed were the bodies, Simonides is said, from his recollection of the place in which each had sat, to have given satisfactory directions for their interment. Admonished by this occurrence, he is reported to have discovered that it is chiefly order that gives distinctness to memory; and that by those, therefore, who would improve this part of the under-

standing, certain places must be fixed upon, and that of the
things which they desire to keep in memory, symbols must be
conceived in the mind, and ranged, as it were, in those places;
thus the order of places would preserve the order of things,
and the symbols of the things would denote the things themselves; so that we should use the places as waxen tablets,
and the symbols as letters.

LXXXVII. "How great the benefit of memory is to the
orator, how great the advantage, how great the power, what
need is there for me to observe? Why should I remark how
excellent a thing it is to retain the instructions which you have
received with the cause, and the opinion which you have formed upon it? to keep all your thoughts upon it fixed in your
mind, all your arrangement of language marked out there?
to listen to him from whom you receive any information, or
to him to whom you have to reply, with such power of reten-
tion, that they seem not to have poured their discourse into
your ears, but to have engraven it on your mental tablet?
They alone, accordingly, who have a vigorous memory, know
what, and how much, and in what manner they are about to
speak; to what they have replied, and what remains unan-
swered; and they also remember many courses that they have
formerly adopted in other cases, and many which they have
heard from others. I must, however, acknowledge that nature
is the chief author of this qualification, as of all those of which
I have previously spoken (but this whole art of oratory, or
image and resemblance of an art, has the power, not of en-
gendering and producing any thing entirely of itself, of which
no part previously existed in our understandings, but of being
able to give education and strength to what has been generated, and has had its birth there); yet there is scarcely any
one of so strong a memory as to retain the order of his language and thoughts without a previous arrangement and observation of heads; nor is any one of so weak a memory as
not to receive assistance from this practice and exercise. For
Simonides, or whoever else invented the art, wisely saw, that
those things are the most strongly fixed in our minds, which
are communicated to them, and imprinted upon them, by the
senses; that of all the senses that of seeing is the most acute;
and that, accordingly, those things are most easily retained in
our minds which we have received from the hearing or the

understanding, if they are also recommended to the imagination by means of the mental eye; so that a kind of form, resemblance, and representation might denote invisible objects,
and such as are in their nature withdrawn from the cognizance
of the sight, in such a manner, that what we are scarcely capable of comprehending by thought we may retain as it were
by the aid of the visual faculty.   By these imaginary forms
and objects, as by all those that come under our corporeal
vision, our memory is admonished and excited; but some place
for them must be imagined; as bodily shape can not be conceived without a place for it.   That I may not, then, be prolix
and impertinent upon so well-known and common a subject;
we must fancy many plain, distinct places at moderate dis-
tances, and such symbols as are impressive, striking, and well
marked, so that they may present themselves to the mind,
and act upon it with the greatest quickness.   This faculty of
artificial memory practice will afford (from which proceeds habit), as well as the derivation of similar words converted and
altered in cases, or transferred from particulars to generals,
and the idea of an entire sentence from the symbol of a single
word, after the manner and method of any skillful painter,
who distinguishes spaces by the variety of what he depicts.

LXXXVIII.   "But the memory of words, which, however,
is less necessary for us,[1] is to be distinguished by a greater
variety of symbols; for there are many words which, like
joints, connect the members of our speech, that can not possibly be represented by any thing similar to them; and for these
we must invent symbols that we may invariably use.   The
memory of things is the proper business of the orator; this
we may be enabled to impress on ourselves by the creation of
imaginary figures, aptly arranged, to represent particular heads,
so that we may recollect thoughts by images, and their order
by place.   Nor is that true which is said by people unskilled
in this artifice, that the memory is oppressed by the weight
of these representations, and that even obscured which unas-
sisted nature might have clearly kept in view; for I have seen
men of consummate abilities, and an almost divine faculty of
memory, as Charmadas at Athens, and Scepsius Metrodorus
in Asia, who is said to be still living, each of whom used to

---

[1] Because words are at the command of the practiced orator, and,
when matter is supplied, easily occur. *Ernesti.*

say that, as he wrote with letters on wax, so he wrote with symbols as it were, whatever he wished to remember, on these places which he had conceived in imagination. Though, therefore, a memory can not be entirely formed by this practice, if there is none given by nature; yet certainly, if there is latent natural faculty, it may be called forth.

"You have now had a very long dissertation from a person whom I wish you may not esteem impudent, but who is certainly not over-modest, in having spoken, so copiously as I have done, upon the art of eloquence, in your hearing, Catulus, and that of Lucius Crassus; for of the rest of the company the age might perhaps reasonably make less impression upon me; but you will certainly excuse me, if you but listen to the motive which impelled me to loquacity so unusual with me."

LXXXIX. "We indeed," said Catulus "(for I make this answer for my brother and myself), not only excuse you, but feel love and great gratitude to you for what you have done; and, as we acknowledge your politeness and good-nature, so we admire your learning and copious store of matter. Indeed, I think that I have reaped this benefit, that I am freed from a great mistake, and relieved from that astonishment which I used always to feel, in common with many others, as to the source from which that divine power of yours in pleading was derived; for I never imagined that you had even slightly touched upon those matters, of which I now perceive that you possess an exact knowledge, gathered from all quarters, and which, taught by experience, you have partly corrected and partly approved. Nor have I now a less high opinion of your eloquence, while I have a far higher one of your general merit and diligence; and I am pleased, at the same time, that my own judgment is confirmed, inasmuch as I always laid it down as a maxim, that no man can attain a character for wisdom and eloquence without the greatest study, industry, and learning. But what was it that you meant, when you said that we should excuse you if we knew the motive which had impelled you to this discourse? What other motive could there be but your inclination to oblige us, and to satisfy the desire of these young gentlemen, who have listened to you with the utmost attention?"

"I was desirous," replied Antonius, "to take away from

Crassus every pretense for refusal, who would, I was sure, engage in such a kind of dissertation either a little too mod- estly, or too reluctantly, for I would not apply the word dis- dainfully to a man of his affability.   But what excuse will he now be able to make?   That he is a person of consular and censorial dignity?   I might have made the same excuse. Will he plead his age?   He is four years younger than I. Can he say that he is ignorant of these matters, of which I indeed have snatched some knowledge late in life, cursorily, and, as people say, at spare times, while he has applied to them from his youth with the most diligent study, under the most able masters?   I will say nothing of his genius, in which no man was ever his equal; for no one that hears me speak has so contemptible an opinion of himself as not to hope to speak better, or at least as well; but while Crassus is speaking, no one is so conceited as to have the presump- tion to think that he shall ever speak like him.   Lest per- sons, therefore, of so much dignity as the present company, should have come to you in vain, let us at length, Crassus, hear you speak."

XC. "If I should grant you, Antonius," replied Crassus, " that these things are so, which, however, are far otherwise, what have you left for me this day, or for any man, that he can possibly say?   For I will speak, my dearest friends, what I really think: I have often heard men of learning (why do I say often?   I should rather say sometimes; for how could I have that opportunity often, when I entered the forum quite a youth, and was never absent from it longer than during my quæstorship?), but I have heard, as I said yesterday, both while I was at Athens, men of the greatest learning, and in Asia that famous rhetorician Scepsius Metrodorus, discours- ing upon these very subjects; but no one of them ever ap- peared to me to have engaged in such a dissertation with greater extent of knowledge, or greater penetration, than our friend has shown to-day; but if it be otherwise, and if I thought any thing had been omitted by Antonius, I should not be so unpolite, nay so almost churlish, as to think that a trouble which I perceived to be your desire."   "Have you then forgotten, Crassus," said Sulpicius, " that Antonius made such a division with you, that he should explain the equip- ment and implements of the orator, and leave it to you to speak of decoration and embellishment?"   "In the first place," rejoined Crassus, "who gave Antonius leave either to make such a partition, or to choose first that part which he liked best? In the next, if I rightly comprehended what I heard with the utmost pleasure, he seemed to me to treat of both these matters in conjunction."   "But," observed Cotta, "he said nothing of the embellishments of language, or on that excellence from which eloquence derives its very name."   "Antonius then," said Crassus, "left me nothing but words, and took the substance for himself."   "Well," remarked Cæsar, "if he has left you the more difficult part, we have reason to desire to hear you; if that which is the easier, you have no reason to refuse."   "And in regard to what you said, Crassus," interposed Catulus, "that if we would stay and pass the day with you here, you would comply with our wishes, do you not think it binding on your honor?"   Cotta then smiled, and said, "I might, Crassus, excuse you; but take care that Catulus has not made it a matter of religious faith; it is a point for the censor's cognizance; and you see how disgraceful it would be for a person of censorial dignity[1] to render himself obnoxious to such censure."   "Do as you please, then," replied Crassus; "but for the present, as it is time, I think we must rise, and take some repose; in the afternoon, if it is then agreeable to you, I will say something on these points, unless perchance you may wish to put me off till to-morrow."   They all replied that they were ready to hear him either at once, or in the afternoon if he preferred; as soon, however, as possible.

BOOK III.

THE ARGUMENT.

CICERO, in the introduction to this book, laments the sad deaths of Crassus and Antonius. He then proceeds to relate Crassus's farther remarks on eloquence, and especially on style and delivery, in which he was thought to excel all other speakers. See Cic., de Clar. Orat., c. 38. He shows that an orator should speak correctly, perspicuously, elegantly, and to the purpose. Style is to be ornamented by a

---

[1] A man who has been censor, as you have been. *Proust.*

tasteful choice of words, and by tropes and figures; and it must have
a certain rhythm or harmony. Some observations are added on
action and delivery in general. In c. 14 a digression is made on the
praises of eloquence, and the combination of a knowledge of philosophy, especially the Academic and Peripatetic, with the study of it.

I. WHEN I proceeded to execute my design, brother Quintus, of relating and committing to writing in this third book,
the remarks which Crassus made after the dissertation of
Antonius, bitter remembrance renewed in my mind its former
concern and regret; for the genius worthy of immortality,
the learning, the virtue that were in Lucius Crassus, were all
extinguished by sudden death, within ten days from the day
which is comprised in this and the former book. When he
returned to Rome on the last day of the theatrical entertain-
ments,[1] he was put into a violent emotion by that oration
which was reported to have been delivered in an assembly of
the people by Philippus, who, it was agreed, had declared,
"that he must look for another council, as he could not carry
on the government with such a senate;" and on the morning
of the thirteenth of September, both Crassus and a full senate
came into the house on the call of Drusus. There, when
Drusus had made many complaints against Philippus, he
brought formally before the senate the fact that the consul
had thrown such grievous obloquy on that order, in his
speech to the people. Here, as I have often heard it unani-
mously said by men of the greatest judgment, although indeed it continually happened to Crassus, whenever he had
delivered a speech more exquisite than ordinary, that he was
always thought never to have spoken better, yet by universal
consent it was then determined that all other orators had always been excelled by Crassus, but that on that day he had
been excelled by himself; for he deplored the misfortune and
unsupported condition of the senate; an order whose hereditary dignity was then being torn from it by a consul, as by
some lawless ruffian, a consul whose duty it was to act the
part of a good parent or trusty guardian toward it; but said
that it was not surprising if, after he had ruined the commonwealth by his own counsels, he should divorce the counsels
of the senate from the commonwealth. When he had applied
these expressions, which were like fire-brands, to Philippus,

[1] Which accompanied the public games. Compare i., 7.

who was a man of violence as well as of eloquence, and of the utmost vigor to resist opposition, he could not restrain himself, but burst forth into a furious flame, and resolved to bind Crassus to good behavior, by forfeiting his securities.[1]   On that occasion, many things are reported to have been uttered by Crassus with a sort of divine sublimity, refusing to acknowledge as a consul him who would not allow him to possess the senatorial dignity : *Do you,* said he, *who, when you thought the general authority of the whole senatorial order intrusted to you as a pledge, yet perfidiously annulled it in the view of the Roman people, imagine that I can be terrified by such petty forfeitures as those?   It is not such pledges that are to be forfeited, if you would bind Lucius Crassus to silence ; for that purpose you must cut out this tongue; and even if it be torn out, the freedom in my very breath will confound your audacity.*

II. It appeared that a multitude of other expressions were then uttered by him with the most vehement efforts of mind, thought, and spirits ; and that that resolution of his, which the senate adopted in a full house, was proposed by him with the utmost magnificence and dignity of language, *That the counsel and fidelity of the senate had never been wanting to the commonwealth, in order to do justice to the Roman people;* and he was present (as appears from the names entered in the register) at the recording of the resolution.   This, however, was the last swan-like note and speech of that divine orator; and, as if expecting to hear it again, we used, after his death, to go into the senate-house, that we might contemplate the spot on which he had last stood to speak ; for we heard that he was seized at the time with a pain in his side while he was speaking, and that a copious perspiration followed ; after which he was struck with a chillness, and, returning home in a fever, died the seventh day after of pleurisy.   O how fallacious are the hopes of mortals, how frail is our condition, and how insignificant all our ambitious efforts, which are often broken and thrown down in the middle of their course, and overwhelmed as it were in their voyage, even before they gain a

---

[1] *Pignoribus ablatis.* The senators and others were obliged to attend the senate when they were summoned, and to be submissive to the superior magistrates, or they might be punished by fine and distraint of their property.   See Livy, iii., 38; xliii., 16; Plin., Ep., iv., 29 ; Cic., Phil., i., 5; Suet., Jul., c. 17; Adam's Roman Antiquities, p. 2.

sight of the harbor! For as long as the life of Crassus was perplexed with the toils of ambition, so long was he more distinguished for the performance of private duties, and the praises due to his genius, than for any benefit that he reaped from his greatness, or for the dignified rank which he bore in the republic; but the first year which, after a discharge of all the honorable offices of the state, opened to him the entrance to supreme authority by universal consent, overthrew all his hopes, and all his future schemes of life, by death. This was a melancholy occurrence to his friends, a grievous calamity to his country, and a heavy affliction to all the virtuous part of mankind; but such misfortunes afterward fell upon the commonwealth, that life does not appear to me to have been taken away from Lucius Crassus by the immortal gods as a privation, but death to have been bestowed on him as a blessing. He did not live to behold Italy blazing with war, or the senate overwhelmed with popular odium, or the leading men of the state accused of the most heinous crimes, or the affliction of his daughter, or the banishment of his son-in-law,[1] or the most calamitous flight of Caius Marius, or that most atrocious of all slaughters after his return, or, finally, that republic in every way disgraced, in which, while it continued most flourishing, he had by far the pre-eminence over all other men in glory

III. But led away as I am by my reflections to touch upon the power and vicissitudes of fortune, my observations shall not expatiate too widely, but shall be confined almost to the very personages who are contained in this dialogue, which I have begun to detail. For who would not call the death of Lucius Crassus, which has been so often lamented by multitudes, a happy one, when he calls to mind the fate of those very persons who were almost the last that held discourse with him? For we ourselves remember, that Quintus Catulus, a man distinguished for almost every species of merit, when he entreated, not the security of his fortunes, but retreat into exile, was reduced to deprive himself of life. It was then, too, that that illustrious head of Marcus Antonius, by whom the lives of so many citizens had been preserved,

---

[1] His daughter Licinia was married to Publius Scipio, the grandson of Serapion, who was instrumental in the death of Tiberius Gracchus. Cic., Brut., 58. *Ellendt.*

was fixed upon the very rostra on which he had so strenuous-
ly defended the republic when consul, and which he had
adorned with imperial trophies when censor. Not far from
his was exposed the head of Caius Julius (who was betrayed
by his Tuscan host), with that of Lucius Julius his brother;
so that he who did not behold such atrocities may justly be
thought to have prolonged his life during the existence of the
constitution, and to have expired together with it. He neither beheld his near relation, Publius Crassus, a man of the
greatest magnanimity, slain by his own hand, nor saw the
image of Vesta sprinkled with the blood of the pontifex, his
colleague; and (such were his feelings toward his country)
even the cruel death of Caius Carbo, his greatest enemy, that
occurred on the same day, would have caused additional grief
to him. He did not behold the horrible and miserable fate
of those young men who had devoted themselves to him ; of
whom Caius Cotta, whom he had left in a promising condition, was expelled, through popular prejudice, from his office
of tribune, a few days after the death of Crassus, and, not
many months afterward, driven from the city. And Sulpicius, who had been involved in the same popular fury, attempted in his tribuneship to spoil of all their honors those
with whom, as a private individual, he had lived in the greatest familiarity; but when he was shooting forth into the
highest glory of eloquence, his life was taken from him by
the sword, and punishment was inflicted on his rashness, not
without great damage to the republic. I am indeed of opinion that you, Crassus, received as well your birth as your
death from the peculiar appointment of divine providence,
both on account of the distinction of your life and the season
of your death; for, in accordance with your virtue and firmness of mind, you must either have submitted to the cruelty
of civil slaughter ; or, if any fortune had rescued you from so
barbarous a death, the same fortune would have compelled
you to be a spectator of the ruins of your country ; and not
only the dominion of ill-designing men, but even the victory
of the honorable party, would, on account of the civil massa-
cres intermingled with it, have been an affliction to you.

IV. Indeed, when I reflect, brother Quintus, upon the
calamities of these great men (whose fates I have just mentioned), and those which we ourselves have felt and experi-

enced from our extraordinary and eminent love for our country, your opinions appear to me to be founded on justice and wisdom, as you have always, on account of such numerous, such violent, and such sudden afflictions as have happened to the most illustrious and virtuous men, dissuaded me from all civil contention and strife. But, because we can not put affairs into the same state as if nothing had occurred, and because our extreme toils are compensated and mitigated by great glory, let us apply ourselves to those consolations, which are not only pleasant to us when troubles have subsided, but may also be salutary while they continue; let us deliver as a memorial to posterity the remaining and almost the last discourse of Lucius Crassus; and let us express the gratitude to him which he so justly merited, although in terms by no means equal to his genius, yet to the best of our endeavors; for there is not any of us, when he reads the admirably written dialogues of Plato, in almost all of which the character of Socrates is represented, who does not, though what is written of him is written in a divine spirit, conceive something still greater of him about whom it is written: and it is also my request, not indeed to you, my brother, who attribute to me perfection in all things, but to others who shall take this treatise into their hands, that they would entertain a nobler conception of Lucius Crassus than any that is expressed by me. For I, who was not present at this dialogue, and to whom Caius Cotta communicated only the topics and heads of the dissertation, have endeavored to shadow forth in the conversation of the speakers those peculiar styles of oratory, in which I knew that each of them was conspicuous. But if any person shall be induced by the common opinion, to think either that Antonius was more jejune, or Crassus more exuberant in style, than they have been respectively described by me, he will be among the number of those who either never heard these great men, or who have not abilities to judge; for each of them was (as I have explained before) superior to all other speakers, in application, and genius, and learning, as well as excellent in his particular style, so that embellishment in language was not wanting in Antonius, nor redundant in Crassus.

V. As soon, therefore, as they had withdrawn before noon, and reposed themselves a little, Cotta said that he particularly observed that Crassus employed all the time about the middle of the day in the most earnest and profound meditation; and that he himself, who was well acquainted with the countenance which he assumed whenever he was going to speak in public, and the nature of his looks when he was fixed in contemplation, and had often remarked them in causes of the greatest importance, came on purpose, while the rest were asleep, into the room in which Crassus had lain down on a couch prepared for him, and that, as soon as he perceived him to be settled in a thoughtful posture, he immediately retired; and that almost two hours passed in that perfect stillness. Afterward, when they all, as the day was now verging to the afternoon, waited upon Crassus, Cæsar said, " Well, Crassus, shall we go and take our seats? though we only come to put you in mind of your promise, and not to demand the performance of it." Crassus then replied, " Do you imagine that I have the assurance to think that I can continue longer indebted to such friends as you, especially in an obligation of this nature?" " What place then will suit you?" said Cæsar; " a seat in the middle of the wood, for that is the most shady and cool?" " Very well," replied Crassus, " for there is in that spot a seat not at all unsuited for this discourse of ours." This arrangement being agreeable to the rest of the company, they went into the wood, and sat down there with the most earnest desire to listen.

Crassus then said, " Not only the influence of your authority and friendship, but also the ready compliance of Antonius, have taken from me all liberty of refusal, though I had an excellent pretext for refusing. In the partition, however, of this dissertation between us, Antonius, when he assumed to himself the part of speaking upon those matters which form the subject of the orator's speech, and left to me to explain how they should be embellished, divided things which are in their nature incapable of separation; for as every speech consists of the matter and the language, the language can have no place if you take away the matter, nor the matter receive any illustration if you take away the language. Indeed, the great men of antiquity, embracing something of superior magnificence in their ideas, appear to me to have seen farther into the nature of things than the visual faculties of our minds can penetrate; as they said that all these things, above and below, formed one system, and were linked together in strict union by one and the same power, and one principle of universal harmony in nature; for there is no order of things which can either of itself, if forcibly separated from the rest, preserve a permanent existence, or without which the rest can maintain their power and eternal duration.

VI. "But, if this reasoning appear to be too comprehensive to be embraced by human sense and understanding, yet that saying of Plato is true, and certainly not unknown to you, Catulus, 'that all the learning of these liberal and polite departments of knowledge is linked together in one bond of union; for when the power of that reason, by which the causes and events of things are known, is once thoroughly discerned, a certain wonderful agreement and harmony, as it were, in all the sciences is discovered.' But, if this also appear to be too sublime a thought for us to contemplate who are prostrate on the earth, it, however, certainly is our duty to know and remember that which we have embraced, which we profess, which we have taken upon ourselves. Since eloquence, as I observed yesterday, and Antonius signified in some passages of his discourse this morning, is one and the same, into whatever tracts or regions of debate it may be carried: for whether it discourses concerning the nature of the heavens or of the earth—whether of divine or human power—whether it speaks from a lower, or an equal, or a superior place—whether to impel an audience, or to instruct, or to deter, or to incite, or to dissuade, or to inflame, or to soothe—whether to a small or to a large assembly—whether to strangers, to friends, or alone—its language is derived through different channels, not from different sources; and, wherever it directs its course, it is attended with the same equipment and decoration. But since we are overwhelmed by opinions, not only those of the vulgar, but those also of men imperfectly instructed, who treat of those things more easily when divided and torn asunder which they have not capacity to comprehend in a general view, and who sever the language from the thoughts like the body from the soul, neither of which separations can be made without destruction, I will not undertake in this discourse more than that which is imposed upon me; I will only signify briefly, that neither can embellishments of language be found without arrangement and expression of thoughts, nor can thoughts be made to shine without the light of language. But before I proceed to touch upon those particulars by which I think language is beautified and illumined, I will state briefly what I think concerning eloquence in general.

VII. " There is no one of the natural senses, in my opinion, which does not include under its general comprehension many things dissimilar one to another, but which are still thought deserving of similar approbation; for we both perceive many things by the ear, which, although they all charm us with their sounds, are yet often so various in themselves, that that which we hear last appears to be the most delightful; and almost innumerable pleasures are received by the eye, which all captivate us in such a manner as to delight the same sense in different ways; and pleasures that bear no sort of resemblance to each other charm the rest of the senses in such a manner that it is difficult to determine which affords the most exquisite enjoyment. But the same observation which is to be made in regard to nature may be applied also to the different kinds of art. Sculpture is a single art, in which Myro, Polycletus, and Lysippus excelled; all of whom differed one from another, but so that you would not wish any one of them to be unlike himself. The art and science of painting is one, yet Zeuxis, Aglaophon, and Apelles are quite unlike one another in themselves, though to none of them does any thing seem wanting in his peculiar style. And if this be wonderful, and yet true, in these, as it were, mute arts, how much more wonderful is it in language and speech? which, though employed about the same thoughts and words, yet admits of the greatest variations; and not so that some speakers are to be censured and others commended, but that those who are allowed to merit praise, merit it for different excellences. This is fully exemplified in poets, who have the nearest affinity to orators: how distinct from each other are Ennius, Pacuvius, and Accius; how distinct, among the Greeks, Æschylus, Sophocles, and Euripides; though almost equal praise may be attributed to them all in different kinds of writing. Then, behold and contemplate those whose art is the subject of our present inquiry; what a wide distinction there is between the accomplishments and natural abilities of orators! Isocrates possessed sweetness, Lysias delicacy, Hyperides pointedness, Æschines sound, and Demosthenes energy ; and which of them was not excellent ? yet which of them resembled any one but himself ? Africanus, had weight, Lælius smoothness, Galba asperity, Carbo something of fluency and harmony ; but which of these was not an orator of the first rank in those times ? and yet every one attained that rank by a style of oratory peculiar to himself.

VIII. "But why should I search into antiquity for examples, when I can point to present and living characters ? What was ever more pleasing to the ear than the language of our friend Catulus ? language of such purity, that he appears to be almost the only orator that speaks pure Latin ; and of such power, that with its peculiar dignity there is yet blended the utmost politeness and wit. In a word, when I hear him, I always think that whatever you should add, or alter, or take away, his language would be impaired and deteriorated. Has not our friend Cæsar here, too, introduced a new kind of oratory, and brought before us an almost peculiar style of eloquence ? Who has ever, besides him, treated tragical subjects in an almost comic manner, serious subjects with pleasantry, grave subjects with gayety, and subjects suited to the forum with a grace peculiar to the stage ? in such a way that neither is the jocular style excluded by the importance of the subject, nor is the weight of the matter lessened by the humor with which it is treated. Here are present with us two young men, almost of equal age, Sulpicius and Cotta ; what things were ever so dissimilar as they are one to another ? yet what is so excellent as they are in their respective styles ? One is polished and refined, explaining things with the greatest propriety and aptitude of expression ; he always adheres to his cause, and, when he has discovered, with his keen discernment, what he ought to prove to the judge, he directs his whole attention and force of oratory to that point, without regarding other arguments ; while Sulpicius has a certain irresistible energy of mind, a most full and powerful voice, a most vigorous action, and consummate dignity of motion, united with such weight and copiousness of language, that he appears of all men the best qualified by nature for eloquence.

IX. "I now return to ourselves (because there has ever been such a comparison made between us, that we are brought,

as it were, into judgment on account of rivalship, in the common conversation of mankind): what two things can be more
dissimilar than Antonius's manner of speaking and my own?
though he is such an orator that no one can possibly surpass
him; and I, though I am altogether dissatisfied with myself,
am yet in preference to others admitted to a comparison with
him.   Do you notice what the manner of Antonius is?   It is
bold, vehement, full of energy and action, fortified and guarded on every point of the cause, spirited, acute, explicit, dwelling upon every circumstance, retiring with honor, pursuing
with eagerness, terrifying, supplicating, exhibiting the greatest variety of language, yet without satiety to the ear; but as
to myself, whatever I am as a speaker (since I appear to you
to hold some place among speakers), I certainly differ very
greatly from his style.   What my talents are it becomes not
me to say, because every one is least known to himself, and it
is extremely difficult for any person to form a judgment of his
own capacity; but the dissimilitude may be easily perceived,
both from the mediocrity of my action, and from the circumstance that I usually conclude in the same track in which I
first set out; and that labor and care in choosing words
causes me greater anxiety than choice of matter, being afraid
that if my language should be a little obsolete, it may appear
unworthy of the expectation and silent attention of the audience.   But if in us who are present there are such remarkable dissimilitudes, such decided peculiarities in each of us, and
in all this variety the better is distinguished from the worse
by difference in ability rather than by difference in kind, and
every thing is praiseworthy that is perfect in its nature, what
do you imagine must be the case if we should take into consideration all the orators that any where exist, or ever existed?   Would it not happen that almost as many kinds of eloquence as of orators would be found?   But from this observation of mine, it may perhaps occur to you, that if there be
almost innumerable varieties and characters of eloquence, dissimilar in species, yet laudable in their kind, things of so diversified a nature can never be formed into an art by the same
precepts and one single method of instruction.   This is not
the case; and it is to be attentively considered by those who
have the conduct and education of others, in what direction
the natural genius of each seems principally to incline him.

For we see that from the same schools of artists and masters, eminent in their respective pursuits, there have gone forth pupils very unlike each other, yet all praiseworthy, because the instruction of the teacher has been adapted to each person's natural genius; a fact of which the most remarkable example (to say nothing of other sciences) is that saying of Isocrates, an eminent teacher of eloquence, that he used to apply the spur to Ephorus, but to put the rein on Theopompus; for the one, who overleaped all bounds in the boldness of his expressions, he restrained; the other, who hesitated and was bashful, as it were, he stimulated: nor did he produce in them any resemblance to each other, but gave to the one such an addition, and retrenched from the other so much superfluity, as to form in both that excellence of which the natural genius of each was susceptible.

X. " I thought it necessary to premise these particulars, that if every remark of mine did not exactly adapt itself to the inclinations of you all, and to that peculiar style of speaking which each of you most admired, you might be sensible that I described that character of eloquence of which I myself most approved.

" Those matters, therefore, of which Antonius has treated so explicitly, are to be endowed with action and elocution by the orator in some certain manner. What manner of elocution can be better (for I will consider action by-and-by) than that of speaking in pure Latin, with perspicuity, with gracefulness, and with aptitude and congruity to the subject in question? Of the two which I mentioned first, purity and clearness of language, I do not suppose that any account is expected from me; for we do not attempt to teach him to be an orator who can not speak; nor can we hope that he who can not speak grammatical Latin will speak elegantly; nor that he who can not speak what we can understand, will ever speak any thing for us to admire. Let us, therefore, omit these matters, which are easy of attainment, though necessary in practice; for the one is taught in school-learning and the rudiments of children; the other[1] is cultivated for this reason, that what every person says may be understood—a qualification which we perceive indeed to be necessary, yet that none

---

[1] Perspicuity.

can be held in less estimation.[1] But all elegance of language, though it receive a polish from the science of grammar, is yet augmented by the reading of orators and poets; for those ancients, who could not then adorn what they expressed, had almost all a kind of nobleness of diction; and those who are accustomed to their style can not express themselves otherwise than in pure Latin, even though they desire to do so. Yet we must not make use of such of their words as our modern mode of speaking does not admit, unless sometimes for the sake of ornament, and but sparingly, as I shall explain; but he who is studious and much conversant with ancient writers, will make such use of common expressions as always to adopt the most eligible.

XI. "In order to speak pure Latin, we must take care not only to use words with which nobody can justly find fault, and preserve the construction by proper cases, and tenses, and genders, and numbers, so that there may be nothing confused, or incongruous, or preposterous; but also that the tongue, and the breath, and the tone of the voice come under proper regulation. I would not have letters sounded with too much affectation, or uttered imperfectly through negligence; I would not have the words dropped out without expression or spirit; I would not have them puffed and, as it were, panted forth, with a difficulty of breathing; for I do not as yet speak of those things relating to the voice which belong to oratorical delivery, but merely of that which seems to me to concern pronunciation. For there are certain faults which every one is desirous to avoid, as a too delicate and effeminate tone of voice, or one that is extravagantly harsh and grating. There is also a fault which some industriously strive to attain; a rustic and rough pronunciation is agreeable to some, that their language, if it has that tone, may seem to partake more of antiquity; as Lucius Cotta, an acquaintance of yours, Catulus, appears to me to take a delight in the broadness of his speech and the rough sound of his voice, and thinks that what he says will savor of the antique if it certainly savor of rusticity. But your harmony and sweetness delight me; I do not refer to the harmony of your words, which is a principal point, but one which method in-

[1] This seems to be speaking rather too lightly of the merit of perspicuity, which Quintilian pronounces the chief virtue of language.

troduces, learning teaches, practice in reading and speaking
confirms ; but I mean the mere sweetness of pronunciation,
which, as among the Greeks it was peculiar to the Athenians,
so in the Latin tongue is chiefly remarkable in this city. At
Athens, learning among the Athenians themselves has long
been entirely neglected ; there remains in that city only the
seat of the studies which the citizens do not cultivate, but
which foreigners enjoy, being captivated in a manner with
the very name and authority of the place ; yet any illiterate
Athenian will easily surpass the most learned Asiatics,[1] not in
his language, but in sweetness of tone, not so much in speaking well as in speaking agreeably. Our citizens[2] pay less
attention to letters than the people of Latium, yet among all
the people that you know in the city, who have the least
tincture of literature, there is not one who would not have
a manifest advantage over Quintus Valerius of Sora,[3] the most
learned of all the Latins, in softness of voice, in conformation
of the mouth, and in the general tone of pronunciation.

XII. " As there is a certain tone of voice, therefore, peculiar to the Roman people and city, in which nothing can offend
or displease, nothing can be liable to animadversion, nothing
sound or savor of what is foreign, let us cultivate that tone,
and learn to avoid not only the asperity of rustic, but the
strangeness of outlandish pronunciation.   Indeed, when I
listen to my wife's mother, Lælia[4] (for women more easily
preserve the ancient language unaltered, because, not having
experience of the conversation of a multitude of people, they
always retain what they originally learned), I hear her with
such attention that I imagine myself listening to Plautus or
Nævius ; she has a tone of voice so unaffected and simple, that
it seems to carry in it nothing of ostentation or imitation ;
from whence I judge that her father and forefathers spoke in
like manner ; not with a rough tone, as he whom I mentioned,
nor with one broad, or rustic, or too open, but with one that
was close, and equable, and smooth.   Our friend Cotta, there-

[1] The Asiatic Greeks.

[2] Those who are born at Rome apply themselves to the liberal
sciences less than the rest of the people of Latium. *Proust.*

[3] See Brut., c. 46.

[4] The daughter of Caius Lælius Sapiens, who was married to Quintus Mucius Scævola, the augur.   See Brut., c. 58 ; Quint., i., 1, 6. *Ellendt.*

fore, whose broad manner of speaking you, Sulpicius, sometimes imitate, so as to drop the letter I and pronounce E as
full as possible, does not seem to me to resemble the ancient
orators, but the modern farmers." As Sulpicius laughed at
this, " I will act with you," said Crassus, " in such a manner,
that, as you oblige me to speak, you shall hear something of
your own faults." " I wish we may," replied Sulpicius, " for
that is what we desire ; and if you do so, we shall to-day,
I fancy, throw off many of our inelegances." " But," said
Crassus, " I can not censure you, Sulpicius, without being in
danger of censure myself; since Antonius has declared that
he thinks you very similar to me."[1] " But," rejoined Sulpicius,
" as Antonius also recommended us to imitate those things
which were most conspicuous in any one,[2] I am afraid in consequence that I may have copied nothing from you but the
stamping of your foot, and a few particular expressions, and
perhaps something of your action." " With what you have
caught from me, then," said Crassus, " I find no fault, lest I
should ridicule myself (but there are many more and greater
faults of mine than you mention) ; of faults, however, which
are evidently your own, or taken by imitation from any third
person, I shall admonish you whenever opportunity may re-
mind me of them.

XIII. " Let us therefore pass over the rules for speaking
the Latin tongue in its purity ; which the teaching given to
children conveys, which refined knowledge and method in
study, or the habit of daily and domestic conversation cher-
ishes, and which books and the reading of the ancient orators
and poets confirm. Nor let us dwell long upon that other
point, so as to discuss by what means we may succeed in
making what we say understood; an object which we shall
doubtless effect by speaking good Latin, adopting words in
common use, and such as aptly express what we wish to communicate or explain, without any ambiguous word or phrase,
not making our sentences too long, not making such observations as are drawn from other subjects, for the sake of comparison, too prolix; avoiding all incoherency of thought, re-
version of the order of time, all confusion of persons, all
irregularity of arrangement whatever. In short, the whole
matter is so easy, that it often appears astonishing to me that

[1] See ii., 21; Brut., c. 55.   [2] See ii., 22.

what the advocate would express should be more difficult to understand, than he who employs the advocate would be if he were to speak on his own business ; for the persons themselves who bring cases to us give us in general such instructions that you would not desire any thing to be delivered in a plainer manner ; but as soon as Fufius, or your equal in age, Pomponius,[1] proceeds to plead those cases, I do not find them equally intelligible, unless I give an extraordinary degree of attention ; their speech is so confused and ill arranged that there is nothing first and nothing second ; there is such a jumble of strange words, that language, which ought to throw a light upon things, involves them in obscurity and darkness ; and the speakers, in what they say, seem in a manner to contradict themselves. But, if it is agreeable, since I think that these topics must appear troublesome and distasteful, at least to you of a more advanced age,[2] let us proceed to other matters which may prove still more unsatisfactory."[3]

XIV. "You see," said Antonius, "how inattentive we are, and how unwillingly we listen to you,[4] when we might be induced (I judge from myself) to neglect all other concerns to follow you and give you our attention ; so elegant are your remarks upon unpleasing, so copious upon barren, so new upon common subjects."

"Those two parts, indeed, Antonius," continued Crassus, "which I have just run over, or rather have almost passed by, that of speaking in pure Latin, and with perspicuity, were easy to treat ; those which remain are important, intricate, diversified, weighty, on which depends all the admiration bestowed upon ability and all the praise given to eloquence ; for nobody ever admired an orator for merely speaking good Latin ; if he speaks otherwise, they ridicule him ; and not only do not think him an orator, but not even a man. Nor has any one ever extolled a speaker for merely speaking in such a manner that those who were present understood what he said ; though every one has despised him who was not able to do so. Whom, then, do men regard with awe? What speaker do they behold with astonishment? At whom do they utter exclamations? Whom do they consider as a deity,

---

[1] See i., 39 ; Brut., c. 57, 62, 90.   *Ellendt.*

[2] Antonius and Catulus.

[3] *Odiosiora. Auditoribus odiosiora.* Schutz.   [4] Ironically.

if I may use the expression, among mortals? Him who
speaks distinctly, explicitly, copiously, and luminously, both
as to matter and words; who produces in his language a sort
of rhythm and harmony; who speaks, as I call it, *gracefully*.
Those also who treat their subject as the importance of things
and persons requires, are to be commended for that peculiar
kind of merit, which I term *aptitude* and *congruity*.   Antonius
said that he had never seen any who spoke in such a manner,
and observed that to such only was to be attributed the distinguishing title of *eloquence*.   On my authority, therefore, de-
ride and despise all those who imagine that from the precepts
of such as are now called rhetoricians they have gained all
the powers of oratory, and have not yet been able to understand what character they hold, or what they profess; for indeed, by an orator, every thing that relates to human life,
since that is the field on which his abilities are displayed, and
is the subject for his eloquence, should be examined, heard,
read, discussed, handled, and considered; since eloquence is
one of the most eminent virtues; and though all the virtues
are in their nature equal and alike, yet one species is more
beautiful and noble than another; as is this power, which,
comprehending a knowledge of things, expresses the thoughts
and purposes of the mind in such a manner, that it can impel the audience whithersoever it inclines its force; and, the
greater is its influence, the more necessary it is that it should
be united with probity and eminent judgment; for if we bestow the faculty of eloquence upon persons destitute of these
virtues, we shall not make them orators, but give arms to
madmen.

XV. "This faculty, I say, of thinking and speaking, this
power of eloquence, the ancient Greeks denominated wisdom.
Hence the Lycurgi, the Pittaci, the Solons; and, compared
with them, our Coruncanii, Fabricii, Catos, and Scipios, were
perhaps not so learned, but were certainly of a like force and
inclination of mind.   Others, of equal ability, but of dissimilar affection toward the pursuits of life, preferred ease and
retirement, as Pythagoras, Democritus, Anaxagoras, and
transferred their attention entirely from civil polity to the
contemplation of nature; a mode of life which, on account
of its tranquillity, and the pleasure derived from science, than
which nothing is more delightful to mankind, attracted a

greater number than was of advantage to public concerns. Accordingly, as men of the most excellent natural talents gave themselves up to that study, in the enjoyment of the greatest abundance of free and unoccupied time, so men of the greatest learning, blessed with excess of leisure and fertility of thought, imagined it their duty to make more things than were really necessary the objects of their attention, investigation, and inquiry. That ancient learning, indeed, appears to have been at the same time the preceptress of living rightly and of speaking well; nor were there separate masters for those subjects, but the same teachers formed the morals and the language; as Phœnix in Homer, who says that he was appointed a companion in war to the young Achilles by his father Peleus, to make him an orator in words and a hero in deeds. But as men accustomed to constant and daily employment, when they are hindered from their occupation by the weather, betake themselves to play at ball, or dice, or draughts, or even invent some new game of their own to amuse their leisure; so they, being either excluded from public employments, as from business, by the state of the times, or being idle from inclination, gave themselves up wholly, some to the poets, some to the geometers, some to music; others even, as the logicians, found out a new study and exercise for themselves, and consumed their whole time and lives in those arts which have been discovered to form the minds of youth to learning and to virtue.

XVI. "But, because there were some, and those not a few, who either were eminent in public affairs, through their twofold excellence in acting and speaking, excellences which are indeed inseparable, as Themistocles, Pericles, Theramenes; or who, though they were not employed themselves in public affairs, were teachers of others in that science, as Gorgias, Thrasymachus, Isocrates; there appeared others who, being themselves men of abundant learning and ingenuity, but averse to political business and employments, derided and despised the exercise of oratory; at the head of which party was Socrates. He, who, by the testimony of all the learned, and the judgment of all Greece, was the first of all men as well in wisdom and penetration, grace and refinement, as in eloquence, variety, and copiousness of language on whatever subject he took in hand, deprived of their common name

those who handled, treated, and gave instruction in those
matters which are the objects of our present inquiry, when
they were previously comprised under one appellation; as all
knowledge in the best arts and sciences, and all exercise in
them, was denominated *philosophy;* and he separated in his
discussions the ability of thinking wisely and speaking gracefully, though they are naturally united; Socrates, I say,
whose great genius and varied conversation Plato has in his
Dialogues consigned to immortality, he himself having left us
nothing in writing.   Hence arose that divorce, as it were, of
the tongue from the heart, a division certainly absurd, useless, and reprehensible, that one class of persons should teach
us to think, and another to speak, rightly; for, as many reasoners had their origin almost from Socrates, and as they
caught up some one thing, some another, from his disputations, which were various, diversified, and diffusive upon all
subjects, many sects as it were became propagated, dissenting
one from another, and much divided and very dissimilar in
opinions, though all the philosophers wished to be called, and
thought that they were, Socratics.

XVII. "First from Plato himself came Aristotle and
Xenocrates, the one of whom founded the Peripatetic sect,
the other the Academy; and from Antisthenes, who was
chiefly delighted with the patience and endurance recommended in the discourses of Socrates, sprung first the Cynics,
afterward the Stoics.   Next, from Aristippus, for whom the
dissertations on pleasure had greater charms, emanated the
Cyrenaic philosophy, which he and his followers maintained
in its simplicity; those who in our days measure all things
by the standard of pleasure, while they act more modestly in
this particular, neither satisfy that dignity which they are far
from rejecting, nor adhere to that pleasure which they are inclined to embrace.   There were also other sects of philosophers, who almost all in general called themselves the followers of Socrates; as those of the Eretrians, Herillians, Mega-
rians, and Pyrrhonians; but these have long since been overthrown and extinguished by the superior arguments of the
others.   Of those which remain, that philosophy which has
undertaken the patronage of pleasure, however true it may
appear to some, is very unsuitable for that personage of whom
we are forming a conception, and whom we would have to be

of authority in public councils, a leader in the administration of government, a consummate master of thought and eloquence, as well in the senate, as in popular assemblies, and in public causes. Yet no injury shall be done to that philosophy by us; for it shall not be repelled from the mark at which it wishes to aim, but shall repose quietly in its gardens, where it wishes, and where, reclining softly and delicately, it calls us away from the rostra, from the courts of justice, and from the senate, and perhaps wisely, especially in such times of the republic as these. But my present inquiry is not which philosophy is the nearest to truth, but which is the best suited to the orator. Let us therefore dismiss those of this sect without any contumely; for they are well-meaning, and, as they seem so to themselves, happy; let us only admonish them to keep that maxim of theirs, though it be eminently true, secret however as a mystery, I mean their denial that it is the part of a wise man to concern himself with public affairs; for if they should convince us, and every man of eminent ability, of the truth of that maxim, they will be unable to remain, as they especially desire, in tranquillity.

XVIII. "The Stoics, too, whom I by no means disapprove, I notwithstanding dismiss; nor am I afraid that they will be angry, as they are proof against anger; and I feel grateful to them on this account, that they alone, of all the philosophers, have declared eloquence to be virtue and wisdom. But there are two peculiarities in their doctrine, which are quite unsuitable to that orator whom we are forming; one, that they pronounce all who are not wise, to be slaves, robbers, enemies, and madmen, and yet do not admit that any person is wise (but it would be very absurd to trust the interests of an assembly of the people, or of the senate, or any other body of men, to one to whom none of those present would appear to be in their senses, none to be citizens, none to be freemen); the other, that they have a manner of speaking which is perhaps subtle, and certainly acute, but for an orator, dry, strange, unsuited to the ear of the populace, obscure, barren, jejune, and altogether of that species which a speaker can not use to a multitude. Other citizens, or rather all other people, have very different notions of good and evil from the Stoics; their estimation of honor and ignominy, rewards and punishments, is entirely different; whether justly or otherwise, is nothing to the present occasion; but if we should adopt their notions, we should never be able to expedite any business by speaking. The remaining sects are the Peripatetic and the Academic; though of the Academics, notwithstanding there is but one name, there are two distinct systems of opinion; for Speusippus, Plato's sister's son, and Xenocrates, who had been a hearer of Plato, and Polemo, who had been a hearer of Xenocrates, and Crantor, differed in no great degree from Aristotle, who had also been a hearer of Plato; in copiousness and variety of diction, however, they were perhaps unequal to him. Arcesilas, who had been a hearer of Polemo, was the first who eagerly embraced the doctrine drawn from the various writings of Plato and the discourses of Socrates, that ' there is nothing certain to be known, either by the senses or the understanding;' he is reported to have adopted an eminently graceful manner of speaking, to have rejected all judgment of the mind and the senses, and to have established first the practice (though it was indeed greatly adopted by Socrates) of not declaring what he himself thought, but of disputing against whatever any other person said that he thought. Hence the *New Academy* derived its origin, in which Carneades distinguished himself by a quickness of wit, that was in a manner divine, and a peculiar force of eloquence. I knew many at Athens who had been hearers of this philosopher, but I can refer for his character to two persons of undoubted authority, my father-in-law Scævola, who heard him when a youth at Rome, and Quintus Metellus, the son of Lucius, my intimate friend, a man of high dignity, who informed me that in the early part of his life at Athens, he attended for many days the lectures of this celebrated philosopher, then almost broken with age.[1]

XIX. " But the streams of learning have flowed from the common summit of science,[2] like rivers from the Apennines, in different directions, so that the philosophers have passed, as it were, into the Upper or Ionian Sea, a Greek sea abound-

---

[1] *Qui illum a se adolescente Athenis jam affectum senectute multos dies auditum esse dicebat.* "Who said that he had been heard by him when a young man for many days at Athens (where he was) now affected with old age."

[2] *Ex communi sapientium jugo.* I read *sapientiæ* with Ellendt. It is a comparison, as he observes, of Socrates to a hill.

ing with harbors, but the orators have fallen into the Lower or Tuscan, a barbarian sea infested with rocks and dangers, in which even Ulysses himself had mistaken his course. If, therefore, we are content with such a degree of eloquence, and such an orator as has the common discretion to know that you ought either to deny the charge which is brought against you, or, if you can not do that, to show that what he who is accused has committed, was either done justifiably, or through the fault or wrong of some other person, or that it is agreeable to law, or at least not contrary to any law, or that it was done without design, or from necessity; or that it does not merit the term given it in the accusation; or that the pleading is not conducted as it ought to have been or might have been; and if you think it sufficient to have learned the rules which the writers on rhetoric have delivered, which, however, Antonius has set forth with much more grace and fullness than they are treated by them; if, I say, you are content with these qualifications, and those which you wished to be specified by me, you reduce the orator from a spacious and immense field of action into a very narrow compass; but if you are desirous to emulate Pericles, or Demosthenes, who is more familiar to us from his numerous writings; and if you are captivated with this noble and illustrious idea and excellence of a perfect orator, you must include in your minds all the powers of Carneades, or those of Aristotle. For, as I observed before, the ancients, till the time of Socrates, united all knowledge and science in all things, whether they appertained to morality, to the duties of life, to virtue, or to civil government, with the faculty of speaking; but afterward, the eloquent being separated by Socrates from the learned (as I have already explained), and this distinction being continued by all the followers of Socrates, the philosophers disregarded eloquence, and the orators philosophy; nor did they at all encroach upon each other's provinces, except that the orators borrowed from the philosophers, and the philosophers from the orators, such things as they would have taken from the common stock if they had been inclined to remain in their pristine union. But as the old pontiffs, on account of the multitude of religious ceremonies, appointed three officers called Epulones,[1] though they

¹ See Liv., xxxiii., 42.

themselves were instituted by Numa to perform the *epulare sacrificium* at the games; so the followers of Socrates excluded the pleaders of causes from their own body, and from the common title of philosophers, though the ancients were of opinion that there was a miraculous harmony between speaking and understanding.

XX. "Such being the case, I shall crave some little indulgence for myself, and beg you to consider that whatever I say, I say not of myself, but of the complete orator. For I am a person, who, having been educated in my boyhood, with great care on the part of my father, and having brought into the forum such a portion of talent as I am conscious of possessing, and not so much as I may perhaps appear to you to have, can not aver that I learned what I now comprehend, exactly as I shall say that it ought to be learned; since I engaged in public business most early of all men, and at one-and-twenty years of age brought to trial a man of the highest rank, and the greatest eloquence;[1] and the forum has been my school, and practice, with the laws and institutions of the Roman people, and the customs of our ancestors, my instructors. I got a small taste of those sciences of which I am speaking, feeling some thirst for them, while I was quæstor in Asia, having procured a rhetorician about my own age from the Academy, that Metrodorus, of whose memory Antonius has made honorable mention; and, on my departure from Asia, at Athens, where I should have staid longer, had I not been displeased with the Athenians, who would not repeat their mysteries, for which I came two days too late. The fact, therefore, that I comprise within my scheme so much science, and attribute so much influence to learning, makes not only not in my favor, but rather against me (for I am not considering what I, but what a perfect orator can do), and against all those who put forth treatises on the art of rhetoric, and who are indeed obnoxious to extreme ridicule; for they write merely about the several kinds of suits, about exordia, and statements of facts; but the real power of eloquence is such, that it embraces the origin, the influence, the changes of all things in the world, all virtues, duties, and all nature, so far as it affects the manners, minds, and lives of mankind. It can give an account of customs, laws, and rights, can gov-

---

[1] Carbo. See note on i., 10.

ern a state, and speak on every thing relating to any subject
whatsoever with elegance and force.   In this pursuit I employ my talents as well as I can, as far as I am enabled by
natural capacity, moderate learning, and constant practice;
nor do I conceive myself much inferior in disputation to those
who have as it were pitched their tent for life in philosophy
alone.

XXI. " For what can my friend Caius Velleius[1] allege to
show why pleasure is the chief good, which I can not either
maintain more fully, if I were so inclined, or refute, with the
aid of those commonplaces which Antonius has set forth, and
that habit of speaking in which Velleius himself is unexercised,
but every one of us experienced?   What is there that either
Sextus Pompeius, or the two Balbi,[2] or my acquaintance
Marcus Vigellius, who lived with Panætius, all men of the
Stoic sect, can maintain concerning virtue, in such a manner
that either I, or any one of you, should give place to them in
debate ?   For philosophy is not like other arts or sciences;
since what can he do in geometry, or in music, who has never
learned?   He must be silent, or be thought a madman; but
the principles of philosophy are discovered by such minds as
have acuteness and penetration enough to extract what is
most probable concerning any subject, and are elegantly expressed with the aid of exercise in speaking.   On such topics, a speaker of ordinary abilities, if he has no great learning,
but has had practice in declaiming, will, by virtue of such
practice, common to others as well as to him, beat our friends
the philosophers, and not suffer himself to be despised and held
in contempt; but if ever a person shall arise who shall have
abilities to deliver opinions on both sides of a question on all
subjects, after the manner of Aristotle, and, from a knowledge
of the precepts of that philosopher, to deliver two contradictory orations on every conceivable topic, or shall be able, after
the manner of Arcesilas or Carneades, to dispute against every proposition that can be laid down, and shall unite with

---

[1] The same that speaks, in the dialogue *De Natura Deorum*, on the
tenets of the Epicureans.
[2] One Balbus is a speaker in the *De Nat. Deorum*, on the doctrines
of the Stoics.   The other, says Ellendt, is supposed to be the lawyer
who is mentioned by Cicero, Brut., c. 42, and who was the master of
Servius Sulpicius.   Of Vigellius nothing is known.

those powers rhetorical skill, and practice and exercise in speaking, he will be the true, the perfect, the only orator. For neither without the nervous eloquence of the forum, can an orator have sufficient weight, dignity, and force ; nor, without variety of learning, sufficient elegance and judgment. Let us suffer that old Corax of yours,[1] therefore, to hatch his young birds in the nest, that they may fly out disagreeable and troublesome bawlers ; and let us allow Pamphilus, whoever he was,[2] to depict a science of such consequence upon flags, as if for an amusement for children ; while we ourselves describe the whole business of an orator, in so short a disputation as that of yesterday and to-day ; admitting, however, that it is of such extent as to be spread through all the books of the philosophers, into which none of those rhetoricians[3] has ever dipped."

XXII. Catulus then said, "It is, indeed, by no means astonishing, Crassus, that there should appear in you either such energy, or such agreeableness, or such copiousness of language ; though I previously supposed that it was merely from the force of natural genius that you spoke in such a way as to seem to me not only the greatest of orators, but the wisest of men ; but I now understand that you have always given precedence to matters relating to philosophy, and your copious stream of eloquence has flowed from that source ; and yet, when I recollect the different stages of your life, and when I consider your manner of living and pursuits, I can neither conceive at what time you acquired that learning, nor can I imagine you to be strongly addicted to those studies, or men, or writings ; nor can I determine at which of these

---

[1] See i., 20. He jokes on the name of Corax, which signifies *a crow*.

[2] *Pamphilum nescio quem.* Some suppose him to be the painter that is mentioned as the instructor of Apelles by Pliny, H. N., xxxv., 36, 8. He seems, whoever he was, to have given some fanciful map-like view of the rules of rhetoric. But it is not intimated by Pliny that the Pamphilus of whom he speaks was, though a learned painter, any thing more than a painter. A Pamphilus is mentioned by Quintilian, iii., 6, 34 ; xii., 10, 6 ; and by Aristotle, Rhet., ii., 23. By *infulæ* in the text, which I have rendered "flags," Ellendt supposes that something similar to our printed cotton handkerchiefs, or flags hung out at booths at fairs, is meant. Talæus thinks that the tables of rules might have been called *infulæ* in ridicule, from their shape.

[3] Such "disagreeable and troublesome bawlers," as those from the nest of Corax just mentioned. *Ernesti.*

two things I ought most to feel surprised, that you could obtain a thorough knowledge of those matters which you persuade me are of the utmost assistance to oratory, amid such important occupations as yours, or that, if you could not do so, you can speak with such effect." Here Crassus rejoined, " I would have you first of all, Catulus, persuade yourself of this, that, when I speak of an orator, I speak not much otherwise than I should do if I had to speak of an actor; for I should say that he could not possibly give satisfaction in his gesture unless he had learned the exercises of the palæstra, and dancing; nor would it be necessary that, when I said this, I should be myself a player, though it perhaps would be necessary that I should be a not unskillful critic in another man's profession. In like manner I am now, at your request, speaking of the orator, that is, the perfect orator; for, about whatever art or faculty inquiry is made, it always relates to it in its state of absolute perfection; and if, therefore, you now allow me to be a speaker, if even a pretty good one, or a positively good one, I will not contradict you (for why should I, at my time of life, be so foolish? I know that I am esteemed such); but, if it be so, I am certainly not perfect. For there is not among mankind any pursuit of greater difficulty or effort, or that requires more aids from learning; but, since I have to speak of the orator, I must of necessity speak of the perfect orator; for unless the powers and nature of a thing be set before the eyes in their utmost perfection, its character and magnitude can not be understood. Yet I confess, Catulus, that I do not at present live in any great familiarity with the writings or the professors of philosophy, and that, as you have rightly observed, I never had much leisure to set apart for the acquisition of such learning, and that I have only given to study such portions of time as my leisure when I was a youth, and vacations from the business of the forum, have allowed me.

XXIII. " But if, Catulus, you inquire my sentiments on that learning, I am of opinion that so much time need not be spent on it by a man of ability, and one who studies with a view to the forum, to the senate, to causes, to civil administration, as those have chosen to give to it whom life has failed while they were learning. For all arts are handled in one manner by those who apply them to practice; in another by

those who, taking delight in treating of the arts themselves,
never intend to do any thing else during the whole course of
their lives. The master of the gladiators[1] is now in the extremity of age, yet daily meditates upon the improvement of
his science, for he has no other care; but Quintus Velocius[2]
had learned that exercise in his youth, and, as he was naturally formed for it, and had thoroughly acquired it, he was,
as it is said in Lucilius,

> " 'Though as a gladiator in the school
> Well skill'd, and bold enough to match with any,'

yet resolved to devote more attention to the duties of the forum, and of friendship, and to his domestic concerns. Valerius[3] sung every day; for he was on the stage; what else
was he to do? But our friend Numerius Furius sings only
when it is agreeable to him; for he is the head of a family,
and of equestrian dignity; he learned when a boy as much as
it was necessary for him to learn. The case is similar with
regard to sciences of the greatest importance; we have seen
Quintus Tubero,[4] a man of eminent virtue and prudence, engaged in the study of philosophy night and day, but his uncle Africanus[5] you could scarcely ever perceive paying any attention to it, though he paid a great deal. Such knowledge
is easily gained, if you only get as much of it as is necessary,
and have a faithful and able instructor, and know how to
learn yourself. But if you are inclined to do nothing else all
your life, your very studies and inquiries daily give rise to
something for you to investigate as an amusement at your
leisure; thus it happens, that the investigation of particular
points is endless, though general knowledge is easy, if practice
establish learning once acquired, moderate exercise be devoted
to it, and memory and inclination continue. But it is pleasant to be constantly learning, if we wish to be thoroughly
masters of any thing; as if I, for instance, had a desire to
play excellently at backgammon, or had a strong attachment
to tennis, though perhaps I should not attain perfection in

---

[1] See note on ii., 80.
[2] This name was introduced on the conjecture of Victorius. Previously the passage was unintelligible.
[3] Of Valerius and Furius nothing is known. *Ellendt.*
[4] Cic., Tusc. Quæst., iv., 2; Fin., iv., 9.
[5] See ii., 37.

those games; but others, because they excel in any performance, take a more vehement delight in it than the object requires, as Titius[1] in tennis, Brulla in backgammon. There is
no reason, therefore, why any one should dread the extent of
the sciences because he perceives old men still learning them;
for either they were old men when they first applied to them,
or have been detained in the study of them till they became
old; or are of more than ordinary stupidity. And the truth
in my opinion is, that a man can never learn thoroughly that
which he has not been able to learn quickly."

XXIV. "Now, now," exclaimed Catulus, "I understand,
Crassus, what you say, and readily assent to it; I see that
there has been time enough for you, a man of vigor and ability
to learn, to acquire a knowledge of what you mention." "Do
you still persist," rejoined Crassus, "to think that I say what
I say of myself, and not of my subject? But, if it be agreeable to you, let us now return to our stated business." "To
me," said Catulus, "it is very agreeable."

"To what end, then," continued Crassus, "does this discourse, drawn out to so great a length, and brought from
such deep sources, tend? The two parts which remain for
me, that of adorning language, and contemplating eloquence
in general in its highest perfection—one of which requires
that we should speak gracefully, the other aptly—have this
influence, that eloquence is rendered by their means product-
ive of the utmost delight, made to penetrate effectually into
the inmost hearts of the audience, and furnished with all possible variety of matter. But the speech which we use in the
forum, adapted for contest, full of acrimony, formed to suit
the taste of the vulgar, is poor indeed and beggarly; and,
on the other hand, even that which they teach who profess
themselves masters of the art of speaking, is not of much
more dignity than the common style of the forum. We have
need of greater pomp,[2] of choice matter collected, imported,
and brought together from all parts; such a provision as
must be made by you, Cæsar, for the next year,[3] with such
pains as I took in my ædileship, because I did not suppose

---

[1] Titius is mentioned ii., 62. Of Brulla nothing is known. *Ellendt.*
[2] *Apparatu.* In allusion, says Petavius, to the shows given by the
ædiles.
[3] *Ad annum.* That of his ædileship. *Ernesti.*

that I could satisfy such a people as ours with ordinary matters, or those of their own country.

" As for choosing and arranging words, and forming them
into proper periods, the art is easy, or, I may say, the mere
practice without any art at all. Of matter, the quantity and
variety are infinite; and as the Greeks[1] were not properly
furnished with it, and our youth in consequence almost grew
ignorant while they were learning, even Latin teachers of
rhetoric, please the gods, have arisen within the last two
years; a class of persons whom I had suppressed by my
edict,[2] when I was censor, not because I was unwilling (as
some I know not who, asserted), that the abilities of our youth
should be improved, but because I did not wish that their
understandings should be weakened and their impudence
strengthened. For among the Greeks, whatever was their
character, I perceived that there was, besides exercise of the
tongue, some degree of learning, as well as politeness suited to
liberal knowledge; but I knew that these new masters could
teach youth nothing but effrontery, which, even when joined
with good qualities, is to be avoided, and in itself especially so;
and as this, therefore, was the only thing that was taught by
the Latins, their school being indeed a school of impudence, I
thought it became the censor to take care that the evil should
not spread farther. I do not, however, determine and decree
on the point, as if I despaired that the subjects which we
are discussing can be delivered, and treated with elegance, in
Latin; for both our language and the nature of things allows
the ancient and excellent science of Greece to be adapted to
our customs and manners; but for such a work are required
men of learning, such as none of our countrymen have been
in this department; but if ever such arise, they will be preferable to the Greeks themselves.

XXV. " A speech, then, is to be made becoming in its
kind, with a sort of complexion and substance of its own; for

---

[1] The Greek rhetoricians. *Pearce.*
[2] Quintilian refers to this passage, ii., 4, 42. . . . . The edict of the
censors Crassus and Ahenobarbus, which was marked by all the ancient
severity, is preserved in Aul. Gell., xv., 11; and Suetonius, De Clar.
Rhet., procem. Crassus intimates that that class of men sprung up
again after his edict; for the censors had not such power that their
mere prohibitions could continue in force after their term of office was
expired. *Ellendt.*

that it be weighty, agreeable, savoring of erudition and liberal knowledge, worthy of admiration, polished, having feeling
and passion in it, as far as is required, are qualities not confined to particular members, but are apparent in the whole
body ; but that it be, as it were, strewed with flowers of language and thought, is a property which ought not to be equally diffused throughout the whole speech, but at such intervals,
that, as in the arrangement of ornaments,[1] there may be certain remarkable and luminous objects disposed here and there.
Such a kind of eloquence, therefore, is to be chosen, as is most
adapted to interest the audience, such as may not only delight, but delight without satiety (for I do not imagine it to
be expected of me, that I should admonish you to beware that
your language be not poor, or rude, or vulgar, or obsolete;
both your age and your geniuses encourage me to something
of a higher nature); for it is difficult to tell what the cause
is why, from those objects which most strongly strike our
senses with pleasure, and occasion the most violent emotions
at their first appearance, we should soonest turn away with a
certain loathing and satiety.   How much more florid, in the
gayety and variety of the coloring, are most objects in modern
pictures than in ancient ones ; which, however, though they
captivate us at first sight, do not afford any lasting pleasure ;
whereas we are strongly attracted by rough and faded coloring in the paintings of antiquity.   How much softer and more
delicate are fanciful[2] modulations and notes in music, than
those which are strict and grave; and yet if the former are
often repeated, not only persons of an austere character, but
even the multitude, raise an outcry against them.   We may
perceive, too, in regard to the other senses, that we take a less
permanent delight in perfumes composed of the sweetest and
most powerful odors, than in those of a more moderate scent ;
that that is more commended which appears to smell like wax,
than that which is as strong as saffron; and that, in the
sense of feeling itself, there is a limit required both to softness
and smoothness.   How soon does even the taste, which of all
our senses is the most desirous of gratification, and is delighted with sweetness beyond the others, nauseate and reject that

---

[1] *In ornatu.*   The arrangement of such ornaments as were displayed
at games and festivals.
[2] *Falsœ.*   Fractæ et molliores.   *Ernesti.*

which is too luscious! Who can take sweet drinks and meats long together? while, in both kinds of nutriment, such things as affect the sense with but a slight pleasure are the farthest removed from that satiating quality; and so, in all other things, loathing still borders upon the most exquisite delights; and therefore we should the less wonder at this effect in language, in which we may form a judgment, either from the poets or the orators, that a style elegant, ornate, embellished, and sparkling, without intermission, without restraint, without variety, whether it be prose or poetry, though painted with the brightest colors, can not possibly give lasting pleasure. And we the sooner take offense at the false locks and paint of the orator or poet, for this cause, that the senses, when affected with too much pleasure, arc satiated, not from reason, but constitutionally; in writings and in speeches these disguised blemishes are even more readily noticed, not only from the judgment of the ear, but from that of the understanding.

XXVI. "Though such expressions of applause, therefore, as 'very well,' 'excellent,' may be often repeated to me, I would not have 'beautifully,' 'pleasantly,' come too often; yet I would have the exclamation, 'Nothing can be better,' very frequent. But this high excellence and merit in speaking should be attended with some portions of shade and obscurity, that the part on which a stronger light is thrown may seem to stand out, and become more prominent. Roscius never delivers this passage with all the spirit that he can,

"'The wise man seeks for honor, not for spoil,
As the reward of virtue;'

but rather in an abject manner, that into the next speech,

"'What do I see? the steel-girt soldier holds
The sacred seats,'

he may throw his whole powers, may gaze, may express wonder and astonishment. How does the other great actor[1] utter

"'What aid shall I solicit?'

How gently, how sedately, how calmly! For he proceeds with

"'O father! O my country! House of Priam!'

---

[1] Æsopus, as I suppose. *Ellendt;* who observes that the verses are from the Andromache of Ennius. See c. 47, 58; Tusc. Disp., iii., 19.

in which so much action could not be exerted if it had been
consumed and exhausted by any preceding emotion. Nor did
the actors discover this before the poets themselves, or, indeed, before even those who composed the music, by both of
whom their tone is sometimes lowered, sometimes heightened,
sometimes made slender, sometimes full, with variation and
distinction. Let our orator, then, be thus graceful and delightful (nor can he indeed be so otherwise); let him have a severe and solid grace, not a luscious and delicious sweetness;
for the precepts relative to the ornament of eloquence, which
are commonly given, are of such a nature that even the worst
speaker can observe them. It is first of all necessary, therefore, as I said before, that a stock of matter and thoughts be
got together; a point on which Antonius has already spoken;
these are to be interwoven into the very thread and essence
of the oration, embellished by words, and diversified by illustrations.

"But the greatest glory of eloquence is to exaggerate a
subject by embellishment; which has effect not only in amplifying and extolling any thing in a speech to an extraordinary degree, but also in extenuating it, and making it appear contemptible. XXVII. This is required on all those
points which Antonius said must be observed in order to gain
credit to our statements, when we explain any thing, or when
we conciliate the feelings, or when we excite the passions of
our audience; but in the particular which I mentioned last,
amplification is of the greatest effect; and excellence in it the
peculiar and appropriate praise of the orator. Even that exercise is of more than ordinary importance which Antonius
illustrated[1] in the latter part of his dissertation (in the beginning[2] he set it aside), I mean that of panegyric and satire;
for nothing is a better preparative for exaggeration and amplification in a speech than the talent of performing both
these parts in a most effective manner. Consequently, even
those topics are of use which, though they ought to be *proper*
to causes, and to be inherent in their very vitals, yet, as they
are commonly applied to general subjects, have been by the
ancients denominated *common places;* of which *some* consist
in bitter accusations and complaints against vices and crimes,
with a certain amplification (in opposition to which nothing

[1] B. ii., c. 84.   [2] B. ii., c. 10.

is usually said, or can be said), as against an embezzler of the public money, or a traitor, or a parricide; remarks which we ought to introduce when the charges have been proved, for otherwise they are jejune and trifling; *others* consist in entreaty or commiseration; *others* relate to contested points of argument, whence you may be enabled to speak fully on either side of any general question, an exercise which is now imagined to be peculiar to those two sects of philosophy[1] of which I spoke before; among those of remote antiquity it belonged to those from whom all the art and power of speaking in forensic pleadings was derived;[2] for concerning virtue, duty, justice and equity, dignity, utility, honor, ignominy, rewards and punishments, and similar subjects, we ought to possess the spirit, and talent, and address, to speak on either side of the question. But since, being driven from our own possessions, we are left in a poor little farm, and even that the subject of litigation, and since, though the patrons of others, we have not been able to preserve and protect our own property, let us borrow what is requisite for us (which is a notable disgrace) from those[3] who have made this irruption into our patrimony.

XXVIII. " Those, then, who take their name from a very small portion[4] of Athens and its neighborhood, and are denominated Peripatetic or Academic philosophers, but who formerly, on account of their eminent knowledge in important affairs, were by the Greeks called political philosophers, being distinguished by a name relating to all public administration, say that every speech on civil affairs is employed on one or other of these two kinds of questions, either that of a definite controversy limited to certain times and parties; as, ' Whether is it proper that our captives be recovered from the Carthaginians by the restitution of theirs?' or on an indefinite question, inquiring about a subject generally; as, ' What should be determined or considered concerning captives in general?' Of these, they term the former kind a cause, or controversy, and limit it to three things, lawsuits, delibera-

---

[1] The Academic and Peripatetic; see iii., 17, 18. *Proust.*
[2] Those who taught forensic eloquence. *Proust.*
[3] The philosophers.
[4] From the Academy, and the gymnasia in the suburbs of Athens. *Ellendt.*

tions, and panegyric; but the other kind of question, or proposition as it were, the indefinite, is denominated a consultation.[1] So far they instruct us. The rhetoricians, however,
use this division in their instructions, but not so that they
seem to recover a lost possession by right, by a decision in
their favor, or by force, but appear, according to the practice of the civil law, to assert their claim to the premises by
breaking off a branch;[2] for they keep possession of that former kind which is restricted to certain times, places, and parties, and that as it were by the hem of the garment;[3] for at
this present time, under Philo,[4] who flourishes, I hear, as chief
of the Academy, the knowledge and practice of even these
causes is much observed; as to the latter kind, they only
mention it in delivering the first principles of the art, and
say that it belongs to the orator; but neither explain its
powers, nor its nature, nor its parts, nor general heads, so
that it had better have been passed over entirely, than left
when it was once attempted; for they are now understood to
say nothing about it for want of something to say; in the
other case, they would have appeared to be silent from judgment.

XXIX. "Every subject, then, has the same susceptibleness
of ambiguity, concerning which it may be inquired and disputed; whether the discussion relate to consultations on indefinite points, or to those causes which are concerned with
civil affairs and contests in the forum; nor is there any that
may not be referred either to the nature and principles of
knowledge or of *action*. For either the knowledge itself and
acquaintance with any affair is the object of inquiry; as,
'Whether virtue be desirable on account of its own intrinsic
worth, or for the sake of some emolument attending it?' or

---

[1] *Consultatio.* See Cic., Part., Orat., i., 18, 20.
[2] A ceremony by which a claim to a possession was made. See Gaius, iv., 17.
[3] *Lacinia.* Like persons who scarcely keep their hold of a thing.
Ellendt.
[4] Philo of Larissa, called by some the founder of a fourth Academy,
was a hearer of Clitomachus, Acad., ii., 6. He fled to Rome, with many
of the chief men of Athens, in the Mithridatic war, when Cicero, then
a young man, attended diligently to his instructions. Brut., 89; Plut.,
Cic., c. 3. He sometimes gave instructions in rhetoric, sometimes in
philosophy, as appears from Tusc. Disp., ii., 3. *Henrichsen.*

counsel with regard to an act is sought; as, 'Whether a wise man ought to concern himself in the administration of government?' And of knowledge there are three kinds—that which is formed by conjecture, that which admits of certain definition, and that which is (if I may so term it) consequential. For whether there be any thing in any other thing, is inquired by conjecture; as, 'Whether there is wisdom in mankind?' But what nature any thing has, a definition explains; as if the inquiry be, 'What is wisdom?' And consequential knowledge is the subject treated of, when the question is, 'What peculiarity attends on any thing?' as, 'Whether it be the part of a good man to tell a falsehood on any occasion?' But to conjecture they return again, and divide it into four kinds; for the question is either, 'What a thing is,' as, 'Whether law among mankind is from nature or from opinions?' or, 'What the origin of a thing is,' as, 'What is the foundation of civil laws and governments?' or the cause and reason of it; as if it is asked, 'Why do the most learned men differ upon points of the greatest importance?' or as to the possible changes in any thing; as if it is disputed, 'Whether virtue can die in men, or whether it be convertible into vice?' With regard to definition, disputes arise, either when the question is, 'What is impressed, as it were, on the common understanding?' as if it be considered, 'Whether that be right which is advantageous to the greater number?' or when it is inquired, 'What is the peculiar property of any character?' as, 'Whether to speak elegantly be peculiar to the orator, or whether any one else can do so?' or when a thing is distributed into parts; as if the question be, 'How many kinds of desirable things there are?' and, 'Whether there be three, those of the body, those of the mind, and external things?' or when it is described what is the form or, as it were, natural characteristic of any person; as if it be inquired, 'What is the exact representation of an avaricious, a seditious, or a vainglorious man?' Of the consequential, two principal kinds of questions are proposed; for the question is either simple, as if it be disputed, 'Whether glory be desirable?' or comparative, 'Whether praise or wealth is more to be coveted?' But of such simple questions there are three sorts, as to things that are to be desired or avoided; as, 'Whether honors are desirable?' 'Whether poverty is to

be avoided ?' as to right and wrong ; as, ' Whether it be right
to revenge injuries, even those of relations ?' as to honor and
ignominy ; as, 'Whether it be honorable to suffer death for
the sake of glory ?'   Of the comparative also there are two
sorts : one, when the question is whether things are the same,
or there be any difference betwixt them ; as betwixt *fear* and
reverence, a king and *a tyrant, a flatterer* and *a friend ;* the
other, when the inquiry is, ' Which of two things is preferable ?' as, ' Whether wise men are led by the approbation of the
most worthy, or by popular applause ?'   Thus are the controversies which relate to knowledge described, for the most
part, by men of the greatest learning.

XXX.   " But those which relate to action, either concern
controverted points of moral duty, under which head it may
be inquired, ' What is right and to be practiced ;' of which
head the whole train of virtues and of vices is the subject-
matter ; or refer to the excitement, or alleviation, or removal
of some emotion of the mind.   Under this head are included
exhortation, reproof, consolation, compassion, and all that
either gives impulse to any emotion of the mind, or, if it so
happen, mitigates it.   These kinds, then, and modes of all
questions being explained, it is of no consequence if the partition of Antonius in any particular disagrees with my division ; for there are the same parts in both our dissertations,
though divided and distributed by me a little otherwise than
by him.   Now I will proceed to the sequel, and recall myself
to my appointed task and business.   For the arguments for
every kind of question are to be drawn from those commonplaces which Antonius enumerated ; but some commonplaces
will be more adapted to some kinds than to others ; concerning which there is no necessity for me to speak, not because
it is a matter of any great length, but of sufficient perspicuity.

" Those speeches, then, are the most ornate which spread
over the widest field, and, from some private and single question, apply and direct themselves to show the nature of such
questions in general, so that the audience, from understanding its nature, and kind, and whole bearing, may determine as
to particular individuals, and as to all suits criminal and civil.
Antonius has encouraged you, young men, to perseverance in
this exercise, and intimated that you were to be conducted by
degrees from small and confined questions to all the power

and varieties of argument. Such qualifications are not to be
gained from a few small treatises, as they have imagined who
have written on the art of speaking ; nor are they work merely for a Tusculan villa, or for a morning walk and afternoon
sitting, such as these of ours ; for we have not only to point
and fashion the tongue, but have to store the mind with the
sweetness, abundance, and variety of most important and numerous subjects.

XXXI. " For ours is the possession (if we are indeed orators, if we are to be consulted as persons of authority and
leaders in the civil contests and perils of the citizens and in
public councils), ours, I say, is the entire possession of all that
wisdom and learning, upon which, as if it were vacant and
had fallen in to them, men abounding in leisure have seized,
taking advantage of us, and either speak of the orator with
ridicule and sarcasm, as Socrates in the Gorgias, or write
something on the art of oratory in a few little treatises, and
call them books on rhetoric ; as if all those things did not
equally concern the orator, which are taught by the same
philosophers on justice, on the duties of life, on the establishment and administration of civil government, and on the
whole systems of moral and even natural philosophy. These
matters, since we can not get them elsewhere, we must now
borrow from those very persons by whom we have been pillaged ; so that we apply them to the knowledge of civil affairs, to which they belong, and have a regard ; nor let us
(as I observed before) consume all our lives in this kind of
learning, but, when we have discovered the fountains (which
he who does not find out immediately will never find at all),
let us draw from them as much as occasion may require, as
often as we need.   For neither is there so sharp a discernment
in the nature and understanding of man, that any one can
descry things of such importance, unless they are pointed out ;
nor yet is there so much obscurity in the things, that a man
of penetrating genius can not obtain an insight into them, if
he only direct his view toward them.   As the orator therefore has liberty to expatiate in so large and immense a field,
and, wherever he stops, can stand upon his own territory, all
the furniture and embellishments of eloquence readily offer
themselves to him.   For copiousness of matter produces copiousness of language ; and, if there be an inherent dignity in

the subjects on which he speaks, there must be, from the nature of the thing, a certain splendor in his expression. If the speaker or writer has but been liberally instructed in the learning proper for youth, and has an ardent attachment to study, and is assisted by natural endowments, and exercised in those indefinite questions on general subjects, and has chosen, at the same time, the most elegant writers and speakers to study and imitate, he will never, be assured, need instruction from such preceptors how to compose or embellish his language; so readily, in an abundance of matter, will nature herself, if she be but stimulated, fall without any guide into all the art of adorning eloquence."

XXXII. Catulus here observed, "Ye immortal gods, what an infinite variety, force, and extent of matter have you, Crassus, embraced, and from how narrow a circle have you ventured to lead forth the orator, and to place him in the domains of his ancestors! For we have understood that those ancient masters and authors of the art of speaking considered no kind of disputation to be foreign to their profession, but were always exercising themselves in every branch of oratory. Of which number was Hippias of Elis, who, when he came to Olympia, at the time of the vast concourse at the games celebrated every fifth year, boasted, in the hearing of almost all Greece, that there was no subject in any art or science of which he was ignorant; as he understood not only those arts in which all liberal and polite learning is comprised, geometry, music, grammar, and poetry, and whatever is said on the natures of things, the moral duties of men, and the science of government, but that he had himself made, with his own hand, the ring which he wore, and the cloak and shoes which he had on.[1] He indeed went a little too far; but, even from his example, we may easily conjecture how much knowledge those very orators desired to gain in the most noble arts, when they did not shrink from learning even the more humble. Why need I allude to Prodicus of Chios, Thrasymachus of Chalcedon, or Protagoras of Abdera? every one of whom in those days disputed and wrote much even on the nature of things. Even Gorgias the Leontine himself, under whose advocacy (as Plato represented) the orator yielded to the philosopher;[2] who

---

[1] See Plato, Hipp. Min., p. 231, G.

[2] Gorgias, in the Dialogue of Plato, undertakes the defense of oratory

was either never defeated in argument by Socrates (and then the Dialogue of Plato is wholly fictitious), or, if he was so defeated, it was because Socrates was the more eloquent and convincing, or, as you term it, the more powerful and better orator; but this Gorgias, in that very book of Plato, offers to speak most copiously on any subject whatever, that could be brought under discussion or inquiry; and he was the first of all men that ventured to demand, in a large assembly, on what subject any one desired to hear him speak; and to whom such honors were paid in Greece, that to him alone, of all great men, a statue was erected at Delphi, not gilded, but of solid gold. Those whom I have named, and many other most consummate masters in the art of speaking, flourished at the same time; from whose examples it may be understood that the truth is really such as you, Crassus, have stated, and that the name of the orator was distinguished among the ancients in Greece in a more extensive sense, and with greater honor than among ourselves. I am therefore the more in doubt whether I should attribute a greater degree of praise to you, or of blame to the Greeks; since you, born under a different language and manners, in the busiest of cities, occupied either with almost all the private causes of the people, or with the government of the world and the direction of the mightiest of empires, have mastered such numbers of subjects, and acquired so extensive a knowledge, and have united all this with the science and practice of one who is of authority in the republic by his counsels and eloquence; while they, born in an atmosphere of learning, ardently attached to such studies, but dissolved in idleness, have not only made no acquisitions, but have not even preserved as their own that which was left and consigned to them."

XXXIII. Crassus then said, "Not only in this particular, Catulus, but in many others, the grandeur of the sciences has been diminished by the distribution and separation of their parts. Do you imagine, that when the famous Hippocrates of Cos flourished, there were then some of the medical faculty who cured diseases, others wounds, and a third class the eyes? Do you suppose that geometry under Euclid and Archimedes, that music under Damon and Aristoxenus, that

against Socrates, whom Plato represents as maintaining the dignity of philosophy. Gorgias is vanquished by Socrates. *Proust.*

grammar itself when Aristophanes and Callimachus treated of it, were so divided into parts, that no one comprehended the universal system of any of those sciences, but different persons selected different parts on which they meant to bestow their labor? I have, indeed, often heard from my father and father-in-law, that even our own countrymen, who were ambitious to excel in renown for wisdom, were wont to comprehend all the objects of knowledge which this city had then learned. They mentioned, as an instance of this, Sextus Ælius; and we ourselves have seen Manius Manilius walking across the forum; a signal that he who did so gave all the citizens liberty to consult him upon any subject; and to such persons, when thus walking or sitting at home upon their seats of ceremony, all people had free access, not only to consult them upon points of civil law, but even upon the settlement of a daughter in marriage, the purchase of an estate, or the cultivation of a farm, and indeed upon any employment or business whatsoever. Such was the wisdom of the well-known elder Publius Crassus, such that of Titus Coruncanius, such that of the great-grandfather Scipio, my son-in-law, a person of great judgment; all of whom were supreme pontiffs, so that they were consulted upon all affairs, divine and human; and the same men gave their counsel and discharged their duty in the senate, before the people, and in the private causes of their friends, in civil and military service, both at home and abroad. What was deficient in Marcus Cato, except the modern polish of foreign and adventitious learning? Did he, because he was versed in the civil law, forbear from pleading causes? or, because he could speak, neglect the study of jurisprudence? He labored in both these kinds of learning, and succeeded in both. Was he, by the popularity which he acquired by attending to the business of private persons, rendered more tardy in the public service of the state? No man spoke with more courage before the people, none was ever a better senator; he was at the same time a most excellent commander-in-chief; and indeed nothing in those days could possibly be known or learned in this city which he did not investigate and thoroughly understand, and on which he did not also write. Now, on the contrary, men generally come to assume offices and the duties of public administration unarmed and defenseless; prepared with no science, nor any knowledge of business. But if any one happen to excel the multitude, he is elevated with pride by the possession of any single talent, as military courage, or a little experience in war (which indeed has now fallen into decay[1]), or a knowledge of the law (not of the whole law, for nobody studies the pontifical law, which is annexed to civil jurisprudence[2]), or eloquence (which they imagine to consist in declamation and a torrent of words), while none have any notion of the alliance and affinity that connects all the liberal arts and sciences, and even the virtues themselves.

XXXIV. "But to direct my remarks to the Greeks (whom we can not omit in a dissertation of this nature; for as examples of virtue are to be sought among our own countrymen, so examples of learning are to be derived from them); seven are said to have lived at one time, who were esteemed and denominated wise men. All these, except Thales of Miletus, had the government of their respective cities. Whose learning is reported, at the same period, to have been greater, or whose eloquence to have received more ornament from literature, than that of Pisistratus? who is said to have been the first that arranged the books of Homer as we now have them, when they were previously confused. He was not indeed of any great service to the community, but was eminent for eloquence, at the same time that he excelled in erudition and liberal knowledge. What was the character of Pericles? —of whose power in speaking we have heard, that when he spoke for the good of his country against the inclinations of the Athenians, that very severity with which he contradicted the favorites of the people became popular and agreeable to all men; and on whose lips the old comic poets declared (even when they satirized him, as was then lawful to be done at Athens) that the graces of persuasion dwelt, and that there was such mighty energy in him that he left, as it were, certain stings in the minds of those who listened to him. Yet no declaimer had taught him to bawl for hours by the water-

---

[1] For, except Metellus Numidicus and Marius, no one in those days had gained any great reputation by his conduct in the field.

[2] *Quod est conjunctum.* That is, "conjunctum cum jure civili." *Proust.* What Cicero says here is somewhat at variance with what he says, De Legg., ii., 19, where he shows, at some length, that only a small part of the civil law is necessary to be combined with the knowledge of the pontifical law. *Ellendt.*

clock, but, as we have it from tradition, the famous Anaxagoras of Clazomenæ, a man eminent in all the most valuable sciences, had instructed him. He, accordingly, excelling as he did in learning, judgment, and eloquence, presided at Athens forty years together over civil and military affairs. What was the character of Critias, or of Alcibiades? They were not, indeed, useful members of the state in which they lived, but were certainly men of learning and eloquence; and were they not improved by conversation with Socrates? Who instructed Dion of Syracuse in every branch of learning? Was it not Plato? The same illustrious philosopher, too, who formed him not to oratory only, but to courage and virtue, impelled, equipped, and armed him to deliver his country. Did Plato, then, instruct Dion in sciences different from those in which Isocrates formed the renowned Timotheus, the son of Conon, the eminent general, and himself a most excellent commander, and a man of extensive learning? Or from those in which Lysis the Pythagorean trained Epaminondas of Thebes, who, perhaps, was the most remarkable man of all Greece? Or from those which Xenophon taught Agesilaus, or Archytas of Tarentum Philolaus, or Pythagoras himself all that old province of Italy which was formerly called Great Greece ? XXXV. I do not imagine that they were different; for I see that one and the same course of study comprised all those branches of knowledge which were esteemed necessary for a man of learning, and one who wished to become eminent in civil administration; and that they who had received this knowledge, if they had sufficient powers for speaking in public, and devoted themselves, without any impediment from nature, to oratory, became distinguished for eloquence.   Aristotle himself, accordingly, when he saw Isocrates grow remarkable for the number and quality of his scholars [because he himself had diverted his lectures from forensic and civil causes to mere elegance of language[1]], changed on a sudden almost his whole system of teaching, and quoted a verse from the tragedy of Philoctetes[2] with a little alteration; for the

---

[1] The words in brackets, says Ellendt, are certainly spurious, for they could not possibly have been written by Cicero. In the original, *quod ipse*, etc., *ipse* necessarily refers to Aristotle, of whom what is here said could never have been true.
[2] The Philoctetes of Euripides, as is generally supposed.

hero said that *It was disgraceful for him to be silent while he allowed barbarians to speak;* but Aristotle said that *it was disgraceful for him to be silent while he allowed Isocrates to speak.* He therefore adorned and illustrated all philosophical learning, and associated the knowledge of things with practice in speaking. Nor did this escape the knowledge of that very sagacious monarch Philip, who sent for him as a tutor for his son Alexander, that he might acquire from the same teacher instructions at once in conduct and in language. Now, if any one desires either to call that philosopher, who instructs us fully in things and words, an *orator,* he may do so without opposition from me; or if he prefer to call that orator, of whom I speak as having wisdom united with eloquence, a *philosopher,* I shall make no objection, provided it be allowed that neither *his* inability to speak, who understands his subject, but can not set it forth in words, nor *his* ignorance, to whom matter is wanting 'though words abound, can merit commendation; and if I had to choose one of the two, I should prefer uneloquent good sense to loquacious folly. But if it be inquired which is the more eminent excellence, the palm is to be given to the learned orator; and if they allow the same person to be a philosopher, there is an end of controversy; but if they distinguish them, they will acknowledge their inferiority in this respect, that all their knowledge is inherent in the *complete orator;* but in the knowledge of the *philosophers* eloquence is not necessarily inherent; which, though it may be undervalued by them, must of necessity be thought to give a finishing grace to their sciences." When Crassus had spoken thus, he made a pause for a while, and the rest kept silence.

XXXVI. Cotta then observed, "I can not indeed complain, Crassus, that you seem to me to have given a dissertation upon a different subject from that on which you had undertaken to speak; for you have contributed to our conversation more than was either laid upon you by us, or given notice of by yourself. But certainly it was the part that belonged to you, to speak upon the embellishments of language, and you had already entered upon it, and distributed the whole excellence of eloquence into four parts; and, when you had spoken upon the first two, as we indeed thought sufficiently, but, as you said yourself, cursorily and slightly, you

had two others left : how we should speak, first, *elegantly*, and
next, *aptly*. But when you were proceeding to these particulars, the tide, as it were, of your genius suddenly hurried you
to a distance from land, and carried you out into the deep,
almost beyond the view of us all; for, embracing all knowledge of every thing, you did not indeed teach it us (for that
was impossible in so short a space of time), but—I know not
what improvement you may have made in the rest of the company—as for myself, you have carried me altogether into the
heart of the academy, in regard to which I could wish that
that were true which you have often asserted that it is not
necessary to consume our lives in it, but that he may see
every thing in it who only turns his eyes toward it : but even
if the view be somewhat obscure, or I should be extraordinarily dull, I shall assuredly never rest, or yield to fatigue,
until I understand their doubtful ways and arts of disputing
for and against every question." Cæsar then said, " One
thing in your remarks, Crassus, struck me very much, that
you said that he who did not learn any thing soon, could
never thoroughly learn it at all; so that I can have no difficulty in making the trial, and either immediately understanding what you extolled to the skies in your observations, or, if
I can not do so, losing no time, as I may remain content with
what I have already acquired." Here Sulpicius observed,
" I, indeed, Crassus, neither desire any acquaintance with
your Aristotle, nor Carneades, nor any of the philosophers;
you may either imagine that I despair of being able to acquire their knowledge, or that, as is really the case, I despise
it. The ordinary knowledge of common affairs, and such as
are litigated in the forum, is great enough for me, for attaining that degree of eloquence which is my object; and even in
that narrow circle of science I am ignorant of a multitude of
things, which I begin to study, whenever any cause in which
I am to speak requires them. If, therefore, you are not now
fatigued, and if we are not troublesome to you, revert to
those particulars which contribute to the merit and splendor
of language; particulars which I desired to hear from you,
not to make me despair that I can ever possibly attain eloquence, but to make some addition to my stock of learning."

XXXVII. " You require of me," said Crassus, " to speak
on matters which are very well known, and with which you,

Sulpicius, are not unacquainted ; for what rhetorician has not treated of this subject, has not given instructions on it, has not even left something about it in writing ? But I will comply with your request, and briefly explain to you at least such points as are known to me ; but I shall still think that you ought to refer to those who are the authors and inventors of these minute precepts. All speech, then, is formed of words, which we must first consider singly, then in composition ; for there is one merit of language which lies in single words, another which is produced by words joined and compounded. We shall therefore either use such words as are the proper and fixed names as it were of things, and apparently almost born at the same time with the things themselves ; or such as are metaphorical, and placed as it were in a situation foreign to them ; or such as we invent and make ourselves. In regard, then, to words taken in their own proper sense, it is a merit in the orator to avoid mean and obsolete ones, and to use such as are choice and ornamental ; such as have in them some fullness and force of sound. But in this kind of *proper* words, selection is necessary, which must be decided in some measure by the judgment of the ear ; in which point the mere habit of speaking well is of great effect. Even what is vulgarly said of orators by the illiterate multitude, *He uses proper words*, or *Such a one uses improper words*, is not the result of any acquired skill, but is a judgment arising from a natural sense of what is right ; in which respect it is no great merit to avoid a fault (though it is of great importance to do so) ; yet this is the groundwork, as it were, and foundation of the whole, namely, the use and command of proper words. But the superstructure which the orator himself is to raise upon this, and in which he is to display his art, appears to be a matter for us to examine and illustrate.

XXXVIII. " There are three qualities, then, in a simple word, which the orator may employ to illustrate and adorn his language ; he may choose either an *unusual* word, or one that is *new* or *metaphorical*. *Unusual* words are generally of ancient date and fashion, and such as have been long out of use in daily conversation ; these are allowed more freely to poetical license than to ours ; yet a poetical word gives occasionally dignity also to oratory ; nor would I shrink from

saying, with Cœlius, *Quâ tempestate Pœnus in Italiam venit,*
' At the season when the Carthaginian came into Italy :' nor
proles, ' progeny ;' nor *suboles,* ' offspring ;' nor *effari,* ' to
utter ;' nor *nuncupari,* ' to declare ;' nor, as you are in the
habit of saying, Catulus, *non rebar,* ' I did not deem ;' nor
non opinabar, ' I did not opine ;' nor many others, from which,
if properly introduced, a speech assumes an air of greater
grandeur. *New* words are such as are produced and formed
by the speaker ; either by joining words together, as these,

> " ' *Tum pavor sapientiam omnem mi exanimato expectorat,*
> Then fear expels all wisdom from the breast
> Of me astonished ;'

or,

> " ' *Num non vis hujus me versutiloquas malitias ?*
> Would you not have me dread his cunning malice ?'

for you see that *versutiloquas* and *expectorat* are words not
newly produced, but merely formed by composition. But
words are often invented, without composition, as the expression of Ennius,[1] *Dii genitales,* ' the genial gods ;' or *bac-
carum ubertate incurviscere,* ' to bend down with the fertile
crop of berries.'

" The third mode, that of using words in a *metaphorical*
sense, is widely prevalent, a mode of which necessity was the
parent, compelled by the sterility and narrowness of language ;
but afterward delight and pleasure made it frequent ; for as
a dress was first adopted for the sake of keeping off the cold,
but in process of time began to be made an ornament of the
body and an emblem of dignity, so the metaphorical use of
words was originally invented on account of their paucity, but
became common from the delight which it afforded. For even
the countrymen say, *gemmare vites,* that ' the vines are bud-
ding ;' *luxuriem esse in herbis,* that ' there is a luxuriancy in
the grass ;' and *lætas segetes,* that ' there is a bountiful crop ;'
for when that which can scarcely be signified by its proper
word is expressed by one used in a metaphorical sense, the
similitude taken from that which we indicate by a foreign
term gives clearness to that which we wish to be understood.

[1] All the editions retain *ille senius,* though universally acknowledged
to be corrupt.   The conjecture of Turnebus, *ille Ennius,* has found most
favor; that of Orellius, *illud Ennii,* is approved by Ellendt.   That the
words *di genitales* were used by Ennius appears from Servius on Virg.,
Æn., vi., 764.

These metaphors, therefore, are a species of borrowing, as you take from something else that which you have not of your own. Those have a greater degree of boldness which do not show poverty, but bring some accession of splendor to our language. But why should I specify to you either the modes of their production or their various kinds?

XXXIX. "A metaphor is a brief similitude contracted into a single word; which word being put in the place of another, as if it were in its own place, conveys, if the resemblance be acknowledged, delight; if there is no resemblance, it is condemned. But such words should be metaphorically used as may make the subject clearer; as all these:[1]

> " ' *Inhorrescit mare,*
> *Tenebræ conduplicantur, noctisque et nimbúm occæcat nigror,*
> *Flamma inter nubes coruscat, cælum tonitru contremit,*
> *Grando mixta imbri largifluo subita præcipitans cadit;*
> *Undique omnes venti erumpunt, sævi existunt turbines;*
> *Fervit æstu pelagus.*
>
> The sea begins to shudder,
> Darkness is doubled; and the black of night
> And of the tempest thickens; fire gleams vivid
> Amid the clouds; the heavens with thunder shake;
> Hail mixed with copious rain sudden descends
> Precipitate; from all sides every blast
> Breaks forth; fierce whirlwinds gather, and the flood
> Boils with fresh tumult.'

Here almost every thing is expressed in words metaphorically adapted from something similar, that the description may be heightened. Or metaphors are employed that the whole nature of any action or design may be more significantly expressed, as in the case of him who indicates, by two metaphorical words, that another person was designedly obscure, in order that what he intended might not be understood,

> " ' *Quandoquidem is se circumvestit dictis, sæpit sedulò,*
> Since thus he clothes himself around with words,
> And hedges constantly.'

"Sometimes, also, brevity is the object attained by metaphor; as, *Si telum manu fugit,* 'If from his hand the javelin fled.' The throwing of a missile weapon unawares could not be described with more brevity in the proper words than it is signified by one used metaphorically. On this head, it often appears to me wonderful why all men are more delighted with

[1] From Pacuvius. See Cic., Divin., i., 14.

words used in a metaphorical or foreign sense than in their own proper and natural signification.   XL. For if a thing has not a name of its own, and a term peculiar to it—as the *pes*, or ' hawser,' in a ship ; *nexum*, a ' bond,' which is a ceremony performed with scales ;[1] *divortium*, a 'divorce,' with reference to a wife[2]—necessity compels you to borrow from another what you have not yourself; but, even in the greatest abundance of proper words, men are much more charmed with such as are uncommon, if they are used metaphorically with judgment.   This happens, I imagine, either because it is some manifestation of wit to jump over such expressions as lie before you, and catch at others from a greater distance ; or because he who listens is led another way in thought, and yet does not wander from the subject, which is a very great pleasure ; or because a subject, and entire comparison, is dispatched in a single word ; or because every metaphor that is adopted with judgment, is directed immediately to our senses, and principally to the sense of sight, which is the keenest of them all.   For such expressions as the *odor* of urbanity, the *softness* of humanity, the *murmur* of the sea, and *sweetness* of language, are derived from the other senses ; but those which relate to the sight are much more striking, for they place almost in the eye of the mind such objects as we can not see and discern by the natural eyes.   There is, indeed, nothing in universal nature, the proper name and term of which we may not use with regard to other matters ; for whencesoever a simile may be drawn (and it may be drawn from any thing), from thence a single word, which contains the resemblance, metaphorically applied, may give illustration to our language. In such metaphorical expressions, dissimilitude is principally to be avoided ; as,

" ' *Cœli ingentes fornices,*
The arch immense of heaven ;'

for though Ennius[3] is said to have brought a globe upon the stage, yet the semblance of an arch can never be inherent in the form of a globe.

---

[1] See Smith's Dict. of Gr. and Rom. Ant., art. *Nexum*.
[2] *Divortium*, in its proper sense, denoted the separation of roads or waters.
[3] In his tragedy of Hecuba, as is supposed by Hermann, ad Eurip., Hec., p. 167. See Varro, L. L., v., p. 8.

> " ' *Vive, Ulixes, dum licet :*
>   *Oculis postremum lumen radiatum rape :*[1]
> Live, live, Ulysses, while you may, and snatch,
> Snatch with thine eyes the last light shining on them.'

He did not say *cape*, ' take,' nor *pete*, ' seek,' for such expressions might have implied delay, as of one hoping to live
longer ; but *rape*, ' snatch,' a word which was peculiarly suitable to what he had said before, *dum licet*, ' while you may.'

XLI. " Care is next to be taken that the simile be not too
far-fetched ; as, for ' the Syrtis of his patrimony,' I should
rather have said, ' the rock ;' for ' the Charybdis of his possessions,' rather ' the gulf :' for the eyes of the mind are more
easily directed to those objects which we have seen, than to
those of which we have only heard. And since it is the
greatest merit in a metaphorical word that what is metaphorical should strike the senses, all offensiveness is to be
avoided in those objects to which the comparison must naturally draw the minds of the audience. I would not have it
said that the republic was ' castrated' by the death of Africanus ; I would not have Glaucia called ' the excrement of the
senate ;' for though there may be a resemblance, yet it is a
depraved imagination in both cases that gives rise to such a
comparison. I would not have the metaphor grander than
the subject requires, as ' a tempest of reveling ;' nor meaner,
as ' the reveling of the tempest.' I would not have the metaphorical be of a more confined sense than the proper and
peculiar term would have been ; as,

> " ' *Quidnam est, obsecro, quid te adiri abnutas ?*[2]
> Why is it, prithee, that thou nodd'st us back
> From coming to thee ?'

Vetas, prohibes, absterres, ' forbid,' ' hinder,' ' terrify,' had been
better, because he had before said,

> " ' Fly quickly hence,'[3]
> Lest my contagion or my shadow fall
> On men of worth.'

Also, if you apprehend that the metaphor may appear too

---

[1] Supposed by Bothe, Trag. Lat. Fragm., p. 278, to be from the
Niptra of Pacuvius. See Cic., Quæst. Acad., ii., 28.

[2] From the Thyestes of Ennius. Cic., Tusc., iii., 12.

[3] Orellius's text has *istim*, which is considered to be the same as *istinc*.
See Victorius, ad Cic. Ep. ad Div., vi., 6.

harsh, it may frequently be softened by prefixing a word or words to it; as if, in old times, on the death of Marcus Cato, any one had said that the senate was left 'an orphan,' the expression had been rather bold; but, 'so to speak, an orphan,' is somewhat milder; for a metaphor ought not to be too daring, but of such a nature that it may appear to have been introduced into the place of another expression, not to have sprung into it; to have come in by entreaty, and not by violence. And there is no mode of embellishment more effective as regards single words, nor any that throws a greater lustre upon language; for the ornament that flows from this figure does not consist merely in a single metaphorical word, but may be connected by a continuation of many, so that one thing may be expressed and another understood; as,

> " 'Nor will I allow
> Myself again to strike the Grecian fleet
> On the same rock and instrument of ruin.'[1]

And this,

> " 'You err, you err, for the strong reins of law
> Shall hold you back, exulting and confiding
> Too much in your own self, and make you bow
> Beneath the yoke of empire.'

Something being assumed as similar, the words which are proper to it are metaphorically transferred (as I termed it before) to another subject.

XLII. "This is a great ornament to language, but obscurity is to be avoided in it; for from this figure arise what are called ænigmas. Nor is this rule to be observed in single words only, but in phrases, that is, in a continuation of words. Nor have metonymy and hypallage[2] their form from a single word, but from a phrase or sentence; as,

> " 'Grim Afric trembles with an awful tumult;'[3]

where for the *Africans* is used *Afric*; not a word newly compounded, as in *Mare saxifragis undis*, 'The sea with its rock-breaking waves;' nor a metaphorical one, as, *Mollitur mare*, 'The sea is softened;' but one proper name exchanged for

---

[1] Whence this and the following quotation are taken is uncertain.

[2] *Traductio atque immutatio.* See Cic., Orat., 27; Quint., viii., 6; ix., 3; infra, c. 43, 54.

[3] From the Annals of Ennius. See Cic., Ep. ad Div., ix., 7; Orat., 27; Festus v. *metonymia.*

another, for the sake of embellishment. Thus, ' Cease, Rome, thy foes to cherish,' and, ' The spacious plains are witnesses.' This figure contributes exceedingly to the ornament of style, and is frequently to be used; of which kind of expression these are examples: that the *Mars*, or fortune, *of war is common;* and to say *Ceres*, for corn; *Bacchus*, for wine; *Neptune*, for the sea; the *curia*, or *house*, for the senate; the *campus*, for the comitia or elections; the *gown*, for peace; *arms* or *weapons*, for war. Under this figure, the virtues and vices are used for the persons in whom they are inherent: ' *Luxury* has broken into that house;' or, ' whither *avarice* has penetrated;' or, ' *honesty* has prevailed;' or, '*justice* has triumphed.' You perceive the whole force of this kind of figure, when, by the variation or change of a word, a thing is expressed more elegantly; and to this figure is closely allied another,[1] which, though less ornamental, ought not to be unknown; as when we would have the whole of a thing understood from a part; as we say *walls* or *roof* for a whole building; or a part from the whole, as when we call one troop *the cavalry of the Roman people;* or when we signify the plural by the singular, as,

> " ' But still the Roman, though the affair has been
> Conducted well, is anxious in his heart;'[2]

or when the singular is understood from the plural,

> " ' We that were *Rudians* once are *Romans* now;'

or in whatever way, by this figure, the sense is to be understood, not as it is expressed, but as it is meant.

XLIII. " We often also put one word catachrestically for another, not with that elegance, indeed, which there is in a metaphor; but, though this is done licentiously, it is sometimes done inoffensively; as when we say a *great speech* for a long one, a *minute soul* for a little one.

" But have you perceived that those elegances which arise from the connection of several metaphors, do not, as I observed,[3] lie in one word, but in a series of words? But all those modes of expression which, I said, lay in the change of a word, or are to be understood differently from what is ex-

---

[1] Synecdoche.
[2] This quotation and the following are from the Annals of Ennius.
[3] C. 41.

pressed, are in some measure metaphorical. Hence it happens, that all the virtue and merit of single words consists in
three particulars: if a word be *antique*, but such, however, as
usage will tolerate; if it be formed *by composition*, or newly
invented, where regard is to be paid to the judgment of the
ear and to custom; or if it be used *metaphorically*; peculiarities which eminently distinguish and brighten language, as
with so many stars.

"The composition of words follows next, which principally
requires attention to two things; first, *collocation*, and, next,
a certain *modulation* and *form*. To collocation it belongs to
compose and arrange the words in such a way that their
junction may not be rough or gaping, but compact, as it
were, and smooth; in reference to which qualities of style,
the poet Lucilius, who could do so most elegantly, has expressed himself wittily and sportively in the character of my
father-in-law :[1]

> " 'How elegantly are his words arranged!
> All like square stones inserted skillfully
> In pavements, with vermiculated emblems!'

And after saying this in ridicule of Albucius, he does not refrain from touching on me:

> " 'I've Crassus for a son-in-law, nor think
> Yourself more of an orator.'

What then? this Crassus, of whose name you, Lucilius, make
such free use, what does he attempt? The very same thing
indeed as Scævola wished, and as I would wish, but with
somewhat better effect than Albucius. But Lucilius spoke
jestingly with regard to me, according to his custom. However, such an arrangement of words is to be observed, as
that of which I was speaking; such a one as may give a com-
pactness and coherence to the language, and a smooth and
equal flow; this you will attain if you join the extremities
of the antecedent words to the commencements of those that
follow in such a manner that there be no rough clashing in
the consonants, nor wide hiatus in the vowels.

XLIV. "Next to diligent attention to this particular follows modulation and harmonious structure of the words; a
point, I fear, that may seem puerile to our friend Catulus
here. The ancients, however, imagined in prose a harmony

[1] Mucius Scævola. He accused Albucius of extortion.

almost like that of poetry; that is, they thought that we
ought to adopt a sort of numbers; for they wished that there
should be short phrases in speeches, to allow us to recover,
and not lose our breath; and that they should be distinguished, not by the marks of transcribers, but according to
the modulation of the words and sentences;[1] and this practice Isocrates is said to have been the first to introduce, that
he might (as his scholar Naucrates writes) 'confine the rude
manner of speaking among those of antiquity within certain
numbers, to give pleasure and captivate the ear.' For musicians, who were also the poets of former ages, contrived these
two things as the ministers of pleasure, verse, and song; that
they might banish satiety from the sense of hearing by gratification, arising from the numbers of language and the modulation of notes. These two things, therefore (I mean the musical management of the voice, and the harmonious structure
of words), should be transferred, they thought, as far as the
strictness of prose will admit, from poetry to oratory. On
this head it is remarkable, that if a verse is formed by the
composition of words in prose, it is a fault; and yet we wish
such composition to have a harmonious cadence, roundness,
and finish, like verse; nor is there any single quality, out of
many, that more distinguishes a true orator from an unskillful and ignorant speaker, than that he who is unpracticed
pours forth all he can without discrimination, and measures
out the periods of his speech, not with art, but by the power
of his breath; but the orator clothes his thoughts in such a
manner as to comprise them in a flow of numbers, at once
confined to measure, yet free from restraint; for, after re-
stricting it to proper modulation and structure, he gives it
an ease and freedom by a variety in the flow, so that the
words are neither bound by strict laws, as those of verse,
nor yet have such a degree of liberty as to wander without
control.

XLV. "In what manner, then, shall we pursue so important an object, so as to entertain hopes of being able to acquire
this talent of speaking in harmonious numbers? It is not a
matter of so much difficulty as it is of necessity; for there is
nothing so pliant, nothing so flexible, nothing which will so
easily follow whithersoever you incline to lead it, as language;

[1] Ellendt aptly refers to Cic., Orat., c. 68; Aristotle, Rhet., iii., 8, 6.

out of which verses are composed; out of which all the variety of poetical numbers; out of which also prose of various
modulation and of many different kinds; for there is not one
set of words for common discourse, and another for oratorical
debate; nor are they taken from one class for daily conversation, and from another for the stage and for display; but,
when we have made our selection from those that lie before us,
we form and fashion them at our pleasure like the softest wax.
According, therefore, as we ourselves are grave, or subtle, or
hold a middle course between both, so the form of our language follows the nature of our thoughts, and is changed and
varied to suit every method by which we delight the ear or
move the passions of mankind.   But as in most things, so in
language, Nature herself has wonderfully contrived, that what
carries in it the greatest utility, should have at the same time
either the most dignity, or, as it often happens, the most
beauty.   We perceive the very system of the universe and of
nature to be constituted with a view to the safety and preservation of the whole; so that the firmament should be
round, and the earth in the middle, and that it should be held
in its place by its own nature and tendency;[1] that the sun
should go round, that it should approach to the winter sign,[2]
and thence gradually ascend to the opposite region; that the
moon, by her advance and retreat, should receive the light of
the sun; and that the five planets should perform the same
revolutions by different motions and courses.   This order of
things has such force, that, if there were the least alteration
in it, they could not possibly subsist together; and such
beauty, that no fairer appearance of nature could even be
imagined.   Turn your thoughts now to the shape and figure of
man, or even that of other animals; you will find no part of
the body fashioned without some necessary use, and the whole
frame perfected, as it were, by art, not by chance.   XLVI.
How is it with regard to trees, of which neither the trunk,
nor the boughs, nor even the leaves, are formed otherwise
than to maintain and preserve their own nature, yet in which
there is no part that is not beautiful?   Or let us turn from
natural objects, and cast our eyes on those of art; what is so

[1] *Nutu.* Compare Cic., De Nat. Deor., ii., 39.   Ellendt thinks that
by *nutus* is meant something similar to our *centripetal force.*
[2] *Brumale signum.* The tropic of Capricorn. De Nat. Deor., iii., 14.

necessary in a ship as the sides, the hold,[1] the prow, the stern, the yards, the sails, the masts? which yet have so much beauty in their appearance, that they seem to have been invented not for safety only, but also for the delight afforded by the spectacle. Pillars support temples and porticoes, and yet have not more of utility than of dignity. It was not regard to beauty, but necessity, that contrived the cupola of the Capitol, and other buildings; for when a plan was contemplated by which the water might run off from each side of the roof, the dignity of the cupola was added to the utility of the temple; but in such a manner, that should the Capitol be built in heaven, where no rain can fall, it would appear to have no dignity without the cupola. It happens likewise in all parts of language, that a certain agreeableness and grace are attendant on utility, and, I may say, on necessity; for the stoppage of the breath, and the confined play of the lungs, introduced periods and the pointing of words. This invention gives such gratification, that, if unlimited powers of breath were granted to a person, yet we could not wish him to speak without stopping; for the invention of stops is pleasing to the ears of mankind, and not only tolerable, but easy, to the lungs.

XLVII. "The largest compass of a period, then, is that which can be rounded forth in one breath. This is the bound set by nature; art has other limits; for as there is a great variety of numbers, your favorite Aristotle, Catulus, inclines to banish from oratorical language the frequent use of the iambus and the trochee; which, however, fall of themselves naturally into our common discourse and conversation; but the strokes of time[2] in those numbers are remarkable, and

---

[1] *Cavernæ.* Some editions have *carinæ*, and Lambinus reads *carina*. If we retain *cavernæ*, it is not easy to say exactly in what sense it should be taken. Servius, on Virgil, Æn., ii., 19, observes that the *fustes curvi navium, quibus extrinsecus fabulæ affiguntur*, were called *cavernæ;* but in this sense, as Ellendt observes, it is much the same with *latera*, which precedes. Ellendt himself, therefore, inclines to take it in the sense of *cavitas alvei*, "hold" or "keel," which, as it is divided into parts, may, he thinks, be expressed in the plural number.

[2] *Percussiones.* The *ictus metrici;* so called, because the musician, in beating time, *struck* the ground with his foot. In a senarius he struck the ground three times, once for every two feet; whence there were said to be in such a verse three *ictus* or *percussiones*. But on pronouncing those syllables, at which the musician struck the ground, the actor

the feet short. He therefore principally invites us to the heroic measure [of the dactyl, the anapæst, and the spondee],[1] in which we may proceed with impunity two feet only, or a little more, lest we plainly fall into verse, or the resemblance of verse ;

"'*Áltæ | sŭnt gĕmĭ|næ quĭbŭs—*'

These three heroic feet fall in gracefully enough with the beginnings of continuations of words. But the pæon is most of all approved by Aristotle; it is of two kinds ;[2] for it either begins with a long syllable which three short syllables follow, as in these words, *dēsĭnĭtĕ, incĭpĭtĕ, cōmprĭmĭtĕ;* or with a succession of three short syllables, the last being produced and made long, as in these words, *dŏmŭĕrānt, sŏnĭpĕdēs;* and it is agreeable to the notions of that philosopher to commence with the former pæon, and to conclude with the latter; and this latter pæon is almost equal, not indeed in the number of the syllables, but by the measure of the ear, which is a more acute and certain method of judgment, to the cretic, which consists of a long, a short, and a long syllable; as in this verse,

"' *Quĭd pĕtām præsĭdī, aut exsĕquār? Quōvĕ nūnc ?*'[3]

With which kind of foot Fannius[4] began, *Sĭ, Quĭrītēs, Mĭnās illius.* This Aristotle thinks better adapted to conclusions of periods, which he wishes to be terminated generally by a syllable that is long.

XLVIII. "But these numbers in oratory do not require such sharp-sighted care and diligence as that which must be used by poets, whom necessity compels, as do the very numbers and measures, so to include the words in versification, as

raised his voice; and hence *percussio* was in Greek ἄρσις, and the raised or accented syllables were said to be ἐν ἄρσει, the others being said to be in θέσει. See Bentley, de Metr. Terentian., init. *Ernesti.*

[1] Madvig and Ellendt justly regard the words in brackets as spurious. I follow those critics also in reading *Altæ sunt geminæ quibus*, though, as Ellendt observes, *Altæ* ought very likely to be *Aræ*. *Aliæ*, which is in most editions, made the passage utterly inexplicable, though Ernesti, Strebæus, and others did what they could to put some meaning into it.

[2] The first and fourth only are meant.

[3] C. 26; where Pearce observes that they are the words of Andromache in Ennius, according to Bentley on Tusc. Disp., iii., 19.

[4] Caius Fannius Strabo, who was consul A.U.C. 632. He left one speech against Caius Gracchus : Cic. Brut., c. 26.

that no part may be, even by the least breath,[1] shorter or longer than the metre absolutely demands. Prose has a more free scope, and is plainly, as it is called, *soluta*, unconfined, yet not so that it may fly off or wander without control, but may regulate itself without being absolutely in fetters; for I agree in this particular with Theophrastus, who thinks that style, at least such as is to a certain degree polished and well constructed,[2] ought to be numerous, yet not as in confinement, but at ease. For, as he suspects, from those feet of which the common hexameter verse is formed, grew forth afterward the anapæstic, a longer kind of measure; thence flowed the still more free and rich dithyramb, the members and feet of which, as the same writer observes, are diffused through all style, that is enriched with the distinguishing ornaments of eloquence. And if that is numerous in all sounds and words, which gives certain strokes as it were, and which we can measure by equal intervals, this harmony of numbers, if it be free from sameness, will be justly considered a merit in the oratorical style. Since, if perpetual and ever-flowing loquacity, without any pauses, is to be thought rude and unpolished, what other reason is there why it should be disliked, except that Nature herself modulates the voice for the human ear? and this could not be the case unless numbers were inherent in the human voice. But in an uninterrupted continuation of sound there are no numbers; distinction, and strokes at equal or often varied intervals, constitute numbers; which we may remark in the falling of drops of water, because they are distinguished by intervals, but which we can not observe in the rolling stream of a river. But as this unrestrained composition of words[3] is more eligible and harmonious, if it be distinguished into parts and members, than if it be carried on without intermission, those members ought to be measured by a certain rule of proportion; for if those at the end are shorter, the compass, as it were, of the words is made irregular; the compass,[4] I say, for so the Greeks denominate these rounded divisions of

[1] *Ne spiritu quidem minimo.*
[2] *Facta.* That is, carefully labored. See Brut., c. 8. *Ellendt.*
[3] *Continuatio verborum soluta.* See above, near the beginning of this chapter, *oratio—verè soluta.*
[4] *Ambitus.* The Greek word is περίοδος. See Orat., c. 61.

style; the subsequent clauses in a sentence, therefore, ought
to be equal to the antecedent, the last to the first; or, which
has a better and more pleasing effect, of a greater length.

XLIX. "These precepts are given by those philosophers
to whom you, Catulus, have the greatest attachment; a remark which I the oftener make, that by referring to my authors, I may avoid the charge of impertinence." "Of what
sort of impertinence?" said Catulus; "or what could be
brought before us more elegant than this discussion of yours,
or expressed more judiciously?" "But still I am afraid,"
said Crassus, "lest these matters should either appear to
these youths[1] too difficult for study, or lest, as they are not
given in the common rules of instruction, I should appear to
have an inclination that they should seem of more importance
and difficulty than they really are." Catulus replied, "You
are mistaken, Crassus, if you imagine that either I or any of
the company expected from you those ordinary or vulgar
precepts; what you say is what we wished to be said; and
not so much indeed to be said, as to be said in the very manner in which you have said it; nor do I answer for myself
only, but for all the rest, without the least hesitation."
"And I," said Antonius, "have at length discovered such a
one as, in the book which I wrote, I said that I had never
found, a *person of eloquence;* but I never interrupted you, not
even to pay you a compliment, for this reason, that no part
of the short time allotted for your discourse might be diminished by a single word of mine."

"To this standard, then," proceeded Crassus, "is your
style to be formed, as well by the practice of speaking as by
writing, which contributes a grace and refinement to other
excellences, but to this in a more peculiar manner. Nor is
this a matter of so much labor as it appears to be; nor are
our phrases to be governed by the rigid laws of the cultiva-
tors of numbers and music; and the only object for our endeavors is, that our sentences may not be loose or rambling,
that they neither stop within too narrow a compass, nor run
out too far; that they be distinguished into clauses, and have
well-rounded periods. Nor are you to use perpetually this
fullness, and, as it were, roundness of language, but a sentence is often to be interrupted by minuter clauses, which

---

[1] Cotta and Sulpicius.

very clauses are still to be modulated by numbers. Nor let the pæon or heroic foot give you any alarm; they will naturally come into your phrases; they will, I say, offer themselves, and will answer without being called; only let it be your care and practice, both in writing and speaking, that your sentences be concluded with verbs, and that the junction of those verbs with other words proceed with numbers that are long and free, especially the heroic feet, the first pæon, or the cretic; but let the cadence be varied and diversified; for it is in the conclusion that sameness is chiefly remarked. And if these measures are observed at the beginning and at the conclusion of sentences, the intermediate numbers may be disregarded; only let the compass of your sentence not be shorter than the ear expects, nor longer than your strength and breath will allow.

L. " But I think that the conclusions of periods ought to be studied more carefully than the former parts; because it is chiefly from these that the finish of style is judged; for in a verse, the commencement of it, the middle, and the extremity are equally regarded; and in whatever part it fails, it loses its force; but in a speech, few notice the beginnings, but almost all the closes, of the periods, which, as they are observable and best understood, should be varied, lest they be disapproved, either by the judgment of the understanding or by the satiety of the ear. For the two or three feet toward the conclusion are to be marked and noted, if the preceding members of the sentence were not extremely short and concise; and these last feet ought either to be trochees, or heroic feet, or those feet used alternately, or to consist of the latter pæon, of which Aristotle approves, or, what is equal to it, the cretic. An interchange of such feet will have these good effects, that the audience will not be tired by an offensive sameness, and that we shall not appear to make similar endings on purpose. But if the famous Antipater of Sidon,[1] whom you, Catulus, very well remember, used to pour forth extempore hexameter and other verses, in various numbers and measures, and if practice had so much power in a man of great ability and memory, that whenever he turned his thoughts and inclinations upon verse, the words followed of

[1] Some of whose epigrams are to be seen in the Greek Anthology. He flourished about 100 B.C.

course, how much more easily shall we attain this facility in oratory, when application and exercise are used!

" Nor let any one wonder how the illiterate part of an audience observe these things when they listen to a speech ; since, in all other things as well as in this, the force of nature is great and extraordinary ; for all men, by a kind of tacit sense, without any art or reasoning, can form a judgment of what is right and wrong in art and reasoning; and as they do this with regard to pictures, statues, and other works, for understanding which they have less assistance from nature, so they display this faculty much more in criticising words, numbers, and sounds of language, because these powers are inherent in our common senses, nor has nature intended that any person should be utterly destitute of judgment in these particulars. All people are accordingly moved, not only by words artfully arranged, but also by numbers and the sounds of the voice. How few are those that understand the science of numbers and measures! yet if in these the smallest offense be given by an actor, so that any sound is made too short by contraction, or too long by extension, whole theatres burst into exclamations. Does not the same thing also happen with regard to musical notes, that not only whole sets and bands of musicians are turned out by the multitude and the populace for varying one from another, but even single performers for playing out of tune?

LI. " It is wonderful, when there is a wide interval of distinction betwixt the learned and illiterate in acting, how little difference there is in judging;[1] for art, being derived from nature, appears to have effected nothing at all if it does not move and delight nature. And there is nothing which so naturally affects our minds as numbers and the harmony of sounds, by which we are excited, and inflamed, and soothed, and thrown into a state of languor, and often moved to cheerfulness or sorrow ; the most exquisite power of which is best suited to poetry and music, and was not, as it seems to me, undervalued by our most learned monarch Numa and our ancestors (as the stringed and wind instruments at the sacred banquets and the verses of the Salii sufficiently indicate), but was most cultivated in ancient Greece; [concerning which subjects, and similar ones, I could wish that you had chosen

[1] See Cic., Brut., c. 49.

to discourse, rather than about these puerile verbal metaphors!]¹ But as the common people notice where there is
any thing faulty in a verse, so they are sensible of any lameness in our language; but they grant the poet no pardon; to
us they show some indulgence; but all tacitly discern that
what we have uttered has not its peculiar propriety and finish. The speakers of old, therefore, as we see some do at the
present day, when they were unable to complete a circuit,
and, as it were, roundness of period (for that is what we have
recently begun, indeed, either to effect or attempt), spoke in
clauses consisting of three, or two words, or sometimes uttered only a single word at a time; and yet in that infancy of
our tongue they understood the natural gratification which
the human ears required, and even studied that what they
spoke should be expressed in correspondent phrases, and that
they should take breath at equal intervals.

LII. " I have now shown, as far as I could, what I deemed
most conducive to the embellishment of language; for I have
spoken of the merits of single words; I have spoken of them
in composition; I have spoken of the harmony of numbers
and structure. But if you wish me to speak also of the form
and, as it were, complexion of eloquence, there is one sort
which has a fullness, but is free from tumor; one which is
plain, but not without nerve and vigor; and one which, par-
ticipating of both these kinds, is commended for a certain
middle quality. In each of these three forms there ought to
be a peculiar complexion of beauty, not produced by the daub-
ing of paint, but diffused throughout the system by the blood.
Then, finally,² this orator of ours is so to be finished as to
his style and thoughts in general, that, as those who study
fencing and polite exercises, not only think it necessary to
acquire a skill in parrying and striking, but also grace and
elegance of motion, so he may use such words as are suited
to elegant and graceful composition, and such thoughts as
contribute to the impressiveness of language. Words and

---

¹ The words in brackets are condemned as spurious by all the recent
editors.

² *Tum denique.* Ellendt incloses *tum* in brackets, and thinks that
much of the language of the rest of the chapter is confused and incorrect. The words *ut ii, qui in armorum tractatione versantur*, which occur a little below, and which are generally condemned, are not translated.

thoughts are formed in almost innumerable ways, as is, I am sure, well known to you; but betwixt the formation of words and that of thoughts there is this difference, that that of the words is destroyed if you change them, that of the thoughts remains, whatever words you think proper to use. But I think that you ought to be reminded (although, indeed, you act agreeably to what I say) that you should not imagine there is any thing else to be done by the orator, at least any thing else to produce a striking and admirable effect, than to observe these three rules with regard to single words; to use frequently *metaphorical* ones, sometimes *new* ones, and rarely *very old* ones.

"But with regard to continuous composition, when we have acquired that smoothness of junction and harmony of numbers which I have explained, our whole style of oratory is to be distinguished and frequently interspersed with brilliant lights, as it were, of thoughts and of words. LIII. For the *dwelling* on a single circumstance has often a considerable effect; and a clear *illustration* and *exhibition* of matters to the eye of the audience, almost as if they were transacted before them. This has wonderful influence in giving a representation of any affair, both to illustrate what is represented, and to amplify it, so that the point which we amplify may appear to the audience to be really as great as the powers of our language can represent it. Opposed to this is *rapid transition* over a thing, which may often be practiced. There is also *signification* that more is to be understood than you have expressed; distinct and concise *brevity;* and *extenuation*, and, what borders upon this, *ridicule*, not very different from that which was the object of Cæsar's instructions; and *digression* from the subject, and when gratification has thus been afforded, the return to the subject ought to be happy and elegant; *proposition* of what you are about to say, *transition* from what has been said, and *retrogression;* there is *repetition;* apt *conclusion* of reasoning; *exaggeration*, or surpassing of the truth, for the sake of amplification or diminution; *interrogation*, and, akin to this, as it were, *consultation* or seeming inquiry, followed by the delivery of your own opinion; and *dissimulation*, the *humor* of saying one thing and signifying another, which steals into the minds of men in a peculiar manner, and which is extremely pleasing when it is well managed, not in a vehement strain of language, but in a

conversational style; also *doubt;* and *distribution;* and *correc-*
tion of yourself, either before or after you have said a thing,
or when you repel any thing from yourself; there is also *pre-*
munition, with regard to what you are going to prove; there
is the *transference of blame* to another person; there is *com-*
munication, or consultation, as it were, with the audience before
whom you are speaking; *imitation* of manners and character,
either with names of persons or without, which is a great ornament to a speech, and adapted to conciliate the feelings even
in the utmost degree, and often also to rouse them; the *intro-*
duction of fictitious characters, the most heightened figure of exaggeration; there is *description; falling into a willful mistake;*
excitement of the audience to cheerfulness; anticipation; compar-
ison and *example*, two figures which have a very great effect;
division; interruption; contention;[1] *suppression; commendation;*
a certain *freedom and even uncontrolledness of language*, for the
purpose of exaggeration; *anger; reproach; promise; depre-*
cation; beseeching; slight *deviation* from your intended course,
but not like digression, which I mentioned before; *expurga-*
tion; conciliation; attack; wishing; execration. Such are the
figures with which thoughts give lustre to a speech.

LIV. " Of words themselves, as of arms, there is a sort of
threatening and attack for use, and also a management for
grace. For the *reiteration* of words has sometimes a peculiar
force, and sometimes elegance; as well as the *variation* or de-
flexion of a word from its common signification; and the frequent *repetition* of the same word in the beginning, and *recur-*
rence to it at the end, of a period; *forcible emphasis* on the
same words; *conjunction;*[2] *adjunction;*[3] *progression;*[4] a sort of
distinction as to some word often used; the *recall* of a word;
the use of words, also, which end similarly, or have similar

---

[1] *Contentio.* This is doubtless some species of comparison; there is
no allusion to it in the Orator. See ad Herenn., iv., 45. *Ellendt.*

[2] *Concursio.* The writer ad Herenn., iv., 14, calls this figure *traduc-*
tio; the Greeks συμπλοκή. *Ellendt.*

[3] *Adjunctio.* It appears to be that which Quintilian (ix., 3) calls
συνεζευγμένον, where several words are connected with the same verb.
Ellendt.

[4] What *progressio* is, no critic has been able to inform us, nor is there
any notice of it in any other writer on rhetoric. I see no mode of explaining the passage, unless we take *adjunctio* and *progressio* together,
and suppose them to signify that the speech proceeds with several words
in conjunction. *Ellendt.*

cadences, or which balance one another, or which correspond to one another. There is also a certain *gradation*, a *conversion*,[1] an elegant *exaggeration* of the sense of words; there is *antithesis*, *asyndeton*, *declination*,[2] *reprehension*,[3] *exclamation*, *diminution*; the use of the *same word in different cases*; the *referring* of what is derived *from many particulars to each particular singly*; *reasoning* subservient to your *proposition*, and *reasoning* suited to the order of *distribution*; *concession*; and again another kind of *doubt*;[4] the introduction of something *unexpected*; *enumeration*; another *correction*;[5] *division*; *continuation*; *interruption*; *imagery*; *answering your own questions*; *immutation*;[6] *disjunction*; *order*; *relation*; *digression*,[7] and *circumscription*. These are the figures, and others like these, or there may even be more, which adorn language by peculiarities in thought or structure of style."

LV. "These remarks, Crassus," said Cotta, "I perceive that you have poured forth to us without any definitions or examples, because you imagined us acquainted with them." "I did not, indeed," said Crassus, "suppose that any of the things which I previously mentioned were new to you, but acted merely in obedience to the inclinations of the whole company. But in these particulars the sun yonder admonished me to use brevity, which, hastening to set, compelled me also to throw out these observations almost too hastily. But explanations, and even rules on this head, are common, though the application of them is most important, and the most difficult of any thing in the whole study of eloquence.

[1] An antithetic position of words, as *esse ut vivas, non vivere ut cdas*. Ellendt.

[2] *Declinatio.* Called ἀντιμεταβολή by Quintilian, ix., 3, 85.

[3] *Reprehensio.* Ἀφορισμὸς or διορισμός. Jul., Rufin., p. 207. Compare Quintil., ix., 2, 18; Ern., p. 332. *Ellendt.*

[4] How this kind of *doubt* differs from that which is mentioned in the preceding chapter, among the figures of thought, it is not easy to say. *Ellendt.*

[5] *Correctio verbi.* Different from that which is mentioned above, in the middle of c. 53. *Ellendt.*

[6] Called ἀλλοίωσις by Quintilian, ix., 3, 92. *Ellendt.*

[7] *Digression* has been twice mentioned before. Strebæus supposes it to be similar to μετάβασις or ἀποστροφή. I have no doubt that the word ought to be rejected. *Circumscription* Quintilian himself could not understand, and has excluded it from his catalogue of figures (ix., 3, 91). *Ellendt.* Most of the figures enumerated in this chapter are illustrated by the writer ad Herennium, b. iv., and by Quintilian, b. ix.

"Since, then, all the points which relate to all the ornamental parts of oratory are, if not illustrated, at least pointed out, let us now consider what is meant by propriety, that is, what is most becoming, in oratory. It is, however, clear that no single kind of style can be adapted to every cause, or every audience, or every person, or every occasion. For capital causes require one style of speaking, private and inferior causes another ; deliberations require one kind of oratory, panegyric another, judicial proceedings another, common conversation another, consolation another, reproof another, disputation another, historical narrative another. It is of consequence also to consider who form the audience, whether the senate, or the people, or the judges ; whether it is a large or a small assembly, or a single person, and of what character ; it ought to be taken into account, too, who the speakers themselves are, of what age, rank, and authority; and the time also, whether it be one of peace or war, of hurry or leisure. On this head, therefore, no direction seems possible to be given but this, that we adopt a character of style, fuller, plainer, or middling,[1] suited to the subject on which we are to speak ; the same ornaments we may use almost constantly, but sometimes in a higher, sometimes in a lower strain ; and it is the part of art and nature to be able *to do* what is becoming on every occasion ; *to know* what is becoming, and when, is an affair of judgment.

LVI. "But all these parts of oratory succeed according as they are delivered. Delivery, I say, has the sole and supreme power in oratory ; without it, a speaker of the highest mental capacity can be held in no esteem ; while one of moderate abilities, with this qualification, may surpass even those of the highest talent. To this Demosthenes is said to have assigned the first place, when he was asked what was the chief requisite in eloquence ; to this the second, and to this the third. For this reason, I am wont the more to admire what was said by Æschines, who, when he had retired from Athens, on account of the disgrace of having lost his cause, and betaken himself to Rhodes, is reported to have read, at the entreaty of the Rhodians, that excellent oration which he had spoken against Ctesiphon, in opposition to Demosthenes ; and when he had concluded it, he was asked to read, next day,

[1] Compare c. 52, *init.*

that also which had been published by Demosthenes on the other side in favor of Ctesiphon ; and when he had read this too in a most pleasing and powerful tone of voice, and all expressed their admiration, *How much more would you have admired it,* said he, *if you had heard him deliver it himself!* By this remark, he sufficiently indicated how much depends on delivery, as he thought the same speech would appear different if the speaker were changed.　What was it in Gracchus —whom you, Catulus, remember better—that was so highly extolled when I was a boy? *Whither shall I, unhappy wretch, betake myself? Whither shall I turn? To the Capitol? But that is drenched with the blood of my brother! Or to my home, that I may see my distressed and afflicted mother in all the agony of lamentation?* These words, it was allowed, were uttered by him with such delivery, as to countenance, voice, and gesture, that his very enemies could not restrain their tears. I dwell the longer on these particulars, because the orators, who are the deliverers of truth itself, have neglected this whole department, and the players, who are only the imitators of truth, have taken possession of it.

LVII. "In every thing, without doubt, truth has the advantage over imitation ; and if truth were efficient enough in delivery of itself, we should certainly have no need for the aid of art.　But as that emotion of mind, which ought to be chiefly expressed or imitated in delivery, is often so confused as to be obscured and almost overwhelmed, the peculiarities which throw that veil over it are to be set aside, and such as are eminent and conspicuous to be selected.　For every emotion of the mind has from nature its own peculiar look, tone, and gesture ; and the whole frame of a man, and his whole countenance, and the variations of his voice, sound[1] like strings in a musical instrument, just as they are moved by the affections of the mind.　For the tones of the voice, like musical chords, are so wound up as to be responsive to every touch, sharp, flat, quick, slow, loud, gentle ; and yet, among all these, each in its kind has its own middle tone.　From these tones, too, are derived many other sorts, as the rough, the smooth, the contracted, the broad, the protracted, and in-

---

[1] *Sonant.* As this word does not properly apply to *vultus*, the countenance, Schutz would make some alteration in the text.　But Müller and others observe that such a *zeugma* is not uncommon.

terrupted; the broken and divided, the attenuated and inflated, with varieties of modulation; for there is none of these, or those that resemble them, which may not be influenced by art and management; and they are presented to the orator, as colors to the painter, to produce variety.

LVIII. "Anger, for instance, assumes a particular tone of voice, acute, vehement, and with frequent breaks:

> "'My impious brother drives me on, ah wretched!
> To tear my children with my teeth!'[1]

and in those lines which you, Antonius, cited a while ago:[2]

> "'Have you, then, dared to separate him from you?'—

and,

> "'Does any one perceive this? Bind him'—

and almost the whole tragedy of Atreus. But lamentation and bewailing assumes another tone, flexible, full, interrupted, in a voice of sorrow: as,

> "'Whither shall I now turn myself? what road
> Shall I attempt to tread? Home to my father,
> Or go to Pelias' daughters?'[3]

and this,

> "'O father, O my country, House of Priam!'

and that which follows,

> "'All these did I behold enwrapt in flames,
> And life from Priam torn by violence.'[4]

Fear has another tone, desponding, hesitating, abject:

> "'In many ways am I encompass'd round!
> By sickness, exile, want. And terror drives
> All judgment from my breast, deprived of sense!
> One threats my life with torture and destruction,
> And no man has so firm a soul, such boldness,
> But that his blood shrinks backward, and his look
> Grows pale with timid fear.'[5]

Violence has another tone, strained, vehement, impetuous, with a kind of forcible excitement:

---

[1] From the Atreus of Accius, whence also the next quotation but one is taken. See Tusc. Quæst., iv., 36.

[2] See ii., 46.

[3] From the Medea of Ennius.

[4] From the Andromache of Ennius. See Tusc. Quæst., i., 35; iii., 19.

[5] From the Alcmæon of Ennius.

> " ' Again Thyestes comes to drag on Atreus :
> Again attacks me, and disturbs my quiet :
> Some greater storm, some greater ill by me
> Must be excited, that I may confound
> And crush his cruel heart.'[1]

Pleasure another, unconstrained, mild, tender, cheerful, languid :

> " ' But when she brought for me the crown design'd
> To celebrate the nuptials, 'twas to thee
> She offer'd it, pretending that she gave it
> To grace another ; then on thee she placed it
> Sportive, and graceful, and with delicacy.'[2]

Trouble has another tone ; a sort of gravity without lamentation ; oppressed, as it were, with one heavy uniform sound :

> " ' 'Twas at the time when Paris wedded Helen
> In lawless nuptials, and when I was pregnant,
> My months being nearly ended for delivery,
> Then, at that very time, did Hecuba
> Bring forth her latest offspring, Polydore.'

LIX. " On all these emotions a proper gesture ought to attend ; not the gesture of the stage, expressive of mere words, but one showing the whole force and meaning of a passage, not by gesticulation, but by emphatic delivery, by a strong and manly exertion of the lungs, not imitated from the theatre and the players, but rather from the camp and the palæstra. The action of the hand should not be too affected,[3] but following the words rather than, as it were, expressing them by mimicry ; the arm should be considerably extended, as one of the weapons of oratory; the stamping of the foot should be used only in the most vehement efforts, at their commencement or conclusion. But all depends on the countenance ; and even in that the eyes bear sovereign sway ; and therefore the oldest of our countrymen showed the more judgment in not applauding even Roscius himself to any great degree when he performed in a mask ; for all the powers of action proceed from the mind, and the countenance is the image of the mind, and the eyes are its interpreters. This, indeed, is the only part of the body that can effectually dis-

[1] From the Atreus of Accius. See Tusc. Quæst., iii., 36 ; De Nat. Deor., iii., 26.

[2] Whence this and the next quotation are taken is unknown.

[3] *Arguta. Argutiæ digitorum.* Orat., c. 18. *Manus inter agendum argutæ admodum et gestuosæ.* Aul. Gell., i., 5.

play as infinite a number of significations and changes, as there is of emotions in the soul; nor can any speaker produce the same effect with his eyes shut,[1] as with them open. Theophrastus indeed has told us that a certain Tauriscus used to say that a player who pronounced his part gazing on any particular object was like one who turned his back on the audience.[2] Great care in managing the eyes is therefore necessary; for the appearance of the features is not to be too much varied, lest we fall into some absurdity or distortion. It is the eyes, by whose intense or languid gaze, as well as by their quick glances and gayety, we indicate the workings of our mind with a peculiar aptitude to the tenor of our discourse; for action is, as it were, the speech of the body, and ought therefore the more to accord with that of the soul. And Nature has given eyes to us, to declare our internal emotions, as she has bestowed a mane, tail, and ears on the horse and the lion. For these reasons, in our oratorical action, the countenance is next in power to the voice, and is influenced by the motion of the eyes. But in every thing appertaining to action there is a certain force bestowed by Nature herself; and it is by action accordingly that the illiterate, the vulgar, and even barbarians themselves, are principally moved. For words move none but those who are associated in a participation of the same language; and sensible thoughts often escape the understandings of senseless men; but action, which by its own powers displays the movements of the soul, affects all mankind; for the minds of all men are excited by the same emotions which they recognize in others, and indicate in themselves by the same tokens.

LX. " To effectiveness and excellence in delivery the voice doubtless contributes most; the voice, I say, which, in its full strength, must be the chief object of our wishes; and next, whatever strength of voice we have, to cherish it. On this point, how we are to assist the voice has nothing to do with precepts of this kind, though, for my part, I think that we should assist it to the utmost. But it seems not unsuitable to the purport of my present remarks, to observe, as I ob-

---

[1] I follow Ellendt in reading *connivens*, instead of *contuens*, the common reading, which Orellius retains.

[2] *Aversum.* " Qui stet aversus à theatro, et spectatoribus tergum obvertat." *Schutz.* Of Tauriscus nothing is known.

served a little while ago, ' that in most things what is most useful is, I know not how, the most becoming;' for nothing is more useful for securing power of voice, than the frequent variation of it; nothing more pernicious than an immoderate straining of it without intermission. And what is more adapted to delight the ear, and produce agreeableness of delivery, than change, variety, and alteration of tone? Caius Gracchus, accordingly (as you may hear, Catulus, from your client Licinius, a man of letters, whom Gracchus formerly had for his amanuensis), used to have a skillful person with an ivory pitch-pipe, to stand concealed behind him when he made a speech, and who was in an instant to sound such a note as might either excite him from too languid a tone, or recall him from one too elevated." " I have heard this before," said Catulus, " and have often admired the diligence of that great man, as well as his learning and knowledge." " And I too," said Crassus; " and am grieved that men of such talents should fall into such miscarriages with regard to the commonwealth; although the same web is still being woven;[1] and such a state of manners is advancing in the country, and held out to posterity, that we now desire to have citizens such as our fathers would not tolerate." " Forbear, Crassus, I entreat you," interposed Cæsar, " from this sort of conversation, and go back to Gracchus's pitch-pipe, of which I do not yet clearly understand the object."

LXI. "There is in every voice," continued Crassus, " a certain middle key; but in each particular voice that key is peculiar. For the voice to ascend gradually from this key is advantageous and pleasing; since to bawl at the beginning of a speech is boorish, and gradation is salutary in strengthening the voice. There is also a certain extreme in the highest pitch (which, however, is lower than the shrillest cry), to which the pipe will not allow you to ascend, but will recall you from too strained an effort of voice. There is also, on the other hand, an extreme in the lowest notes, to which, as being of a full sound, we by degrees descend. This variety and this gradual progression of the voice throughout all the notes, will preserve its powers, and add agreeableness to delivery. But you will leave the piper at home, and carry with you into the forum merely the intention of the custom.

[1] As to the state of the republic at that time, see i., 7. *Ellendt.*

"I have said what I could, though not as I wished, but as the shortness of the time obliged me; for it is wise to lay the blame upon the time, when you can not add more even if you desired." "But," said Catulus, "you have, as far as I can judge, brought together every thing upon the subject, and that in so excellent a manner, that you seem not to have received instructions in the art from the Greeks, but to be able to instruct the Greeks themselves. I rejoice that I have been present at your conversation; and could wish that my son-in-law, your friend Hortensius,[1] had also been present; who, I trust, will excel in all those good qualities of which you have treated in this dissertation." "Will excel!" exclaimed Crassus; "I consider that he already excels. I had that opinion of him when he pleaded, in my consulship, the cause of Africa[2] in the senate; and I found myself still more confirmed in it lately, when he spoke for the King of Bithynia. You judge rightly, therefore, Catulus; for I am convinced that nothing is wanting to that young man, on the part either of nature or of learning. You, therefore, Cotta, and you, Sulpicius, must exert the greater vigilance and industry; for he is no ordinary orator, who is springing up to rival those of your age; but one of a penetrating genius, and an ardent attachment to study, of eminent learning, and of singular powers of memory; but, though he is a favorite of mine, I only wish him to excel those of his own standing; for to desire that he, who is so much younger,[3] should outstrip you, is hardly fair. But let us now arise, and refresh ourselves, and at length relieve our minds and attention from this fatiguing discussion."

[1] The orator afterward so famous.

[2] He pleaded this cause, observes Ellendt, at the age of nineteen; but the nature of it, as well as that of the King of Bithynia, is unknown.

[3] He was ten years younger than Cotta and Sulpicius.   Brut., c. 88. *Ellendt.*

END OF "DE ORATORE."

BRUTUS;

OR,

REMARKS ON EMINENT ORATORS.

THE ARGUMENT.

This treatise was the fruit of Cicero's retirement, during the remains of the civil war in Africa, and was composed in the form of a dialogue. It contains a few short, but very masterly sketches of all the speakers who had flourished either in Greece or Rome, with any reputation of eloquence, down to his own time; and as he generally touches the principal incidents of their lives, it will be considered, by an attentive reader, as a *concealed epitome of the Roman history.* The conference is supposed to have been held with Atticus, and their common friend Brutus, in Cicero's garden at Rome, under the statue of Plato, whom he always admired, and usually imitated in his Dialogues.

I. WHEN I had left Cilicia, and arrived at Rhodes, word was brought me of the death of Hortensius. I was more affected with it than, I believe, was generally expected; for, by the loss of my friend, I saw myself forever deprived of the pleasure of his acquaintance, and of our mutual intercourse of good offices. I likewise reflected, with concern, that the dignity of our college must suffer greatly by the decease of such an eminent augur. This reminded me that *he* was the person who first introduced me to the college, where he attested my qualification upon oath, and that it was *he* also who installed me as a member; so that I was bound by the constitution of the order to respect and honor him as a parent. My affliction was increased, that, in such a deplorable dearth of wise and virtuous citizens, this excellent man, my faithful associate in the service of the public, expired at the very time when the commonwealth could least spare him, and when we had the greatest reason to regret the want of his prudence and authority. I can add, very sincerely, that in *him* I lamented the loss, not (as most people imagined) of a

dangerous rival who opposed my reputation, but of a generous associate who engaged with me in the pursuit of fame.
For if we have instances in history, though in studies of less
importance, that some distinguished poets have been greatly
afflicted at the death of their contemporary bards, with what
tender concern should I honor the memory of a man with
whom it is more glorious to have disputed the prize of eloquence, than never to have combated as an antagonist, especially as he was always so far from obstructing *my* endeavors, or I *his*, that, on the contrary, we mutually assisted each
other with our credit and advice! But as *he*, who had a
perpetual run of felicity,[1] left the world at a happy moment
for himself, though a most unfortunate one for his fellow-
citizens, and died when it would have been much easier for
him to lament the miseries of his country than to assist it,
after living in it as long as he *could* have lived with honor
and reputation, we may, indeed, deplore his death as a heavy
loss to *us* who survive him.   If, however, we consider it
merely as a personal event, we ought rather to congratulate
his fate than to pity it; that, as often as we revive the memory of this illustrious and truly happy man, we may appear
at least to have as much affection for him as for ourselves.
For if we only lament that we are no longer permitted to enjoy him, it must, indeed, be acknowledged that this is a
heavy misfortune to *us;* which it however becomes us to
support with moderation, lest our sorrow should be suspected to arise from motives of interest, and not from friendship.
But if we afflict ourselves, on the supposition that *he* was the
sufferer, we misconstrue an event, which to *him* was certainly
a very happy one.
    II. If Hortensius were now living, he would probably re-
gret many other advantages in common with his worthy fellow-citizens.   But when he beheld the forum, the great theatre in which he used to exercise his genius, no longer acces-
sible to that accomplished eloquence which could charm the

---

[1] *Quoniam perpetuâ quâdam felicitate usus ille, cessit è vitâ, suo magis
quam suorum civium tempore.*   This fine sentiment, conveyed in such
elegant language, carries an allusion to the conversation of Solon with
Crœsus, in which the former maintained the seeming paradox, that he
alone can be deemed happy who meets a happy death.   See Herod.,
Clio, 32.

ears of a Roman or a Grecian audience, he must have felt a
pang of which none, or at least but few, besides himself could
be susceptible.   Even *I* indulge heartfelt anguish, when I behold my country no longer supported by the talents, the wisdom, and the authority of law—the only weapons which I
have learned to wield, and to which I have long been accustomed, and which are most suitable to the character of an illustrious citizen, and of a virtuous and well-regulated state.
But if there ever was a time when the authority and eloquence of an honest individual could have wrested their arms
from the hands of his distracted fellow-citizens, it was then
when the proposal of a compromise of our mutual differences
was rejected, by the hasty imprudence of some and the tim-
orous mistrust of others.   Thus it happened, among other
misfortunes of a more deplorable nature, that when my declining age, after a life spent in the service of the public,
should have reposed in the peaceful harbor, not of an indolent
and total inactivity, but of a moderate and honorable retirement, and when my eloquence was properly mellowed and had
acquired its full maturity—thus it happened, I say, that recourse was then had to those fatal arms, which the persons
who had learned the use of them in honorable conquest could
no longer employ to any salutary purpose.   Those, therefore,
appear to me to have enjoyed a fortunate and happy life (of
whatever state they were members, but especially in *ours*),
who, together with their authority and reputation, either for
their military or political services, are allowed to enjoy the
advantages of philosophy; and the sole remembrance of them,
in our present melancholy situation, was a pleasing relief to
me, when we lately happened to mention them in the course
of conversation.

III. For, not long ago, when I was walking for my amusement in a private avenue at home, I was agreeably interrupted by my friend Brutus and Titus Pomponius, who came, as
indeed they frequently did, to visit me—two worthy citizens,
who were united to each other in the closest friendship, and
were so dear and so agreeable to me, that on the first sight
of them, all my anxiety for the commonwealth subsided.
After the usual salutations, " Well, gentlemen," said I, " how
go the times?   What news have you brought?"   " None,"
replied Brutus, " that you would wish to hear, or that I can

venture to tell you for truth." "No," said Atticus; "we are come with an intention that all matters of state should be dropped, and rather to hear something from you, than to say any thing which might serve to distress you." "Indeed," said I, "your company is a present remedy for my sorrow; and your letters, when absent, were so encouraging, that they first revived my attention to my studies." "I remember," replied Atticus, "that Brutus sent you a letter from Asia, which I read with infinite pleasure; for he advised you in it like a man of sense, and gave you every consolation which the warmest friendship could suggest." "True," said I; "for it was the receipt of that letter which recovered me from a growing indisposition to behold once more the cheerful face of day; and as the Roman state, after the dreadful defeat near Cannæ, first raised its drooping head by the victory of Marcellus at Nola, which was succeeded by many other victories, so, after the dismal wreck of our affairs, both public and private, nothing occurred to me, before the letter of my friend Brutus, which I thought to be worth my attention, or which contributed, in any degree, to ease the anxiety of my heart." "That was certainly my intention," answered Brutus; "and if I had the happiness to succeed, I was sufficiently rewarded for my trouble. But I could wish to be informed what you received from Atticus, which gave you such uncommon pleasure." "That," said I, "which not only entertained me, but I hope has restored me entirely to myself." "Indeed!" replied he; "and what miraculous composition could that be?" "Nothing," answered I, "could have been a more acceptable or a more seasonable present than that excellent treatise of his, which roused me from a state of languor and despondency." "You mean," said he, "his short and, I think, very accurate abridgment of universal history." "The very same," said I; "for that little treatise has absolutely saved me."

IV. "I am heartily glad of it," said Atticus; "but what could you discover in it which was either new to you or so wonderfully beneficial as you pretend?" "It certainly furnished many hints," said I, "which were entirely new to me; and the exact order of time which you observed through the whole, gave me the opportunity I had long wished for, of beholding the history of all nations in one regular and comprehensive view. The attentive perusal of it proved an excellent remedy for my sorrows, and led me to think of attempting something on your own plan, partly to amuse myself, and partly to return your favor by a grateful, though not an equal, acknowledgment. We are commanded, it is true, in that precept of Hesiod, so much admired by the learned, to return with the same measure we have received, or, if possible, with a larger. As to a friendly inclination, I shall certainly return you a full proportion of it; but as to a recompense in kind, I confess it to be out of my power, and therefore hope you will excuse me; for I have not, as husbandmen are accustomed to have, gathered a fresh harvest out of which to repay the kindness[1] I have received; my whole harvest having sickened and died, for want of the usual manure; and as little am I able to present you with any thing from those hidden stores which are now consigned to perpetual darkness, and to which I am denied all access, though formerly I was almost the only person who was able to command them at pleasure. I must, therefore, try my skill in a long-neglected and uncultivated soil, which I will endeavor to improve with so much care, that I may be able to repay your liberality with interest, provided my genius should be so happy as to resemble a fertile field, which, after being suffered to lie fallow a considerable time, produces a heavier crop than usual."

"Very well," replied Atticus, "I shall expect the fulfillment of your promise; but I shall not insist upon it till it suits your convenience; though, after all, I shall certainly be better pleased if you discharge the obligation." "And I also," said Brutus, "shall expect that you perform your promise to my friend Atticus; nay, though I am only his voluntary solicitor, I shall, perhaps, be very pressing for the discharge of a debt which the creditor himself is willing to submit to your own choice." V. "But I shall refuse to pay you," said I, "unless the original creditor takes no farther part in the suit." "This is more than I can promise," replied he; "for I can easily foresee that this easy man, who disclaims all se-

---

[1] *Non enim ex novis, ut agricolæ solent, fructibus est, unde tibi reddam quod accepi.* The allusion is to a farmer, who, in time of necessity, borrows corn or fruit of his more opulent neighbor, which he repays in kind as soon as his harvest is gathered home. Cicero was not, he says, in a situation to make a similar return.

verity, will urge his demand upon you, not indeed to distress you, but yet with earnestness and importunity." "To speak ingenuously," said Atticus, "my friend Brutus, I believe, is not much mistaken ; for as I now find you in good spirits for the first time, after a tedious interval of despondency, I shall soon make bold to apply to you ; and as this gentleman has promised his assistance to recover what you owe me, the least I can do is to solicit, in my turn, for what is due to him." "Explain your meaning," said I. "I mean," replied he, "that you must write something to amuse us ; for your pen has been totally silent this long time ; and since your treatise on politics, we have had nothing from you of any kind, though it was the perusal of that which fired me with the ambition to write an abridgment of universal history. But we shall, however, leave you to answer this demand when and in what manner you shall think most convenient. At present, if you are not otherwise engaged, you must give us your sentiments on a subject on which we both desire to be better informed." "And what is that?" said I. "A work which you had just begun," replied he, "when I saw you last at Tusculanum—the History of Eminent Orators— *when* they made their appearance, and *who* and *what* they were ; which furnished such an agreeable train of conversation, that when I related the substance of it to *your*, or I ought rather to have said *our common* friend Brutus, he expressed an ardent desire to hear the whole of it from your own mouth. Knowing you, therefore, to be at leisure, we have taken the present opportunity to wait upon you ; so that, if it is really convenient, you will oblige us both by resuming the subject." "Well, gentlemen," said I, "as you are so pressing, I will endeavor to satisfy you in the best manner I am able." "You are *able* enough," replied he ; "only unbend, or rather, if possible, set at full liberty your mind." "If I remember right," said I, "Atticus, what gave rise to the conversation was my observing that the cause of Deiotarus, a most excellent sovereign and a faithful ally, was pleaded by our friend Brutus, in my hearing, with the greatest elegance and dignity."

VI. "True," replied he ; "and you took occasion, from the ill success of Brutus, to lament the loss of a fair administration of justice in the forum." "I did so," answered I, "as indeed I frequently do ; and whenever I see you, my Brutus, I am concerned to think where your wonderful genius, your finished erudition, and unparalleled industry will find a theatre to display themselves. For after you had thoroughly improved your abilities by pleading a variety of important causes, and when my declining vigor was just giving way and lowering the ensigns of dignity to your more active talents, the liberty of the state received a fatal overthrow, and that eloquence, of which we are now to give 'the history, was condemned to perpetual silence." "Our other misfortunes," replied Brutus, "I lament sincerely, and I think I ought to lament them ; but as to eloquence, I am not so fond of the influence and the glory it bestows, as of the study and the practice of it, which nothing can deprive me of, while you are so well disposed to assist me ; for no man can be an eloquent speaker who has not a clear and ready conception. Whoever, therefore, applies himself to the study of eloquence, is at the same time improving his judgment, which is a talent equally necessary in all military operations." "Your remark," said I, "is very just ; and I have a higher opinion of the merit of eloquence, because, though there is scarcely any person so diffident as not to persuade himself that he either has or may acquire every other accomplishment which formerly could have given him consequence in the state, I can find no person who has been made an orator by the success of his military prowess. But that we may carry on the conversation with greater ease, let us seat ourselves." As my visitors had no objection to this, we accordingly took our seats in a private lawn, near a statue of Plato. Then resuming the conversation—"To recommend the study of eloquence," said I, "and describe its force, and the great dignity it confers upon those who have acquired it, is neither our present design, nor has any necessary connection with it. But I will not hesitate to affirm, that whether it is acquired by art or practice, or the mere powers of nature, it is the most difficult of all attainments ; for each of the five branches of which it is said to consist is of itself a very important art ; from whence it may easily be conjectured how great and arduous must be the profession which unites and comprehends them all.

VII. "Greece alone is a sufficient witness of this ; for

though she was fired with a wonderful love of eloquence, and
has long since excelled every other nation in the practice of
it, yet she had all the rest of the arts much earlier; and had
not only invented, but even completed them, a considerable
time before she was mistress of the full powers of elocution.
But when I direct my eyes to Greece, your beloved Athens,
my Atticus, first strikes my sight, and is the brightest object
in my view; for in that illustrious city the *orator* first made
his appearance, and it is there we shall find the earliest records of eloquence, and the first specimens of a discourse conducted by rules of art. But even in Athens there is not a
single production now extant which discovers any taste for
ornament, or seems to have been the effort of a real orator,
before the time of Pericles (whose name is prefixed to some
orations which still remain) and his contemporary Thucydides; who flourished, not in the infancy of the state, but
when it had arrived at its full maturity of power. It is,
however, supposed that Pisistratus (who lived many years
before), together with Solon, who was something older, and
Clisthenes, who survived them both, were very able speakers
for the age they lived in. But some years after these, as may
be collected from the Attic annals, came Themistocles, who
is said to have been as much distinguished by his eloquence
as by his political abilities;. and after him the celebrated Pericles, who, though adorned with every kind of excellence, was
most admired for his talents as a speaker. Cleon also, their
contemporary, though a turbulent citizen, was allowed to be
a tolerable orator. These were immediately succeeded by
Alcibiades, Critias, and Theramenes; the character of their
eloquence may be easily inferred from the writings of Thucydides, who lived at the same time; their discourses were
nervous and stately, full of sententious remarks, and so excessively concise as to be sometimes obscure.

VIII. "But as soon as the force of a regular and well-ad-
justed style was understood, a crowd of rhetoricians immediately appeared, such as Gorgias the Leontine, Thrasymachus the Chalcedonian, Protagoras the Abderite, and Hippias the Elean, who were all held in great esteem, with many
others of the same age, who professed (it must be owned rather too arrogantly) to teach their scholars *how the worse might
be made, by the force of eloquence, to appear the better cause.*

But these were openly opposed by Socrates, who, by a subtle method of arguing peculiar to himself, took every opportunity to refute the principles of their art. His instructive conferences produced a number of intelligent men, and *Philosophy* is said to have derived her birth from him; not the doctrine of *Physics*, which was of an earlier date, but that Philosophy which treats of men and manners, and of the nature of good and evil. But as this is foreign to our present subject, we must defer the philosophers to another opportunity, and return to the orators, from whom I have ventured to make a short digression. When the professors, therefore, above mentioned were in the decline of life, Isocrates made his appearance, whose house stood open to all Greece as the *school of eloquence.* He was an accomplished orator and an excellent teacher; though he did not display his talents in the splendor of the forum, but cherished and improved within the walls of an obscure academy, that glory which, in my opinion, no orator has since acquired. He composed many valuable specimens of his art, and taught the principles of it to others; and not only excelled his predecessors in every part of it, but first discovered that a certain rhythm and modulation should be observed in prose, care being taken, however, to avoid making verses. Before *him*, the artificial structure and harmony of language was unknown—or, if there are any traces of it to be discovered, they appear to have been made without design; which, perhaps, will be thought a beauty; but, whatever it may be deemed, it was, in the present case, the effect rather of native genius, or of accident, than of art and observation. For Nature herself teaches us to close our sentences within certain limits; and when they are thus confined to a moderate flow of expression, they will frequently have a harmonious cadence; for the ear alone can decide what is full and complete, and what is deficient; and the course of our language will necessarily be regulated by our breath, in which it is excessively disagreeable, not only to fail, but even to labor.

IX. "After Isocrates came Lysias, who, though not personally engaged in forensic causes, was a very accurate and elegant composer, and such an one as you might almost venture to pronounce a complete orator; for Demosthenes is the man who approaches the character so nearly, that you may apply it to him without hesitation. No keen, no artful turns could have been contrived for the pleadings he has left behind him, which he did not readily discover; nothing could have been expressed with greater nicety, or more clearly and poignantly, than it has been already expressed by him; and nothing greater, nothing more rapid and forcible, nothing adorned with a nobler elevation, either of language or sentiment, can be conceived, than what is to be found in his orations. He was soon rivaled by his contemporaries Hyperides, Æschines, Lycurgus, Dinarchus, and Demades (none of whose writings are extant), with many others that might be mentioned; for this age was adorned with a profusion of good orators; and to the end of this period appears to me to have flourished that vigorous and blooming eloquence, which is distinguished by a natural beauty of composition, without disguise or affectation. When these orators were in the decline of life, they were succeeded by Phalereus, then in the prime of youth. He indeed surpassed them all in learning, but was fitter to appear on the parade than in the field; and, accordingly, he rather pleased and entertained the Athenians, than inflamed their passions; and marched forth into the dust and heat of the forum, not from a weather-beaten tent, but from the shady recesses of Theophrastus, a man of consummate erudition. He was the first who relaxed the force of Eloquence, and gave her a soft and tender air; and he rather chose to be agreeable, as indeed he was, than great and striking; but agreeable in such a manner as rather charmed, than warmed the mind of the hearer. His greatest ambition was to impress his audience with a high opinion of his elegance, and not, as Eupolis relates of Pericles, to *animate* as well as to *please*.

X. "You see, then, in the very city in which Eloquence was born and nurtured, how late it was before she grew to maturity; for before the time of Solon and Pisistratus, we meet with no one who is so much as mentioned as an able speaker. These, indeed, if we compute by the Roman date, may be reckoned very ancient; but if by that of the Athenians, we shall find them to be moderns. For though they flourished in the reign of Servius Tullius, Athens had then subsisted much longer than Rome has at present. I have not, however, the least doubt that the power of eloquence has been always more or less conspicuous. For Homer, we may suppose, would not have ascribed such superior talents of elocution to Ulysses and Nestor (one of whom he celebrates for his force, and the other for his sweetness), unless the art of speaking had then been held in some esteem; nor could the poet himself have attained a style so finished, nor exhibited such fine specimens of oratory, as we actually find in him. The time, indeed, in which he lived is undetermined; but we are certain that he flourished many years before Romulus, and as early at least as the elder[1] Lycurgus, the legislator of the Spartans. But a more particular attention to the art, and a greater ability in the practice of it, may be observed in Pisistratus. He was succeeded in the following century by Themistocles, who, according to the Roman date, was a person of the remotest antiquity; but according to that of the Athenians, he was almost a modern. For he lived when Greece was in the height of her power, and when the city of Rome had but lately been emancipated from the shackles of regal tyranny; for the dangerous war with the Volsci, who were headed by Coriolanus (then a voluntary exile), happened nearly at the same time as the Persian war; and we may add, that the fate of both commanders was remarkably similar. Each of them, after distinguishing himself as an excellent citizen, being driven from his country by the insults of an ungrateful people, went over to the enemy; and each of them repressed the efforts of his resentment by a voluntary death. For though you, my Atticus, have represented the death of Coriolanus in a different manner, you must pardon me if I do not subscribe to the justness of your representation."

XI. "You may use your pleasure," replied Atticus, with a smile; "for it is the privilege of rhetoricians to exceed the truth of history, that they may have an opportunity of embellishing the fate of their heroes; and accordingly, Clitarchus and Stratocles have entertained us with the same pretty fiction about the death of Themistocles, which you have invented for Coriolanus. Thucydides, indeed, who was himself an Athenian of the highest rank and merit, and lived nearly at the same time, has only informed us that he died, and was privately buried in Attica, adding, that it was sus-

---

[1] *Superiorem.* So called, as Orellius observes, to distinguish him from Lycurgus the Athenian orator, mentioned in the preceding chapter.

pected by some that he had poisoned himself. But these ingenious writers have assured us that, having slain a bull at the altar, he caught the blood in a large bowl, and, drinking it off, fell suddenly dead upon the ground. For this species of death had a tragical air, and might be described with all the pomp of rhetoric; whereas the ordinary way of dying afforded no opportunity for ornament. As it will, therefore, suit your purpose that Coriolanus should resemble Themistocles in every thing, I give you leave to introduce the fatal bowl; and you may still farther heighten the catastrophe by a solemn sacrifice, that Coriolanus may appear in all respects to have been a second Themistocles." "I am much obliged to you," said I, "for your courtesy; but, for the future, I shall be more cautious in meddling with history when you are present; whom I may justly commend as a most exact and scrupulous relator of the Roman history; but nearly at the time we are speaking of (though somewhat later) lived the above-mentioned Pericles, the illustrious son of Xantippus, who first improved his eloquence by the friendly aids of literature—not that kind of literature which treats professedly of the art of speaking, of which there was then no regular system; but after he had studied under Anaxagoras, the naturalist, he directed with alacrity his attention from abstruse and intricate speculations to forensic and popular debates. All Athens was charmed with the sweetness of his language, and not only admired him for his fluency, but was awed by the superior force and terrors of his eloquence.

XII. "This age, therefore, which may be considered as the infancy of the art, furnished Athens with an orator who almost reached the summit of his profession; for an emulation to shine in the forum is not usually found among a people who are either employed in settling the form of their government, or engaged in war, or struggling with difficulties, or subjected to the arbitrary power of kings. Eloquence is the attendant of peace, the companion of ease and prosperity, and the tender offspring of a free and well-established constitution. Aristotle, therefore, informs us, that when the tyrants were expelled from Sicily, and private property, after a long interval of servitude, was secured by the administration of justice, the Sicilians, Corax and Tisias (for this people, in general, were very quick and acute, and had a natural turn for disquisition), first attempted to write precepts on the art of speaking. Before them, he says, no one spoke by prescribed method, conformably to rules of art, though many discoursed very sensibly, and generally from written notes; but Protagoras took the pains to compose a number of dissertations, on such leading and general topics as are now called *commonplaces*. Gorgias, he adds, did the same, and wrote panegyrics and invectives on every subject; for he thought it was the province of an orator to be able either to exaggerate or extenuate, as occasion might require. Antiphon the Rhamnusian composed several essays of the same species; and (according to Thucydides, a very respectable writer, who was present to hear him) pleaded a capital cause in his own defense, with as much eloquence as had ever yet been displayed by any man. But Lysias was the first who openly professed the *art;* and, after him, Theodorus, being better versed in the theory than the practice of it, began to compose orations for others to pronounce, but confined to himself the art of composing them. In the same manner, Isocrates at first declined to teach the art, but wrote speeches for other people to deliver; on which account, being often prosecuted for assisting, contrary to law, to circumvent one or another of the parties in judgment, he left off composing orations for other people, and wholly applied himself to prescribe rules, and reduce them into a system.

XIII. "Thus, then, we have traced the birth and origin of the orators of Greece, who were, indeed, very ancient, as I have before observed, if we compute by the Roman annals; but of a much later date, if we reckon by their own; for the Athenian state had signalized itself by a variety of great exploits, both at home and abroad, a considerable time before she became enamored of the charms of eloquence. But this noble art was not common to Greece in general, but almost peculiar to Athens. For who has ever heard of an Argive, a Corinthian, or a Theban orator, at the times we are speaking of? unless, perhaps, some merit of the kind may be allowed to Epaminondas, who was a man of uncommon erudition. But I have never read of a Lacedemonian orator, from the earliest period of time to the present. For Menelaus himself, though said by Homer to have possessed a sweet elocution, is likewise described as a man of few words. Brevity, indeed, upon some occasions, is a real excellence; but it is very far from being compatible with the general character of eloquence. The art of speaking was likewise studied, and admired, beyond the limits of Greece; and the extraordinary honors which were paid to oratory have perpetuated the names of many foreigners who had the happiness to excel in it. For no sooner had eloquence ventured to sail from the Piræeus, but she traversed all the isles, and visited every part of Asia; till at last, infected with their manners, she lost all the purity and the healthy complexion of the Attic style, and indeed almost forgot her native language. The Asiatic orators, therefore, though not to be undervalued for the rapidity and the copious variety of their elocution, were certainly too loose and luxuriant. But the Rhodians were of a sounder constitution, and more resembled the Athenians. So much, then, for the Greeks; for, perhaps, what I have already said of them is more than was necessary." "Respecting the necessity of it," answered Brutus, "there is no occasion to speak; but what you have said of them has entertained me so agreeably, that instead of being longer, it has been much shorter than I could have wished." "A very handsome compliment," said I; "but it is time to begin with our countrymen, of whom it is difficult to give any farther account than what we are able to conjecture from our annals.

XIV. "For who can question the address and the capacity of Brutus, the illustrious founder of your family—that Brutus, who so readily discovered the meaning of the oracle, which promised the supremacy to him who should first salute his mother[1]—that Brutus, who, under the appearance of stupidity, concealed the most exalted understanding—who dethroned and banished a powerful monarch, the son of an illustrious sovereign—who settled the state, which he had rescued from arbitrary power, by the appointment of an annual magistracy, a regular system of laws, and a free and open course of justice—and who abrogated the authority of his colleague, that he might banish from the city the smallest ves-

---

[1] The words here alluded to occur in Livy: "Imperium summum Romæ habebit, qui vestrûm primus, O juvenes, osculum matri tulerit." This at first was interpreted of Tarquin, who kissed his mother. But Brutus gave the words a different and more ingenious turn; he illustrated their meaning by falling down and kissing the earth, the common mother of all mankind.

tige of the regal name ?—events which could never have been
produced without exerting the powers of persuasion. We are
likewise informed that a few years after the expulsion of the
kings, when the Plebeians retired to the banks of the Anio,
about three miles from the city, and had possessed themselves
of what is called the *Sacred* Mount, Marcus Valerius the dictator appeased their fury by a public harangue ; for which he
was afterward rewarded with the highest posts of honor, and
was the first Roman who was distinguished by the surname
of *Maximus.* Nor can Lucius Valerius Potitus be supposed
to have been destitute of the powers of utterance, who, after
the odium which had been excited against the Patricians by
the tyrannical government of the Decemviri, reconciled the
people to the senate by his prudent laws and conciliatory
speeches. We may likewise suppose, that Appius Claudius
was a man of some eloquence ; since he dissuaded the senate
from consenting to a peace with King Pyrrhus, though they
were much inclined to it. The same might be said of Caius
Fabricius, who was dispatched to Pyrrhus to treat for the
ransom of his captive fellow-citizens ; and of Tiberius Coruncanius, who appears, by the memoirs of the pontifical college,
to have been a person of the greatest genius ; and likewise of
Manius Curius (then a tribune of the people), who, when the
Interrex Appius *the Blind,* an able speaker, held the Comitia
contrary to law, refusing to admit any consul of plebeian rank,
prevailed upon the senate to protest against the conduct of his
antagonist ; which, if we consider that the Mænian law was
not then in being, was a very bold attempt. We may also
conclude that Marcus Pompilius was a man of abilities, who,
in the time of his consulship, when he was solemnizing a public sacrifice in the proper habit of his office (for he was also a
Flamen Carmentalis), hearing of the mutiny and insurrection
of the people against the senate, rushed immediately into the
midst of the assembly, covered as he was with his sacerdotal
robes, and quelled the sedition by his authority and the force
of his elocution. I do not pretend to have historical evidence
that the persons here mentioned were then reckoned orators,
or that any sort of reward or encouragement was given to
eloquence ; I only infer what appears very probable. It is
also recorded that Caius Flaminius, who, when tribune of the
people, proposed the law for dividing the conquered territories

of the Gauls and Piceni among the citizens, and who, after his promotion to the consulship, was slain near the lake Thrasimenus, became very popular by historical talents.   Quintus Maximus Verrucosus was likewise reckoned a good speaker by his contemporaries ; as was also Quintus Metellus, who, in the second Punic war, was joint consul with Lucius Vetu rius Philo.

XV.   "But the first person we have any certain account of, who was publicly distinguished as an *orator*, and who really appears to have been such, was Marcus Cornelius Cethegus, whose eloquence is attested by Quintus Ennius, a voucher of the highest credibility, since he actually heard him speak, and gave him this character after his death, so that there is no reason to suspect that he was prompted by the warmth of his friendship to exceed the bounds of truth.   In the ninth book of his Annals, he has mentioned him in the following terms :

" 'Additur orator Corneliu' suaviloquenti
Ore Cethegus Marcu', Tuditano collega,
Marci filius.'

' Add the *orator* Marcus Cornelius Cethegus, so much admired for his mellifluent tongue, who was the colleague of Tuditanus, and the son of Marcus.'   He expressly calls him an *orator*, you see, and attributes to him a remarkable sweetness of elocution ; which, even in the present times, is an excellence of which few are possessed : for some of our modern orators are so insufferably harsh, that they may be said rather to bark than to speak.   But what the poet so much admires in his friend, may certainly be considered as one of the principal ornaments of eloquence.   He adds :

" 'is dictus, ollis popularibus olim,
Qui tum vivebant homines, atque ævum agitabant,
Flos delibatus populi.'

' He was called by his contemporaries the choicest flower of the state.'   A very elegant compliment ; for as the glory of a man is the strength of his mental capacity, so the brightest ornament of genius is eloquence ; in which, whoever had the happiness to excel, was beautifully styled, by the ancients, the *flower* of the state ; and, as the poet immediately subjoins,

" 'suadæque medulla :'

' the very marrow and quintessence of persuasion.'   That which the Greeks call πειθώ (i. e., *persuasion*), and which it is

the chief business of an orator to effect, is here called *suada*
by Ennius ; and of this he commends Cethegus as the *quintessence ;* so that he makes the Roman orator to be himself the
very substance of that amiable goddess, who is said by Eupolis
to have dwelt on the lips of Pericles. This Cethegus was
joint consul with Publius Tuditanus in the second Punic
war ; at which time also Marcus Cato was quæstor, about one
hundred and forty years before I myself was promoted to the
consulship ; which circumstance would have been absolutely
lost, if it had not been recorded by Ennius ; and the memory
of that illustrious citizen, as has probably been the case of
many others, would have been buried in the ruins of antiquity.
The manner of speaking which was then in vogue may easily
be collected from the writings of Nævius ; for Nævius died,
as we learn from the memoirs of the times, when the persons
above mentioned were consuls ; though Varro, a most accurate investigator of historical truth, thinks there is a mistake
in this, and fixes the death of Nævius something later.   For
Plautus died in the consulship of Publius Claudius and Lucius
Porcius, twenty years after the consulship of the persons we
have been speaking of, and when Cato was censor.   Cato,
therefore, must have been younger than Cethegus, for he was
consul nine years after him ; but we always consider him as
a person of the remotest antiquity, though he died in the consulship of Lucius Marcius and Manius Manilius, and but
eighty-three years before my own promotion to the same office.

XVI. " He is certainly, however, the most ancient orator
we have, whose writings may claim our attention ; unless any
one is pleased, on account of the above-mentioned speech respecting the peace with Pyrrhus, or a series of panegyrics on
the dead, which, I own, are still extant, to compliment Appius
with that character.   For it was customary, in most families
of note, to preserve their images, their trophies of honor, and
their memoirs, either to adorn a funeral when any of the family deceased, or to perpetuate the fame of their ancestors, or
prove their own nobility.   But the truth of history has been
much corrupted by these encomiastic essays ; for many circumstances were recorded in them which never existed, such
as false triumphs, a pretended succession of consulships, and
false alliances and elevations, when men of inferior rank were

confounded with a noble family of the same name ; as if I
myself should pretend that I am descended from Manius Tullius, who was a patrician, and shared the consulship with
Servius Sulpicius, about ten years after the expulsion of the
kings. But the real speeches of Cato are almost as numerous as those of Lysias the Athenian, under whose name a
great number are still extant. For Lysias was certainly an
Athenian ; because he not only died, but received his birth at
Athens, and served all the offices of the city ; though Timæus,
as if he acted by the Licinian or the Mucian law, orders his
return to Syracuse. There is, however, a manifest resemblance between *his* character and that of *Cato ;* for they are
both of them distinguished by their acuteness, their elegance,
their agreeable humor, and their brévity. But the Greèk has
the happiness to be most admired ; for there are some who
are so extravagantly fond of him, as to prefer a graceful air
to a vigorous constitution, and who are perfectly satisfied with
a slender and an easy shape, if it is only attended with a moderate share of health.   It must, however, be acknowledged,
that even Lysias often displays a vigor of mind, which no human power can excel ; though his mental frame is certainly
more delicately wrought than that of Cato. Notwithstanding,
he has many admirers, who are charmed with him, merely on
account of his delicacy.

XVII. "But as to Cato, where will you find a modern
orator who condescends to read him ?—nay, I might have
said, who has the least knowledge of him?   And yet, good
gods ! what a wonderful man !   I say nothing of his merit as
a citizen, a senator, and a general ; we must confine our attention to the orator.   Who, then, has displayed more dignity
as a panegyrist ?—more severity as an accuser ?—greater acuteness of sentiments ?—or greater address in relating and informing ?   Though he composed above a hundred and fifty orations (which I have seen and read), they are crowded with all
the beauties of language and sentiment.   Let us select from
these what deserves our notice and applause ; they will supply
us with all the graces of oratory.   Not to omit his *Antiquities,*
who will deny that these also are adorned with every flower,
and with all the lustre of eloquence ? and yet he has scarcely
any admirers ; which some ages ago was the case of Philistus
the Syracusan, and even of Thucydides himself.   For as the

lofty and elevated style of Theopompus soon diminished the reputation of their pithy and laconic harangues, which were sometimes scarcely intelligible from excessive brevity and quaintness; and as Demosthenes eclipsed the glory of Lysias, so the pompous and stately elocution of the moderns has obscured the lustre of Cato. But many of us are deficient in taste and discernment, for we admire the Greeks for their antiquity, and what is called their Attic neatness, and yet have never noticed the same quality in Cato. This was the distinguishing character, say they, of Lysias and Hyperides. I own it, and I admire them for it; but why not allow a share of it to Cato? They are fond, they tell us, of the *Attic* style of eloquence; and their choice is certainly judicious, provided they not only copy the dry bones, but imbibe the animal spirits of those models. What they recommend, however, is, to do it justice, an agreeable quality. But why must Lysias and Hyperides be so fondly admired, while Cato is entirely overlooked? His language indeed has an antiquated air, and some of his expressions are rather too harsh and inelegant. But let us remember that this was the language of the time; only change and modernize it, which it was not in his power to do; add the improvements of number and cadence, give an easier turn to his sentences, and regulate the structure and connection of his words (which was as little practiced even by the older Greeks as by him), and you will find no one who can claim the preference to Cato. The Greeks themselves acknowledge that the chief beauty of composition results from the frequent use of those *tralatitious* forms of expression which they call *tropes*, and of those various attitudes of language and sentiment which they call *figures;* but it is almost incredible in what copiousness, and with what amazing variety, they are all employed by Cato.

XVIII. " I know, indeed, that he is not sufficiently polished, and that recourse must be had to a more perfect model for imitation; for he is an author of such antiquity, that he is the oldest now extant whose writings can be read with patience; and the ancients, in general, acquired a much greater reputation in every other art than in that of speaking. But who that has seen the statues of the moderns, will not perceive in a moment that the figures of Canachus are too stiff and formal to resemble life? Those of Calamis, though evidently harsh,

are somewhat softer. Even the statues of Myron are not sufficiently alive; and yet you would not hesitate to pronounce
them beautiful. But those of Polycletes are much finer, and,
in my mind, completely finished. The case is the same in
painting; for in the works of Zeuxis, Polygnotus, Timanthes,
and several other masters, who confined themselves to the use
of four colors, we commend the air and the symmetry of their
figures; but in Echion, Nicomachus, Protogenes, and Apelles,
every thing is finished to perfection. This, I believe, will hold
equally true in all the other arts; for there is not one of them
which was invented and carried to perfection at the same time.
I can not doubt, for instance, that there were many poets before Homer; we may infer it from those very songs which
he himself informs us were sung at the feasts of the Phæa-
cians, and of the profligate suitors of Penelope. Nay, to go
no farther, what is become of the ancient poems of our own
countrymen?

> " 'Such as the fauns and rustic bards composed,
> When none the rocks of poetry had cross'd,
> Nor wish'd to form his style by rules of art,
> Before this vent'rous man,' etc.

" Old Ennius here speaks of himself; nor does he carry his
boast beyond the bounds of truth; the case being really as
he describes it. For we had only an Odyssey in Latin, which
resembled one of the rough and unfinished statues of Dædalus;
and some dramatic pieces of Livius, which will scarcely bear
a second reading. This Livius exhibited his first performance
at Rome in the consulship of Marcus Tuditanus, and Caius
Clodius the son of Cæcus, the year before Ennius was born,
and, according to the account of my friend Atticus (whom I
choose to follow), the five hundred and fourteenth from the
building of the city. But historians are not agreed about the
date of the year. Attius informs us that Livius was taken
prisoner at Tarentum by Quintus Maximus in his fifth consulship, about thirty years after he is said by Atticus, and
our ancient annals, to have introduced the drama. He adds,
that he exhibited his first dramatic piece about eleven years
after, in the consulship of Caius Cornelius and Quintus Minu-
cius, at the public games which Salinator had vowed to the
Goddess of Youth for his victory over the Senones. But in
this, Attius was so far mistaken, that Ennius, when the per-

sons above mentioned were consuls, was forty years old ; so
that if Livius was of the same age, as in this case he would
have been, the first dramatic author we had must have been
younger than Plautus and Nævius, who had exhibited a great
number of plays before the time he specifies.

XIX. "If these remarks, my Brutus, appear unsuitable to
the subject before us, you must throw the whole blame upon
Atticus, who has inspired me with a strange curiosity to inquire into the age of illustrious men, and the respective times
of their appearance." "On the contrary," said Brutus, "I am
highly pleased that you have carried your attention so far ;
and I think your remarks well adapted to the curious task you
have undertaken, the giving us a history of the different classes
of orators in their proper order." "You understand me rightly," said I ; "and I heartily wish those venerable Odes were
still extant, which Cato informs us, in his Antiquities, used
to be sung by every guest in his turn at the homely feasts of
our ancestors, many ages before, to commemorate the feats of
their heroes.   But the *Punic War* of that antiquated poet,
whom Ennius so proudly ranks among the *fauns and rustic
bards*, affords me as exquisite a pleasure as the finest statue
that was ever formed by Myron.   Ennius, I allow, was a more
finished writer ; but if he had really undervalued the other,
as he pretends to do, he would scarcely have omitted such a
bloody war as the first *Punic*, when he attempted professedly
to describe all the wars of the Republic.   Nay, he himself as-
signs the reason :
      "'Others (said he) that cruel war have sung.'
Very true, and they have sung it with great order and precision, though not, indeed, in such elegant strains as yourself.
This you ought to have acknowledged, as you must certainly
be conscious that you have borrowed many ornaments from
Nævius ; or if you refuse to own it, I shall tell you plainly
that you have pilfered them.

"Contemporary with the Cato above mentioned (though
somewhat older) were Caius Flaminius, Caius Varro, Quintus
Maximus, Quintus Metellus, Publius Lentulus, and Publius
Crassus, who was joint consul with the elder Africanus.   This
Scipio, we are told, was not destitute of the powers of elocution ; but his son, who adopted the younger Scipio (the son
of Paulus Æmilius), would have stood foremost in the list of

orators, if he had possessed a firmer constitution. This is
evident from a few speeches, and a Greek History of his,
which are very agreeably written.

XX. "In the same class we may place Sextus Ælius, who
was the best lawyer of his time, and a ready speaker. A little
after these, flourished Caius Sulpicius Gallus, who was better
acquainted with the Grecian literature than all the rest of
the nobility, and to his reputation as a graceful orator, he
added the highest accomplishments in every other respect;
for a more copious and splendid way of speaking began now
to prevail. When this Sulpicius, in quality of prætor, was
celebrating the public shows in honor of Apollo, died the
poet Ennius, in the consulship of Quintus Marcius and Cneius
Servilius, after exhibiting his tragedy of *Thyestes*. At the
same time lived Tiberius Gracchus, the son of Publius, who
was twice consul and censor; a Greek oration of his to the
Rhodians is still extant, and he bore the character of a worthy
citizen and an eloquent speaker. We are likewise told that
Publius Scipio Nasica, surnamed *Corculum*,[1] as a favorite of
the people, and who also had the honor to be twice chosen
consul and censor, was esteemed an able orator. To him we
may add Lucius Lentulus, who was joint consul with Caius
Figulus; Quintus Nobilior, the son of Marcus, who was inclined to the study of literature by his father's example, and
presented Ennius (who had served under his father in Ætolia)
with the freedom of the city, when he founded a colony in
quality of triumvir; and his colleague Titus Annius Luscus,
who is said to have been tolerably eloquent. We are likewise informed that Lucius Paulus, the father of Africanus,
defended the character of an eminent citizen in a public speech;
and that Cato, who died in the eighty-third year of his age,
was then living, and actually pleaded that very year against
the defendant Servius Galba, in the open forum, with great
energy and spirit; he has left a copy of this oration behind
him.

XXI. "But when Cato was in the decline of life, a crowd
of orators, all younger than himself, made their appearance

---

[1] His name was Publius *Cornelius* Scipio Nasica. From *Cornelius*,
as being a favorite of the people, he was called *Corculum*, the "little
heart" of the people. In our language, with nearer affinity to his real
name, he might have been styled "kernel" of the people.

at the same time; for Aulus Albinus, who wrote a history in
Greek, and shared the consulship with Lucius Lucullus, was
greatly admired for his learning and elocution; and nearly
ranked with him were. Servius Fulvius and Servius Fabius
Pictor, the latter of whom was well acquainted with the laws
of his country, the belles-lettres, and the history of antiquity.
Quintus Fabius Labeo likewise excelled in the same accomplishments.   But Quintus Metellus, whose four sons attained
the consular dignity, was admired for his eloquence beyond
the rest; he undertook the defense of Lucius Cotta, when accused by Africanus, and composed many other speeches, particularly that against Tiberius Gracchus, of which we have a
full account in the annals of Caius Fannius.   Lucius Cotta
himself was likewise reckoned a skillful speaker;[1] but Caius
Lælius and Publius Africanus were allowed by all to be more
finished orators; their orations are still extant, and may serve
as specimens of their respective abilities.   But Servius Galba,
who somewhat preceded either of them in years, was indisputably the best speaker of the age.   He was the first among
the Romans who displayed the proper and distinguishing talents of an orator; such as, digressing from his subject to embellish and diversify it—soothing or alarming the passions,
exhibiting every circumstance in the strongest light—implor-
ing the compassion of his audience—and artfully enlarging on
those topics, or general principles of prudence or morality, on
which the stress of his argument depended; and yet, I know
not how, though he is allowed to have been the greatest orator of his time, the orations he has left are more inanimate,
and have more the air of antiquity, than those of Lælius, or
Scipio, or even of Cato himself.   Their beauties have so de-
cayed with age, that scarcely any thing remains of them but
the bare skeleton.   In the same manner, though both Lælius
and Scipio are greatly extolled for their abilities, the preference was given to Lælius as a speaker; and yet his oration,
in defense of the privileges of the Sacerdotal college, has no
greater merit than any one that might be named of the
numerous speeches of Scipio.   Nothing, indeed, can be sweet-

---

[1] The original is *veterator habitus.*   He was deemed "a veteran," *i. e.*,
he possessed all the skill of long-continued practice.   Sextus Pompeius
interprets *veteratores,* " callidi dicti à multâ rerum gerendarum vetus-
tate."

er and milder than that of Lælius, nor could any thing have been urged with greater dignity to support the honor of religion; but, of the two, Lælius appears to me to be less polished, and to speak more of the mould of time than Scipio; and, as different speakers have different tastes, he had, in my mind, too strong a relish for antiquity, and was too fond of using obsolete expressions. But such is the jealousy of mankind, that they will not allow the same person to be possessed of too many perfections. For, as in military prowess they thought it impossible that any man could vie with Scipio, though Lælius had not a little distinguished himself in the war with Viriathus; so for learning, eloquence, and wisdom, though each was allowed to be above the reach of any other competitor, they adjudged the preference to Lælius. Nor was this the opinion of the public only, but it seems to have been allowed by mutual consent between themselves; for it was then a general custom, as candid in this respect as it was fair and just in every other, to give his due to each.

XXII. "I accordingly remember that Publius Rutilius Rufus once told me at Smyrna, that when he was a young man, the two consuls Publius Scipio and Decimus Brutus, by order of the Senate, tried a capital cause of great consequence. For several persons of note having been murdered in the Silan Forest, and the domestics and some of the sons of a company of gentlemen who farmed the taxes of the pitch-manufactory, being charged with the fact, the consuls were ordered to try the cause in person. Lælius, he said, spoke very sensibly and elegantly, as indeed he always did, on the side of the farmers of the customs. But the consuls, after hearing both sides, judging it necessary to refer the matter to a second trial, the same Lælius, a few days after, pleaded their cause again with more accuracy, and much better than at first. The affair, however, was once more put off for a farther hearing. Upon this, when his clients attended Lælius to his own house, and, after thanking him for what he had already done, earnestly begged him not to be disheartened by the fatigue he had suffered, he assured them he had exerted his utmost to defend their reputation; but frankly added, that he thought their cause would be more effectually supported by Servius Galba, who possessed talents more powerful and penetrating than his own. They, accordingly, by the advice of Lælius, requested Galba to undertake it. To this he consented, but with the greatest modesty and reluctance, out of respect to the illustrious advocate he was going to succeed; and as he had only the next day to prepare himself, he spent the whole of it in considering and digesting his cause. When the day of trial was come, Rutilius himself, at the request of the defendants, went early in the morning to Galba, to give him notice of it, and conduct him to the court in proper time. But till word was brought that the consuls were going to the bench, he confined himself in his study, where he suffered no one to be admitted; and continued very busy in dictating to his amanuenses, several of whom (as indeed he often used to do) he kept fully employed at the same time. While he was thus engaged, being informed that it was high time for him to appear in court, he left his house with that animation and glow of countenance, that you would have thought he had not only *prepared* his cause, but actually *carried* it. Rutilius added, as another circumstance worth noticing, that his scribes, who attended him to the bar, appeared excessively fatigued, from whence he thought it probable that he was equally warm and vigorous in the composition as in the delivery of his speeches. But to conclude the story, Galba pleaded his cause before Lælius himself, and a very numerous and attentive audience, with such uncommon force and dignity, that every part of his oration received the applause of his hearers; and so powerfully did he move the feelings and insure the sympathy of the judges, that his clients were immediately acquitted of the charge, to the satisfaction of the whole court.

XXIII. "As, therefore, the two principal qualities required in an orator are perspicuity in stating the subject, and dignified ardor in moving the passions; and as he who fires and inflames his audience, will always effect more than he who can barely inform and amuse them; we may conjecture from the above narrative, with which I was favored by Rutilius, that Lælius was most admired for his elegance, and Galba for his pathetic force. But the energy peculiar to him was most remarkably exerted, when, having in his prætorship put to death some Lusitanians, contrary, it was believed, to his previous and express engagement, Titus Libo, the tribune, exasperated the people against him, and preferred a bill which was to operate against his conduct as a subsequent law. Marcus Cato, as I have before mentioned, though extremely old, spoke in support of the bill with great vehemence; which speech he inserted in his book of *Antiquities*, a few days, or at most only a month or two, before his death. On this occasion, Galba not refusing to plead to the charge, and submitting his fate to the generosity of the people, recommended his children to their protection, with tears in his eyes; and particularly his young ward, the son of Caius Gallus Sulpicius, his deceased friend, whose orphan state and piercing cries, which were the more regarded for the sake of his illustrious father, excited their pity in a wonderful manner; and thus, as Cato informs us in his History, he escaped the flames which would otherwise have consumed him, by employing the children to move the compassion of the people. I likewise find (what may be easily judged from his orations still extant) that his prosecutor, Libo, was a man of some eloquence." As I concluded these remarks with a short pause, "What can be the reason," said Brutus, " if there was so much merit in the oratory of Galba, that there is no trace of it to be seen in his orations? a circumstance which I have no opportunity to be surprised at in others, who have left nothing behind them in writing."

XXIV. " The reasons," said I, ".why some have not written any thing, and others not so well as they spoke, are very different. Some of our orators, as being indolent, and unwilling to add the fatigue of private to public business, do not practice composition; for most of the orations we are now possessed of were written, not before they were spoken, but some time afterward. Others did not choose the trouble of improving themselves, to which nothing more contributes than frequent writing; and as to perpetuating the fame of their eloquence, they thought it unnecessary, supposing that their eminence in that respect was sufficiently established already, and that it would be rather diminished than increased by submitting any written specimen of it to the arbitrary test of criticism. Some also were sensible that they spoke much better than they were able to write; which is generally the case of those who have a great genius, but little learning, such as Servius Galba. When he spoke, he was perhaps so much animated by the force of his abilities, and the natural warmth and impetuosity of his temper, that his language was rapid, bold, and striking; but afterward, when he took up the pen in his leisure hours, and his passion had sunk into a calm, his elocution became dull and languid. This indeed can never happen to those whose only aim is to be neat and polished; because an orator may always be master of that discretion which will enable him both to speak and write in the same agreeable manner; but no man can revive at pleasure the ardor of his passions; and when that has once subsided, the fire and pathos of his language will be extinguished. This is the reason why the calm and easy spirit of Lælius seems still to breathe in his writings; whereas the vigor of Galba is entirely withered away.

XXV. "We may also reckon in the number of middling orators, the two brothers Lucius and Spurius Mummius, both whose orations are still in being; the style of Lucius is plain and antiquated; but that of Spurius, though equally unembellished, is more close and compact; for he was well versed in the doctrine of the Stoics. The orations of Spurius Alpinus, their contemporary, are very numerous; and we have several by Lucius and Caius Aurelius Oresta, who were esteemed indifferent speakers. Publius Popilius also was a worthy citizen, and had a moderate share of elocution; but his son Caius was really eloquent. To these we may add Caius Tuditanus, who was not only very polished and graceful in his manners and appearance, but had an elegant turn of expression; and of the same class was Marcus Octavius, a man of inflexible constancy in every just and laudable measure; and who, after being insulted and disgraced in the most public manner, defeated his rival Tiberius Gracchus by the mere dint of his perseverance. But Marcus Æmilius Lepidus, who was surnamed Porcina, and flourished at the same time as Galba, though he was indeed something younger, was esteemed an orator of the first eminence; and really appears, from his orations which are still extant, to have been a masterly writer. For he was the first speaker among the Romans who gave us a specimen of the easy gracefulness of the Greeks; and who was distinguished by the measured flow of his language, and a style regularly polished and improved by art. His manner was carefully studied by Caius Carbo and Tiberius Gracchus, two accomplished youths, who were nearly of an age : but we must defer their character as public speakers, till we have finished our account of their elders.   For Quintus Pompeius, considering the time in which he lived, was no contemptible orator, and actually raised himself to the highest honors of the state by his own personal merit, and without being recommended, as usual, by the quality of his ancestors.   Lucius Cassius too derived his influence, which was very considerable, not, indeed, from the highest powers, yet from a tolerable share of eloquence ; for it is remarkable that he made himself popular, not as others did, by his complaisance and liberality, but by the gloomy rigor and severity of his manners.   His law for collecting the votes of the people by way of ballot, was strongly opposed by the tribune Marcus Antius Briso, who was supported by Marcus Lepidus, one of the consuls : and it was afterward objected to Africanus, that Briso dropped the opposition by his advice.   At this time the two Cæpios were very serviceable to a number of clients by their superior judgment and eloquence, but still more so by their extensive interest and popularity.   But the written speeches of Pompeius (though it must be owned they have rather an antiquated air) discover an amazing sagacity, and are very far from being dry and spiritless.

XXVI. " To these we must add Publius Crassus, an orator of uncommon merit, who was qualified for the profession by the united efforts of art and nature, and enjoyed some other advantages which were almost peculiar to his family.   For he had contracted an affinity with that accomplished speaker Servius Galba above mentioned, by giving his daughter in marriage to Galba's son ; and being likewise himself the son of Mucius, and the brother of Publius Scævola, he had a fine opportunity at home (which he made the best use of) to gain a thorough knowledge of the civil law.   He was a man of unusual application, and was much beloved by his fellow-citizens, being constantly employed either in giving his advice, or pleading causes in the forum.   Contemporary with the speakers I have mentioned were the two Caii Fannii, the sons of Caius and Marcus, one of whom (the son of Caius), who was joint consul with Domitius, has left us an excellent speech against Gracchus, who proposed the admission of the Latin and Italian allies to the freedom of Rome."   " Do you really think, then," said Atticus, " that Fannius was the au-

thor of that oration? For when we were young, there were
different opinions about it. Some asserted that it was written by Caius Persius, a man of letters, and much extolled for
his learning by Lucilius; and others believed it the joint production of a number of noblemen, each of whom contributed
his best to complete it." "This I remember," said I; "but
I could never persuade myself to coincide with either of them.
Their suspicion, I believe, was entirely founded on the character of Fannius, who was only reckoned among the *middling*
orators; whereas the speech in question is esteemed the best
which the time afforded. But, on the other hand, it is too
much of a piece to have been the mingled composition of
many; for the flow of the periods, and the turn of the language, are perfectly similar, throughout the whole of it. And
as to *Persius*, if *he* had composed it for Fannius to pronounce,
Gracchus would certainly have taken some notice of it in his
reply; because Fannius rallies Gracchus pretty severely, in
one part of it, for employing Menelaus of Maratho, and several others, to compose his speeches. We may add, that Fannius himself was no contemptible orator; for he pleaded a
number of causes, and his tribuneship, which was chiefly conducted under the management and direction of Publius Africanus, exhibited much oratory. But the other Caius Fannius (the son of Marcus and son-in-law of Caius Lælius) was of
a rougher cast, both in his temper and manner of speaking.
By the advice of his father-in-law (of whom, by-the-by, he
was not remarkably fond, because he had not voted for his
admission into the college of augurs, but gave the preference
to his younger son-in-law, Quintus Scævola; though Lælius
politely excused himself, by saying that the preference was
not given to the youngest son, but to his wife the eldest
daughter), by his advice, I say, he attended the lectures of
Panætius. His abilities as a speaker may be easily inferred
from his history, which is neither destitute of elegance, nor a
perfect model of composition. As to his brother Mucius, the
augur, whenever he was called upon to defend himself, he always pleaded his own cause; as, for instance, in the action
which was brought against him for bribery by Titus Albucius.
But he was never ranked among the orators, his chief merit
being a critical knowledge of the civil law, and an uncommon
accuracy of judgment. Lucius Cælius Antipater, likewise (as

you may see by his works), was an elegant and a perspicuous writer for the time he lived in; he was also an excellent lawyer, and taught the principles of jurisprudence to many others, particularly to Lucius Crassus.

XXVII. "As to Caius Carbo and Tiberius Gracchus, I wish they had been as well inclined to maintain peace and good order in the state as they were qualified to support it by their eloquence; their glory would then have never been excelled. But the latter, for his turbulent tribuneship, which he entered upon with a heart full of resentment against the great and good, on account of the odium he had brought upon himself by the treaty of Numantia, was slain by the hands of the republic; and the other, being impeached of a seditious affectation of popularity, rescued himself from the severity of the judges by a voluntary death. That both of them were excellent speakers, is very plain from the general testimony of their contemporaries; for, as to their speeches now extant, though I allow them to be very skillful and judicious, they are certainly defective in elocution. Gracchus had the advantage of being carefully instructed by his mother Cornelia from his very childhood, and his mind was enriched with all the stores of Grecian literature; for he was constantly attended by the ablest masters from Greece, and particularly, in his youth, by Diophanes of Mitylene, who was the most eloquent Grecian of his age; but, though he was a man of uncommon genius, he had but a short time to improve and display it. As to Carbo, his whole life was spent in trials and forensic debates. He is said, by very sensible men who heard him, and among others by our friend Lucius Gellius, who lived in his family in the time of his consulship, to have been a sonorous, a fluent, and a spirited speaker, and likewise, upon occasion, very pathetic, very engaging, and excessively humorous: Gellius used to add, that he applied himself very closely to his studies, and bestowed much of his time in writing and private declamation. He was, therefore, esteemed the best pleader of his time; for no sooner had he begun to distinguish himself in the forum, but the depravity of the age gave birth to a number of lawsuits; and it was first found necessary, in the time of his youth, to settle the form of public trials, which had never been done before. We accordingly find that Lucius Piso, then a tribune of the people, was the first who proposed a law against bribery, which he did when Censorinus and Manilius were consuls. This Piso, too, was a professed pleader, who moved and opposed a great number of laws; he left some orations behind him, which are now lost, and a book of annals very indifferently written. But in the public trials, in which Carbo was concerned, the assistance of an able advocate had become more necessary than ever, in consequence of the law for voting by ballots, which was proposed and carried by Lucius Cassius, in the consulship of Lepidus and Mancinus.

XXVIII. " I have likewise been often assured by the poet Attius (an intimate friend of his) that your ancestor Decimus Brutus, the son of Marcus, was no inelegant speaker; and that, for the time he lived in, he was well versed both in the Greek and Roman literature. He ascribed the same accomplishments to Quintus Maximus, the grandson of Lucius Paulus; and added that, a little prior to Maximus, the Scipio, by whose instigation (though only in a private capacity) Tiberius Gracchus was assassinated, was not only a man of great ardor in all other respects, but very warm and spirited in his manner of speaking. Publius Lentulus too, the father of the senate, had a sufficient share of eloquence for an honest and useful magistrate. About the same time Lucius Furius Philus was thought to speak our language as elegantly and more correctly than any other man; Publius Scævola to be very acute and judicious, and rather more fluent than Philus; Manius Manilius to possess almost an equal share of judgment with the latter; and Appius Claudius to be equally fluent, but more warm and pathetic. Marcus Fulvius Flaccus, and Caius Cato the nephew of Africanus, were likewise tolerable orators; some of the writings of Flaccus are still in being, in which nothing, however, is to be seen but the mere scholar. Publius Decius was a professed rival of Flaccus; he too was not destitute of eloquence; but his style was too bold, as his temper was too violent. Marcus Drusus, the son of Claudius, who, in his tribuneship, baffled[1] his colleague Gracchus

---

[1] *Baffled.* In the original it runs, *Caium Gracchum collegam, iterum Tribunum, fecit:* but this was undoubtedly a mistake of the transcriber, as being contrary not only to the truth of history, but to Cicero's own account of the matter in lib. iv., De Finibus. Pighius, therefore, has very properly recommended the word *fregit* instead of *fecit.*

(then raised to the same office a second time), was a nervous speaker, and a man of great popularity; and next to him was his brother Caius Drusus. Your kinsman also, my Brutus (Marcus Pennus), successfully opposed the tribune Gracchus, who was something younger than himself. For Gracchus was quæstor, and Pennus (the son of that Marcus, who was joint consul with Quintus Ælius) was tribune, in the consulship of Marcus Lepidus and Lucius Orestes; but after enjoying the ædileship, and a prospect of succeeding to the highest honors, he was snatched off by an untimely death. As to Titus Flamininus, whom I myself have seen, I can learn nothing but that he spoke our language with great accuracy.

XXIX. "To these we may join Caius Curio, Marcus Scaurus, Publius Rutilius, and Caius Gracchus. It will not be amiss to give a short account of Scaurus and Rutilius; neither of whom, indeed, had the reputation of being a first-rate orator, though each of them pleaded a number of causes. But some deserving men, who were not remarkable for their genius, may be justly commended for their industry; not that the persons I am speaking of were really destitute of genius, but only of that particular kind of it which distinguishes the orator. For it is of little consequence to discover what is *proper* to be said, unless you are able to express it in a free and agreeable manner; and even that will be insufficient, if not recommended by the voice, the look, and the gesture. It is needless to add, that much depends upon *art;* for though, even without this, it is possible, by the mere force of nature, to say many striking things; yet, as they will after all be nothing more than so many lucky hits, we shall not be able to repeat them at our pleasure. The style of Scaurus, who was a very sensible and an honest man, was remarkably grave, and commanded the respect of the hearer; so that, when he was speaking for his client, you would rather have thought he was giving evidence in his favor than pleading his cause. This manner of speaking, however, though but indifferently adapted to the bar, was very much so to a calm debate in the senate, of which Scaurus was then esteemed the father; for it not only bespoke his prudence, but, what was still a more important recommendation, his credibility. This advantage, which it is not easy to acquire by art, he derived entirely from nature; though you know that even *here* we have some precepts to assist us. We have several of his orations still extant, and three books inscribed to Lucius Fufidius, containing the history of his own life, which, though a very useful work, is scarcely read by any body. But the *Institution of Cyrus*, by Xenophon, is read by every one; which, though an excellent performance of the kind, is much less adapted to our manners and form of government, and not superior in merit to the honest simplicity of Scaurus.

XXX. "Fufidius himself was likewise a tolerable pleader; but Rutilius was distinguished by his solemn and austere way of speaking; and both of them were naturally warm and spirited. Accordingly, after they had rivaled each other for the consulship, he who had lost his election immediately sued his competitor for bribery; and Scaurus, the defendant, being honorably acquitted of the charge, returned the compliment to Rutilius by commencing a similar prosecution against *him*. Rutilius was a man of great industry and application, for which he was the more respected, because, besides his pleadings, he undertook the office (which was a very troublesome one) of giving advice to all who applied to him in matters of law. His orations are very dry, but his juridical remarks are excellent; for he was a learned man, and well versed in the Greek literature, and was likewise an attentive and constant hearer of Panætius, and a thorough proficient in the doctrine of the Stoics; whose method of discoursing, though very close and artful, is too precise, and not at all adapted to engage the attention of common people. That self-confidence, therefore, which is so peculiar to the sect, was displayed by *him* with amazing firmness and resolution; for though he was perfectly innocent of the charge, a prosecution was commenced against him for bribery (a trial which raised a violent commotion in the city), and yet, though Lucius Crassus and Marcus Antonius, both of consular dignity, were at that time in very high repute for their eloquence, he refused the assistance of either, being determined to plead his cause himself, which he accordingly did. Caius Cotta, indeed, who was his nephew, made a short speech in his vindication, which he spoke in the true style of an orator, though he was then but a youth. Quintus Mucius too said much in his defense, with his usual accuracy and elegance, but not with that force and extension which the mode of trial and the

importance of the cause demanded.   Rutilius, therefore, was
an orator of the *Stoical*, and Scaurus of the *Antique* cast ; but
they are both entitled to our commendation, because in *them*
even this formal and unpromising species of elocution has appeared among us with some degree of merit.   For as in the
theatre, so in the forum, I would not have our applause confined to those alone who act the busy and more important
characters, but reserve a share of it for the quiet and unam-
bitious performer, who is distinguished by a simple truth of
gesture, without any violence.

XXXI.   "As I have mentioned the Stoics, I must take
some notice of Quintus Ælius Tubero, the grandson of Lucius
Paullus, who made his appearance at the time we are speaking of.   He was never esteemed an orator, but was a man of
the most rigid virtue, and strictly conformable to the doctrine
he professed; but, in truth, he had not sufficient ease and
polish.   In his Triumvirate, he declared, contrary to the
opinion of Publius Africanus his uncle, that the augurs had
no right of exemption from sitting in the courts of justice;
and as in his temper, so in his manner of speaking, he was
harsh, unpolished, and austere, on which account he could
never raise himself to the honorable posts which were enjoyed by his ancestors.   But he was a brave and steady citizen,
and a warm opposer of Gracchus, as appears from Gracchus's
oration against him ; we have likewise some of Tubero's
speeches against Gracchus.   He was not, indeed, a shining
orator, but he was a learned and very skillful disputant."
" I find," said Brutus, " that the case is much the same among
us, as with the Greeks ; and that the Stoics, in general, are
very judicious at an argument, which they conduct by certain rules of art, and are likewise very neat and exact in their
language ; but if we take them from this, to speak in public,
they make a poor appearance.   Cato, however, must be ex-
cepted ; in whom, though as rigid a Stoic as ever existed, I
could not wish for a more consummate degree of eloquence.
I can likewise discover a moderate share of it in Fannius—
not so much in Rutilius; but none at all in Tubero."
" True," said I ; " and we may easily account for it; their
whole attention was so closely confined to the study of logic,
that they never troubled themselves to acquire the free, diffusive, and variegated style which is so necessary for a pub-

lic speaker. But your uncle, you doubtless know, was wise enough to borrow only that from the Stoics which they were able to furnish for his purpose (the art of reasoning); but for the art of speaking, he had recourse to the masters of rhetoric, and exercised himself in the manner they directed. If, however, we must be indebted for every thing to the philosophers, the Peripatetic discipline is, in my mind, much the most proper to form our language. For which reason, my Brutus, I the more approve your choice, in attaching yourself to a sect (I mean the philosophers of the old Academy) in whose system a just and accurate way of reasoning is enlivened by a perpetual sweetness and fluency of expression; but even the delicate and flowing style of the Peripatetics and Academics is not sufficient to complete an orator; nor yet can he be complete without it. For as the language of the Stoics is too close and contracted to suit the ears of common people, so that of the latter is too diffusive and luxuriant for a spirited contest in the forum, or a pleading at the bar. Who had a richer style than Plato? The philosophers tell us, that if Jupiter himself was to converse in Greek, he would speak like *him*. Who also was more nervous than Aristotle? Who sweeter than Theophrastus? We are told that even Demosthenes attended the lectures of Plato, and was fond of reading what he published; which, indeed, is sufficiently evident from the turn and majesty of his language; and he himself has expressly mentioned it in one of his letters. But the style of this excellent orator is, notwithstanding, much too violent for the academy; as that of the philosophers is too mild and placid for the forum.

XXXII. "I shall now, with your leave, proceed to the age and merits of the rest of the Roman orators." "Nothing," said Atticus—"for I can safely answer for my friend Brutus—would please us better." "Curio, then," said I, "was nearly of the age I have just mentioned; a celebrated speaker, whose genius may be easily ascertained from his orations. For, among several others, we have a noble speech of his for Servius Fulvius, in a prosecution for incest. When we were children, it was esteemed the best then extant; but now it is almost overlooked among the numerous performances of the same kind which have been lately published." "I am very sensible," replied Brutus, " to whom we are obliged for the numerous performances you speak of." "And I am equally sensible," said I, "who is the person you intend; for I have at least done a service to my young countrymen, by introducing a loftier and more embellished way of speaking than was used before; and, perhaps, I have also done some harm, because after *mine* appeared, the speeches of our predecessors began to be neglected by most people; though never by *me*, for I can assure you I always prefer them to my own." "But you must reckon me," said Brutus, "among the *most people;* though I now see, from your recommendation, that I have a great many books to read, of which before I had very little opinion." "But this celebrated oration," said I, "in the prosecution for incest, is in some places excessively puerile; and what is said in it of the passion of love, the inefficacy of questioning by tortures, and the danger of trusting to common hearsay, is indeed pretty enough, but would be insufferable to the chastened ears of the moderns, and to a people who are justly distinguished for the solidity of their knowledge. He likewise wrote several other pieces, spoke a number of good orations, and was certainly an eminent pleader; so that I much wonder, considering how long he lived and the character he bore, that he was never preferred to the consulship.

XXXIII. "But I have a man here[1] (Caius Gracchus) who had an amazing genius, and the most ardent application; and was a scholar from his very childhood; for you must not imagine, my Brutus, that we have ever yet had a speaker whose language was richer and more copious than his." "I really think so," answered Brutus; "and he is almost the only author we' have, among the ancients, that I take the trouble to read." "And he well *deserves* it," said I; "for the Roman name and literature were great losers by his untimely fate. I wish he had transferred his affection for his brother to his country! How easily, if he had thus prolonged his life, would he have rivaled the glory of his father and grandfather! In eloquence, I scarcely know whether we should yet have had his equal. His language was noble; his sentiments manly and judicious; and his whole manner great and

---

[1] He refers, perhaps, to the works of Gracchus, which he might then have in his hand; or, more probably, to a statue of him, which stood near the place where he and his friends were sitting.

striking. He wanted nothing but the finishing touch; for, though his first attempts were as excellent as they were numerous, he did not live to complete them. In short, my Brutus, *he*, if any one, should be carefully studied by the Roman youth; for he is able, not only to sharpen, but to enrich and ripen their talents. After *him* appeared Caius Galba, the son of the eloquent Servius, and the son-in-law of Publius Crassus, who was both an eminent speaker and a skillful civilian. He was much commended by our fathers, who respected him for the sake of *his;* but he had the misfortune to be stopped in his career; for, being tried by the Mamilian law as a party concerned in the conspiracy to support Jugurtha, though he exerted all his abilities to defend himself, he was unhappily condemned. His peroration, or, as it is often called, his epilogue, is still extant; and was so much in repute, when we were school-boys, that we used to learn it by heart; he was the first member of the Sacerdotal College, since the building of Rome, who was publicly tried and condemned.

XXXIV. "As to Publius Scipio, who died in his consulship, he neither spoke much, nor often; but he was inferior to no one in purity of language, and superior to all in wit and pleasantry. His colleague, Lucius Bestia, who began his tribuneship very successfully (for, by a law which he preferred for the purpose, he procured the recall of Popilius, who had been exiled by the influence of Caius Gracchus), was a man of spirit, and a tolerable speaker; but he did not finish his consulship equally happily. For, in consequence of the invidious law of Mamilius above mentioned, Caius Galba, one of the priests, and the four consular gentlemen, Lucius Bestia, Caius Cato, Spurius Albinus, and that excellent citizen Lucius Opimius, who killed Gracchus, of which he was acquitted by the people, though he had constantly sided against them, were all condemned by their judges, who were of the Gracchan party. Very unlike him in his tribuneship, and, indeed, in every other part of his life, was that infamous citizen Caius Licinius Nerva; but he was not destitute of eloquence. Nearly at the same time (though, indeed, he was somewhat older) flourished Caius Fimbria, who was rather rough and abusive, and much too warm and hasty; but his application, and his great integrity and firmness, made him a serviceable speaker in the senate. He was likewise a tolerable pleader and civilian, and distinguished by the same rigid freedom in the turn of his language as in that of his virtues. When we were boys, we used to think his orations worth reading, though they are now scarcely to be met with. But Caius Sextius Calvinus was equally elegant, both in his taste and his language, though, unhappily, of a very infirm constitution; when the pain in his feet intermitted, he did not decline the trouble of pleading, but he did not attempt it very often. His fellow-citizens, therefore, made use of his advice whenever they had occasion for it, but of his patronage only when his health permitted. Contemporary with these, my good friend, was your namesake Marcus Brutus, the disgrace of your noble family; who, though he bore that honorable name, and had the best of men and an eminent civilian for his father, confined his practice to accusations, as Lycurgus is said to have done at Athens. He never sued for any of our magistracies, but was a severe and troublesome prosecutor; so that we easily see that in *him* the natural goodness of the stock was corrupted by the vicious inclinations of the man. At the same time lived Lucius Cæsulenus, a man of plebeian rank, and a professed accuser, like the former; I myself heard him in his old age, when he endeavored, by the Aquilian law, to subject Lucius Sabellius to a fine for a breach of justice. But I should not have taken any notice of such a low-born wretch, if I had not thought that no person I ever heard could give a more suspicious turn to the cause of the defendant, or exaggerate it to a higher degree of criminality.

XXXV. "Titus Albucius, who lived in the same age, was well versed in the Grecian literature, or, rather, was almost a Greek himself. I speak of him as I think, but any person who pleases may judge what he was by his orations. In his youth, he studied at Athens, and returned from thence a thorough proficient in the doctrine of Epicurus, which, of all others, is the least adapted to form an orator. His contemporary, Quintus Catulus, was an accomplished speaker, not in the ancient taste, but (unless any thing more perfect can be exhibited) in the finished style of the moderns. He had copious stores of learning; an easy, winning elegance, not only in his manners and disposition, but in his very language, and an unblemished purity and correctness of style. This may be easily seen by his orations, and particularly by the

History of his Consulship, and of his subsequent transactions, which he composed in the soft and agreeable manner of Xenophon, and made a present of to the poet Aulus Furius, an intimate acquaintance of his. But this performance is as little known as the three books of Scaurus before mentioned." "Indeed, I must confess," said Brutus, "that both the one and the other are perfectly unknown to me; but that is entirely my *own* fault. I shall now, therefore, request a sight of them from *you;* and am resolved, in future, to be more careful in collecting such valuable curiosities." "This Catulus," said I, "as I have just observed, was distinguished by the purity of his language; which, though a material accomplishment, is too much neglected by most of the Roman orators; for as to the elegant tone of his voice, and the sweetness of his accent, as you knew his son, it will be needless to take any notice of them. His son, indeed, was not in the list of orators; but whenever he had occasion to deliver his sentiments in public, he neither wanted judgment, nor a neat and liberal turn of expression. Nay, even the father himself was not reckoned the foremost in the rank of orators; but still he had that kind of merit, that notwithstanding after you had heard two or three speakers who were particularly eminent in their profession, you might judge him inferior; yet, whenever you hear him *alone*, and without an immediate opportunity of making a comparison, you would not only be satisfied with him, but scarcely wish for a better advocate. As to Quintus Metellus Numidicus, and his colleague Marcus Silanus, they spoke, on matters of government, with as much eloquence as was really necessary for men of their illustrious character, and of consular dignity. But Marcus Aurelius Scaurus, though he spoke in public but seldom, always spoke very neatly, and he had a more elegant command of the Roman language than most men. Aulus Albinus was a speaker of the same kind; but Albinus the flamen was esteemed an *orator*. Quintus Cæpio, too, had a great deal of spirit, and was a brave citizen; but the unlucky chance of war was imputed to him as a crime, and the general odium of the people proved his ruin.

XXXVI. "Caius and Lucius Memmius were likewise indifferent orators, and distinguished by the bitterness and asperity of their accusations; for they prosecuted many, but

seldom spoke for the defendant. Spurius Thorius, on the
other hand, was distinguished by his *popular* way of speaking; the very same man who, by his corrupt and frivolous
law, diminished[1] the taxes that were levied on the public
lands. Marcus Marcellus, the father of Æserninus, though
not reckoned a professed pleader, was a prompt, and, in some
degree, a practiced speaker; as was also his son Publius Lentulus. Lucius Cotta likewise, a man of prætorian rank, was
esteemed a tolerable orator; but he never made any great
progress; on the contrary, he purposely endeavored, both in
the choice of his words and the rusticity of his pronunciation,
to imitate the manner of the ancients. I am indeed sensible
that in this instance of Cotta, and in many others, I have and
shall again insert in the list of orators those who, in reality,
had but little claim to the character. For it was, professedly, my design to collect an account of all the Romans, without exception, who made it their business to excel in the profession of *eloquence;* and it may be easily seen from this account by what slow gradations they advanced, and how excessively difficult it is in every thing to rise to the summit of
perfection. As a proof of this, how many orators have been
already recounted, and how much time have we bestowed
upon them, before we could ascend, after infinite fatigue and
drudgery, as, among the Greeks, to *Demosthenes* and *Hyperides,*
so now, among our own countrymen, to *Antonius* and *Crassus!*
For, in my mind, these were consummate orators, and the
first among the Romans whose diffusive eloquence rivaled the
glory of the Greeks.

XXXVII. "Antonius comprehended every thing which
could be of service to his cause, and he arranged his materials
in the most advantageous order; and as a skillful general
posts the cavalry, the infantry, and the light-troops, where
each of them can act to most advantage, so Antonius drew
up his arguments in those parts of his discourse, where they
were likely to have the best effect. He had a quick and retentive memory, and a frankness of manner which precluded
any suspicion of artifice. All his speeches were, in appearance, the unpremeditated effusions of an honest heart, and
yet, in reality, they were preconcerted with so much skill,
that the judges were sometimes not so well prepared as they

[1] By dividing great part of them among the people.

should have been to withstand the force of them. His language, indeed, was not so refined as to pass for the standard of elegance; for which reason he was thought to be rather a careless speaker; and yet, on the other hand, it was neither vulgar nor incorrect, but of that solid and judicious turn which constitutes the real merit of an orator as to the choice of his words. For, though a purity of style is certainly, as has been observed, a very commendable quality, it is not so much so for its intrinsic consequence as because it is too generally neglected. In short, it is not so meritorious to speak our native tongue correctly, as it is disgraceful to speak it otherwise, nor is it so much the characteristic of a good orator as of a well-bred citizen. But in the choice of his words (in which he had more regard to their weight than their brilliance), and likewise in the structure of his language and the compass of his periods, Antonius conformed himself to the dictates of reason, and, in a great measure, to the nicer rules of art, though his chief excellence was a judicious management of the figures and decorations of sentiment. This was likewise the distinguishing excellence of Demosthenes; in which he was so far superior to all others, as to be allowed, in the opinion of the best judges, to be the prince of orators. For the *figures* (as they are called by the Greeks) are the principal ornaments of an able speaker—I mean those which contribute not so much to paint and embellish our language, as to give a lustre to our sentiments.

XXXVIII. "But besides these, of which Antonius had a great command, he had a peculiar excellence in his manner of delivery, both as to his voice and gesture; for the latter was such as to correspond to the meaning of every sentence, without beating time to the words. His hands, his shoulders, the turn of his body, the stamp of his foot, his posture, his air, and, in short, all his motions, were adapted to his language and sentiments; and his voice was strong and firm, though naturally hoarse—a defect which he alone was capable of improving to his advantage; for in capital causes, it had a mournful dignity of accent, which was exceedingly proper, both to win the assent of the judges, and excite their compassion for a suffering client; so that in *him* the observation of Demosthenes was eminently verified; who, being asked what was the *first* quality of a good orator, what the *second*,

and what the *third*, constantly replied, 'A good enunciation.'
But many thought that he was equaled, and others that he
was even excelled, by Lucius Crassus. All, however, were
agreed in this, that whoever had either of them for his advocate, had no cause to wish for a better. For my own part,
notwithstanding the uncommon merit I have ascribed to Antonius, I must also acknowledge that there can not be a more
finished character than that of Crassus. He possessed a
wonderful dignity of elocution, with an agreeable mixture of
wit and pleasantry, which was perfectly polished, and without the smallest tincture of scurrility. His style was correct
and elegant, without stiffness or affectation; his method of
reasoning was remarkably clear and distinct; and when his
cause turned upon any point of law or equity, he had an inexhaustible fund of arguments and comparative illustrations.

XXXIX. "For as Antonius had an admirable turn for
suggesting apposite hints, and either suppressing or exciting
the suspicions of the hearer, so no man could explain and define, or discuss a point of equity, with a more copious facility
than Crassus, as sufficiently appeared upon many other occasions, but particularly in the cause of Manius Curius, which
was tried before the centumviri. For he urged a great variety of arguments in the defense of right and equity, against
the literal *jubet* of the law; and supported them by such a
numerous series of precedents, that he overpowered Quintus
Scævola (a man of uncommon penetration, and the ablest
civilian of his time), though the case before them was only a
matter of regal right. But the cause was so ably managed
by the two advocates, who were nearly of an age, and both
of consular rank, that while each endeavored to interpret the
law in favor of his client, Crassus was universally allowed to
be the best lawyer among the orators, and Scævola to be the
most eloquent civilian of the age; for the latter could not
only discover with the nicest precision what was agreeable to
law and equity, but had likewise a conciseness and propriety
of expression which was admirably adapted to his purpose.
In short, he had such a wonderful vein of oratory in com-
menting, explaining, and discussing, that I never beheld his
equal; though in amplifying, embellishing, and refuting, he
was rather to be dreaded as a formidable critic, than admired
as an eloquent speaker."

XL. "Indeed," said Brutus, "though I always thought I sufficiently understood the character of Scævola, by the account I had heard of him from Caius Rutilius, whose company I frequented for the sake of his acquaintance with him, I had not the least idea of his merit as an orator. I am now, therefore, not a little pleased to be informed that our republic has had the honor of producing so accomplished a man and such an excellent genius." "Really, my Brutus," said I, "you may take it from me, that the Roman state had never been adorned with two finer characters than these. For, as I have before observed that the one was the best lawyer among the orators, and the other the best speaker among the civilians of his time ; so the difference between them, in all other respects, was of such a nature, that it would almost be impossible for you to determine which of the two you would rather choose to resemble. For, as Crassus was the oldest of all our elegant speakers, so Scævola was the most elegant among those who were distinguished by the concise accuracy of their language ; and as Crassus tempered his affability with a proper share of severity, so the rigid air of Scævola was not destitute of the milder graces of an affable condescension. Though this was really their character, it is very possible that I may be thought to have embellished it beyond the bounds of truth, to give an agreeable air to my narrative ; but as your favorite sect, my Brutus, the old Academy, has defined all virtue to be a just mediocrity, it was the constant endeavor of these two eminent men to pursue this golden mean ; and yet it so happened, that while each of them shared a part of the other's excellence, he preserved his own entire." "To speak what I think," replied Brutus, "I have not only acquired a proper acquaintance with their characters from your account of them, but I can likewise discover that the same comparison might be drawn between *you* and Servius Sulpicius, which you have just been making between Crassus and Scævola." "In what manner?" said I. "Because *you*," replied Brutus, "have taken the pains to acquire as extensive a knowledge of the law as is necessary for an orator ; and Sulpicius, on the other hand, took care to furnish himself with sufficient eloquence to support the character of an able civilian. Besides, your age corresponded as nearly to his, as the age of Crassus did to that of Scævola."

XLI. " As to my own abilities," said I, "the rules of decency forbid me to speak of them ; but your character of Servius is a very just one, and I may freely tell you what I think of him. There are few, I believe, who have applied themselves more assiduously to the art of speaking than he did, or indeed to the study of every useful science. In our youth, we both of us followed the same liberal exercises ; and he afterward accompanied me to Rhodes, to pursue those studies which might equally improve him as a man and a scholar; but when he returned from thence, he appears to me to have been rather ambitious of being the foremost man in a secondary profession, than the second in that which claims the highest dignity. I will not pretend to say that he could not have ranked himself among the first in the latter profession ; but he rather chose to be, what he actually made himself, the first lawyer of his time." " Indeed!" said Brutus : " and do you really prefer Servius to Quintus Scævola ?" " My opinion," said I, " Brutus, is, that Quintus Scævola and many others had a thorough practical knowledge of the law, but that Servius alone understood it as a *science*, which he could never have done by the mere study of the law, and without a previous acquaintance with the art, which teaches us to divide a whole into its subordinate parts, to explain an indeterminate idea by an accurate definition ; to illustrate what is obscure by a clear interpretation ; and first to discover what things are of a *doubtful* nature, then to distinguish them by their different degrees of probability ; and, lastly, to be provided with a certain rule or measure by which we may judge what is true and what false, and what inferences fairly may or may not be deduced from any given premises. This important art he applied to those subjects which, for want of it, were necessarily managed by others without due order and precision."

XLII. " You mean, I suppose," said Brutus, " the art of logic." " You suppose very rightly," answered I ; " but he added to it an extensive acquaintance with polite literature, and an elegant manner of expressing himself, as is sufficiently evident from the incomparable writings he has left behind him. And as he attached himself, for the improvement of his eloquence, to Lucius Lucilius Balbus and Caius Aquilius Gallus, two very able speakers, he effectually thwarted the prompt celerity of the latter (though a keen, experienced man) both in supporting and refuting a charge, by his accuracy and precision, and overpowered the deliberate formality of Balbus (a man of great learning and erudition) by his adroit and dexterous method of arguing; so that he equally possessed the good qualities of both, without their defects. As Crassus, therefore, in my mind, acted more prudently than Scævola (for the latter was very fond of pleading causes, in which he was certainly inferior to Crassus; whereas the former never engaged himself in an unequal competition with Scævola, by assuming the character of a civilian), so Servius pursued a plan which sufficiently discovered his wisdom; for as the profession of a pleader and a lawyer are both of them held in great esteem, and give those who are masters of them the most extensive influence among their fellow-citizens, he acquired an undisputed superiority in the one, and improved himself as much in the other as was necessary to support the authority of the civil law, and promote him to the dignity of consul." "This is precisely the opinion I had formed of him," said Brutus. "For a few years ago I heard him often, and very attentively, at Samos, when I wanted to be instructed by him in the pontifical law, as far as it is connected with the civil; and I am now greatly confirmed in my opinion of him, by finding that it coincides so exactly with yours. I am likewise not a little pleased to observe that the equality of your ages, your sharing the same honors and preferments, and the affinity of your respective studies and professions, has been so far from precipitating either of you into that envious detraction of the other's merit, which most people are tormented with, that, instead of interrupting your mutual friendship, it has only served to increase and strengthen it; for, to my own knowledge, he had the same affection for, and the same favorable sentiments of *you*, which I now discover in you toward *him*. I can not, therefore, help regretting very sincerely that the Roman state has so long been deprived of the benefit of his advice and of your eloquence; a circumstance which is indeed calamitous enough in itself, but must appear much more so to him who considers into what hands that once respectable authority has been of late, I will not say transferred, but forcibly wrested." "You certainly forget," said Atticus, "that I proposed, when we began the conversation, to drop all matters of state; by all means, therefore, let us keep to our plan ; for if we once begin to repeat our grievances, there will be no end, I need not say to our inquiries, but to our sighs and lamentations."

XLIII. " Let us proceed, then," said I, " without any farther digression, and pursue the plan we set out upon. Crassus (for he is the orator we were just speaking of) always came into the forum ready prepared for the combat. He was expected with impatience, and heard with pleasure. When he first began his oration (which he always did in a very accurate style), he seemed worthy of the great expectations he had raised. He was very moderate in the movements of his body, had no remarkable variation of voice, never advanced from the ground he stood upon, and seldom stamped his foot ; his language was forcible, and sometimes warm and pathetic ; he had many strokes of humor, which were always tempered with a becoming dignity ; and, what is difficult to attain, he was at once very florid and very concise. In a close contest, he never met with his equal ; and there was scarcely any kind of causes in which he had not signalized his abilities ; so that he enrolled himself very early among the first orators of the time. He accused Caius Carbo, though a man of great eloquence, when he was but a youth ; and displayed his talents in such a manner, that they were not only applauded, but admired by every body. He afterward defended the virgin Licinia, when he was only twenty-seven years of age ; on which occasion he discovered an uncommon share of eloquence, as is evident from those parts of his oration which he left behind him in writing. As he was then desirous to have the honor of settling the colony of Narbonne (as he afterward did), he thought it advisable to recommend himself by undertaking the management of some popular cause. His oration in support of the act which was proposed for that purpose is still extant, and discovers a greater maturity of genius than might have been expected at that time of life. He afterward pleaded many other causes ; but his tribuneship was so remarkably silent, that if he had not supped with Granius the beadle when he enjoyed that office (a circumstance which has been twice mentioned by Lucilius), we should scarcely have known that a tribune of that name had existed." " I believe so," replied Brutus ; " but I have heard as little of the tribuneship of Scævola, though I must naturally suppose that he was the colleague of Crassus." "He was so," said I, "in all his other preferments; but he was not tribune till the year after him; and when he sat in the rostrum in that capacity, Crassus spoke in support of the Servilian law. I must observe, however, that Crassus had not Scævola for his colleague in the censorship, for none of the Scævolas ever solicited that office. But when the last-mentioned oration of Crassus was published (which I dare say you have frequently read), he was thirty-four years of age, which was exactly the difference between his age and mine. For he supported the law I have just been speaking of, in the very consulship under which I was born; whereas he himself was born in the consulship of Quintus Cæpio and Caius Lælius, about three years later than Antonius. I have particularly noticed this circumstance, to specify the time when the Roman eloquence attained its first *maturity*, and was actually carried to such a degree of perfection as to leave no room for any one to carry it higher, unless by the assistance of a more complete and extensive knowledge of philosophy, jurisprudence, and history."

XLIV. "But does there," said Brutus, "or will there ever exist a man, who is furnished with all the united accomplishments you require?" "I really do not know," said I; "but we have a speech made by Crassus in his consulship in praise of Quintus Cæpio, intermingled with a defense of his conduct, which, though a short one if we consider it as an oration, is not so as a panegyric; and another, which was his last, and which he spoke in the forty-eighth year of his age, at the time he was censor. In these we have the genuine complexion of eloquence, without any painting or disguise; but his periods (I mean those of Crassus) were generally short and concise; and he was fond of expressing himself in those minuter sentences, or members, which the Greeks call *colons*." "As you have spoken so largely," said Brutus, "in praise of the two last-mentioned orators, I heartily wish that Antonius had left us some other specimen of his abilities than his trifling essay on the art of speaking, and Crassus more than he has; by so doing, they would have transmitted their fame to posterity, and to us a valuable system of eloquence. For as to the elegant language of Scævola, we have sufficient proofs of it in the orations he has left behind him." "For my part," said I, "the oration I was speaking of, on Cæpio's case, has been a model which served to instruct me from my very childhood. It supports the dignity of the senate, which was deeply interested in the debate, and excites the jealousy of the audience against the party of the judges and accusers, whose powers it was necessary to expose in the most popular terms. Many parts of it are very strong and nervous; many others very cool and composed; and some are distinguished by the asperity of their language, and not a few by their wit and pleasantry; but much more was said than was committed to writing, as is sufficiently evident from several heads of the oration, which are merely proposed without any enlargement or explanation. But the oration in his censorship against his colleague Cneius Domitius is not so much an oration as an analysis of the subject, or a general sketch of what he had said, with here and there a few ornamental touches, by way of specimen; for no contest was ever conducted with greater spirit than this. Crassus, however, was eminently distinguished by the popular turn of his language; but that of Antonius was better adapted to judicial trials than to a public debate.

XLV. "As we have had occasion to mention him, Domitius himself must not be left unnoticed; for, though he is not enrolled in the list of orators, he had a sufficient share, both of utterance and genius, to support his character as a magistrate and his dignity as a consul. I might likewise observe of Caius Cælius that he was a man of great application and many eminent qualities, and had eloquence enough to support the private interests of his friends, and his own dignity in the state. At the same time lived Marcus Herennius, who was reckoned among the middling orators, whose principal merit was the purity and correctness of their language; and yet, in a suit for the consulship, he got the better of Lucius Philippus, a man of the first rank and family, and of the most extensive connections, and who was likewise a member of the college, and a very eloquent speaker. Then also lived Caius Clodius, who, besides his consequence as a nobleman of the first distinction and a man of the most powerful influence, was likewise possessed of a moderate share of eloquence. Nearly of the same age was Caius Titius, a Roman knight, who, in my judgment, arrived at as high a degree of perfection as a Roman orator was able to do, without the assist-

ance of the Grecian literature, and a good share of practice.
His orations have so many delicate turns, such a number of
well-chosen examples, and such an agreeable vein of politeness, that they almost seem to have been composed in the
true Attic style. He likewise transferred his delicacies into
his tragedies, with ingenuity enough, I confess, but not in the
tragic taste. But the poet Lucius Afranius, whom he studiously imitated, was a very lively writer, and, as you well know,
possessed great dramatic eloquence. Quintus Rubrius Varro,
who with Caius Marius was declared an enemy by the senate,
was likewise a warm and very spirited prosecutor. My relation, Marcus Gratidius, was a plausible speaker of the same
kind, well versed in Grecian literature, formed by nature for
the profession of eloquence, and an intimate acquaintance of
Marcus Antonius ; he commanded under him in Cilicia, where
he lost his life ; and he once commenced a prosecution against
Caius Fimbria, the father of Marcus Marius Gratidianus.

XLVI. "There have likewise been several among the allies, and the Latins, who were esteemed good orators ; as, for
instance, Quintus Vettius of Vettium, one of the Marsi, whom
I myself was acquainted with, a man of sense, and a concise speaker ; the Valerii, Quintus and Decimus, of Sora, my
neighbors and acquaintances, who were not so remarkable for
their talent in speaking, as for their skill both in Greek and
Roman literature ; and Caius Rusticellus of Bononia, an experienced orator, and a man of great natural volubility. But
the most eloquent of all those who were not citizens of Rome
was Tiberius Betucius Barrus of Asculum, some of whose orations, which were spoken in that city, are still extant ; that
which he made at Rome against Cæpio is really excellent ;
the speech which Cæpio delivered in answer to it, was made
by Ælius, who composed a number of orations, but pronounced
none himself. But among those of a remoter date, Lucius
Papirius of Fregellæ in Latium, who was almost contemporary
with Tiberius Gracchus, was universally esteemed the most
eloquent ; we have a speech of his in vindication of the Fre-
gellans and the Latin colonies, which was delivered before the
senate." "And what then is the merit," said Brutus, "which
you mean to ascribe to these provincial orators ?" "What
else," replied I, "but the very same which I have ascribed to
the city orators, excepting that their language is not tinctured

with the same fashionable delicacy." "What fashionable delicacy do you mean?" said he. "I can not," said I, "pretend to define it; I only know that there is such a quality existing. When you go to your province in Gaul, you will be convinced of it. You will there find many expressions which are not current in Rome; but these may be easily changed and corrected. But, what is of greater importance, our orators have a particular accent in their manner of pronouncing, which is more elegant, and has a more agreeable effect than any other. This, however, is not peculiar to the orators, but is equally common to every well-bred citizen. I myself remember that Titus Tincas, of Placentia, who was a very facetious man, once engaged in raillery with my old friend Quintus Granius, the public crier." "Do you mean that Granius," said Brutus, "of whom Lucilius has related such a number of stories?" "The very same," said I; "but, though Tincas said as many smart things as the other, Granius at last overpowered him by a certain vernacular *goût*, which gave an additional relish to his humor; so that I am no longer surprised at what is said to have happened to Theophrastus, when he inquired of an old woman who kept a stall, what was the price of something which he wanted to purchase. After telling him the value of it, 'Honest *stranger*,' said she, 'I can not afford it for less;' an answer which nettled him not a little, to think that *he* who had resided almost all his life at Athens, and spoke the language very correctly, should be taken at last for a foreigner. In the same manner, there is, in my opinion, a certain accent as peculiar to the native citizens of Rome, as the other was to those of Athens. But it is time for us to return home; I mean, to the orators of our own growth.

XLVII. "Next, therefore, to the two capital speakers above mentioned (that is, Crassus and Antonius) came Lucius Philippus—not, indeed, till a considerable time afterward; but still he must be reckoned the next. I do not mean, however, though nobody appeared in the interim who could dispute the prize with him, that he was entitled to the second, or even the third post of honor. For as in a chariot-race I can not properly consider *him* as either the second or third winner who has scarcely got clear of the starting-post before the first has reached the goal ; so, among orators, I can scarcely honor him with the name of a competitor who has been so far distanced by the foremost as hardly to appear on the same ground with him. But yet there were certainly some talents to be observed in Philippus, which any person who considers them, without subjecting them to a comparison with the superior merits of the two before mentioned, must allow to have been respectable. He had an uncommon freedom of address, a large fund of humor, great facility in the invention of his sentiments, and a ready and easy manner of expressing them. He was likewise, for the time he lived in, a great adept in the literature of the Greeks ; and, in the heat of a debate, he could sting and lash, as well as ridicule his opponents. Almost contemporary with these was Lucius Gellius, who was not so much to be valued for his positive as for his negative merits ; for he was neither destitute of learning, nor invention, nor unacquainted with the history and the laws of his country ; besides which, he had a tolerable freedom of expression. But he happened to live at a time when many excellent orators made their appearance ; and yet he served his friends upon many occasions to good purpose ; in short, his life was so long, that he was successively contemporary with a variety of orators of different periods, and had an extensive series of practice in judicial causes. Nearly at the same time lived Decimus Brutus, who was fellow-consul with Mamercus, and was equally skilled both in the Grecian and Roman literature. Lucius Scipio likewise was not an unskillful speaker ; and Cnæus Pompeius, the son of Sextus, had some reputation as an orator ; for his brother Sextus applied the excellent genius he was possessed of to acquire a thorough knowledge of the civil law, and a complete acquaintance with geometry and the doctrine of the Stoics. A little before these, Marcus Brutus, and very soon after him Caius Bilienus, who was a man of great natural capacity, made themselves, by nearly the same application, equally eminent in the profession of the law ; the latter would have been chosen consul if he had not been thwarted by the repeated promotion of Marius, and some other collateral embarrassments which attended his suit. But the eloquence of Cnæus Octavius, which was wholly unknown before his elevation to the consulship, was effectually displayed, after his preferment to that office, in a great variety of speeches. It is, however, time for us to drop those who were only classed in the number of good *speakers*, and turn our attention to such as were really *orators*."

"I think so too," replied Atticus; "for I understood that you meant to give us an account, not of those who took great pains to be eloquent, but of those who were so in reality."

XLVIII. "Caius Julius then," said I, "(the son of Lucius), was certainly superior, not only to his predecessors, but to all his contemporaries, in wit and humor; he was not, indeed, a nervous and striking orator, but, in the elegance, the pleasantry, and the agreeableness of his manner, he has not been excelled by any man. There are some orations of his still extant, in which, as well as in his tragedies, we may discover a pleasing tranquillity of expression with very little energy. Publius Cethegus, his equal in age, had always enough to say on matters of civil regulation; for he had studied and comprehended them with the minutest accuracy, by which means he acquired an equal authority in the senate with those who had served the office of consul, and, though he made no figure in a public debate, he was a serviceable veteran in any suit of a private nature. Quintus Lucretius Vispillo was an acute speaker, and a good civilian in the same kind of causes; but Osella was better qualified for a public harangue than to conduct a judicial process. Titus Annius Velina was likewise a man of sense, and a tolerable pleader; and Titus Juventius had a great deal of practice in the same way: the latter, indeed, was rather too heavy and inanimate, but at the same time was keen and artful, and knew how to seize every advantage which was offered by his antagonist; to which we may add, that he was far from being a man of no literature, but had an extensive knowledge of the civil law. His scholar, Publius Orbius, who was almost contemporary with me, had no great practice as a pleader; but his skill in the civil law was in no respect inferior to his master's. As to Titus Aufidius, who lived to a great age, he was a professed imitator of both, and was, indeed, a worthy inoffensive man; but he seldom spoke at the bar. His brother, Marcus Virgilius, who, when he was a tribune of the people, commenced a prosecution against Lucius Sylla, then advanced to the rank of general, had as little practice as Aufidius. Virgilius's colleague, Publius Magius, was more copious and diffusive. But

of all the orators, or rather *ranters*, I ever knew, who were
totally illiterate and unpolished, and (I might have added) absolutely coarse and rustic, the readiest and keenest were Quintus Sertorius, and Caius Gorgonius, the one of consular, and
the other of equestrian rank. Titus Junius (the son of Lucius), who had served the office of tribune, and prosecuted and
convicted Publius Sextius of bribery, when he was prætor
elect, was a prompt and an easy speaker; he lived in great
splendor, and had a very promising genius; and, if he had
not been of a weak, and indeed a sickly constitution, he
would have advanced much farther than he did in the road
to preferment.

XLIX. "I am sensible, however, that in the account I
have been giving, I have included many who were neither
real nor reputed orators, and that I have omitted others,
among those of a remoter date, who well deserved not only to
have been mentioned, but to be recorded with honor. But
this I was forced to do for want of better information; for
what could I say concerning men of a distant age, none of
whose productions are now remaining, and of whom no mention is made in the writings of other people? But I have
omitted none of those who have fallen within the compass of
my own knowledge, or that I myself remember to have heard.
For I wish to make it appear, that in such a powerful and
ancient republic as ours, in which the greatest rewards have
been proposed to eloquence, though all have desired to be
good speakers, not many have attempted the task, and but
very few have succeeded. But I shall give my opinion of
every one in such explicit terms, that it may be easily understood whom I consider as a mere declaimer, and whom as an
orator. About the same time, or rather something later than
the above-mentioned Julius, but almost contemporary with
each other, were Caius Cotta, Publius Sulpicius, Quintus
Varius, Cnæus Pomponius, Caius Curio, Lucius Fufius, Marcus Drusus, and Publius Antistius; for no age whatsoever
has been distinguished by a more numerous progeny of orators. Of these, Cotta and Sulpicius, both in my opinion and
in that of the public at large, had an evident claim to the
preference." "But wherefore," interrupted Atticus, "do you
say, *in your own opinion, and in that of the public at large?*
In deciding the merits of an orator, does the opinion of the

vulgar, think you, always coincide with that of the learned? Or, rather, does not one receive the approbation of the populace, while another of a quite opposite character is preferred by those who are better qualified to give their judgment?" " You have started a very pertinent question," said I, " but, perhaps, *the public at large* will not approve my answer to it." " And what concern need *that* give you," replied Atticus, " if it meets the approbation of Brutus?"   " Very true," said I; " for I had rather my *sentiments* on the qualifications of an orator should please you and Brutus, than all the world besides; but as to my *eloquence,* I should wish *this* to please every one.   For he who speaks in such a manner as to please the people, must inevitably receive the approbation of the learned.   As to the truth and propriety of what I hear, I am indeed to judge of this for myself, as well as I am able; but the general merit of an orator must and will be decided by the effects which his eloquence produces.   For (in my opinion at least) there are three things which an orator should be able to effect; viz., to *inform* his hearers, to *please* them, and to *move their passions.*   By what qualities in the speaker each of these effects may be produced, or by what deficiencies they are either lost, or but imperfectly performed, is an inquiry which none but an artist can resolve; but whether an audience is really so affected by an orator as shall best answer his purpose, must be left to their own feelings, and the decision of the public.   The learned therefore, and the people at large, have never disagreed about who was a good orator, and who was otherwise.

L. " For do you suppose that while the speakers above mentioned were in being, they had not the same degree of reputation among the learned as among the populace?   If you had inquired of one of the latter *who was the most eloquent man in the city,* he might have hesitated whether to say *Antonius* or *Crassus;* or this man, perhaps, would have mentioned the one, and that the other.   But would any one have given the preference to *Philippus,* though otherwise a smooth, a sensible, and a facetious speaker?—that *Philippus* whom we, who form our judgment upon these matters by rules of art, have decided to have been the next in merit?   Nobody would, I am certain.   For it is the invariable prerogative of an accomplished orator, to be reckoned such in the opinion of the people. Though Antigenidas, therefore, the musician, might say to his scholar, who was but coldly received by the public, *Play on, to please me and the Muses;* I shall say to my friend Brutus, when he mounts the rostra, as he frequently does, *Play to me and the people;* that those who hear him may be sensible of the *effect* of his eloquence, while I can likewise amuse myself with remarking the *causes* which produce it. When a citizen hears an able orator, he readily credits what is said; he imagines every thing to be true, he believes and relishes the force of it; and, in short, the persuasive language of the speaker wins his absolute, his hearty assent.   You, who are possessed of a critical knowledge of the art, what more will you require?   The listening multitude is charmed and captivated by the force of his eloquence, and feels a pleasure which is not to be resisted.   What here can you find to censure?   The whole audience is either flushed with joy, or overwhelmed with grief; it smiles or weeps, it loves or hates, it scorns or envies, and, in short, is alternately seized with the various emotions of pity, shame, remorse, resentment, wonder, hope, and fear, according as it is influenced by the language, the sentiments, and the action of the speaker.   In this case, what necessity is there to await the sanction of a critic?   For here, whatever is approved by the feelings of the people, must be equally so by men of taste and erudition; and, in this instance of public decision, there can be no disagreement between the opinion of the vulgar and that of the learned.   For, though many good speakers have appeared in every species of oratory, which of them who was thought to excel the rest in the judgment of the populace was not approved as such by every man of learning? or which of our ancestors, when the choice of a pleader was left to his own option, did not immediately fix it either upon Crassus or Antonius?   There were certainly many others to be had; but, though any person might have hesitated to which of the above two he should give the preference, there was nobody, I believe, who would have made choice of a third.   And in the time of my youth, when Cotta and Hortensius were in such high reputation, who, that had liberty to choose for himself, would have employed any other?"

LI. "But what occasion is there," said Brutus, "to quote the example of other speakers to support your assertion?

have we not seen what has always been the wish of the defendant, and what the judgment of Hortensius, concerning yourself? for whenever the latter shared a cause with you (and I was often present on those occasions), the peroration, which requires the greatest exertion of the powers of eloquence, was constantly left to *you*." "It was," said I; "and Hortensius (induced, I suppose, by the warmth of his friendship) always resigned the post of honor to *me*. But, as to myself, what rank I hold in the opinion of the people I am unable to determine; as to others, however, I may safely assert, that such of them as were reckoned most eloquent in the judgment of the vulgar, were equally high in the estimation of the learned. For even Demosthenes himself could not have said what is related of Antimachus, a poet of Claros, who, when he was rehearsing to an audience, assembled for the purpose, that voluminous piece of his which you are well acquainted with, and was deserted by all his hearers except Plato, in the midst of his performance, cried out, *I shall proceed notwithstanding; for Plato alone is of more consequence to me than many thousands.* The remark was very just. For an abstruse poem, such as his, only requires the approbation of the judicious few, but a discourse intended for the people should be perfectly suited to their taste. If Demosthenes, therefore, after being deserted by the rest of his audience, had even Plato left to hear him, and no one else, I will answer for it, he could not have uttered another syllable. Nor could you yourself, my Brutus, if the whole assembly were to leave you, as it once did Curio?" "To open my whole mind to you," replied he, "I must confess that even in such causes as fall under the cognizance of a few select judges, and not of the people at large, if I were to be deserted by the casual crowd who came to hear the trial, I should not be able to proceed." "The case, then, is plainly this," said I; "as a flute, which will not return its proper sound when it is applied to the lips, would be laid aside by the musician as useless, so the ears of the people are the instrument upon which an orator is to play; and if these refuse to admit the breath he bestows upon them, or if the hearer, like a restive horse, will not obey the spur, the speaker must cease to exert himself any farther.

LII. "There is, however, this exception to be made; the

people sometimes give their approbation to an orator who does not deserve it. But even here they approve what they have had no opportunity of comparing with something better; as, for instance, when they are pleased with an indifferent, or, perhaps, a bad speaker. His abilities satisfy their expectation; they have seen nothing preferable; and, therefore, the merit of the day, whatever it may happen to be, meets their full applause. For even a middling orator, if he is possessed of any degree of eloquence, will always captivate the ear; and the order and beauty of a good discourse has an astonishing effect upon the human mind. Accordingly, what common hearer who was present when Quintus Scævola pleaded for Mucius Coponius, in the cause above mentioned, would have wished for, or indeed thought it possible to find any thing which was more correct, more elegant, or more complete? When he attempted to prove, that, as Mucius Curius was left heir to the estate only in case of the death of his future ward before he came of age, he could not possibly be a legal heir, when the expected ward was never born; what did he leave unsaid of the scrupulous regard which should be paid to the literal meaning of every testament? what of the accuracy and preciseness of the old and established forms of law? and how carefully did he specify the manner in which the will would have been expressed, if it had intended that Curius should be the heir in case of a total default of issue? in what a masterly manner did he represent the ill consequences to the public if the letter of a will should be disregarded, its intention decided by arbitrary conjectures, and the written bequests of plain illiterate men left to the artful interpretation of a pleader? how often did he urge the authority of his father, who had always been an advocate for a strict adherence to the letter of a testament? and with what emphasis did he enlarge upon the necessity of supporting the common forms of law? All which particulars he discussed not only with great art and ingenuity, but in such a neat, such a close, and, I may add, in so florid and so elegant a style, that there was not a single person among the common part of the audience who could expect any thing more complete, or even think it possible to exist.

LIII. "But when Crassus, who spoke on the opposite side, began with the story of a notable youth, who, having found an oar-niche of a boat as he was rambling along the shore, took it into his head that he would build a boat to it; and when he applied the tale to Scævola, who, from the *oar-niche* of an argument [which he had deduced from certain imaginary ill consequences to the public], represented the decision of a private will to be a matter of such importance as to deserve the attention of the *centumviri;* when Crassus, I say, in the beginning of his discourse, had thus taken off the edge of the strongest plea of his antagonist, he entertained his hearers with many other turns of a similar kind, and in a short time changed the serious apprehensions of all who were present into open mirth and good-humor, which is one of those three 'effects which I have just observed an orator should be able to produce. He then proceeded to remark that it was evidently the intention and the will of the testator, that in case, either by death, or default of issue, there should happen to be no son to fall to his charge, the inheritance should devolve to Curius; that most people in a similar case would express themselves in the same manner, and that it would certainly stand good in law, and always had. By these, and many other observations of the same kind, he gained the assent of his hearers, which is another of the three duties of an orator. Lastly, he supported, at all events, the true meaning and spirit of a will, against the literal construction; justly observing, that there would be an endless caviling about words, not only in wills, but in all other legal deeds, if the real intention of the party were to be disregarded, and hinting very smartly that his friend Scævola had assumed a most unwarrantable degree of importance, if no person must afterward presume to indite a legacy but in the musty form which he himself might please to prescribe. As he enlarged on each of these arguments with great force and propriety, supported them by a number of precedents, exhibited them in a variety of views, and enlivened them with many occasional turns of wit and pleasantry, he gained so much applause, and gave such general satisfaction, that it was scarcely remembered that any thing had been said on the contrary side of the question. This was the third, and the most important duty we assigned to an orator. Here, if one of the people were to be judge, the same person who had heard the first speaker with a degree of admiration, would, on hearing the second, despise himself for his former want of judgment;

whereas a man of taste and erudition, on hearing Scævola, would have observed that he was really master of a rich and ornamental style; but if, on comparing the manner in which each of them concluded his cause, it was to be inquired which of the two was the best orator, the decision of the man of learning would not have differed from that of the vulgar.

LIV. "What advantage, then, it will be said, has the skillful critic over the illiterate hearer? A great and very important advantage; if it is, indeed, a matter of any consequence to be able to discover by what means that which is the true and real end of speaking is either obtained or lost. He has likewise this additional superiority, that when two or more orators, as has frequently happened, have shared the applauses of the public, he can judge, on a careful observation of the principal merits of each, what is the most perfect character of eloquence, since whatever does not meet the approbation of the people must be equally condemned by a more intelligent hearer. For as it is easily understood by the sound of a harp, whether the strings are skillfully touched; so it may likewise be discovered from the manner in which the passions of an audience are affected, how far the speaker is able to command them. A man, therefore, who is a real connoisseur in the art, can sometimes, by a single glance, as he passes through the forum, and without stopping to listen attentively to what is said, form a tolerable judgment of the ability of the speaker. When he observes any of the bench either yawning, or speaking to the person who is next to him, or looking carelessly about him, or sending to inquire the time of day, or teazing the quæsitor to dismiss the court, he concludes very naturally that the cause upon trial is not pleaded by an orator who understands how to apply the powers of language to the passions of the judges, as a skillful musician applies his fingers to the harp. On the other hand, if, as he passes by, he beholds the judges looking attentively before them, as if they were either receiving some material information, or visibly approved what they had already heard; if he sees them listening to the voice of the pleader with a kind of ecstasy, like a fond bird to some melodious tune; and, above all, if he discovers in their looks any strong indications of pity, abhorrence, or any other emotion of the mind; though he should not be near enough to hear a single word, he imme diately discovers that the cause is managed by a real orator, who is either performing, or has already played his part to good purpose."

LV. After I had concluded these digressive remarks, my two friends were kind enough to signify their approbation, and I resumed my subject. "As this digression," said I, "took its rise from Cotta and Sulpicius, whom I mentioned as the two most approved orators of the age they lived in, I shall first return to *them*, and afterward notice the rest in their proper order, according to the plan we began upon. I have already observed that there are two classes of *good* orators (for we have no concern with any others), of which the former are distinguished by the simple neatness and brevity of their language, and the latter by their copious dignity and elevation; but although the preference must always be given to that which is great and striking; yet, in speakers of real merit, whatever is most perfect of the kind is justly entitled to our commendation. It must, however, be observed, that the close and simple orator should be careful not to sink into a dryness and poverty of expression; while, on the other hand, the copious and more stately speaker should be equally on his guard against a swelling and empty parade of words. To begin with Cotta, he had a ready, quick invention, and spoke correctly and freely; and as he very prudently avoided every forcible exertion of his voice, on account of the weakness of his lungs, so his language was equally adapted to the delicacy of his constitution. There was nothing in his style but what was neat, compact, and healthy; and (what may justly be considered as his greatest excellence) though he was scarcely able, and therefore never attempted to force the passions of the judges by a strong and spirited elocution, yet he managed them so artfully, that the gentle emotions he raised in them answered exactly the same purpose, and produced the same effect, as the violent ones which were excited by Sulpicius; for Sulpicius was really the most striking, and, if I may be allowed the expression, the most tragical orator I ever heard; his voice was strong and sonorous, and yet sweet and flowing; his gesture and his deportment were graceful and ornamental, but in such a style as to appear to have been formed for the forum, and not for the stage; and his language, though rapid and voluble, was neither loose nor

exuberant. He was a professed imitator of Crassus, while
Cotta chose Antonius for his model; but the latter wanted
the force of Antonius, and the former the agreeable humor of
Crassus."

"How extremely difficult, then," said Brutus, "must be
the art of speaking, when such consummate orators as these
were each of them destitute of one of its principal beauties !"
LVI. "We may likewise observe," said I, "in the present instance, that two orators may have the highest degree of merit, who are totally unlike each other; for none could be more
so than Cotta and Sulpicius, and yet both of them were far
superior to any of their contemporaries. It is therefore the
business of every intelligent master to notice what is the natural bent of his pupil's capacity, and taking that for his guide,
to imitate the conduct of Isocrates with his two scholars
Theopompus and Ephorus, who, after remarking the lively
genius of the former, and the mild and timid bashfulness of
the latter, is reported to have said that he applied a spur to
the one and a curb to the other. The orations now extant,
which bear the name of Sulpicius, are supposed to have been
written after his decease by my contemporary Publius Canu-
tius, a man, indeed, of inferior rank, but who, in my mind,
had a great command of language. But we have not a single
speech of Sulpicius that was really his own; for I have often
heard him say that he neither had, nor ever could commit
any thing of the kind to writing. And as to Cotta's speech
in defense of himself, called a vindication of the Varian law,
it was composed, at his own request, by Lucius Ælius. This
Ælius was a man of merit, and a very worthy Roman knight,
who was thoroughly versed in Greek and Roman literature.
He had likewise a critical knowledge of the antiquities of his
country, both as to the date and particulars of every new improvement, and every memorable transaction, and was perfectly well read in the ancient writers; a branch of learning
in which he was succeeded by our friend Varro, a man of
genius, and of the most extensive erudition, who afterward
enlarged the plan by many valuable collections of his own,
and gave a much fuller and more elegant system of it to the
public; for Ælius himself chose to assume the character of a
Stoic, and neither aimed to be, nor ever was an orator; but
he composed several orations for other people to pronounce,

as for Quintus Metellus, Fabius Quintus Cæpio, and Quintus Pompeius Rufus; though the latter composed those speeches himself which he spoke in his own defense, but not without the assistance of Ælius. For I myself was present at the writing of them, in the younger part of my life, when I used to attend Ælius for the benefit of his instructions. But I am surprised that Cotta, who was really an excellent orator, and a man of good learning, should be willing that the trifling speeches of Ælius should be published to the world as *his*.

LVII. "To the two above mentioned no third person of the same age was esteemed an equal; Pomponius, however, was a speaker much to my taste, or, at least, I have very little fault to find with him. But there was no employment for any in capital causes, excepting for those I have already mentioned; because Antonius, who was always courted on these occasions, was very ready to give his service; and Crassus, though not so compliable, generally consented, on any pressing solicitation, to give *his*. Those who had not interest enough to engage either of these, commonly applied to Philippus or Cæsar; but when Cotta and Sulpicius were at liberty, they generally had the preference; so that all the causes in which any honor was to be acquired were pleaded by these six orators. We may add, that trials were not so frequent then as they are at present, neither did people employ, as they do now, several pleaders on the same side of the question; a practice which is attended with many disadvantages. For hereby we are often obliged to speak in reply to those whom we had not an opportunity of hearing; in which case, what has been alleged on the opposite side is often represented to us either falsely or imperfectly; and besides, it is a very material circumstance, that I myself should be present to see with what countenance my antagonist supports his allegations, and, still more so, to observe the effect of every part of his discourse upon the audience. And as every defense should be conducted upon one uniform plan, nothing can be more improperly contrived than to recommence it by assigning the peroration, or pathetical part of it, to a second advocate. For every cause can have but one natural introduction and conclusion, and all the other parts of it, like the members of an animal body, will best retain their proper strength and beauty when they are regularly disposed and connected. We may add, that, as it is very difficult in a single oration of any length to avoid saying something which does not comport with the rest of it só well as it ought to do, how much more difficult must it be to contrive that nothing shall be said which does not tally exactly with the speech of another person who has spoken before you? But as it certainly requires more labor to plead a whole cause than only a part of it, and as many advantageous connections are formed by assisting in a suit in which several persons are interested, the custom, however preposterous in itself, has been readily adopted.

LVIII. "There were some, however, who esteemed Curio the third best orator of the age; perhaps because his language was brilliant and pompous, and because he had a habit (for which I suppose he was indebted to his domestic education) of expressing himself with tolerable correctness; for he was a man of very little learning. But it is a circumstance of great importance what sort of people we are used to converse with at home, especially in the more early part of life, and what sort of language we have been accustomed to hear from our tutors and parents, not excepting the mother. We have all read the letters of Cornelia, the mother of the Gracchi, and are satisfied that her sons were not so much nurtured in their mother's lap, as in the elegance and purity of her language. I have often, too, enjoyed the agreeable conversation of Lælia, the daughter of Caius, and observed in her a strong tincture of her father's elegance. I have likewise conversed with his two daughters, the Muciæ, and his grand-daughters, the two Liciniæ, with one of whom (the wife of Scipio) you, my Brutus, I believe, have sometimes been in company." "I have," replied he, "and was much pleased with her conversation; and the more so, because she was the daughter of Crassus." "And what think you," said I, "of Crassus, the son of that Licinia, who was adopted by Crassus in his will?" "He is said," replied he, "to have been a man of great genius; and the Scipio you have mentioned, who was my colleague, likewise appears to me to have been a good speaker and an elegant companion." "Your opinion, my Brutus," said I, "is very just. For this family, if I may be allowed the expression, seems to have been the offspring of wisdom. As to their two grandfathers, Scipio and Crassus, we have taken notice of them already, as we also have of their great-grandfathers, Quintus Metellus, who had four sons; Publius Scipio, who, when a private citizen, rescued the republic from the arbitrary influence of Tiberius Gracchus; and Quintus Scævola, the augur, who was the ablest and most affable civilian of his time. And, lastly, how illustrious are the names of their next immediate progenitors, Publius Scipio, who was twice consul, and was called the darling of the people; and Caius Lælius, who was esteemed the wisest of men." "A generous stock indeed!" cried Brutus, "into which the wisdom of many has been successively ingrafted, like a number of scions on the same tree!"

LIX. "I have likewise a suspicion," replied I, "(if we may compare small things with great), that Curio's family, though he himself was left an orphan, was indebted to his father's instruction and good example for the habitual purity of their language; and so much the more, because, of all those who were held in any estimation for their eloquence, I never knew one who was so totally uninformed and unskilled in every branch of liberal science. He had not read a single poet or studied a single orator, and he knew little or nothing either of public, civil, or common law. We might say almost the same, indeed, of several others, and some of them very able orators, who (we know) were but little acquainted with these useful parts of knowledge; as, for instance, of Sulpicius and Antonius. But this deficiency was supplied in them by an elaborate knowledge of the art of speaking; and there was not one of them who was totally unqualified in any of the five[1] principal parts of which it is composed; for whenever this is the case (and it matters not in which of those parts it happens), it entirely incapacitates a man to shine as an orator. Some, however, excelled in one part, and some in another. Thus Antonius could readily invent such arguments as were most in point, and afterward digest and methodize them to the best advantage; and he could likewise retain the plan he had formed with great exactness; but his chief merit was the goodness of his delivery, in which he was justly allowed to excel. In some of these qualifications he was upon an equal footing with Crassus, and in others he was superior; but then the language of Crassus was indisputably preferable to *his*. In the same manner, it can not be said

[1] Invention, disposition, elocution, memory, and pronunciation.

that either Sulpicius or Cotta, or any other speaker of repute, was absolutely deficient in any one of the five parts of oratory. But we may justly infer from the example of Curio that nothing will more recommend an orator than a brilliant and ready flow of expression; for he was remarkably dull in the invention, and very loose and unconnected in the disposition of his arguments.

LX. "The two remaining parts are pronunciation and memory, in each of which he was so miserably defective as to excite the laughter and the ridicule of his hearers. His gesture was really such as Caius Julius represented it, in a severe sarcasm that will never be forgotten; for, as he was swaying and reeling his whole body from side to side, Julius facetiously inquired *who it was that was speaking from a boat?* To the same purpose was the jest of Cnæus Sicinius, a man very vulgar, but exceedingly humorous, which was the only qualification he had to recommend him as an orator. When this man, as tribune of the people, had summoned Curio and Octavius, who were then consuls, into the forum, and Curio had delivered a tedious harangue, while Octavius sat silently by him, wrapped up in flannels, and besmeared with ointments, to ease the pain of the gout; *Octavius*, said he, *you are infinitely obliged to your colleague; for if he had not tossed and flung himself about to-day in the manner he did, you would certainly have been devoured by the flies.* As to his memory, it was so extremely treacherous, that after he had divided his subject into three general heads, he would sometimes, in the course of speaking, either add a fourth, or omit the third. In a capital trial, in which I had pleaded for Titinia, the daughter of Cotta, when he attempted to reply to me in defense of Servius Nævius, he suddenly forgot every thing he intended to say, and attributed it to the pretended witchcraft and magic artifices of Titinia. These were undoubted proofs of the weakness of his memory. But, what is still more inexcusable, he sometimes forgot, even in his written treatises, what he had mentioned but a little before. Thus, in a book of his, in which he introduces himself as entering into conversation with our friend Pansa, and his son Curio, when he was walking home from the senate-house; the senate is supposed to have been summoned by Cæsar in his first consulship; and the whole conversation arises from the son's inquiry, what the house had resolved upon. Curio launches out into a long invective against the conduct of Cæsar, and, as is generally the custom in dialogues, the parties are engaged in a close dispute on the subject; but very unhappily, though the conversation commences at the breaking up of the senate which Cæsar held when he was first consul, the author censures those very actions of the same Cæsar, which did not happen till the next, and several other succeeding years of his government in Gaul."

LXI. "Is it possible, then," said Brutus, with an air of surprise, "that any man (and especially in a written performance) could be so forgetful as not to discover, upon a subsequent perusal of his own work, what an egregious blunder he had committed?" "Very true," said I; "for if he wrote with a design to discredit the measures which he represents in such an odious light, nothing could be more stupid than not to commence his dialogue at a period which was subsequent to those measures. But he so entirely forgets himself as to tell us that he did not choose to attend a senate which was held in one of Cæsar's future consulships, in the very same dialogue in which he introduces himself as returning home from a senate which was held in his first consulship. It can not, therefore, be wondered at, that he who was so remarkably defective in a faculty which is the handmaid of our other intellectual powers, as to forget, even in a written treatise, a material circumstance which he had mentioned but a little before, should find his memory fail him, as it generally did, in a sudden and unpremeditated harangue. It accordingly happened, though he had many connections, and was fond of speaking in public, that few causes were intrusted to his management. But, among his contemporaries, he was esteemed next in merit to the first orators of the age; and that merely, as I said before, for his good choice of words, and his uncommon readiness, and great fluency of expression. His orations, therefore, may deserve a cursory perusal. It is true, indeed, they are much too languid and spiritless; but they may yet be of service to enlarge and improve an accomplishment, of which he certainly had a moderate share; and which has so much force and efficacy, that it gave Curio the appearance and reputation of an orator without the assistance of any other good quality.

LXII. "But to return to our subject; Caius Carbo, of the same age, was likewise reckoned an orator of the second class; he was the son, indeed, of the truly eloquent man before mentioned, but was far from being an acute speaker himself; he was, however, esteemed an orator. His language was tolerably nervous, he spoke with ease; and there was an air of authority in his address that was perfectly natural. But Quintus Varius, was a man of quicker invention, and, at the same time, had an equal freedom of expression; besides which, he had a bold and spirited delivery, and a vein of elocution which was neither poor, nor coarse and vulgar; in short, you need not hesitate to pronounce him an *orator*. Cnæus Pomponius was a vehement, a rousing, and a fierce and eager speaker, and more inclined to act the part of a prosecutor than of an advocate. But far inferior to these was Lucius Fufius; though his application was, in some measure, rewarded by the success of his prosecution against Manius Aquilius. For as to Marcus Drusus, your great uncle, who spoke like an orator only upon matters of government; Lucius Lucullus, who was, indeed, an artful speaker, and your father, my Brutus, who was well acquainted with the common and civil law; Marcus Lucullus, and Marcus Octavius, the son of Cnæus, who was a man of so much authority and address as to procure the repeal of Sempronius's corn-act by the suffrages of a full assembly of the people; Cnæus Octavius, the son of Marcus; and Marcus Cato, the father, and Quintus Catulus, the son; we must excuse *these* (if I may so express myself) from the fatigues and dangers of the field—that is, from the management of judicial causes, and place them in garrison over the general interests of the republic, a duty to which they seem to have been sufficiently adequate. I should have assigned the same post to Quintus Cæpio if he had not been so violently attached to the equestrian order as to set himself at variance with the senate. I have also remarked that Cnæus Carbo, Marcus Marius, and several others of the same stamp, who would not have merited the attention of an audience that had any taste for elegance, were extremely well suited to address a tumultuous crowd. In the same class (if I may be allowed to interrupt the series of my narrative) Lucius Quintius lately made his appearance; though Palicanus, it must be owned, was still better adapted to please the ears of the populace. But, as I have mentioned this inferior kind of speakers, I must be so just to Lucius Apuleius Saturninus as to observe that, of all the factious declaimers since the time of the Gracchi, he was generally esteemed the ablest; and yet he caught the attention of the public more by his appearance, his gesture, and his dress, than by any real fluency of expression, or even a tolerable share of good sense. But Caius Servilius Glaucia, though the most abandoned wretch that ever existed, was very keen and artful, and excessively humorous; and, notwithstanding the meanness of his birth, and the depravity of his life, he would have been advanced to the dignity of a consul in his prætorship if it had been judged lawful to admit his suit; for the populace were entirely at his devotion, and he had secured the interest of the knights by an act he had procured in their favor. He was slain in the open forum, while he was prætor, on the same day as the tribune Saturninus, in the consulship of Marius and Flaccus; and bore a near resemblance to Hyperbolus, the Athenian, whose profligacy was so severely stigmatized in the old Attic comedies. These were succeeded by Sextus Titius, who was indeed a voluble speaker, and possessed a ready comprehension : but he was so loose and effeminate in his gesture as to furnish room for the invention of a dance, which was called the *Titian jig;* so careful should we be to avoid every peculiarity in our manner of speaking, which may afterward be exposed to ridicule by a ludicrous imitation.

LXIII. " But we have rambled back insensibly to a period which has been already examined; let us, therefore, return to that which we were reviewing a little before. Contemporary with Sulpicius was Publius Antistius, a plausible declaimer, who, after being silent for several years, and exposed (as he often was) not only to the contempt, but the derision of his hearers, first spoke with applause in his tribuneship in a real and very interesting protest against the illegal application of Caius Julius for the consulship; and that so much the more, because, though Sulpicius himself, who then happened to be his colleague, spoke on the same side of the debate, Antistius argued more copiously, and to better purpose. This raised his reputation so high, that many, and (soon afterward) every cause of importance, was eagerly recommended to his patronage. To speak the truth, he had a quick conception, a methodical judgment, and a retentive memory; and though his language was not much embellished, it was very far from being low. In short, his style was easy and flowing, and his appearance rather gentlemanly than otherwise; but his action was a little defective, partly through the disagreeable tone of his voice, and partly by a few ridiculous gestures, of which he could not entirely break himself. He flourished in the time between the flight and the return of Sylla, when the republic was deprived of a regular administration of justice, and of its former dignity and splendor. But the reception which he met with was the more favorable, as the forum was in a measure destitute of good orators; for Sulpicius was dead; Cotta and Curio were abroad; and no pleaders of eminence were left but Carbo and Pomponius, from each of whom he easily carried off the palm.

LXIV. "His nearest successor in the following age was Lucius Sisenna, who was a man of learning, had a taste for the liberal sciences, spoke the Roman language with accuracy, was well acquainted with the laws and constitution of his country, and had a tolerable share of wit; but he was not a speaker of any great application or extensive practice; and as he happened to live in the intermediate time between the appearance of Sulpicius and Hortensius, he was unable to equal the former, and forced to yield to the superior talents of the latter. We may easily form a judgment of his abilities from the historical works he has left behind him, which, though evidently preferable to any thing of the kind which had appeared before, may serve as a proof that he was far below the standard of perfection, and that this species of composition had not then been improved to any great degree of excellence among the Romans. But the genius of Quintus Hortensius, even in his early youth, like one of Phidias's statues, was no sooner beheld than it was universally admired! He spoke his first oration in the forum in the consulship of Lucius Crassus and Quintus Scævola, to whom it was personally addressed; and though he was then only nineteen years old, he descended from the rostra with the hearty approbation not only of the audience in general, but of the two consuls themselves, who were the most intelligent judges in the whole city. He died in the consulship of Lucius Paulus and

Caius Marcellus, from which it appears that he was four-and-forty years a pleader. We shall review his character more at large in the sequel ; but in this part of my history, I chose to include him in the number of orators who were rather of an earlier date. This, indeed, must necessarily happen to all whose lives are of any considerable length, for they are equally liable to a comparison with their elders and their juniors ; as in the case of the poet Attius, who says that both he and Pacuvius applied themselves to the cultivation of the drama under the same ædiles, though, at the time, the one was eighty, and the other only thirty years old. Thus Hortensius may be compared not only with those who were properly his contemporaries, but with me, and you, my Brutus, and with others of a prior date. For he began to speak in public while Crassus was living ; but his fame increased when he appeared as a joint advocate with Antonius and Philippus (at that time in the decline of life) in defense of Cnæus Pompeius —a cause in which (though a mere youth) he distinguished himself above the rest. He may therefore be included in the list of those whom I have placed in the time of Sulpicius ; but among his proper coevals, such as Marcus Piso, Marcus Crassus, Cnæus Lentulus, and Publius Lentulus Sura, he excelled beyond the reach of competition ; and after these he happened upon me, in the early part of my life (for I was eight years younger than himself), and spent a number of years with me in pursuit of the same forensic glory ; and at last (a little before his death), he once pleaded with *you*, in defense of Appius Claudius, as I have frequently done for others.

LXV. "Thus you see, my Brutus, I am come insensibly to *yourself*, though there was undoubtedly a great variety of orators between my first appearance in the forum and yours. But as I determined, when we began the conversation, to make no mention of those among them who are still living, to prevent your inquiring too minutely what is my opinion concerning each, I shall confine myself to such as are now no more." "That is not the true reason," said Brutus, "why you choose to be silent about the living." "What then do you suppose it to be?" said I. "You are only fearful," replied he, "that your remarks should afterward be mentioned by us in other company, and that by this means you should

expose yourself to the resentment of those whom you may not
think it worth your while to notice." "Indeed," answered I,
"I have not the least doubt of your secrecy." "Neither
have you any reason," said he ; " but, after all, I suppose you
had rather be silent *yourself* than rely upon *our* taciturnity."
"To confess the truth," replied I, "when I first entered upon
the subject, I never imagined that I should have extended
it to the age now before us; whereas I have been drawn
by a continued series of history among the moderns of latest
date." "Introduce, then," said he, "those intermediate orators you may think worthy of our notice, and afterward let
us return to yourself and Hortensius." "To Hortensius,"
replied I, " with all my heart ; but as to my *own* character, I
shall leave it to other people to examine, if they choose to
take the trouble." "I can by no means agree to *that*," said
he ; "for, though every part of the account you have favored
us with has entertained me very agreeably, it now begins to
seem tedious, because I am impatient to hear something of
yourself; I do not mean the wonderful qualities, but the *pro-
gressive steps*, and the advances of your eloquence ; for the
former are sufficiently known already both to *me* and the
whole world." "As you do not require me," said I, "to
sound the praises of my own genius, but only to describe my
labor and application to improve it, your request shall be
complied with. But, to preserve the order of my narrative,
I shall first introduce such other speakers as I think ought to
be previously noticed.

"And I shall begin with Marcus Crassus, who was contemporary with Hortensius. LXVI. With a tolerable share
of learning, and a very moderate capacity, his application, assiduity, and interest procured him a place among the ablest
pleaders of the time for several years. His language was
pure, his expression neither low nor vulgar, and his ideas well
digested ; but he had nothing in him that was florid and ornamental ; and the real ardor of his mind was not supported
by any vigorous exertion of his voice, so that he pronounced
almost every thing in the same uniform tone. His equal, and
professed antagonist, Caius Fimbria, was not able to maintain his character so long ; and though he always spoke with
a strong and elevated voice, and poured forth a rapid torrent
of well-chosen expressions, he was so immoderately vehement

that you might justly be surprised that the people should have been so absent and inattentive as to admit a *madman* like him into the list of orators. As to Cnæus Lentulus, his action acquired him a reputation for his eloquence very far beyond his real abilities; for though he was not a man of any great penetration (notwithstanding he carried the appearance of it in his countenance), nor possessed any real fluency of expression (though he was equally specious in this respect as in the former), yet by his sudden breaks and exclamations he affected such an ironical air of surprise, with a sweet and sonorous tone of voice, and his whole action was so warm and lively, that his defects were scarcely noticed; for as Curio acquired the reputation of an orator with no other quality than a tolerable freedom of elocution, so Cnæus Lentulus concealed the mediocrity of his other accomplishments by his *action*, which was really excellent. Much the same might be said of Publius Lentulus, whose poverty of invention and expression was secured from notice by the mere dignity of his presence, his correct and graceful gesture, and the strength and sweetness of his voice; and his merit depended so entirely upon his action, that he was more deficient in every other quality than his namesake.

LXVII. "But Marcus Piso derived all his talents from his erudition; for he was much better versed in Grecian literature than any of his predecessors. He had, however, a natural keenness of discernment, which he greatly improved by art, and exerted with great address and dexterity, though in very indifferent language; but he was frequently warm and choleric, sometimes cold and insipid, and now and then rather smart and humorous. He did not long support the fatigue and emulous contention of the forum, partly on account of the weakness of his constitution, and partly because he could not submit to the follies and impertinences of the common people (which we orators are forced to swallow), either, as it was generally supposed, from a peculiar moroseness of temper, or from a liberal and ingenuous pride of heart. After acquiring, therefore, in his youth, a tolerable degree of reputation, his character began to sink; but in the trial of the Vestals he again recovered it with some additional lustre, and being thus recalled to the theatre of eloquence, he kept his rank as long as he was able to support the fatigue of it, after which his credit declined in proportion as he remitted his application. Publius Murena had a moderate genius, but was passionately fond of the study of antiquity ; he applied himself with equal diligence to the belles-lettres, in which he was tolerably versed ; in short, he was a man of great industry, and took the utmost pains to distinguish himself. Caius Censorinus had a good stock of Grecian literature, explained whatever he advanced with great neatness and perspicuity, and had a graceful action, but was too cold and inanimate for the forum. Lucius Turius, with a very indifferent genius, but the most indefatigable application, spoke in public very often, in the best manner he was able ; and, accordingly, he only wanted the votes of a few centuries to promote him to the consulship. Caius Macer was never a man of much interest or authority, but was one of the most active pleaders of his time ; and if his life, his manners, and his very looks had not ruined the credit of his genius, he would have ranked higher in the list of orators. He was neither copious, nor dry and barren ; neither neat and embellished, nor wholly inelegant ; and his voice, his gesture, and every part of his action, was without any grace ; but in inventing and digesting his ideas he had a wonderful accuracy, such as no man I ever saw either possessed or exerted in a more eminent degree ; and yet, somehow, he displayed it rather with the air of a quibbler than of an orator. Though he had acquired some reputation in public causes, he appeared to most advantage and was most courted and employed in private ones.

LXVIII. " Caius Piso, who comes next in order, had scarcely any exertion, but he was a speaker who adopted a very familiar style ; and though, in fact, he was far from being slow of invention, he had more penetration in his look and appearance than he really possessed. His contemporary, Marcus Glabrio, though carefully instructed by his grandfather Scævola, was prevented from distinguishing himself by his natural indolence and want of attention. Lucius Torquatus, on the contrary, had an elegant turn of expression, and a clear comprehension, and was perfectly polite and well-bred in his whole manner. But Cnæus Pompeius, my coeval, a man who was born to excel in every thing, would have acquired a more distinguished reputation for his eloquence if he had not been diverted from the pursuit of it by the more dazzling charms of military fame. His language was naturally bold and elevated, and he was always master of his subject; and as to his powers of enunciation, his voice was sonorous and manly, and his gesture noble and full of dignity. Decimus Silanus, another of my contemporaries, and your father-in-law, was not a man of much application, but he had a very competent share of discernment and elocution. Quintus Pompeius, the son of Aulus, who had the title of *Bithynicus*, and was about two years older than myself, was, to my own knowledge, remarkably fond of the study of eloquence, had an uncommon stock of learning, and was a man of indefatigable industry and perseverance; for he was connected with Marcus Piso and me, not only as an intimate.acquaintance, but as an associate in our studies and private exercises. His elocution was but ill recommended by his action; for though the former was sufficiently copious and diffusive, there was nothing graceful in the latter. His contemporary, Publius Autronius, had a very clear and strong voice, but he was distinguished by no other accomplishment. Lucius Octavius Reatinus died in his youth, while he was in full practice; but he ascended the rostra with more assurance than ability. Caius Staienus, who changed his name into Ælius by a kind of self-adoption, was a warm, an abusive, and indeed a furious speaker; which was so agreeable to the taste of many, that he would have risen to some rank in the state if it had not been for a crime of which he was clearly convicted, and for which he afterward suffered.

LXIX. "At the same time were the two brothers Caius and Lucius Cæpasius, who, though men of an obscure family and little previous consequence, were yet, by mere dint of application, suddenly promoted to the quæstorship, with no other recommendation than a provincial and unpolished kind of oratory. That I may not seem willfully to omit any declaimer, I must also notice Caius Cosconius Calidianus, who, without any discernment, amused the people with a rapidity of language (if such it might be called) which he attended with a perpetual hurry of action, and a most violent exertion of his voice. Of much the same cast was Quintus Arrius, who may be considered as a second-hand Marcus Crassus. He is a striking proof of what consequence it is in such a city as ours to devote one's self to the interests of *the many*, and to be as active as possible in promoting their safety or their honor; for by these means, though of the lowest parentage, having raised himself to the offices of rank, and to considerable wealth and influence, he likewise acquired the reputation of a tolerable patron, without either learning or abilities. But as inexperienced champions, who, from a passionate desire to distinguish themselves in the circus, can bear the blows of their opponents without shrinking, are often overpowered by the heat of the sun, when it is increased by the reflection of the sand, so *he*, who had hitherto supported even the sharpest encounters with good success, could not stand the severity of that year of judicial contest, which blazed upon him like a summer's sun."

"Upon my word," cried Atticus, "you are now treating us with the very *dregs* of oratory, and you have entertained us in this manner for some time; but I did not offer to interrupt you, because I never dreamed you would have descended so low as to mention the *Staieni* and *Autronii!*" "As I have been speaking of the dead, you will not imagine, I suppose," said I, "that I have done it to court their favor; but in pursuing the order of history, I.was necessarily led by degrees to a period of time which falls within the compass of our own knowledge. But I wish it to be noticed, that after recounting all who ever ventured to speak in public, we find but few (very few indeed!) whose names are worth recording, and not many who had even the *repute* of being orators. Let us, however, return to our subject.

LXX. "Titus Torquatus, then, the son of Titus, was a man of learning (which he first acquired in the school of Molo in Rhodes), and of a free and easy elocution which he received from nature. If he had lived to a proper age, he would have been chosen consul without any solicitation; but he had more ability for speaking than inclination; so that, in fact, he did not do justice to the art he professed; and yet he was never wanting to his duty, either in the private causes of his friends and dependents, or in his senatorial capacity. My townsman, too, Marcus Pontidius, pleaded a number of private causes. He had a rapidity of expression, and a tolerable quickness of comprehension; but he was very warm, and, indeed, rather too choleric and irascible; so that he often wrangled, not only with his antagonist, but (what appears very strange) with the judge himself, whom it was rather his business to soothe and gratify. Marcus Messala, who was something younger than myself, was far from being a poor and abject pleader, and yet he was not a very elegant one. He was judicious, penetrating, and wary, very exact in digesting and methodizing his subject, and a man of uncommon diligence and application, and of very extensive practice. As to the two Metelli (Celer and Nepos), these also had a moderate share of employment at the bar; but, being destitute neither of learning nor abilities, they chiefly applied themselves (and with some success) to debates of a more popular kind. But Cnæus Lentulus Marcellinus, who was never reckoned a bad speaker, was esteemed a very eloquent one in his consulship. He wanted neither sentiment nor expression; his voice was sweet and sonorous; and he had a sufficient stock of humor. Caius Memmius, the son of Lucius, was a perfect adept in the learning of the Greeks; for he had an insuperable disgust to the literature of the Romans. He was a neat and polished speaker, and had a sweet and harmonious turn of expression; but as he was equally averse to every laborious effort either of the mind or the tongue, his eloquence declined in proportion as he lessened his application."

LXXI. "But I heartily wish," said Brutus, "that you would give us your opinion of those orators who are still living; or, if you are determined to say nothing of the rest, there are two at least (that is, Cæsar and Marcellus, whom I have often heard you speak of with the highest approbation), whose characters would give me as much entertainment as any of those you have already specified." "But why," answered I, "should you expect that I should give you my opinion of men who are as well known to yourself as to me?" "Marcellus, indeed," replied he, "I am very well acquainted with; but as to Cæsar, I know little of *him*. For I have heard the former very often; but by the time I was able to judge for myself, the latter had set out for his province." "But what," said I, "think you of him whom you have heard so often?" "What else can I think," replied he, "but that you will soon have an orator who will very nearly resemble yourself?" "If that is the case," answered I, "pray think of him as favorably as you can." "I do," said he;

"for he pleases me very highly, and not without reason. He is absolutely master of his profession, and, neglecting every other, has applied himself solely to *this;* and, for that purpose, has persevered in the rigorous task of composing a daily essay in writing. His words are well chosen; his language is full and copious; and every thing he says receives an additional ornament from the graceful tone of his voice, and the dignity of his action. In short, he is so complete an orator, that there is no quality I know of in which I can think him deficient. But he is still more to be admired for being able, in these unhappy times (which are marked with a distress that, by some cruel fatality, has overwhelmed us all), to console himself, as opportunity offers, with the consciousness of his own integrity, and by the frequent renewal of his literary pursuits. I saw him lately at Mitylene, and then (as I have already hinted) I saw him a *thorough man;* for though I had before discovered in him a strong resemblance of yourself, the likeness was much improved after he was enriched by the instructions of your learned and very intimate friend Cratippus." "Though I acknowledge," said I, "that I have listened with pleasure to your eulogies on a very worthy man, for whom I have the warmest esteem, they have led me insensibly to the recollection of our common miseries, which our present conversation was intended to suspend. But I would willingly hear what is Atticus's opinion of Cæsar."

LXXII. "Upon my word," replied Atticus, "you are wonderfully consistent with your plan, to say nothing *yourself* of the living; and, indeed, if you were to deal with *them,* as you already have with the *dead,* and say something of every paltry fellow that occurs to your memory, you would plague us with *Autronii* and *Staieni* without end. But though you might possibly have it in view not to encumber yourself with such a numerous crowd of insignificant wretches; or perhaps, to avoid giving any one room to complain that he was either unnoticed, or not extolled according to his imaginary merit, yet certainly you might have said something of Cæsar, especially as your opinion of *his* abilities is well known to every body, and his concerning *yours* is very far from being a secret. But, however," said he (addressing himself to Brutus), "I really think of Cæsar, and every body else says the same of this accurate master in the art of speaking, that he has the purest and the most elegant command of the Roman language of all the orators that have yet appeared; and that not merely by domestic habit, as we have lately heard it observed of the families of the Lælii and the Mucii (though even here, I believe, this might partly have been the case), but he chiefly acquired and brought it to its present perfection by a studious application to the most intricate and refined branches of literature, and by a careful and constant attention to the purity of his style. But that *he*, who, involved as he was in a perpetual hurry of business, could dedicate to *you*, my Cicero, a labored treatise on the art of speaking correctly; that *he*, who, in the first book of it, laid it down as an axiom that an accurate choice of words is the foundation of eloquence; and who has bestowed," said he (addressing himself again to Brutus), "the highest encomiums on this friend of ours, who yet chooses to leave Cæsar's character to *me*—that *he* should be a perfect master of the language of polite conversation, is a circumstance which is almost too obvious to be mentioned. I said, *the highest encomiums*," pursued Atticus, "because he says in so many words, when he addresses himself to Cicero, 'If others have bestowed all their time and attention to acquire a habit of expressing themselves with ease and correctness, how much is the name and dignity of the Roman people indebted to you, who are the highest pattern, and indeed the first inventor of that rich fertility of language which distinguishes your performances.'"

LXXIII. "Indeed," said Brutus, "I think he has extolled your merit in a very friendly and a very magnificent style; for you are not only the *highest pattern*, and even the *first inventor* of all our *fertility* of language, which alone is praise enough to content any reasonable man, but you have added fresh honors to the name and dignity of the Roman people; for the very excellence in which we had hitherto been conquered by the vanquished Greeks has now been either wrested from their hands, or equally shared, at least, between us and them. So that I prefer this honorable testimony of Cæsar, I will not say to the public thanksgiving which was decreed for your *own* military services, but to the triumphs of many heroes." "Very true," replied I, "provided this honorable testimony was really the voice of Cæsar's judgment, and not of his friendship; for *he* certainly has added more to the dignity of the Roman people, whoever he may be (if indeed any such man has yet existed), who has not only exemplified and enlarged, but first produced this rich fertility of expression, than the doughty warriors who have stormed a few paltry castles of the Ligurians, which have furnished us, you know, with many repeated triumphs. In reality, if we can submit to hear the truth, it may be asserted (to say nothing of those godlike plans, which, supported by the wisdom of our generals, have frequently saved the sinking state both abroad and at home) that an orator is justly entitled to the preference to any commander in a petty war. But the general, you will say, is the more serviceable man to the public. Nobody denies it; and yet (for I am not afraid of provoking your censure, in a conversation which leaves each of us at liberty to say what he thinks) I had rather be the author of one single oration of Crassus in defense of Curius, than be honored with two Ligurian triumphs. You will, perhaps, reply, that the storming a castle of the Ligurians was a thing of more consequence to the state than that the claim of Curius should be ably supported. This I own to be true. But it was also of more consequence to the Athenians that their houses should be securely roofed, than to have their city graced with a most beautiful statue of Minerva; and yet, notwithstanding this, I would much rather have been a Phidias than the most skillful joiner in Athens. In the present case, therefore, we are not to consider a man's usefulness, but the strength of his abilities; especially as the number of painters and statuaries who have excelled in their profession is very small; whereas there can never be any want of joiners and mechanical laborers. LXXIV. But proceed, my Atticus, with Cæsar, and oblige us with the remainder of his character." "We see then," said he, "from what has just been mentioned, that a pure and correct style is the groundwork, and the very basis and foundation, upon which an orator must build his other accomplishments; though it is true that those who had hitherto possessed it derived it more from early habit than from any principles of art. It is needless to refer you to the instances of Lælius and Scipio; for a purity of language, as well as of manners, was the characteristic of the age they lived in. It could not, indeed, be applied to every one; for their two contemporaries, Cæcilius and Pacuvius, spoke very incorrectly; but yet people in general who had not resided out of the city nor been corrupted by any domestic barbarisms, spoke the Roman language with purity. Time, however, as well at Rome as in Greece, soon altered matters for the worse; for this city (as had formerly been the case at Athens) was resorted to by a crowd of adventurers from different parts, who spoke very corruptly, which shows the necessity of reforming our language, and reducing it to a certain standard, which shall not be liable to vary like the capricious laws of custom. Though we were then very young, we can easily remember Titus Flamininus, who was joint consul with Quintus Metellus; he was supposed to speak his native language with correctness, but was a man of no literature. As to Catulus, he was far indeed from being destitute of learning, as you have already observed; but his reputed purity of diction was chiefly owing to the sweetness of his voice and the delicacy of his accent. Cotta, who, by his broad pronunciation, lost all resemblance of the elegant tone of the Greeks, and affected a harsh and rustic utterance, quite opposite to that of Catulus, acquired the same reputation of correctness by pursuing a wild and unfrequented path. But Sisenna, who had the ambition to think of reforming our phraseology, could not be lashed out of his whimsical and new-fangled turns of expression, by all the raillery of Caius Rufius." "What do you refer to?" said Brutus; "and who was the Caius Rufius you are speaking of?" "He was a noted prosecutor," replied he, "some years ago. When this man had supported an indictment against one Caius Rutilius, Sisenna, who was counsel for the defendant, told him that several parts of his accusation were *spitatical*.[1] LXXV. *My lords*, cried Rufius to the judges, *I shall be cruelly overreached, unless you give me your assistance. His charge overpowers my comprehension; and I am afraid he has some unfair design upon me. What, in the name of heaven, can he intend by* SPITAT- ICAL? *I know the meaning of* SPIT, *or* SPITTLE; *but this hor- rid* ATICAL, *at the end of it, absolutely puzzles me:* The whole bench laughed very heartily at the singular oddity of the expression; my old friend, however, was still of opinion

---

[1] In the original *sputatilica*, worthy to be spit upon. It appears, from the connection, to have been a word whimsically derived by the author of it from *sputa*, spittle.

that to speak correctly was to speak differently from other people.

"But Cæsar, who was guided by the principles of art, has corrected the imperfections of a vicious custom by adopting the rules and improvements of a good one, as he found them occasionally displayed in the course of polite conversation. Accordingly, to the purest elegance of expression (which is equally necessary to every well-bred citizen, as to an orator), he has added all the various ornaments of elocution, so that he seems to exhibit the finest painting in the most advantageous point of view. As he has such extraordinary merit even in the tenor of his language, I must confess that there is no person I know of to whom he should yield the preference. Besides, his manner of speaking, both as to his voice and gesture, is splendid and noble, without the least appearance of artifice or affectation; and there is a dignity in his very presence which bespeaks a great and elevated mind." "Indeed," said Brutus, "his orations please me highly; for I have had the satisfaction to read several of them. He has likewise written some commentaries, or short memoirs, of his own transactions." "And such," said I, "as merit the highest approbation; for they are plain, correct, and graceful, and divested of all the ornaments of language, so as to appear (if I may be allowed the expression) in a kind of undress. But while he pretended only to furnish the loose materials, for such as might be inclined to compose a regular history, he may, perhaps, have gratified the vanity of a few literary *frisseurs*, but he has certainly prevented all sensible men from attempting any improvement on his plan. For, in history, nothing is more pleasing than a correct and elegant brevity of expression. With your leave, however, it is high time to return to those orators who have quitted the stage of life.

LXXVI. "Caius Sicinius, then, who was a grandson of the censor Quintus Pompey, by one of his daughters, died after his advancement to the quæstorship. He was a speaker of some merit and reputation, which he derived from the system of Hermagoras, who, though he furnished but little assistance for acquiring an ornamental style, gave many useful precepts to expedite and improve the invention of an orator. For in this system we have a collection of fixed and determinate rules for public speaking, which are delivered indeed without any show or parade (and I might have added, in a trivial and homely form), but yet are so plain and methodical that it is almost impossible to mistake the road. By keeping close to these, and always digesting his subject before he ventured to speak upon it (to which we may add, that he had a tolerable fluency of expression), he so far succeeded, without any other assistance, as to be ranked among the pleaders of the day. As to Caius Visellius Varro, who was my cousin, and a contemporary of Sicinius, he was a man of great learning. He died while he was a member of the court of inquests, into which he had been admitted after the expiration of his ædileship. The public, I confess, had not the same opinion of his abilities that I have, for he never passed as a man of sterling eloquence among the people. His speech was excessively quick and rapid, and consequently indistinct; for, in fact, it was embarrassed and obscured by the celerity of its course; and yet, after all, you will scarcely find a man who had a better choice of words, or a richer vein of sentiment. He had, besides, a complete fund of polite literature, and a thorough knowledge of the principles of jurisprudence, which he learned from his father Aculeo. To proceed in our account of the dead, the next that presents himself is Lucius Torquatus, whom you will not so readily pronounce a proficient in the art of speaking (though he was by no means destitute of elocution) as what is called by the Greeks *a political adept.* He had a plentiful stock of learning, not indeed of the common sort, but of a more abstruse and curious nature; he had likewise an admirable memory, and a very sensible and elegant turn of expression; all which qualities derived an additional grace from the dignity of his deportment and the integrity of his manners. I was also highly pleased with the style of his contemporary Triarius, which expressed to perfection the character of a worthy old gentleman, who had been thoroughly polished by the refinements of literature. What a venerable severity was there in his look! what forcible solemnity in his language! and how thoughtful and deliberate every word he spoke!" At the mention of Torquatus and Triarius, for each of whom he had the most affectionate veneration, "It fills my heart with anguish," said Brutus, "(to omit a thousand other circumstances), when I reflect, as I can not help doing, on your mentioning the names of these

worthy men, that your long-respected authority was insufficient to procure an accommodation of our differences. The
republic would not otherwise have been deprived of these,
and many other excellent citizens." "Not a word more,"
said I, "on this melancholy subject, which can only aggravate
our sorrow; for as the remembrance of what is already past
is painful enough, the prospect of what is yet to come is still
more afflicting. Let us, therefore, drop our unavailing complaints, and (agreeably to our plan) confine our attention to
the forensic merits of our deceased friends.

LXXVII. "Among those, then, who lost their lives in
this unhappy war, was Marcus Bibulus, who, though not a
professed orator, was a very accurate writer, and a solid and
experienced advocate; and Appius Claudius, your father-in-
law, and my colleague and intimate acquaintance, who was
not only a hard student, and a man of learning, but a practiced orator, a skillful augurist and civilian, and a thorough
adept in the Roman history. As to Lucius Domitius, he was
totally unacquainted with any rules of art; but he spoke his
native language with purity, and had a great freedom of address. We had likewise the two Lentuli, men of consular
dignity; one of whom (I mean Publius), the avenger of my
wrongs and the author of my restoration, derived all his powers and accomplishments from the assistance of art, and not
from the bounty of nature; but he had such a great and noble disposition, that he claimed all the honors of the most illustrious citizens, and supported them with the utmost dignity of character. The other (Lucius Lentulus) was an animated speaker; for it would be saying too much, perhaps, to
call him an orator; but, unhappily, he had an utter aversion
to the trouble of thinking. His voice was sonorous; and his
language, though not absolutely harsh and forbidding, was
warm and vigorous, and carried in it a kind of terror. In a judicial trial, you would probably have wished for a more agreeable and a keener advocate; but in a debate on matters of
government, you would have thought his abilities sufficient.
Even Titus Postumius had such powers of utterance as were
not to be despised; but in political matters he spoke with the
same unbridled ardor he fought with; in short, he was much
too warm; though it must be owned he possessed an extensive knowledge of the laws and constitution of his country."

"Upon my word," cried Atticus, "if the persons you have mentioned were still living, I should be apt to imagine that you were endeavoring to solicit their favor. For you introduce every body who had the courage to stand up and speak his mind; so that I almost begin to wonder how Marcus Servilius has escaped your notice." LXXVIII. "I am, indeed, very sensible," replied I, "that there have been many who never spoke in public that were much better qualified for the task than those orators I have taken the pains to enumerate;[1] but I have, at least, answered one purpose by it, which is to show you that in this populous city we have not had very many who had the resolution to speak at all, and that even among these there have been few who were entitled to our applause. I can not, therefore, neglect to take some notice of those worthy knights, and my intimate friends, very lately deceased, Publius Cominius Spoletinus, against whom I pleaded in defense of Caius Cornelius, and who was a methodical, spirited, and ready speaker; and Tiberius Accius, of Pisaurum, to whom I replied in behalf of Aulus Cluentius, and who was an accurate and a tolerably copious advocate: he was also well instructed in the precepts of Hermagoras, which, though of little service to embellish and enrich our elocution, furnish a variety of arguments, which, like the weapons of the light-infantry, may be readily managed, and are adapted to every subject of debate. I must add, that I never knew a man of greater industry and application. As to Caius Piso, my son-in-law, it is scarcely possible to mention any one who was blessed with a finer capacity. He was constantly employed either in public speaking, and private declamatory exercises, or, at least, in writing and thinking; and, consequently, he made such a rapid progress, that he rather seemed to fly than to run. He had an elegant choice of expression, and the structure of his periods was perfectly neat and harmonious; he had an astonishing variety and strength of argument, and a lively and agreeable turn of thought; and his gesture was naturally so graceful, that it appeared to have been formed (which it really was not) by the nicest rules of art. I am rather fearful, indeed, that I should be thought to have been prompted by my affection for him to have given him a greater character than he deserved; but this is so far from being the case, that

[1] This was probably intended as an indirect compliment to Atticus.

I might justly have ascribed to him many qualities of a different and more valuable nature; for in continence, social ardor, and every other kind of virtue, there was scarcely any of his contemporaries who was worthy to be compared with him.

LXXIX. "Marcus Cælius, too, must not pass unnoticed, notwithstanding the unhappy change, either of his fortune or disposition, which marked the latter part of his life. As long as he was directed by my influence, he behaved himself so well as a tribune of the people, that no man supported the interests of the senate, and of all the good and virtuous, in opposition to the factious and unruly madness of a set of abandoned citizens, with more firmness than *he* did; a part in which he was enabled to exert himself to great advantage, by the force and dignity of his language, and his lively humor and polite address. He spoke several harangues in a very sensible style, and three spirited invectives, which originated from our political disputes; and his defensive speeches, though not equal to the former, were yet tolerably good, and had a degree of merit which was far from being contemptible. After he had been advanced to the ædileship by the hearty approbation of all the better sort of citizens, as he had lost my company (for I was then abroad in Cilicia) he likewise lost himself, and entirely sunk his credit by imitating the conduct of those very men whom he had before so successfully opposed. But Marcus Calidius has a more particular claim to our notice for the singularity of his character; which can not so properly be said to have entitled him to a place among our other orators, as to distinguish him from the whole fraternity; for in him we beheld the most uncommon and the most delicate sentiments arrayed in the softest and finest language imaginable. Nothing could be so easy as the turn and compass of his periods; nothing so ductile; nothing more pliable and obsequious to his will; so that he had a greater command of words than any orator whatever. In short, the flow of his language was so pure and limpid that nothing could be clearer, and so free that it was never clogged or obstructed. Every word was exactly in the place where it should be, and disposed (as Lucilius expresses it) with as much nicety as in a curious piece of mosaic work. We may add, that he had not a single expression which was either harsh, unnatural, abject, or far-fetched; and yet he was so far from confining himself to the plain and ordinary mode of speaking, that he abounded greatly in the metaphor—but such metaphors as did not appear to usurp a post that belonged to another, but only to occupy their own. These delicacies were displayed, not in a loose and effeminate style, but in such a one as was strictly *numerous*, without either appearing to be so, or running on with a dull uniformity of sound. He was likewise master of the various ornaments of language and thought which the Greeks call *figures*, whereby he enlivened and embellished his style as with so many forensic decorations. We may add that he readily discovered, upon all occasions, what was the real point of debate, and where the stress of the argument lay; and that his method of ranging his ideas was extremely artful, his action gentlemanly, and his whole manner very engaging and very sensible. LXXX. In short, if to speak agreeably is the chief merit of an orator, you will find no one who was better qualified than Calidius.

"But as we have observed a little before that it is the business of an orator to instruct, to please, and *to move the passions*, he was, indeed, perfectly master of the first two; for no one could better elucidate his subject, or charm the attention of his audience. But as to the third qualification, the moving and alarming the passions, which is of much greater efficacy than the former, he was wholly destitute of it. He had no force, no exertion; either by his own choice, and from an opinion that those who had a loftier turn of expression, and a more warm and spirited action, were little better than madmen; or because it was contrary to his natural temper and habitual practice; or, lastly, because it was beyond the strength of his abilities. If, indeed, it is a useless quality, his want of it was a real excellence; but if otherwise, it was certainly a defect. I particularly remember, that when he prosecuted Quintus Gallius for an attempt to poison him, and pretended that he had the plainest proofs of it, and could produce many letters, witnesses, informations, and other evidences to put the truth of his charge beyond a doubt, interspersing many sensible and ingenious remarks on the nature of the crime—I remember, I say, that when it came to my turn to reply to him, after urging every argument which the case itself suggested, I insisted upon it as a material circumstance in favor of my client that the prosecutor, while he charged him with a design against his life, and assured us that he had the most indubitable proofs of it then in his hands, related his story with as much ease, and as much calmness and indifference, as if nothing had happened. 'Would it have been possible,' said I (addressing myself to Calidius), 'that you should speak with this air of unconcern, unless the charge was purely an invention of your own? And, above all, that you, whose eloquence has often vindicated the wrongs of other people with so much spirit, should speak so coolly of a crime which threatened your life? Where was that expression of resentment which is so natural to the injured? Where that ardor, that eagerness, which extorts the most pathetic language even from men of the dullest capacities? There was no visible disorder in your mind, no emotion in your looks and gesture, no smiting of the thigh or the forehead, nor even a single stamp of the foot. You were, therefore, so far from interesting our feelings in your favor, that we could scarcely keep our eyes open while you were relating the dangers you had so narrowly escaped.' Thus we employed the natural defect, or, if you please, the sensible calmness of an excellent orator, as an argument to invalidate his charge." "But is it possible to doubt," cried Brutus, "whether this was a sensible quality or a defect? For as the greatest merit of an orator is to be able to inflame the passions, and give them such a bias as shall best answer his purpose, he who is destitute of this must certainly be deficient in the most capital part of his profession."

LXXXI. "I am of the same opinion," said I; "but let us now proceed to him (Hortensius) who is the only remaining orator worth noticing; after which, as you seem to insist upon it, I shall say something of myself. I must first, however, do justice to the memory of two promising youths, who, if they had lived to a riper age, would have acquired the highest reputation for their eloquence." "You mean, I suppose," said Brutus, "Caius Curio and Caius Licinius Calvus." "The very same," replied I. "One of them, besides his plausible manner, had such an easy and voluble flow of expression, and such an inexhaustible variety, and sometimes accuracy of sentiment, that he was one of the most ready and ornamental speakers of his time. Though he had received but little instruction from the professed masters of the art, nature had furnished him with an admirable capacity for the practice of it. I never, indeed, discovered in him any great degree of application; but he was certainly very ambitious to distinguish himself; and if he had continued to listen to my advice, as he had begun to do, he would have preferred the acquisition of real honor to that of untimely grandeur." "What do you mean?" said Brutus; "or in what manner are these two objects to be distinguished?" "I distinguish them thus," replied I; "as honor is the reward of virtue, conferred upon a man by the choice and affection of his fellow-citizens, he who obtains it by their free votes and suffrages is to be considered, in my opinion, as an honorable member of the community. But he who acquires his power and authority by taking advantage of every unhappy incident, and without the consent of his fellow-citizens, as Curio aimed to do, acquires only the name of honor, without the substance. Whereas, if he had hearkened to me, he would have risen to the highest dignity in an honorable manner, and with the hearty approbation of all men, by a gradual advancement to public offices, as his father and many other eminent citizens had done before. I often gave the same advice to Publius Crassus, the son of Marcus, who courted my friendship in the early part of his life, and recommended it to him very warmly to consider *that* as the truest path to honor which had been already marked out to him by the example of his ancestors. For he had been extremely well educated, and was perfectly versed in every branch of polite literature; he had likewise a penetrating genius, and an elegant variety of expression; and appeared grave and sententious without arrogance, and modest and diffident without dejection. But, like many other young men, he was carried away by the tide of ambition; and after serving a short time with reputation as a volunteer, nothing could satisfy him but to try his fortune as a general, an employment which was confined by the wisdom of our ancestors to men who had arrived at a certain age, and who, even then, were obliged to submit their pretensions to the uncertain issue of a public decision. Thus, by exposing himself to a fatal catastrophe, while he was endeavoring to rival the fame of Cyrus and Alexander, who lived to finish their desperate career, he lost all resemblance of Lucius Crassus and his other worthy progenitors. LXXXII. But let us return to Calvus, whom we have just mentioned,

an orator who had received more literary improvements than
Curio, and had a more accurate and delicate manner of speaking, which he conducted with great taste and elegance ; but
(by being too minute and nice a critic upon himself), while
he was laboring to correct and refine his language, he suffered all the force and spirit of it to evaporate. In short, it
was so exquisitely polished as to charm the eye of every skillful observer; but it was little noticed by the common people in a crowded forum, which is the proper theatre of eloquence." " His aim," said Brutus, " was to be admired as
an *Attic* orator ; and to this we must attribute that accurate
exility of style which he constantly affected."   " This, indeed, was his professed character," replied I ; " but he was
deceived himself, and led others into the same mistake.   It
is true, whoever supposes that to speak in the *Attic* taste is
to avoid every awkward, every harsh, every vicious expression, has, in this sense, an undoubted right to refuse his approbation to every thing which is not strictly *Attic*.   For he
must naturally detest whatever is insipid, disgusting, or incorrect, while he considers correctness and propriety of language as the religion and good manners of an orator ; and
every one who pretends to speak in public should adopt the
same opinion.   But if he bestows the name of Atticism on a
meagre, a dry, and a niggardly turn of expression, provided
it is neat, correct, and polished, I can not say, indeed, that
he bestows it improperly ; as the Attic orators, however, had
many qualities of a more important nature, I would advise
him to be careful that he does not overlook their different
kinds and degrees of merit, and their great extent and variety of character.   The Attic speakers, he will tell me, are the
models upon which he wishes to form his eloquence.   But
which of them does he mean to fix upon ? for they are not
all of the same cast.   Who, for instance, could be more unlike each other than Demosthenes and Lysias ? or than Demosthenes and Hyperides ?   Or who more different from either of them than Æschines?   Which of them, then, do you
propose to imitate ?   If only *one*, this will be a tacit implica-
tion that none of the rest were true masters of Atticism ; if
all, how can you possibly succeed, when their characters are
so opposite ?   Let me farther ask you, whether Demetrius
Phalereus spoke in the Attic style ?   In my opinion, his ora-

tions have the very taste of Athens. But he is certainly more florid than either Hyperides or Lysias ; partly from the natural turn of his genius, and partly by choice.

LXXXIII. "There were likewise two others at the time we are speaking of, whose characters were equally dissimilar, and yet both of them were truly *Attic.* The first (Charisius) was the author of a number of speeches, which he composed for his friends, professedly in imitation of Lysias; and the other (Demochares, the nephew of Demosthenes) wrote several orations, and a regular history of what was transacted in Athens under his own observation; not so much, indeed, in the style of a historian as of an orator. Hegesias took the former for his model, and was so vain of his own taste for Atticism that he considered his predecessors, who were really masters of it, as mere rustics in comparison of himself. But what can be more insipid, more frivolous, or more puerile, than that very concinnity of expression which he actually acquired? 'But still we wish to resemble the Attic speakers.' Do so, by all means. But were not those, then, true Attic speakers we have just been mentioning? 'Nobody denies it; and these are the men we imitate.' But how? when they are so very different, not only from each other, but from all the rest of their contemporaries? 'True ; but Thucydides is our leading pattern.' This, too, I can allow, if you design to compose histories instead of pleading causes. For Thucydides was both an exact and a stately historian ; but he never intended to write models for conducting a judicial process. I will even go so far as to add, that I have often commended the speeches which he has inserted in his history in great numbers; though I must frankly own that I neither *could* imitate them if I *would,* nor indeed *would* if I *could ;* like a man who would neither choose his wine so new as to have been tunned off in the preceding vintage, nor so excessively old as to date its age from the consulship of Opimius or Anicius. 'The latter,' you will say, 'bears the highest price.' Very probably ; but when it has too much age, it has lost that delicious flavor which pleases the palate, and, in my opinion, is scarcely tolerable. 'Would you choose, then, when you have a mind to regale yourself, to apply to a fresh, unripened cask?' By no means ; but still there is a certain age when good wine arrives at its utmost perfection. In the same manner,

I would recommend neither a raw, unmellowed style, which (if I may so express myself) has been newly drawn off from the vat, nor the rough and antiquated language of the grave and manly Thucydides. For even *he*, if he had lived a few years later, would have acquired a much softer and mellower turn of expression.

"'Let us, then, imitate Demosthenes.' LXXXIV. Good gods! to what else do I direct all my endeavors, and my wishes! But it is, perhaps, my misfortune not to succeed. These *Atticizers*, however, acquire with ease the paltry character they aim at; not once recollecting that it is not only recorded in history, but must have been the natural consequence of his superior fame, that when Demosthenes was to speak in public, all Greece flocked in crowds to hear him. But when our *Attic* orators venture to speak, they are presently deserted, not only by the little throng around them who have no interest in the dispute (which alone is a mortifying proof of their insignificance), but even by their associates and fellow-advocates. If to speak, therefore, in a dry and lifeless manner, is the true criterion of Atticism, they are heartily welcome to enjoy the credit of it; but if they wish to put their abilities to the trial, let them attend the comitia, or a judical process of real importance. The open forum demands a fuller and more elevated tone; and *he* is the orator for me who is so universally admired that when he is to plead an interesting cause all the benches are filled beforehand, the tribunal crowded, the clerks and notaries busy in adjusting their seats, the populace thronging about the rostra, and the judge brisk and vigilant; *he* who has such a commanding air that when he rises up to speak, the whole audience is hushed into a profound silence, which is soon interrupted by their repeated plaudits and acclamations, or by those successive bursts of laughter, or violent transports of passion, which he knows how to excite at his pleasure; so that even a distant observer, though unacquainted with the subject he is speaking upon, can easily discover that his hearers are pleased with him, and that a *Roscius* is performing his part on the stage. Whoever has the happiness to be thus followed and applauded, is, beyond dispute, an Attic speaker; for such was Pericles, such was Hyperides, and Æschines, and such, in the most eminent degree, was the great Demosthenes! If, indeed, these connoisseurs, who have so much, dislike to every thing bold and ornamental, only mean to say that an accurate, a judicious, and a neat and compact, but unembellished style, is really an Attic one, they are not mistaken. For in an art of such wonderful extent and variety as that of speaking, even this subtile and confined character may claim a place ; so that the conclusion will be that it is very possible to speak in the Attic taste without deserving the name of an orator ; but that all, in general, who are truly eloquent are likewise Attic speakers.

"It is time, however, to return to Hortensius." LXXXV. "Indeed, I think so," cried Brutus; "though I must acknowledge that this long digression of yours has entertained me very agreeably." "But I made some remarks," said Atticus, "which I was several times inclined to mention, only I was loth to interrupt you. As your discourse, however, seems to be drawing toward an end, I think I may venture to state them." "By all means," replied I. "I readily grant, then," said he, "that there is something very humorous and elegant in that continued *irony*, which Socrates employs to so much advantage in the dialogues of Plato, Xenophon, and Æschines ; for when a dispute commences on the nature of wisdom, he professes, with a great deal of humor and ingenuity, to have no pretensions to it himself, while, with a kind of concealed raillery, he ascribes the highest degree of it to those who had the arrogance to lay an open claim to it. Thus, in Plato, he extols Protagoras, Hippias, Prodicus, Gorgias, and several others, to the skies, but represents himself as quite ignorant. This in *him* was peculiarly becoming ; nor can I agree with Epicurus, who thinks it censurable. But in a professed history (for such, in fact, is the account you have been giving us of the Roman orators), I shall leave you to judge whether an application of the *irony* is not equally reprehensible as it would be in giving judicial evidence." "Pray, what are you driving at?" said I; "for I can not comprehend you." "I mean," replied he, "in the first place, that the commendations which you have bestowed upon some of our orators have a tendency to mislead the opinion of those who are unacquainted with their true characters. There were likewise several parts of your account at which I could scarcely forbear laughing ; as, for instance, when you compared old Cato to Lysias. He was, indeed, a great and a very extraordinary man. Nobody, I believe, will say to the contrary. But shall we call him an orator? Shall we pronounce him the rival of Lysias who was the most finished character of the kind? If we mean to jest, this comparison of yours would form a pretty *irony;* but if we are talking in real earnest, we should pay the same scrupulous regard to truth as if we were giving evidence upon oath. As a citizen, a senator, a general, and, in short, a man who was distinguished by his prudence, his activity, and every other virtue, your favorite Cato has my highest approbation. I can likewise applaud his speeches, considering the time he lived in. They exhibit the outlines of a great genius, but such, however, as are evidently rude and imperfect. In the same manner, when you represented his *Antiquities* as replete with all the graces of oratory, and compared Cato with Philistus and Thucydides, did you really imagine that you could persuade Brutus and me to believe you? or would you seriously degrade those, whom none of the Greeks themselves have been able to equal, into a comparison with a stiff country gentleman, who scarcely suspected that there was any such thing in being as a copious and ornamental style?

LXXXVI. "You have likewise said much in commendation of Galba—if as the best speaker of his age, I can so far agree with you, for such was the character he bore—but if you meant to recommend him as an *orator*, produce his orations (for they are still extant), and then tell me honestly whether you would wish your friend Brutus here to speak as *he* did? Lepidus, too, was the author of several speeches which have received your approbation, in which I can partly join with you if you consider them only as specimens of our ancient eloquence. The same might be said of Africanus and Lælius, than whose language (you tell us) nothing in the world can be sweeter; nay, you have mentioned it with a kind of veneration, and endeavored to dazzle our judgment by the great character they bore, and the uncommon elegance of their manners. Divest it of these adventitious graces, and this sweet language of theirs will appear so homely as to be scarcely worth noticing. Carbo, too, was mentioned as one of our capital orators; and for this only reason—that in speaking, as in all other professions, whatever is the best of its kind, for the time being, how deficient soever in reality, is always admired and applauded. What I have said of Carbo is equally true of the Gracchi; though, in some particulars, the character you have given them was no more than they deserved. But, to say nothing of the rest of your orators, let us proceed to Antonius and Crassus, your two paragons of eloquence, whom I have heard myself, and who were certainly very able speakers. To the extraordinary commendation you have bestowed upon them I can readily give my assent, but not, however, in such an unlimited manner as to persuade myself that you have received as much improvement from the speech in support of the Servilian law as Lysippus said he had done by studying the famous statue[1] of Polycletus. What you have said on *this* occasion I consider as absolute *irony;* but I shall not inform you why I think so, lest you should imagine I design to flatter you. I shall therefore pass over the many fine encomiums you have bestowed upon *these;* and what you have said of Cotta and Sulpicius, and but very lately of your pupil Cælius. I acknowledge, however, that we may call them orators; but as to the nature and extent of their merit, let your own judgment decide. It is scarcely worth observing that you have had the additional good-nature to crowd so many daubers into your list, that there are some, I believe, who will be ready to wish they had died long ago, that you might have had an opportunity to insert *their* names among the rest." LXXXVII. "You have opened a wide field of inquiry," said I, "and started a subject which deserves a separate discussion, but we must defer it to a more convenient time; for, to settle it, a great variety of authors must be examined, and especially Cato, which could not fail to convince you that nothing was wanting to complete his pieces but those rich and glowing colors which had not then been invented. As to the above oration of Crassus, he himself, perhaps, could have written better if he had been willing to take the trouble; but nobody else, I believe, could have mended it. You have no reason, therefore, to think I spoke *ironically* when I mentioned it as the guide and *tutoress* of my eloquence; for, though you seem to have a higher opinion of my capacity in its present state, you must remember that, in our youth, we could find nothing better to imitate among the

---

[1] *Doryphorus.* A spearman.

Romans. And as to my admitting so *many* into my list of orators, I only did it (as I have already observed) to show how few have succeeded in a profession in which all were desirous to excel. I therefore insist upon it that you do not consider *me* in the present case as a *practicer of irony*, though we are informed by Caius Fannius, in his history, that *Africanus* was a very excellent one." "As you please about *that*," cried Atticus; "though, by-the-by, I did not imagine it would have been any disgrace to you to be what Africanus and Socrates have been before you." "We may settle *this* another time," interrupted Brutus; "but will you be so obliging," said he (addressing himself to me), "as to give us a critical analysis of some of the old speeches you have mentioned?" "Very willingly," replied I; "but it must be at Cuma, or Tusculum, when opportunity offers; for we are near neighbors, you know, in both places. LXXXVIII. At present, let us return to *Hortensius*, from whom we have digressed a second time.

"Hortensius, then, who began to speak in public when he was very young, was soon employed even in causes of the greatest moment; and though he first appeared in the time of Cotta and Sulpicius (who were only ten years older), and when Crassus and Antonius, and afterward Philippus and Julius, were in the height of their reputation, he was thought worthy to be compared with either of them in point of eloquence. He had such an excellent memory as I never knew in any person; so that what he had composed in private, he was able to repeat, without notes, in the very same words he had made use of at first. He employed this natural advantage with so much readiness, that he not only recollected whatever he had written or premeditated himself, but remembered every thing that had been said by his opponents, without the help of a prompter. He was likewise inflamed with such a passionate fondness for the profession, that I never saw any one who took more pains to improve himself; for he would not suffer a day to elapse without either speaking in the forum, or composing at home; and very often he did both in the same day. He had, besides, a turn of expression which was very far from being low and unelevated, and possessed two other accomplishments, in which no one could equal him—an uncommon clearness and accuracy in stating the points he was to discuss, and a neat and easy manner of collecting the substance of what had been said by his antagonist and by himself. He had likewise an elegant choice of words, an agreeable flow in his periods, and a copious elocution, for which he was partly indebted to a fine natural capacity, and which was partly acquired by the most laborious rhetorical exercises. In short, he had a most retentive view of his subject, and always divided and distributed it into distinct parts with the greatest exactness; and he very seldom overlooked any thing which the case could suggest that was proper either to support his *own* allegations or to refute those of his opponent. Lastly, he had a sweet and sonorous voice; but his gesture had rather more art in it, and was managed with more precision than is requisite in an orator.

"While *he* was in the height of his glory, Crassus died, Cotta was banished, our public trials were intermitted by the Marsic war, and I myself made my first appearance in the forum. LXXXIX. Hortensius joined the army, and served the first campaign as a volunteer, and the second as a military tribune; Sulpicius was made a lieutenant general; and Antonius was absent on a similar account. The only trial we had was that upon the Varian law; the rest, as I have just observed, having been intermitted by the war. We had scarcely any body left at the bar but Lucius Memmius and Quintus Pompeius, who spoke mostly on their own affairs; and, though far from being orators of the first distinction, were yet tolerable ones (if we may credit Philippus, who was himself a man of some eloquence), and, in supporting evidence, displayed all the poignancy of a prosecutor, with a moderate freedom of elocution. The rest, who were esteemed our capital speakers, were then in the magistracy, and I had the benefit of hearing their harangues almost every day. Caius Curio was chosen a tribune of the people, though he left off speaking after being once deserted by his whole audience. To him I may add Quintus Metellus Celer, who, though certainly no orator, was far from being destitute of utterance; but Quintus Varius, Caius Carbo, and Cnæus Pomponius were men of real elocution, and might almost be said to have lived upon the rostra. Caius Julius too, who was then a curule ædile, was daily employed in making speeches to the people, which were composed with great neatness and accuracy. But while I attended the forum with this eager curiosity, my first disappointment was the banishment of Cotta; after which I continued to hear the rest with the same assiduity as before; and though I daily spent the remainder of my time in reading, writing, and private declamation, I can not say that I much relished my confinement to these preparatory exercises. The next year Quintus Varius was condemned, and banished by his own law; and I, that I might acquire a competent knowledge of the principles of jurisprudence, then attached myself to Quintus Scævola, the son of Publius, who, though he did not choose to undertake the charge of a pupil, yet, by freely giving his advice to those who consulted him, answered every purpose of instruction to such as took the trouble to apply to him. In the succeeding year, in which Sylla and Pompey were consuls, as Sulpicius, who was elected a tribune of the people, had occasion to speak in public almost every day, I had opportunity to acquaint myself thoroughly with his manner of speaking. At this time Philo, a philosopher of the first name in the Academy, with many of the principal Athenians, having deserted their native home, and fled to Rome, from the fury of Mithridates, I immediately became his scholar, and was exceedingly taken with his philosophy; and, besides the pleasure I received from the great variety and sublimity of his matter, I was still more inclined to confine my attention to that study, because there was reason to apprehend that our laws and judicial proceedings would be wholly overturned by the continuance of the public disorders. In the same year Sulpicius lost his life; and Quintus Catulus, Marcus Antonius, and Caius Julius, three orators who were partly contemporary with each other, were most inhumanly put to death. Then also I attended the lectures of Molo the Rhodian, who was newly come to Rome, and was both an excellent pleader and an able teacher of the art.

XC. "I have mentioned these particulars, which, perhaps, may appear foreign to our purpose, that *you*, my Brutus (for Atticus is already acquainted with them), may be able to mark my progress, and observe how closely I trod upon the heels of Hortensius. The three following years the city was free from the tumult of arms; but either by the death, the voluntary retirement, or the flight of our ablest orators (for even Marcus Crassus, and the two Lentuli, who were then in the bloom of youth, had all left us), Hortensius, of course, was the first speaker in the forum. Antistius, too, was daily rising into reputation; Piso pleaded pretty often; Pomponius, not so frequently; Carbo, very seldom; and Philippus, only once or twice. In the mean while I pursued my studies of every kind, day and night, with unremitting application. I lodged and boarded at my own house (where he lately died) Diodotus the Stoic, whom I employed as my preceptor in various other parts of learning, but particularly in logic, which may be considered as a close and contracted species of eloquence, and without which you yourself have declared it impossible to acquire that full and perfect eloquence, which they suppose to be an open and dilated kind of logic. Yet, with all my attention to Diodotus, and the various arts he was master of, I never suffered even a single day to escape me without some exercise of the oratorical kind. I constantly declaimed in private with Marcus Piso, Quintus Pompeius, or some other of my acquaintance; pretty often in Latin, but much oftener in Greek; because the Greek furnishes a greater variety of ornaments, and an opportunity of imitating and introducing them into Latin; and because the Greek masters, who were far the best, could not correct and improve us unless we declaimed in that language. This time was distinguished by a violent struggle to restore the liberty of the republic; the barbarous slaughter of the three orators, Scævola, Carbo, and Antistius; the return of Cotta, Curio, Crassus, Pompey, and the Lentuli; the re-establishment of the laws and courts of judicature, and the entire restoration of the commonwealth; but we lost Pomponius, Censorinus, and Murena from the roll of orators. I now began, for the *first* time, to undertake the management of causes, both private and public; not, as most did, with a view to learn my profession, but to make a trial of the abilities which I had taken so much pains to acquire. I had then a second opportunity of attending the instructions of Molo, who came to Rome while Sylla was dictator, to solicit the payment of what was due to his countrymen for their services in the Mithridatic war. My defense of Sextus Roscius, which was the first cause I pleaded, met with such a favorable reception, that from that moment I was looked upon as an advocate of the first class, and equal to the greatest and most important causes; and after this I pleaded many others, which I precomposed with all the care and accuracy I was master of.

XCI. "But as you seem desirous not so much to be acquainted with any incidental marks of my character, or the first sallies of my youth, as to know me thoroughly, I shall mention some particulars, which otherwise might have seemed unnecessary. At this time my body was exceedingly weak and emaciated; my neck long and slender; a shape and habit which I thought to be liable to great risk of life, if engaged in any violent fatigue or labor of the lungs. And it gave the greater alarm to those who had a regard for me, that I used to speak without any remission or variation, with the utmost stretch of my voice, and a total agitation of my body. When my friends, therefore, and physicians, advised me to meddle no more with forensic causes, I resolved to run any hazard rather than quit the hopes of glory which I had proposed to myself from pleading; but when I considered that by managing my voice, and changing my way of speaking, I might both avoid all future danger of that kind and speak with greater ease, I took a resolution of traveling into Asia merely for an opportunity to correct my manner of speaking; so that after I had been two years at the bar, and acquired some reputation in the forum, I left Rome. When I came to Athens, I spent six months with Antiochus, the principal and most judicious philosopher of the old Academy, and under this able master I renewed those philosophical studies which I had laboriously cultivated and improved from my earliest youth. At the same time, however, I continued my *rhetorical exercises* under Demetrius the Syrian, an experienced and reputable master of the art of speaking. After leaving Athens I traversed every part of Asia, where I was voluntarily attended by the principal orators of the country, with whom I renewed my rhetorical exercises. The chief of them was Menippus of Stratonica, the most eloquent of all the Asiatics; and if to be neither tedious nor impertinent is the characteristic of an Attic orator, he may be justly ranked in that class. Dionysius also of Magnesia, Æschylus of Cnidos, and Xenocles of Adramyttium, who were esteemed the first rhetoricians of Asia, were continually with me. Not contented with these, I went to Rhodes, and applied myself again to

Molo, whom I had heard before at Rome, and who was both an experienced pleader and a fine writer, and particularly judicious in remarking the faults of his scholars, as well as in his method of teaching and improving them. His principal trouble with me was to restrain the luxuriancy of a juvenile imagination, always ready to overflow its banks, within its due and proper channel. Thus, after an excursion of two years, I returned to Italy, not only much improved, but almost changed into a new man. The vehemence of my voice and action was considerably abated; the excessive ardor of my language was corrected; my lungs were strengthened; and my whole constitution confirmed and settled.

XCII. "Two orators then reigned in the forum (I mean Cotta and Hortensius), whose glory fired my emulation. Cotta's way of speaking was calm and easy, and distinguished by the flowing elegance and propriety of his language. The other was splendid, warm, and animated; not such as you, my Brutus, have seen him, when he had shed the blossom of his eloquence, but far more lively and pathetic both in his style and action. As Hortensius, therefore, was nearer to me in age, and his manner more agreeable to the natural ardor of my temper, I considered him as the proper object of my competition. For I observed that when they were both engaged in the same cause (as, for instance, when they defended Marcus Canuleius, and Cneius Dolabella, a man of consular dignity), though Cotta was generally employed to open the defense, the most important parts of it were left to the management of Hortensius. For a crowded audience and a clamorous forum require an orator who is lively, animated, full of action, and able to exert his voice to the highest pitch. The first year, therefore, after my return from Asia, I undertook several capital causes; and in the interim I put up as a candidate for the quæstorship, Cotta for the consulate; and Hortensius for the ædileship. After I was chosen quæstor I passed a year in Sicily, the province assigned to me by lot; Cotta went as consul into Gaul; and Hortensius, whose new office required his presence at Rome, was left of course the undisputed sovereign of the forum. In the succeeding year, when I returned from Sicily, my oratorical talents, such as they were, displayed themselves in their full perfection and maturity.

"I have been saying too much, perhaps, concerning myself; but my design in it was not to make a parade of my eloquence and ability, which I have no temptation to do, but only to specify the pains and labor which I have taken to improve it. After spending the five succeeding years in pleading a variety of causes, and with the ablest advocates of the time, I was declared an ædile, and undertook the patronage of the Sicilians against Hortensius, who was then one of the consuls elect. XCIII. But as the subject of our conversation not only requires an historical detail of orators, but such preceptive remarks as may be necessary to elucidate their characters, it will not be improper to make some observations of this kind upon that of Hortensius. After his appointment to the consulship (very probably because he saw none of consular dignity who were able to rival him, and despised the competition of others of inferior rank) he began to remit that intense application which he had hitherto persevered in from his childhood, and having settled himself in very affluent circumstances, he chose to live for the future what he thought an *easy* life, but which, in truth, was rather an indolent one. In the three succeeding years, the beauty of his coloring was so much impaired as to be very perceptible to a skillful connoisseur, though not to a common observer. After that, he grew every day more unlike himself than before, not only in other parts of eloquence, but by a gradual decay of the former celerity and elegant texture of his language. I, at the same time, spared no pains to improve and enlarge my talents, such as they were, by every exercise that was proper for the purpose, but particularly by that of writing. Not to mention several other advantages I derived from it, I shall only observe, that about this time, and but a very few years after my ædileship, I was declared the first prætor, by the unanimous suffrages of my fellow-citizens. For, by my diligence and assiduity as a pleader, and my accurate way of speaking, which was rather superior to the ordinary style of the bar, the novelty of my eloquence had engaged the attention and secured the good wishes of the public. But I will say nothing of myself; I will confine my discourse to our other speakers, among whom there is not one who has gained more than a common acquaintance with those parts of literature which feed the springs of eloquence; not one who has

been thoroughly nurtured at the breast of Philosophy, which
is the mother of every excellence either in deed or speech;
not one who has acquired an accurate knowledge of the civil
law, which is so necessary for the management even of private causes, and to direct the judgment of an orator; not
one who is a complete master of the Roman history, which
would enable us, on many occasions, to appeal to the venerable evidence of the dead; not one who can entangle his
opponent in such a neat and humorous manner as to relax
the severity of the judges into a smile or an open laugh; not
one who knows how to dilate and expand his subject by reducing it from the limited considerations of time and person
to some general and indefinite topic; not one who knows how
to enliven it by an agreeable digression; not one who can
rouse the indignation of the judge, or extort from him the
tear of compassion; or who can influence and bend his soul
(which is confessedly the capital perfection of an orator) in
such a manner as shall best suit his purpose.

XCIV. "When Hortensius, therefore, the once eloquent
and admired Hortensius, had almost vanished from the forum,
my appointment to the consulship, which happened about six
years after his own promotion to that office, revived his dying
emulation; for he was unwilling that, after I had equaled
him in rank and dignity, I should become his superior in any
other respect. But in the twelve succeeding years, by a mutual deference to each other's abilities, we united our efforts
at the bar in the most amicable manner; and my consulship,
which had at first given a short alarm to his jealousy, afterward cemented our friendship, by the generous candor with
which he applauded my conduct. But our emulous efforts
were exerted in the most conspicuous manner just before the
commencement of that unhappy period when Eloquence herself was confounded and terrified by the din of arms into a
sudden and total silence; for after Pompey had proposed and
carried a law, which allowed even the party accused but
three hours to make his defense, I appeared (though comparatively as a mere *novitiate* by this new regulation) in a number
of causes which, in fact, were become perfectly the same, or
very nearly so; most of which, my Brutus, you were present
to hear, as having been my partner and fellow-advocate in
many of them, though you pleaded several by yourself; and

Hortensius, though he died a short time afterward, bore his share in these limited efforts. He began to plead about ten years before the time of your birth; and in his sixty-fourth year, but a very few days before his death, he was engaged with you in the defense of Appius, your father-in-law. As to our respective talents, the orations we have published will enable posterity to form a proper judgment of them.

XCV. "But if we mean to inquire why Hortensius was more admired for his eloquence in the younger part of his life than in his latter years, we shall find it owing to the following causes. The first was, that an *Asiatic* style is more allowable in a young man than in an old one. Of this there are two different kinds. The former is sententious and sprightly, and abounds in those turns of thought which are not so much distinguished by their weight and solidity as by their neatness and elegance; of this cast was Timæus the historian, and the two orators so much talked of in our younger days, Hierocles of Alabanda, and his brother Menecles, but particularly the latter, both whose orations may be reckoned master-pieces of this kind. The other sort is not so remarkable for the plenitude and richness of its thoughts as for its rapid volubility of expression, which at present is the ruling taste in Asia; but, besides its uncommon fluency, it is recommended by a choice of words which are peculiarly delicate and ornamental; of this kind were Æschylus the Cnidian, and my contemporary Æschines the Milesian; for they had an admirable command of language, with very little elegance of sentiment. These showy kinds of eloquence are agreeable enough in young people, but they are entirely destitute of that gravity and composure which befits a riper age. As Hortensius, therefore, excelled in both, he was heard with applause in the earlier part of his life. For he had all that fertility and graceful variety of sentiment which distinguished the character of Menecles; but, as in Menecles, so in him, there were many turns of thought which were more delicate and entertaining than really useful, or indeed sometimes convenient. His language also was brilliant and rapid, and yet perfectly neat and accurate, but by no means agreeable to men of riper years. I have often seen it received by Philippus with the utmost derision, and, upon some occasions, with a contemptuous indignation; but the younger part of the audi-

ence admired it, and the populace were highly pleased with
it. In his youth, therefore, he met the warmest approbation
of the public, and maintained his post with ease as the first
orator in the forum. For the style he chose to speak in,
though it has little weight or authority, appeared very suitable to his age; and as it discovered in him the most visible
marks of genius and application, and was recommended by
the numerous cadence of his periods, he was heard with universal applause. But when the honors he afterward rose to,
and the dignity of his years, required something more serious
and composed, he still continued to appear in the same character, though it no longer became him; and as he had, for
some considerable time, intermitted those exercises, and relaxed that laborious attention which had once distinguished
him, though his former neatness of expression and luxuriancy
of conception still remained, they were stripped of those brilliant ornaments they had been used to wear. For this reason,
perhaps, my Brutus, he appeared less pleasing to you than he
would have done if you had been old enough to hear him
when he was fired with emulation, and flourished in the full
bloom of his eloquence."

XCVI. "I am perfectly sensible," said Brutus, "of the
justice of your remarks; and yet I have always looked upon
Hortensius as a great orator, but especially when he pleaded
for Messala, in the time of your absence." "I have often
heard of it," replied I; "and his oration, which was afterward published, they say, in the very same words in which he
delivered it, is no way inferior to the character you give it.
Upon the whole, then, his reputation flourished from the time
of Crassus and Scævola (reckoning from the consulship of the
former), to the consulship of Paullus and Marcellus; and I
held out in the same career of glory from the dictatorship of
Sylla to the period I have last mentioned. Thus the eloquence of Hortensius was extinguished by his *own* death, and
mine by that of the commonwealth." "Presage more favorably, I beg of you," cried Brutus. "As favorably as you
please," said I, "and that, not so much upon my own account as yours. But *his* death was truly fortunate, who did
not live to behold the miseries which he had long foreseen; for
we often lamented, between ourselves, the misfortunes which
hung over the state, when we discovered the seeds of a civil

war in the insatiable ambition of a few private citizens, and
saw every hope of an accommodation excluded by the rashness and precipitancy of our public counsels. But the felicity which always marked his life seems to have exempted
him, by a seasonable death, from the calamities that followed.
But as, after the decease of Hortensius, we seem to have been
left, my Brutus, as the sole guardians of an *orphan* eloquence,
let us cherish her, within our own walls at least, with a generous fidelity ; let us discourage the addresses of her worth-
less and impertinent suitors; let us preserve her pure and unblemished in all her virgin charms, and secure her, to the utmost of our ability, from the lawless violence of every armed
ruffian. I must own, however, though I am heartily grieved
that I entered so late upon the road of life as to be overtaken
by a gloomy night of public distress before I had finished my
journey, that I am not a little relieved by the tender consolation which you administered to me in your very agreeable
letters, in which you tell me I ought to recollect my courage,
since my past transactions are such as will speak for me when
I am silent, and survive my death ; and such as, if the gods
permit, will bear an ample testimony to the prudence and integrity of my public counsels by the final restoration of the
republic ; or, if otherwise, by burying me in the ruins of my
country.

XCVII. "But when I look upon *you*, my Brutus, it fills
me with anguish to reflect that, in the vigor of your youth,
and when you were making the most rapid progress in the
road to fame, your career was suddenly stopped by the fatal
overthrow of the commonwealth. This unhappy circumstance
has stung me to the heart ; and not *me* only, but my worthy
friend here, who has the same affection for you and the same
esteem for your merit which I have. We have the warmest
wishes for your happiness, and heartily pray that you may
reap the rewards of your excellent virtues, and live to find a
republic in which you will be able, not only to revive, but
even to add to the fame of your illustrious ancestors. For
the forum was your birthright, your native theatre of action ;
and you were the only person that entered it who had not
only formed his elocution by a rigorous course of private practice, but enriched his oratory with the furniture of philosophical science, and thus united the highest virtue to the most

consummate eloquence. Your situation, therefore, wounds us with the double anxiety that *you* are deprived of the *republic*, and the republic of *you*. But still continue, my Brutus (notwithstanding the career of your genius has been checked by the rude shock of our public distress), continue to pursue your favorite studies, and endeavor (what you have almost, or rather entirely effected already) to distinguish yourself from the promiscuous crowd of pleaders with which I have loaded the little history I have been giving you. For it would ill befit you (richly furnished as you are with those liberal arts which, unable to acquire at home, you imported from that celebrated city which has always been revered as the seat of learning) to pass after all as an ordinary pleader. For to what purposes have you studied under Pammenes, the most eloquent man in Greece? or what advantage have you derived from the discipline of the old Academy, and its hereditary master Aristus (my guest and very intimate acquaintance), if you still rank yourself in the common class of orators? Have we not seen that a whole age could scarcely furnish two speakers who really excelled in their profession? Among a crowd of contemporaries, Galba, for instance, was the only orator of distinction; for old Cato (we are informed) was obliged to yield to his superior merit, as were likewise his two juniors, Lepidus and Carbo. But, in a public harangue, the style of his successors, the Gracchi, was far more easy and lively; and yet, even in their time, the Roman eloquence had not reached its perfection. Afterward came Antonius and Crassus; and then Cotta, Sulpicius, Hortensius, and—but I say no more; I can only add, that if I had been so fortunate—
[*The conclusion is lost.*]

INDEX.

THE END